DIVIDED WORLDS?

SEMEIA STUDIES

Jacqueline M. Hidalgo, General Editor

Editorial Board:
Eric D. Barreto
Jin Young Choi
L. Juliana M. Claassens
Rhiannon Graybill
Emmanuel Nathan
Kenneth Ngwa
Shively T. J. Smith

Number 100

DIVIDED WORLDS?

Challenges in Classics and New Testament Studies

Edited by

Caroline Johnson Hodge, Timothy A. Joseph,
and Tat-siong Benny Liew

Atlanta

Copyright © 2023 by SBL Press

All rights reserved. No part of this work may be reproduced or transmitted in any form or by any means, electronic or mechanical, including photocopying and recording, or by means of any information storage or retrieval system, except as may be expressly permitted by the 1976 Copyright Act or in writing from the publisher. Requests for permission should be addressed in writing to the Rights and Permissions Office, SBL Press, 825 Houston Mill Road, Atlanta, GA 30329 USA.

Library of Congress Control Number: 2023940271

Contents

Acknowledgments vii
Abbreviations ix

Introduction: Divided Worlds?
    Caroline Johnson Hodge, Timothy Joseph, and
    Tat-siong Benny Liew 1

An Argument for Being Less Disciplined
    Denise Kimber Buell 39

The World of *Kandake*: Foregrounding Ethiopian
Queens and Empires
    Gay L. Byron 65

An Apocalyptic Epidemiology of Foreignness: The Use of
Revelation in American Associations of Immigrants with Disease
    Yii-Jan Lin 83

What Large Letters: Invisible Labor, Invisible
Disabilities, and Paul's Use of Scribes
    Candida R. Moss 105

Wayward and Willful Members: Twisting Figures Past
Porneia in Paul's Letters
    Joseph A. Marchal 123

Master Jesus and the Enslaved Apostles
    Jennifer A. Glancy 155

Visualizing Oppression: Slavery and the Arts of Domination
    Abraham Smith 175

$r > g$
    Allen Dwight Callahan 203

Equality: A Modern, Ancient Greek, and Pauline
History of the Concept
> Jorann Økland 217

Aesthetics: New Testament, the Classics, and a Case
Study in 1 Corinthians
> Laura Salah Nasrallah 247

Responses

On Polycentrism, Simultaneity, and the Priority of Ethical Urgency:
The Example of Walker's *Appeal*
> Timothy A. Joseph 279

Divided Worlds: How Divided Are They?
> Shelley P. Haley 289

A Classicist's Reflections on Greco-Roman Epidemiologies of
Foreignness and Categorizations of Disability
> Thomas R. Martin 297

Freedom, Slavery, and Beyond: A Reflection
> Dominic Machado 315

Two Approaches to Equality, Inequality, and Justice in the
Ancient World
> Douglas Boin 329

On Being Disciplined
> Katherine Lu Hsu 337

Afterword: The Ancient World and the Ancient World
> Joy Connolly 343

List of Contributors..355
Ancient Sources Index...361
Modern Authors Index..368
Subject Index..378

Acknowledgments

This volume originated from a two-day conference sponsored by the McFarland Center for Religion, Ethics, and Culture (CREC) at the College of the Holy Cross. We are grateful for this sponsorship and want to thank the director, Tom Landy, as well as Pat Hinchliffe and Danielle Kane for their support. The online conference in November of 2020 would not have been possible without the Holy Cross ITS Department. Special thanks to James Cahill, Thomas Alatalo, Holly Hunt, Luigi Piarulli, and Anne Barry for technical help.

We would also like to thank the Committee on Faculty Scholarship at Holy Cross for the publication grant that covered professional copyediting, and to Katie Van Heest of Tweed Academic Editing for her excellent work copyediting the contributions to the volume.

We are grateful to Steed Davidson (outgoing series editor) and the Semeia Studies series board for accepting the proposal and to Jacqueline M. Hidalgo (new series editor), Bob Buller, and Nicole L. Tilford of SBL Press for shepherding the project to completion.

We appreciate all the intellectual energy and labor that went into the project, especially from our contributors to the volume, both those who participated in the initial conference and those who joined us at the publication stage.

Abbreviations

Greek and Latin Primary Sources

Ab ubre cond.	Livy, *Ab ubre condita*
Agr.	Tacitus, *Agricola*
A.J.	Josephus, *Antiquitates judaicae*
Ann.	Tacitus, *Annales*
Apol.	Plato, *Apologia*
Ars	Ovid, *Ars amatoria*
Att.	Cicero, *Epistulae ad Atticum*
Aug.	Suetonius, *Divus Augustus*
B.J.	Josephus, *Bellum judaicum*
Bell.	Procopius, *De bellis*
Bib. hist.	Diodorus Siculus, *Bibliotheca historica*
Cat.	Cicero, *In Catilinam*
Chaer.	Chariton, *De Chaerea et Callirhoe*
Civ.	Augustine, *De civitate Dei*
Comp.	Dionysius of Halicarnassus, *De compositione verborum*
Contr.	Seneca the Elder, *Controversiae*
De capt.	Galen, *De captionibus*
De med.	Celsus, *De medicina*
De or.	Cicero, *De oratore*
Dig.	Digesta
Ep.	Julian, *Epistulae*; Pliny the Younger, *Epistulae*; Seneca the Younger, *Epistulae morales*
Epigr.	Martial, *Epigrammata*
Epit.	Lucius Annaeus Florus, *Epitome rerum Romanorum*
Eth. eud.	Aristotle, *Ethica eudemia*
Fam.	Cicero, *Epistulae ad familiares*

Fin.	Cicero, *De finibus bonorum et malorum*
Flor.	Stobaeus, *Floreligium*
Geogr.	Strabo, *Geographica*; Virgil, *Georgics*
Haer.	Irenaeus, *Adversus haereses*
Hel.	Historia Augustae, *Antoninus Heliogobalus*
Hist.	Cassius Dio, *Historia Romana*; Herodian, *Historia de imperio post Marcum Aurelium*; Herodotus, *Historia*
Hist. Aug., Hel.	Historia Augusta, Heliogabalus
Hist. Aug., Ver.	Historia Augusta, Verus
Hist. eccl.	Eusebius, *Historia ecclesiastica*; Evagrius Scholasticus, *Historia ecclesiastica*
Hymn Apoll.	Homeric Hymns, *Hymn to Apollo*
Hymn Heph.	Homeric Hymns, *Hymn to Hephaestus*
Il.	Homer, *Iliad*
Inst.	Quintilian, *Institutio oratoria*
Lac.	Xenophon, *Respublica Lacedaemoniorum*
Leg.	Plato, *Leges*
Mon.	Pseudo-Plutarch, *De Monarchia*
Nat.	Lucretius, *De rerum natura*; Pliny the Elder, *Naturalis historia*
Noct. att.	Aulus Gellius, *Noctes atticae* (*Attic Nights*)
Nub.	Aristophanes, *Nubes* (*Clouds*)
Off.	Cicero, *De officiis* (*On Duties*)
P.W.	Thucydides, *Historia belli peloponnesiaci*
Pol.	Aristotle, *Politica*
Praec. ger. rei publ.	Plutarch, *Praecepta gerendae rei publicae*
Praep. ev.	Eusebius, *Praeparatio evangelica*
Quint. fratr.	Cicero, *Epistulae ad Quintum fratrem*
Rep.	Cicero, *De republica*
Rhet. Her.	Rhetorica ad Herennium
Rust.	Columella, *De re rustica*
Sat.	Juvenal, *Satirae*
Spec.	Philo, *De specialibus legibus*
Theog.	Hesiod, *Theogonia*
Ther. Pis.	Galen, *De theriaca ad Pisonem*
Tris.	Ovid, *Tristia*
Tusc.	Cicero, *Tusculanae disputations*
Verus	Historia Augustae, *Lucius Verus*
Vesp.	Suetonius, *Vespasianus*

Abbreviations

Secondary Sources

AB	The Anchor Bible
ABD	Freedman, David Noel, ed. *Anchor Bible Dictionary*. 6 vols. New York: Doubleday, 1992.
ABSA	Annual of the British School at Athens
AHB	*Ancient History Bulletin*
AJA	*American Journal of Archaeology*
AJP	*American Journal of Philology*
ANRW	Temporini, Hildegard, and Wolfgang Haase, eds. *Aufstieg und Niedergang der römischen Welt: Geschichte und Kultur Roms im Spiegel der neueren Forschung*. Part 2, *Principat*. Berlin: de Gruyter, 1972–.
AYBRL	Anchor Yale Bible Reference Library
BAR	*Biblical Archaeology Review*
Bib	*Biblica*
BibInt	Biblical Interpretation Series
BibInt	*Biblical Interpretation*
BJRL	*Bulletin of the John Rylands University Library of Manchester*
BWANT	Beiträge zur Wissenschaft vom Alten und Neuen Testament
CBQ	*Catholic Biblical Quarterly*
CCSL	Corpus Christianorum: Series Latina
ChrLit	*Christianity and Literature*
CIL	Corpus Inscriptionum Latinarum
CJ	*Classical Journal*
ClAnt	*Classical Antiquity*
ClQ	*Classical Quarterly*
CP	*Classical Philology*
CSEL	Corpus Scriptorum Ecclesiasticorum Latinorum
CW	*Classical World*
ECL	Early Christianity and Its Literature
ExpTim	*Expository Times*
GR	*Greece and Rome*
HBT	*Horizons in Biblical Theology*
HTR	*Harvard Theological Review*
HTS	Harvard Theological Studies

HvTSt	*Hervormde Teologiese Studies* (HTS *Teologiese Studies*/HTS *Theological Studies*)
JAAR	*Journal of the American Academy of Religion*
JBL	*Journal of Biblical Literature*
JBR	*Journal of Bible and Religion*
JCRT	*Journal for Cultural and Religious Theory*
JdI	*Jahrbuch des deutschen archäologischen Instituts*
JECS	*Journal of Early Christian Studies*
JFSR	*Journal of Feminist Studies in Religion*
JRAS	*Journal of the Royal Asiatic Society*
JRS	*Journal of Roman Studies*
JSHJ	*Journal for the Study of the Historical Jesus*
JSJ	*Journal for the Study of Judaism*
JSNT	*Journal for the Study of the New Testament*
JTS	*Journal of Theological Studies*
LCL	Loeb Classical Library
LSJ	Liddell, Henry George, Robert Scott, Henry Stuart Jones. *A Greek-English Lexicon*. 9th ed. with revised supplement. Oxford: Clarendon, 1996.
LSNT	Library of New Testament Studies
MAAR	Memoirs of the American Academy in Rome
MTSR	*Method and Theory in the Study of Religion*
Neot	*Neotestamentica*
NovTSup	Supplements to Novum Testamentum
NTS	*New Testament Studies*
PG	Patrologia Graeca [= *Patrologiae Cursus Completus: Series Graeca*]. Edited by Jacques-Paul Migne. 162 vols. Paris, 1857–1886.
PL	Patrologia Latina [= *Patrologiae Cursus Completus: Series Latina*]. Edited by Jacques-Paul Migne. 217 vols. Paris, 1844–1864.
PRSt	*Perspectives in Religious Studies*
PW	*Paulys Real-Encyclopadie der classischen Altertumswissenschaft*. New edition by Georg Wissowa and Wilhelm Kroll. 50 vols. in 84 parts. Stuttgart: Metzler & Druckenmuller, 1894–1980.
R&T	*Religion & Theology*
RThom	*Revue thomiste*
SBLDS	Society of Biblical Literature Dissertation Series

SemeiaSt	Semeia Studies
SNTSMS	Society for New Testament Studies Monograph Series
TAPA	*Transactions of the American Philological Association*
Theol	*Theologica*
WBC	Word Biblical Commentary
WGRWSup	Writings from the Greco-Roman World Supplement Series
WUNT	Wissenschaftliche Untersuchungen zum Neuen Testament
WW	*Word and World*
ZPE	*Zeitschrift fur Papyrologie und Epigraphik*

Introduction: Divided Worlds?

Caroline Johnson Hodge, Timothy A. Joseph, and Tat-siong Benny Liew

This volume grew out of a question that continues to puzzle us: Why do classics and New Testament scholars talk with one another so infrequently despite several important overlaps between their two disciplines? Biblical scholars, for instance, often refer to the context from which the New Testament writings emerged as the "Greco-Roman world." Classics scholars examine works such as those composed by Seneca, Lucan, Plutarch, Juvenal, Dio Chrysostom, and Tacitus that were written during the same time frame when the New Testament writings were written. We also know New Testament colleagues who are employed by departments of classics, though these arrangements are infrequent. What is preventing a more regular and robust engagement between scholars of these two disciplines? Don't these scholars share the same ancient Mediterranean landscape? When working together, might scholars in these fields find ways to expand that landscape and create new and more expansive approaches of study? In exploring these questions, we hope to illustrate the value of thinking against the grain with respect to some of our traditional disciplinary boundaries while also calling attention to our potential to contribute to issues of justice in the past and present. As readers will readily note, all of the authors and respondents in this volume stress the contemporary urgency of their work on ancient sources. As editors, we aim to lay the groundwork for these contributions by thinking through the divides between these disciplines and the ethical and political issues that attend these barriers and their potential removal.

Confronting the Gap

Without claiming to know all the reasons for the general lack of interaction between scholars in these two overlapping disciplines, we would like to highlight three probable reasons: entanglements with the church, legacies of anti-Judaism, and professionalization in disciplinary formations.

Church and Faith Concerns

One reason for this disciplinary divide may have to do with the origins of New Testament studies having developed under the watchful eye or even the control of the church, as well as the discipline's continuing and intricate connections with the practice of the Christian faith. Historically, the church has held suspicions about and prohibitions of certain classical texts. In the thirteenth century, for example, papal approval for teaching Aristotle and his Arab commentators was finally granted after a long and passionate debate among people of the church (Bazan 1998, 19–20). During the Enlightenment, "the study of dead languages and classical texts was much criticized as a waste of time and talent" by the church when modern languages and knowledge were becoming available in a more technologically advanced Europe (Grafton, Most, and Zetzel 1985, 11). In contrast, at that time the New Testament writings were still held in high esteem because of the power of the church, which also explains why Hermann Reimarus ([1879] 1970) felt it necessity to circulate his writings anonymously in eighteenth-century Germany when arguing that early Christianity originated through a basic manipulation of the population. The Statute of 1800 at Oxford, England, specified that anyone "who has been found to have neglected the element of religion" would not be awarded a degree (quoted in Ellis 2007, 55). At the same time, people worried that ecclesiastical tutors might take advantage of their position to push their religion on the students placed in their charge, with the result that there was much disagreement in the nineteenth century regarding the place of religion in schools and universities. Given this looming mutual skepticism, it is no surprise that the church and the academy eventually became two disparate—though by no means totally disconnected—circles (Engel 1983).

Intellectual work in nineteenth-century Europe, including work in religion, was characterized in many ways by a turn to history (Crane 2000; Ameriks 2006; Howard 2009; Klein 2018), a shift that further complicated the relationship between the study of the New Testament and classical texts. With historical consciousness on the rise, the New Testament writings also came under scrutiny, particularly because of all the miracles found within the gospels. Through textual criticism and source criticism, *ad fontes* scholarship of sorting through and sorting out the histories behind the New Testament texts became a major obsession (Longstaff and Thomas 1988; Kraus 2007; Thatcher and Williams 2013). Another important shift was the growing recognition that the New Testament writings must be placed within a larger linguistic and cultural world. The English translators of a nineteenth-century book on the grammar of New Testament Greek, for example, wrote that the "general classical scholar also will find [the book] full of interest, both in its numerous references to ancient authors, and in its copious illustration of grammatical principles, in their application to the Greek language of classical writers" (Agnew and Ebbeke 1839, vi). In 1835 David Friedrich Strauss published *The Life of Jesus, Critically Examined* (see Strauss 1892), where he proposed that the gospels should be understood as mythological rather than historical. This incurred not only a high cost to his professorial career but also created a watershed moment in New Testament studies. His book provoked a fierce search for historical facts that continued to dominate New Testament studies well into the latter half of the twentieth century, including what is now known as the "Quest for the Historical Jesus." Some viewed these attempts to ground the gospels in history, including historical-critical methods such as source criticism and form criticism, as having "freed [New Testament studies] in varying degrees from constraints imposed by rigid political and religious powers" (Hauser and Watson 2017, viii). Others, however, resisted or suppressed these methods for fear that they might endanger people's faith commitment.

It would be a mistake to think that all who developed or pursued the historical-critical study of the New Testament in the nineteenth century were enemies of the church. Constantin von Tischendorf (1896, 20), articulated that his textual critical work, which he identified as both a "learned labor" and a "science," had two goals: "to clear up ... the history of the sacred text, and to discover if possible the genuine apostolic text which is the foundation of our faith." Writing about his discovery of the Codex Sinaiticus, von Tischendorf confidently declares that "Providence has given to our age, in which attacks on Christianity are so common, the Sinaitic Bible, to be to us a full and clear light as to what is the real text of God's Word written, and to assist us in defending the truth by establishing its authentic form" (32). Another such example is the story of F. D. Maurice (Morris 2005). Maurice saw his study of the New Testament as an opportunity to reinvigorate and renew the church by making it more ecumenical and inclusive. Working with these goals, his philological work on New Testament Greek led him to reject the church's teaching on eternal punishment. For this Maurice was dismissed from his professorial chair at King's College, London. The historical-critical turn of New Testament studies in the nineteenth century thus had different meanings for different people. Although some viewed the turn with skepticism and saw it as an assault on Christianity, others embraced it for apologetic reasons, seeing it as reinforcing the faith by ascertaining the essence of Jesus's greatness (Sobrino 1977–1978; Morgan 2005; Bock 2011; Myles 2016).

In schools and universities within the Western world during the eighteenth and early nineteenth centuries—most of which had a Christian affiliation—the New Testament was commonly taught alongside classical texts, as "the education of Christian gentlemen [was] essentially synonymous with classical learning" (in the United States, see Winterer 2002, 10; in Oxford in the early 1800s, see Ellis 2007). The coexistence of the New Testament and, for example, the Homeric poems in curricula was not always harmonious, but "many Protestant ministers happily reconciled the ethics of the heathens with the morality of Christianity," on the grounds that "the great Greek and Roman philosophers and moralists had groped near enough to Christian truth" (Winterer 2002, 14). But the historical-critical turn that was transforming New Testament scholarship was at the same time moving scholars of classical texts toward specialized training in source criticism, with divisive consequences for the longtime coexistence of New Testament and classical texts in curricula and in the academy (Goldhill 2020b explores a number of causes and consequences). As training became more specialized and often narrower in focus, academic departments began to form and grow increasingly independent and competitive (Adler 2016, 51–67). This trend toward professionalization and the palisading of departments began in German universities but in time spread broadly (for further discussion of this development and Foucault's critique of it, see below).

A representative demonstration of the expanding fissures between New Testament and classical studies at this time can be identified in the scholarly process of assembling Henry George Liddell, Robert Scott, and Henry Stuart Jones's, *A Greek-English Lexicon* (LSJ). First published in 1843, this resource remains an authoritative ancient Greek dictionary among classics scholars. As one scholar has put it, the prioritizing of classical texts in LSJ is evident in its "treatment of New Testament Greek [as] superficial, shoddy and shambolic" (James 2019, 180). This dictionary, which is "part of what defines the classical canon and our privileged engagement with it" (Goldhill 2020a), stands as a living—and still thriving—reminder of the nineteenth-century schism between New Testament and classical studies.

With the distance between the disciplines growing greater, many scholars in classics might have felt alarmed when someone such as T. S. Eliot (1936, 174) could state that "it is only upon readers who wish to see a Christian civilization survive and develop that I am urging the importance of the study of Latin and Greek." To ensure that the discipline would have an independent place and value within educational systems, it makes sense that classicists might have wanted to distance themselves from New Testament studies, especially given the ongoing influence that the church and faith commitments seemed to have on the discipline. One of the ways to achieve this was for classicists to see their discipline as having a "privileged relationship" with humanism and particularly its "opposition to Christianity" (Leonard and Porter 2014, 298; see also Adler 2016, 43–48).

The emergence of other critical approaches within New Testament studies in the twentieth century has not demonstrably changed the discipline's associations with faith. Literary criticism or formalist analysis becomes for some not only a manifestation of literary artistry but also a proof of biblical authority, since "the autonomist view of the text ... supports a high view of Scripture" and Scripture can "come alive" through literary criticism as "a living word of address to its readers" (Johnston 1982, 38, 45). New Testament passages or books have a *sensus plenior* that narrative criticism unlocks, and the intricate and integral design of the text—through the use of, for example, chiasm, inclusion, intercalation, irony, parallelism, or plot kernels—reveals "the intentions of author human and divine" (Carson 2016, 12). Apologetics can be at work even when the study of the New Testament takes an imperial turn to interrogate empire, so the empire-critical lens is criticized for focusing on politics rather than on God and theology (McKnight and Modica 2013) or the New Testament writings are shown to be completely and purely on the side of liberation (Stowers 1998, 297–302; Moore 2012; Punt 2012).

Since a faith-preserving agenda continues to be present within New Testament studies and since faith commitments do not sit easily with secular education, classicists may understandably prefer to reject this arena and labor on another stage. Citing A. B. Cook's study of Zeus as an example, Simon Goldhill (2020b, 60) suggests that classicists desiring to work on Greco-Roman cults would often depend on the works of anthropologists rather than on those by scholars of religion and theology. Even though New Testament scholars do not necessarily understand their scholarship as doing theology, nor do all classicists stay away from religion, we think Douglas Boin (2016) is largely on target to say that classicists generally have a "Christian problem," which, in our view, causes them to "quarantine" the New Testament.

Language and the Jewish Question

A second possible reason for the gap is the differentiation of Classical Greek from Koine Greek and the latter's association with Judaism. Goldhill (2020b, 57) makes the observation that classics scholars rarely work on Josephus, Philo, or the Septuagint (but see recently Redondo 2000 and the essays in Chapman and Rodgers 2016). What is interesting to us is that these areas frequently neglected in classics actually have something in common with the New Testament writings: they are all associated with the Jewish people. We know that the New Testament writings were written in Koine, or "common" Greek (LSJ, a.i), but is it possible that these Greek writings authored by Jews were considered "profane" (LSJ, a.vii) and hence less worthy of consideration and study? Is the Greek of the New Testament writings written by Jews "Greek" enough? While scholars may not agree on the causes, they recognize that anti-Semitism was a considerable problem in the academy of nineteenth-century Europe and in society at large (Oldson 1991; Jensen 2007; Godsey 2008; Kolstø 2014; Bell 2018). Before Jewish seminaries were established in various European cities in the second part of the nineteenth century, Jews with secular doctorates had to convert to Christianity if they wanted a chance to get an academic appointment, and Jewish studies was rarely viewed as a legitimate area of research (Dunkelgrün 2020, 68, 77).

Anti-Semitism reared its ugly head not only in how academic positions were selected but also in how academic research was produced. Friedrich August Wolf, whose work on Homer was recognized not only as being "the first 'history of a text in antiquity'" but also as having "effected a 'revolution in philology'" (Grafton, Most, and Zetzel 1985, 15, 26), had no hesitation to teach "his students that '[t]he Hebrew Nation has not elevated itself to the degree of culture, such that one might consider it a learned people,'" and that the discipline of classics should "be the exclusive study of [a]ncient Greece and Rome" (Dunkelgrün 2020, 65–66). There is, of course, no shortage of anti-Jewish material in the Greco-Roman writings of antiquity (Gager 1985; Schäfer 1998; Gruen 2002). Just like religion, academic study (including language study and philology) influences and is influenced by nationalism and racial understandings (Goldhill 2020b, 48–49). Our opinions of a people or a race and our view of their language(s) are deeply intertwined, so language facility can be embraced or resisted to establish one's status (Goldhill 2002). If, as Wolf surmised, Jews in antiquity were not "a learned people," then what they wrote in "profane" Greek would likely matter less to scholars; if their writings were not studied, then their characterization as unlearned would be reinforced.

As our earlier discussion of Liddell, Scott, and Jones's *Greek-English Lexicon* has already shown, language competence has been key in the disciplinary policing of New Testament studies and classics. Since the New Testament texts were written in Koine Greek, many New Testament scholars feel intimidated and reluctant to engage scholars of classics, especially if they lack mastery of Classical Greek and Latin (see the discussion in Bond 2019). These issues are tied up in a larger dynamic, as ideology often shapes disciplinary decisions regarding which or whose language should be learned and what materials need to be studied.

Scholars of the New Testament also need to acknowledge that an antithetical assumption about "Hellenism" and "Hebraism" was pervasive across the culture of nineteenth-century Europe, including New Testament studies. As Miriam Leonard (2012) shows, European Enlightenment thinking in many ways revolved around the polarity between Greeks and Jews, and this assumed polarity ended up impacting various disciplinary formations in relation to race. For instance, in his early work, Georg Wilhelm Friedrich Hegel contrasted a beautiful Greek spirit of unity and harmony with an unhappy Jewish emphasis on severance and longing, only to conclude in his later work that Jewish life after Christianity's emergence was meaningless, alienated, and devoid of genuine history (Yovel 1997, 4–13; Wake 2014). The change from Hegel's early and frequent mention of the Jews to the limited references to the Jews in his arguably best known and most influential work, *The Phenomenology of Spirit* (2018), is telling. Hegel moved from talking about "Socrates and the Jews" to "Socrates and the Christ(ians)"; the Jews and their history were aborted with their rejection of Christ (Leonard 2012, 68; cf. Hattersley 2009), and Jesus and his early followers had somehow stopped being Jewish.

Indeed, questions regarding the relations between Hellenism and Hebraism have consumed New Testament scholars for a long time (Fairweather 1924; Macgregor 1936; Hengel 1974; Borgen 1996; Collins and

Sterling 2001; Engberg-Pedersen 2001). These questions at times also entail, once again, the issue of language, as we can see from Jan Nicholaas Sevenster's 1968 book with the telling title *Do You Know Greek? How Much Greek Could the First Jewish Christians Have Known?* as well as Hughson T. Ong's 2015 book, *The Multilingual Jesus and the Sociolinguistic World of the New Testament* (see also Fitzmyer 1970; Redondo 2000). There is no denying that Enlightenment debates in Europe influenced the development of New Testament studies in the nineteenth century and beyond (Blanton 2007; Moore and Sherwood 2011). Yii-Jan Lin (2016) has shown in a recent study, for example, that biological sciences, along with their racial(ized) assumptions, have been key to the evolution of New Testament textual criticism since the eighteenth century. To go back to Hegel, his shadow and fingerprints were all over Strauss's influential book that we mentioned earlier.

We would be wrong, however, to think that New Testament scholars simply inherited the Hellenism–Hebraism divide from someone such as Hegel, whose anti-Jewish sentiments were first nurtured by Christian traditions "primarily in the Lutheran version" (Yovel 1997, 4). After the Holocaust, New Testament scholars have also become more aware of and sensitive to the pervasive blindness about and prejudice against Jews in our discipline (Segal 1990; Fredriksen and Reinhartz 2002; Nanos 2002; Kloppenborg and Marshall 2005; Levine 2006; Donaldson 2010; Langton 2010; Chazan 2016; Levine and Brettler 2017; Boyarin 2019). At the same time, we must not forget that Christian supersessionism existed long before the eighteenth or nineteenth century and that troubling polemic and rhetoric among Jews can be found in the New Testament (Boyarin 2012; Schäfer 2012). Our interest here is not to argue about the roots of anti-Judaism or anti-Semitism (e.g., Gerdmar 2008; Chazan 2016) but to affirm that the New Testament with all of its Jewish dimensions should be a part of, rather than apart from, other Greco-Roman writings. This is not our way to make the New Testament rational or "Western," but to emphasize the value of Jewish Greek as well as the reality of a Jewish Hellenism. To follow up on this affirmation, we will need to attend to the history of disciplinary formation.

Disciplinary Specialization and Professionalization

The third and final reason for the disciplinary gap between New Testament and classics is an ongoing commitment to the constraints of specialization and professionalization, a topic addressed in brief above but worthy of further exploration. Here we will not attempt to trace the formation history of our different fields. Indeed, this is a formidable task, especially with disciplines that look at texts from ancient history and which have developed in specific ways depending on geographical location. These challenges are evident in the work of recent scholars who have limited their focus geographically or temporally. For example, Christopher Stray (1998, 2003, 2007) has provided detailed studies of the discipline of classics in England, while Caroline Winterer (2002), focusing on the eighteenth and nineteenth centuries, and Eric Adler (2016), focusing on the twentieth and early twenty-first centuries, have examined the study of the classics in the United States. In New Testament studies, William Baird (1992–2003) has produced a three-volume work on the history of New Testament research; Larry Hurtado (2009) has written an article on the discipline's development in the twentieth century; and Jerry H. Bentley (1983) has published an interesting study on how Renaissance humanists, such as Lorenza Valla and Desiderius Erasmus, set the course for the beginning of modern critical research on the New Testament.

Instead, we will think about disciplinary development in more general and modest terms, building on the work of Michel Foucault. When considering that the boundaries of different modern academic disciplines began to solidify in the eighteenth century with the organization of modern university structures, we refer to Foucault's (2002a) analysis of how knowledge production changed between the Renaissance and the end of the nineteenth century, especially with modernity's epistemological challenge brought about by the rise of the sciences starting in the eighteenth century. We choose Foucault's analysis not because it is perfect but because it seems aware of the contextual specificity of the geopolitical West. Starting with a preface about Jorge Luis Borges's Chinese encyclopedia (Foucault 2002a, xvi–xx), Foucault's *The Order of Things* shows how "the lingual properties to which Western civilization has long been accustomed may be just local flora and fauna" (Chow 2021, 45).

Considering the division of human intellectual pursuits into three main areas (humanities and social sciences, language and linguistics, and physical sciences), Foucault emphasizes the importance of specialization and institutionalization. The division of different forms of knowledge means that "from the nineteenth century the field of knowledge can no longer provide the ground for a reflection that will be homogeneous and uniform at all points"; hence, "from now on each form of positivity will have the 'philosophy' that suits it" (Foucault 2002a, 304). Furthermore, as Foucault (1988, 308–9) explains in an interview, we need to analyze

> how, out of the mass of things said, out of the totality of actual discourse, a number of these discourses ... are given a particular sacralization and function ... among all the narratives, why is it that a number of them are sacralized ?... They are immediately taken up with an institution ... the university institution.... So here we already have the truth of something ... through an interplay of ... sacralization and institutional validation, of which the university is both the operator and the receiver.

As specialized knowledge emerges with specific epistemes, rules, territories, and boundaries, they not only become compartmentalized but also must be validated by the university. This is the process behind the making of disciplines. After citing Émile Durkheim's definition of sociology as "the science of institutions, of their genesis and functioning," Sara Ahmed (2012, 19) goes on to comment that "if the institution can be understood as the object of the social sciences, then the institution might be how the social derives its status as science." In addition to the university, we also need to highlight our respective academic guilds in this process. These institutions set the questions that we may ask, the texts that we should read, and the procedures that we are obliged to follow in our work as disciplinary and disciplined scholars. Our discipline, whether classics or New Testament studies, is also an institution that legitimizes and institutionalizes us as its members.

This process of legitimation and institutionalization is inseparable from the assumptions and developments of professionalism, which characterize not only modern forms of production in general but also the production of knowledge in particular. After all, anyone who desires can read the writings of Homer or those in the New Testament, but they are not professors or recognized scholars in the field. This claim to be a professional takes us back to Foucault's emphasis on specialization. Burton Bledstein explains in his 1976 book *The Culture of Professionalism* that what distinguishes professionals is their mastery of a field that is coherent and self-contained in and of itself. Only after a field—or a discipline—has been isolated and established as autonomous can specific rules and larger paradigms be developed or debated *within* it to certify and evaluate the competence, promotion, and tenure of an institutional or institutionalized professional. Professional authority and institutional autonomy are mutually reinforcing processes. Professionalization often means the ever-proliferating or, perhaps more accurately, the ever-splitting and ever-shrinking spheres of specialization, resulting in what Stephen Moore and Yvonne Sherwood (2011, 84) call in the context of biblical studies "a subspecialist in a subdiscipline of a subdiscipline." Among New Testament scholars, there are gospel scholars, Pauline scholars, and Revelation scholars—with gospel scholars further separating into Matthean, Markan, Lukan, and Johannine scholars. In classics, there are Latinists and Hellenists, often with specializations in epic, tragedy, comedy, historiography, or oratory, as well as specialists in historical linguistics, classical history, archaeology, art history, and other aspects of material culture.

Acknowledging our respective disciplines as institutions will perhaps enable us to see and question the game rather than just to go on playing the game while trying to be competitive players. This acknowledgment may also enable us to understand a discipline's difficulty with change and with interdisciplinary pursuits, insofar as such pursuits challenge and violate the discipline's tendency to isolate its turf and control its borders. As Alfred North Whitehead (1925, 179) professed a century ago, the professionalization of knowledge

> is exclusive and intolerant, and rightly so. It fixes attention on a definite group of abstractions, neglects everything else, and elicits every scrap of information and theory which is relevant to what it has retained. This method is triumphant.

With this mentality, limiting one's range signifies both professional focus and scholarly expertise. It is not surprising that scholars are inclined to work in small circles within their own identified discipline. There is little motivation in this institutional and professional setting for one to engage scholars who labor in another identifiable discipline.

Encouraging a Conversation

Though not specifically about New Testament studies, some recent calls indicate that the time may be ripe for New Testament and classics scholars to converse and collaborate (see Boin 2016; Bond 2019; Mendonca 2019; Conybeare and Goldhill 2020). Interdisciplinary work is often encouraged by university administrators, but such encouragement can occasionally, and unfortunately, be used to cover up budgetary cuts or departmental mergers. Without dismissing the reality that our work is inseparable from the economy and neoliberal capitalism, we attempt to provide here some better reasons for why a more regular and active engagement between scholars of these two disciplines may make sense.

Past Precedents

We can see the artificial and arbitrary separation of classics and New Testament studies if we look at how scholars of earlier generations operated. Erasmus the Renaissance man worked on the New Testament as well as edited and translated many classical texts (Rummel 1985; Sider 2019). Karl Lachmann contributed to source criticism within New Testament studies through his work on the Synoptic problem (Poirier 2009), but his development of stemmatics was important to textual criticism in both classics and New Testament studies (Müller-Sievers 2001, 166–69; Most 2019; see also Garrison 2020). Although Benjamin Jowett is better known among classicists, particularly because of his work on Plato's writings (Higgins 1993), he also commented on the New Testament, including Paul's letters (Atherstone 2003; Hinchliff 1987). In a way, the work of these scholars defies disciplinary classification, possibly because they worked before the redrawing of disciplinary boundaries became fixed and rigid in the twentieth century. The good news is that even today, there are still scholars who occasionally transgress the divide between the New Testament and classics (e.g., Boin 2013, 2014, 2015; Jones 2014, 2015; Most 1985, 2005; Sick 2007, 2011, 2016, 2017).

Shared Research Methods and Overlapping Research Topics

In *Classical Philology and Theology* (2020), an edited volume that shares our interest in the destabilization of disciplinary boundaries (and that also contains helpful contributions to which we have already referred), Catherine Conybeare and Simon Goldhill offer an abiding argument upon which we would like to build. Philology and textual criticism are key to both New Testament studies and classics. Without getting into the tedious debates about whether the first credit of developing these research methods should go to New Testament scholars or classicists (e.g., Timpanaro 2005), we want to suggest that, if research method is one criterion in setting disciplinary boundaries, the shared use of philology and textual criticism shows that interdisciplinary work *occurred* in the past and *can occur* in the future of these two disciplines.

Besides sharing research methods, New Testament studies and classics also have research questions that can be productively pursued by scholars from both disciplines. Just as we have discussed how the New Testament writings might be read to inform our thinking and understanding of a Jewish Hellenism, scholars in both fields can go beyond looking at the Greco-Roman world as the mere background of the New Testament. Instead, we can consider how the New Testament writings and the Greco-Roman world interacted more dynamically in and through each other. How might the New Testament writings have helped bring about changes in Greco-Roman culture, even or especially when they were also molded by the ethos and contexts of the Greco-Roman world? For instance, in addition to reading Jesus and Caesar as competing lords, as some New Testament scholars of the empire-critical persuasion have argued (Horsley 2003; Carter 2021), what if we think about how the Jesus-is-the-Son-of-God argument in the New Testament and the divine-emperor claims in the larger Greco-Roman world might be mutually informative and inflective (cf. Botha 2004; Gupta 2014; Elm 2020)? What about issues such as gender, slavery, sexuality, status, disability, domesticity, ethnicity, and life and death when examined across New Testament and classical texts? The Greco-Roman world was organized by various forces: social, religious, economic, material, military, political, textual, and ideological. Just like every other text in the Greco-Roman period, the New Testament, as a collection of Jewish *and* early Christian writings, was both shaped by *and* shaped these forces. Suggesting both resistance and assimilation, these writings became a force among many others that impacted the structure and development of the Greco-Roman world (Johnson 2009; Boin 2015). To further our understanding of how people negotiated these various forces with nuance will require the collaboration of New Testament and classics scholars.

Impetus from Other Disciplines

Although conversations between New Testament and classics scholars do not happen as much as we would like, scholars outside our two disciplines often engage both classics and the New Testament in their own work. This is arguably most obvious among philosophers. Jacques Derrida (1995) looks at Plato's *Phaedo* and Matthew's Sermon on the Mount (Matt 5–7), the latter in a couple of different French translations, to discuss religion and an ethics of responsibility. He also discusses the "partition between

Plato and Socrates" alongside the book of Revelation to illustrate how texts are "without origin, or a verifiable, decidable, presentable, appropriable identity" (Derrida 1984, 13, 34). His works, as a result, have led scholars in both of our fields to analyze and evaluate his use of the New Testament and classical texts, though they do so separately rather than collaboratively (cf. Twomey 2005; Leonard 2010). In her ambitious attempt to conceptualize the human more holistically and to reimagine a new kind of living, the feminist philosopher Luce Irigaray (2017, 44–45, 100–104) mentions not only Plato's *Symposium* but also the Gospel of John in the New Testament.

Philosophers teaching in North America also engage both sets of resources. Richard Kearney (2021) refers to the New Testament (e.g., Matthew, Philippians, 1 Corinthians) and classics (e.g., Aristotle, Elysian rites, and various Greek myths) in his recent book on touch. Charles Taylor (1989, xi) refers not only to Platonism, Aristotelian ethics, Stoicism, and Greek religious traditions but also to the Gospels of Mark, Matthew, and John, as well as Paul's letters (such as Romans) in his argument that "understanding modern identity is an exercise in retrieval."

In the field of literature, it is not unusual to see works of literary criticism sprinkled with references to both classics and the New Testament. Such examples can be found in the works of Northrop Frye (1982, 2020), Harold Bloom (1997, 2019), and even Terry Eagleton (2018, 2020). Sigmund Freud is known for reading the Greco-Roman classics in his work of developing psychoanalysis (Gamwell and Wells 1989; Barker 1996; Armstrong 2018), but we should not lose sight of his attraction to the apostle Paul of the New Testament. While Paul does not appear in the title of Freud's book *Moses and Monotheism*, "the book is almost as much about the apostle Paul as about Moses, for it proposes to explain how the religion of the one logically emerged from the religion of the other" (Langton 2010, 265). When Bonnie H. Honig (2013, xviii, 155), a feminist scholar in political and legal theory, takes on Sophocles's *Antigone* to argue for what she calls an "agonistic humanism," she also refers, albeit briefly, to Mary Magdalene's attempt to perform the proper burial rites for Jesus's crucified body.

Impetus from other disciplines for classics and New Testament scholars to converse and to engage one another comes out in both positive and negative ways. In his work on the boldness of speech (παρρησία), we see Foucault refer not only to Pericles's orations, Plato's works, and Isocrates's writings but also to the New Testament and New Testament scholarship (e.g., Foucault 2001, 11; 2010, 134; 11; 2011, 325–31). However, when Foucault argues in his three-volume *The History of Sexuality* (1980, 1985,

1986) that a "search for personal ethics" in Greco-Roman antiquity had given way to a "morality of obedience" with Christianity (see also Foucault 1988, 49), he basically skips over the New Testament writings in his actual arguments. For a work that emphasized "the art of not being governed quite so much" (Foucault 2002b, 193) and made the "outside" a consistent "thematic" (Chow 2021, 15), Foucault's history of sexuality, by depending only on Christian writers of the fourth and fifth centuries such as Augustine, leaves the New Testament outside, as though it belongs to neither Greco-Roman antiquity nor Christianity. Given Foucault's concern in this history not only with sexuality but also with subject formation, why would Paul's letters, for example, not be an important resource to consider alongside other Greco-Roman resources (see Moxnes 2003)? Would engagement with both New Testament studies and classics not further nuance and enrich Foucault's genealogical work here?

Similarly, in his distinguished career as a political theorist, J. Peter Euben did much with the classics as a resource for taking contemporary political theory in radially democratic directions (see Euben 1990, 2003; Euben, Wallach, and Ober 1994). In his proposal that "the charges leveled against Socrates anticipate those leveled against the multiculturalists by conservative canonists in [the culture wars of] our own day" (1997, 33), however, Euben seems to have forgotten his own acknowledgment that "the master canon" for those "conservative canonists" includes not only Greco-Roman but also Judeo-Christian texts (16, 22). Would his attempt to use "the master's tools" to "remodel" if not "to destroy the master's house" (22) have been even more effective had he incorporated the New Testament in his readings, particularly given how both Socrates and Jesus were sentenced to die for their respective questioning of traditions and doctrinal closures? The important yet, in some sense, unfinished work of the likes of Foucault and Euben points us to promising possibilities for future cross-disciplinary work.

Emphasizing the Worldliness of Our Disciplines

Our mention of culture wars brings us to another problem related to how New Testament studies and classics have been specialized, professionalized, and conditioned by both guild and university validation. According to Terry Eagleton (1984, 66), the university is "an institution which permits the critic's voice to be 'disinterested' to the precise extent that it is effectively inaudible to society as a whole." Disciplinary territory or its territorial isolation relates to criticism's withdrawal from the public sphere into the university, where the scientific, objectivist, or positivist ethos is the norm. If the word *permits* implies the university's power as an institution to legitimize, it also points to the insularity of institutions (as Eagleton suggests). Institutions and institutionalized professionals are, for various reasons, prone to prioritizing their own growth and advancement over attending to the needs and affairs of the larger world. Professionalization, status promotion, and privatization are all related and accepted modes of operation in our respective guilds and schools. For many in the guilds of New Testament studies and classics, it is business as usual with our respective guild-sanctioned and guild-sanctified sense of scholarly and scientific antiquarianism, even though our work is always already embedded in, influenced by, and, despite our intentions or lack thereof, impactful to our own sociopolitical contexts. The so-called culture wars have led us to realize that not engaging in the politics of the world beyond one's guild and university is in itself political, because it translates into the conservative stance of upholding the status quo. With the term *worldliness*, Edward W. Said (1983, 1–16) points to the multiple connections that our intellectual work has in and with the world. Despite the fact that we work with ancient materials, we still operate in what Mikhail M. Bakhtin (1981, 11) calls a "zone of maximal contact with the present (with contemporary reality)."

Colonial Entanglements and Racist Genealogies

Texts from both the New Testament and classics have been used by white supremacists and for colonial purposes. While the justification for colonialism and racism provided by the Great Commission of Matthew's Jesus to "go … and make disciples of all nations" (Matt 28:16–20) is better known (Lalitha and Smith 2014), one must not lose sight of the role that classical texts and ideas have also played in the hands of both colonialists and racists. Upon Christopher Columbus's arrival in what Europeans would soon call America, justification for Spain's seizure of land from indigenous peoples came not only from appeals to the Christian God's providence but also from Aristotle's influential assertion that "authority and subordination are conditions not only inevitable but also expedient; some things are marked out from the moment of birth to rule or to be ruled" (*Pol.* 1254a.8 [trans. Rackham, LCL, with some adjustments]; see Lepore 2018, 20–22). It is telling that Hubert Evans (1988, 26), a British "Collector and Magistrate" of the Indian Civil Service (ICS) in the 1920s, remembers in his memoir that on his first trip to India he brought with him Homer's *Odyssey*, Virgil's *Aeneid*, and, from the British and Foreign Bible Society, an "attractively got-up, gilt-edged *New Testament in Urdu*." Afraid that his Urdu was not up to standard, Evans "took the precaution of throwing in [his] *Novum Testamentum Graece* for use as a crib" (26). One can further see the important and mingling roles of the New Testament and classics in the minds and practices of the British colonials when Evans mentions how "a notable teacher of the classics like Dean Gaisford could end a Christmas sermon to the undergraduates of Oxford with the inspiring words: 'Nor can I do better, in conclusion, than impress upon you the study of Greek literature, which not only elevates above the vulgar herd, but leads not infrequently to positions of considerable emolument'" (10). As can be reasonably assumed, Gaisford's Christmas sermon involved certain references to the New Testament, and the positions he had in mind were colonial services on behalf of the British Empire.

Evans's choice of books to bring to India was not surprising, "since Greek and Latin were almost indispensable for successful entry into the ICS" (Vasunia 2013, 136; see also 193–236). The Greek and Latin classics meant so much to ICS members that many educated Indians began to see classics as some kind of "secret knowledge" that gave these colonial officers a sense of superiority and right to rule (Hagerman 2013, 169–86), causing not only the British to compare themselves to what they found in classics but also Mohandas Gandhi and Jawaharlal Nehru to identify with and appropriate classical works during their struggle against the British Empire (Vasunia 2013, 335–49).

The same story can be told in the continent of Africa (Harlow and Carter 2003, esp. 328–50, 496–528, 538–60). We will give but a few examples. Whether wittingly or unwittingly, those who translate the New Testament into African languages can challenge and help bring about changes in a people's worldview, religious beliefs, and cultural practices (Dube 1999, 2015; Mothoagae 2017, 2018). In terms of classics, Cecil Rhodes, the ardent agent of the British colonial project in Africa, was known for treasuring two particular books: Marcus Aurelius's *Meditations* and Edward Gibbon's *Decline and Fall of the Roman Empire* (Lambert 2011, 61; see also Wardle 2017). Supposedly, one of Rhodes's favorite sayings was "remember always that you are a Roman" (cited in Parchami 2015, 117). Rhodes was not an exception but an example that shows how classics helped instill in the colonialists of Africa a sense of superiority (Hilton 2017).

Case in point, knowledge of Latin was a prerequisite in nineteenth-century South Africa for university study or a career in law or medicine—a reality that led to passionate debates over whether Blacks in mission schools should be allowed to study classics (Lambert 2011, 102–4). Just as what we saw with Gandhi and Nehru in India, we read in Nelson Mandela's (1994, 456) autobiography that, during his imprisonment on Robben Island, he not only read some "classic Greek plays" but also participated in performing *Antigone*. These Greek plays gave him two important understandings. In Mandela's own words, he learned that "character was measured by facing up to difficult situations ... a hero was a man who would not break even under the most trying circumstances" and that "Antigone ... was ... a freedom fighter, for she defied the law on the grounds that it was unjust" (456). For Mandela, this fifth century BCE play by Sophocles "symbolized our struggle" (456; see also Parker 2017, 21–27). The influence of the New Testament and classics on South African history can be seen in the novel *Elizabeth Costello* by the Nobel Prize–winning South African author J. M. Coetzee (2004, 113–50); both disciplines are featured as the foci of debates about the future of South Africa between the Australian protagonist and her sister, who revealingly was a classicist before she became a missionary nun in South Africa (see also Lambert 2011, 125–32).

These uses of the New Testament and classics have much to do with the assumed authority, whether religions or cultural, being given to these texts. More specifically, Ali Parchami (2015, 105) explains that the Roman Empire carries a particular appeal to modern North Atlantic colonialists and racists because "they were the first hegemonic power in the Western world to adopt a sophisticated language that justified interventionist expansionism under a veneer of altruism and even humanitarianism." The rhetoric of *Pax Romana* claimed its colonial/imperial expansion as self-defense or as a divinely ordained responsibility to bring order (peace, civilization, and even spiritual well-being) to an otherwise chaotic world. While there are, of course, many differences, this fits hand in glove with the claims of *Pax Britannica* and *Pax Americana*. Just as the Roman historian Livy could declare that "it should be clear to all nations that the forces of the Roman people brought not slavery to free peoples, but on the contrary, freedom for the enslaved" (*Ab ubre cond.* 45.18.1 [Schlesinger, LCL]), James Bryce would say in 1914, "let anyone think of the general state of the ancient world before the conquest of Rome ... [and] what Rome did for her subjects, or what England has done in India," and Woodrow Wilson would state in 1917 that the United States "seek no indemnities for ourselves, no material compensation for the sacrifices we shall freely make. We are but one of the champions of the rights of mankind" (cited in Parchami 2015, 107, 110, 112). More recently, the invasion of Iraq by the United States was justified as self-defense because Iraq had supposedly stocked "weapons of mass destruction." When such weapons were not found, the United States quickly turned to the tried-and-true rhetoric of "liberation" by stating that they were bringing Iraqis freedom and humanitarian aid (Parchami 2015, 113), with US President George Bush reportedly justifying the invasion on the grounds that he was "driven with a mission from God" (MacAskill 2005). Like the Roman Empire, the imperialism of the United States also tends to avoid direct control if possible (Parchami 2015, 105, 115, 119; see also Hardt and Negri 2000, 160–83).

Jacques Berlinerblau (2008, 2) also gives a more specific reason why the New Testament is often used for colonial, imperial, racial, and other politically charged issues when he shares a "most profound insight" that a well-known Bible scholar shared during a heated discussion about the Bible and homosexuality: "the Bible in and of itself is neither good or evil. It can be used for both. It says everything. It says nothing. The Bible is just raw power." What this unnamed professor said about the Bible applies, of course, to the New Testament. Regardless of whether one agrees or disagrees with these monikers, the New Testament and classics come together again in the self-identification of the United States as "the New Jerusalem" (Rev 21:2) and in the critique of it as "the new Rome" (Boruchoff 2008; Malamud 2009; Smil 2010; Richmann 2020).

Ongoing Contention and Convergence

We can see, therefore, that the use of both the New Testament and classics in the so-called culture wars is not exactly new (e.g., Underwood 2006; Adler 2016). Just as some call the COVID vaccine "the mark of the beast" (Rev 13:16–18) and others refer to Matthew's greatest commandment (Matt 22:36–40) or to Luke's parable of the Good Samaritan (Luke 10:25–37) to support people getting the COVID vaccination (e.g., McCammon 2021), classics can be invoked in court to argue for and against the criminality of homosexuality (e.g., Finnis 1994; Nussbaum 1994). Let's not forget that the New Testament has long been embroiled in debates about homosexuality (Scroggs 1983; Brooten 1996; Marchal 2020) and that classical works such as Homer's *Iliad*, Sophocles's *Oedipus Rex*, Thucydides's *History of the Peloponnesian War*, Lucretius's *On the Nature of Things*, and Virgil's *Geor-

gics have plenty to say about plagues (Stover 1999; Burton 2001; Heerink 2011; Michelakis 2019; Botting 2021).

Although appealing to these ancient texts in sociopolitical debates is nothing new, this does not make the matter any less serious. Looking at both biblioblogs and academic writings, James Crossley (2008) shows that much of New Testament studies has (unreflectively?) assumed and reinforced orientalist stereotypes of Arabs and Islam in ways that reinforce Anglo-American political power and "the War on Terror," as well as advocated for Jesus's Jewishness due to national and religious biases against Palestinians and Muslims. Douglas Boin (2016) similarly warns that simplistic presentations of early Christians and Romans as being engaged in a "culture clash" fits too easily into Samuel P. Huntington's (1996) "clash of civilization" thesis and the Islamophobia that Huntington's thesis helped promote, especially when the fall of the Roman Empire was invoked again in response to the decade-old Syrian refugee crisis and the 2015 Paris massacre. Such problematic talks of culture clash not only minimize the disagreements among early Christians and among Romans but also questionably maximize the differences between early Christians and Romans. Besides underscoring the relevance of classics for today, Boin's warning also points to the need for classics and New Testament scholars to learn from one another. Not only did the worlds of the early Christians and Romans collide and elide, but so too these ancient worlds also collide and elide with our world today. This latter point has been recognized and promoted separately by scholars in classics (Malamud 2009; Bassi and Euben 2010b; Hardwick and Harrison 2013; Zuckerberg 2018) and in New Testament studies (Schüssler Fiorenza 1988; Wimbush 2011; Segovia 2015), but the former point is partly what we are trying to encourage via this volume.

Canons of Chance and Choice

Besides the question of what a particular New Testament text or a specific Greco-Roman philosopher might say or not say about colonialism, disease, or homosexuality, there is also the issue of what texts we choose to read and not to read from the past. Classics and New Testament studies are both in the discipline of saving something from the ancient world. At the same time, we know full well that what these two disciplines save is partial in both senses of the word: fragmentary and partisan.

We cannot save everything from either the classical world of Greece and Rome or that of the early Christians. Much of what we have lost (just like much of what has been saved) is the historical result of both accidents and intentions. What history has preserved for us, however, we also do not necessarily keep in the same way. Instead, classics and New Testament studies have their respective canons because of a process of selection. Certain authors and texts have been archived and affirmed, but others have been archived and avoided. What Derrida says about archives in general is applicable to the formation of disciplinary canons: it "begins by selection, and this selection is a violence" (cited in Naas 2015, 135).

While this political—that is to say, power-based—process of selection (much of which we do not know and cannot understand) started long before us, we are now part of this *ongoing* process by virtue of our guild memberships. What we continue to canonize and what we continue to bracket or leave out (Buell 2014) is a responsibility we cannot deny. For the purposes of this volume, this responsibility includes (1) what we do with and how we classify the canons of each other's disciplines and (2) whether and how we address the socially divisive issues of our own times. As Derrida (2006, 18, 67) writes, an inheritance is something that "*one must* filter, sift, criticize, one must sort out several different possibilities that inhabit the same injunction.... This inheritance must be reaffirmed by transforming it as radically as will be necessary."

Conjuring Interconnected Worlds-to-Come?

How may New Testament and classics scholars approach our work dialogically and face these contemporary and interdisciplinary challenges? This is what the contributors in this volume attempt to explore with their essays and responses. Since we want our readers to read each entry in its entirety, we will not provide any summaries here. As the editors of this volume, we do want to emphasize that, as readers of the New Testament and classical texts, we do not think these ancient texts can tell us what we should do today, but they can help us question what we think, especially when we are confronted with controversial issues. Appealing to ancient authorities such as the classics or the New Testament as if they can dictate what or how things should be effectually but ineffectively flattens all kinds of worlds. Instead, by continuing to think with these libraries of texts *together*, we may be able to better rethink our present and our future worlds.

A related point we would like to emphasize is that Said's worldliness must be taken in a passive and an active sense. Our intellectual work is inevitably influenced by the realities of the world; at the same time, our intellectual work also has the potential to make worlds—or what Gayatri Spivak (1990, 1–2) calls "worlding" (see also Cheah 2016, 95–130). Although Spivak's coining of the term refers to colonial representations, we should keep in mind, without denying the existence of power differentials, that representations are not monopolized by colonialists. In the words of Toni Morrison (1993), "word-work is sublime … because it is generative." Just as one uses the reverse gear and the rearview mirror of an automobile not to continue driving backward but to facilitate a transition to a forward moving journey, our reading and retelling of classical and New Testament stories can generate different worlds in an open future rather than govern or safeguard the world in a foreclosed future. Having experienced the 2008 recession, the ever-worsening climate crisis, and now COVID-19, we should know that our world is not only fragile but also contingent (Connolly 2013). Since our world is (1) constantly changing and becoming and (2) not devoid of power relations and inequities, the question is if and how our collaborative work across New Testament and classical studies may intervene in these worlding processes, particularly those processes of imperialism and systems of oppression. Will our word-work open up or close down "the coming of other worlds" (Cheah 2016, 194)?

To do so, we must challenge the Eurocentric assumptions of both disciplines. For example, the scholarly convention of contextualizing New Testament studies by referring to the Greco-Roman world often erases the Afro-Asiatic provenance of the New Testament writings (Sadler 2007; Byron 2009). In classics, one may talk similarly about geographical and cultural proximities in the interchanges of multiple axes—between Greek and Roman societies and those in the Near and Middle East, India, and Africa, not to mention Islamic scholarly engagement with and contribution to ancient Greco-Roman works in the medieval period (Rosenthal 1975, 1990; Pormann 2009, 2012). It is our hope that conversations between New Testament and classics scholars will make our disciplines "less the stable source of Western identity and more a source of political and cultural self-critique" (Bassi and Euben 2010a, x).

In this spirit of self-critique that can expose and potentially transcend divides, we also think it is important to acknowledge that the disciplinary designations classics and New Testament studies have themselves long been markers of division. The term *classics* has its very etymology in class distinction, as the early Roman king Servius Tullius is said to have used the adjective *classicus* of the men in the wealthiest tier of the six groups (*classes*; sing. *classis*) of society (Livy, *Ad urbe cond.* 1.43.5, with Hall 2008, 387–88 and Schein 2008, 76–77). The second-century CE author Aulus Gellius (*Noct. att.* 19.8.15) is the first to attest to how the term *classicus* could be applied to certain authors (and not to others), showing the "transfer [of] the language of economic and social stratification to the realm of literature" (Schein 2008, 76). This designation of some texts—and, by extension, their readers—as classic and thus exclusive and superior has had a long and enduring hold, as both the preceding pages in this introduction and many of the ensuing essays in this volume explore.[1] It has led to the privileging not only of certain texts and cultures but also of particular temporal periods and geographical areas. At the same time, the term *New Testament* has long been considered problematic for its implications that the Jewish scriptures of the Old Testament were outdated or even replaced (Edwards 1999; Seitz 1998). Alternatives to both these designations have emerged (e.g., "Greco-Roman studies" or "ancient Mediterranean studies" for classics; "Christian Testament" or "Christian Scriptures" for New Testament) but have not taken hold broadly. Both classics and New Testament are problematic yet entrenched categories; their staying power requires some energy and volition on our part to address and possibly change.

We do not know if or what worlds will emerge out of this volume, but we do know how our volume began. The process originated from a two-day conference sponsored by the McFarland Center for Religion, Ethics, and Culture at the College of the Holy Cross because of our curiosity about the relationship between classics and New Testament studies. New Testament scholars presented papers and classicists served as respondents, with discussion among the group in attendance following each paper. In putting together their written responses, the respondents had the opportunity to read and work from the papers that the New Testament scholars submitted for publication. The dialogue among contributors thus took place in a number of ways and at several stages. It is difficult for the inherently linear, page-to-page setup of a print volume to replicate this interchange

---

1. In this introduction we have opted not to capitalize *classics* because the uppercase "C" may seem to imply a superior status to the study of ancient Greek and Latin texts in particular. We do not, however, assume that this implication is embraced by scholars who capitalize the term.

in a representative but clear way, and so we have opted to present the ten papers first and then the set of seven responses.

Each of the papers contextualizes its treatment of New Testament texts within a broader look at the ancient Mediterranean world while also directly addressing issues of marginalization and oppression that remain vital in the twenty-first century. After beginning with a paper questioning disciplinary boundaries and the structures that have kept them up (Denise Kimber Buell), we have two papers (Gay L. Byron, Yii-Jan Lin) that focus on the question of race. From there we move to other issues of marginalization and oppression: namely, disability (Candida R. Moss), sexuality (Joseph A. Marchal), slavery (Jennifer A. Glancy, Abraham Smith), and economic inequity (Allen Dwight Callahan). Then we go to a paper that reflects broadly on the concept of equality (Jorann Økland) and one that argues for interdisciplinarity through a specific case study (Laura Salah Nasrallah).

Each of the responses by classics scholars sets out to bring new texts or images into dialogue with the ideas explored in these papers. The first response by Timothy Joseph and the concluding response by Katherine Lu Hsu aim to respond to the volume's papers as a whole. The four other responses focus more on particular papers, with Shelley P. Haley responding to the papers by Byron and Marchal; Thomas R. Martin responding to those by Lin and Moss; Dominic Machado responding to Glancy and Smith, and Douglas Boin responding to Callahan and Økland. The volume closes with an afterword by Joy Connolly, a scholar in the field of classics who also brings a particularly broad cross-disciplinary perspective from her tenure, beginning in 2019, as the president of the American Council of Learned Societies. Connolly's afterword takes into consideration all of the preceding contents of the volume and thus the dialogue in which the papers and responses engage.

With this volume we hope our effort is not the end but rather the beginning of a sustained dialogue that will include many of our readers. Since disciplinary formation depends on shared research methods and topics as well as the company we keep, classics and New Testament scholars will need to cultivate not only conversation but also relationships if we are to destabilize disciplinary boundaries.

Works Cited

Adler, Eric. 2016. *Classics, The Culture Wars, and Beyond*. Ann Arbor: University of Michigan Press.

Agnew, J. H., and O. G. Ebbeke. 1839. "Preface." Pages v–viii in *A Grammar of the Idioms of the Greek Language of the New Testament*. By Georg Benedikt Winter. New York: Carter & Brothers.

Ahmed, Sara. 2012. *On Being Included: Racism and Diversity in Institutional Life*. Durham, NC: Duke University Press.

Ameriks, Karl. 2006. *Kant and the Historical Turn: Philosophy as Critical Interpretation*. New York: Oxford University Press.

Aristotle. 1932. *Politics*. Translated by H. Rackham. LCL. Cambridge: Harvard University Press.

Armstrong, Richard H. 2018. *A Compulsion for Antiquity: Freud and the Ancient World*. Ithaca, NY: Cornell University Press.

Atherstone, Andrew. 2003. "Benjamin Jowett's Pauline Commentary: An Atonement Controversy." *JTS* 54:139–53.

Baird, William. 1992–2003. *History of New Testament Research*. 3 vols. Minneapolis: Fortress.

Bakhtin, Mikhail M. 1981. *The Dialogic Imagination: Four Essays*. Edited by Michael Holquist. Translated by Caryl Emerson and Michael Holquist. Austin: University of Texas Press

Barker, Stephen, ed. 1996. *Excavation and Their Objects: Freud's Collection of Antiquity*. Albany: State University of New York Press.

Bassi, Karen, and J. Peter Euben. 2010a. "Introduction." Pages ix–xxi in *When Worlds Elide: Classics, Politics, Culture*. Edited by Karen Bassi and J. Peter Euben. Lanham, MD: Lexington.

——, eds. 2010b. *When Worlds Elide: Classics, Politics, Culture*. Lanham, MD: Lexington.

Bazan, B. Carlos. 1998. "The Original Idea of the University." Pages 3–27 in *Rethinking the Future of the University*. Edited by David Lyle Jeffrey and Dominic Manganiello. Ottawa: University of Ottawa Press.

Bell, Dorian. 2018. *Globalizing Race: Antisemitism and Empire in French and European Culture*. Evanston, IL: Northwestern University Press.

Bentley, Jerry H. 1983. *Humanists and Holy Writ: New Testament Scholarship in the Renaissance*. Princeton: Princeton University Press.

Berlinerblau, Jacques. 2008. *Thumpin' It: The Use and Abuse of the Bible*. Louisville: Westminster John Knox.

Blanton, Ward. 2007. *Displacing Christian Origins: Philosophy, Secularity, and the New Testament.* Chicago: University of Chicago Press.

Bledstein, Burton J. 1976. *The Culture of Professionalism: The Middle Class and the Development of Higher Education in America.* New York: Norton.

Bloom, Harold. 1997. *The Anxiety of Influence: A Theory of Poetry.* 2nd ed. New York: Oxford University Press.

———. 2019. *Possessed by Memory: The Inward Light of Criticism.* New York: Vintage.

Bock, Darrell L. 2011. "Faith and the Historical Jesus: Does a Confessional Position and Respect for the Jesus Tradition Preclude Serious Historical Engagement?" *JSHJ* 9:3–25.

Boin, Douglas. 2013. *Ostia in Late Antiquity.* Cambridge: Cambridge University Press.

———. 2014. "Hellenistic 'Judaism' and the Social Origins of the 'Pagan–Christian' Debate." *JECS* 22:167–96.

———. 2015. *Coming Out Christian in the Roman World: How the Followers of Jesus Made a Place in Caesar's Empire.* New York: Bloomsbury.

———. 2016. "Classicists' Christian Problem." *The Chronicle of Higher Education.* January 10, 2016. https://www.chronicle.com/article/classicists-christian-problem/.

Bond, Sarah E. 2019. "Addressing the Divide between Biblical Studies and Classics. Society for Classical Studies." April 13, 2019. https://tinyurl.com/SBL06104a.

Borgen, Peder. 1996. *Early Christianity and Hellenistic Judaism.* Edinburgh: T&T Clark.

Boruchoff, David A. 2008. "New Spain, New England, and the New Jerusalem: The "Translation" of Empire, Faith, and Learning (*translatio imperii, fidei ac scientiae*) in Colonial Missionary Project." *Early American Literature* 43:5–34.

Botha, Pieter J. J. 2004. "Assessing Representations of the Imperial Cult in New Testament Studies." *Verbum et ecclesia* 25:14–45.

Botting, Eileen Hunt. 2021. "The Politics of Epidemics, from Thucydides to Mary Shelley to COVID-19." *Current History* 120:35–37.

Boyarin, Daniel. 2012. *The Jewish Gospels: The Story of the Jewish Christ.* New York: The New Press.

———. 2019. *Judaism: The Genealogy of a Modern Notion.* New Brunswick, NJ: Rutgers University Press.

Brooten, Bernadette. 1996. *Love between Women: Early Christian Responses to Female Homoeroticism.* Chicago: University of Chicago Press.

Buell, Denise Kimber. 2014. "Canons Unbound." Pages 293–306 in *Feminist Biblical Studies in the Twentieth Century.* Edited by Elisabeth Schüssler Fiorenza. Atlanta: SBL Press.

Burton, Paul. 2001. "Avian Plague: Sophocles' *Oedipus Tyrannus* and Alfred Hitchcock's *The Birds.*" *Mouseion* 1:313–41.

Byron, Gay L. 2009. "Ancient Ethiopia and the New Testament: Ethnic (Con)Texts and Racialized (Sub)Texts." Pages 161–90 in *They Were All Together in One Place? Toward Minority Biblical Criticism.* Edited by Randall C. Bailey, Tat-siong Benny Liew, and Fernando F. Segovia. SemeiaSt 57. Atlanta: Society of Biblical Literature.

Carson, D. A. 2016. "The Many Facets of the Current Discussion." Pages 3–40 in *The Enduring Authority of the Christian Scriptures.* Edited by D. A. Carson. Grand Rapids: Eerdmans.

Carter, Warren. 2021. *Jesus and the Empire of God: Reading the Gospels in the Roman Empire.* Eugene, OR: Cascade.

Chapman, Honora, and Zuleika Rodgers, eds. 2016. *A Companion to Josephus.* Malden, MA: Wiley-Blackwell.

Chazan, Robert. 2016. *From Anti-Judaism to Anti-Semitism: Ancient and Medieval Christian Constructions of Jewish History.* Cambridge: Cambridge University Press.

Cheah, Pheng. 2016. *What Is a World? On Postcolonial Literature as World Literature.* Durham, NC: Duke University Press.

Chow, Rey. 2021. *A Face Drawn in Sand: Humanistic Inquiry and Foucault in the Present.* New York: Columbia University Press.

Coetzee, J. M. 2004. *Elizabeth Costello.* New York: Penguin.

Collins, John J., and Gregory Sterling, eds. 2001. *Hellenism in the Land of Israel.* Notre Dame: University of Notre Dame Press.

Connolly, William E. 2013. *On the Fragility of Things: Self-Organizing Processes, Neoliberal Fantasies, and Democratic Activism.* Durham, NC: Duke University Press.

Conybeare, Catherine, and Simon Goldhill, eds. 2020. *Classical Philology and Theology: Entanglement, Disavowal, and the Godlike Scholar.* Cambridge: Cambridge University Press.

Crane, Susan A. 2000. *Collecting and Historical Consciousness in Early Nineteenth-Century Germany.* Ithaca, NY: Cornell University Press.

Crossley, James G. 2008. *Jesus in an Age of Terror: Scholarly Projects for a New American Century.* London: Equinox.

Derrida, Jacques. 1984. "Of an Apocalyptic Tone Recently Adopted in Philosophy." Translated by John P. Leavey Jr. *Oxford Literary Review* 6.2:3–37.

———. 1995. *The Gift of Death*. Translated by David Wills. Chicago: University of Chicago Press.

———. 2006. *Specter of Marx: The State of the Debt, the Work of Mourning, and the New International*. Translated by Peggy Kamuf. Introduction by Bernd Magnus and Stephen Cullenberg. New York: Routledge.

Donaldson, Terrance L. 2010. *Jews and Anti-Judaism in the New Testament*. Waco, TX: Baylor University Press.

Dube, Musa W. 1999. "Consuming a Cultural Bomb: Translating *Badimo* into "Demons" in the Setswana Bible (Matthew 8.28–34; 15.22; 10.8)." *JSNT* 73:33–58.

———. 2015. "Translating Cultures: The Creation of Sin in the Public Space of Batswana." *Scriptura* 114.1:1–11.

Dunkelgrün, Theodor. 2020. "The Philology of Judaism: Zacharias Frankel, the Septuagint, and the Jewish Study of Ancient Greek in the Nineteenth Century." Pages 63–85 in *Classical Philology and Theology: Entanglement, Disavowal, and the Godlike Scholar*. Edited by Catherine Conybeare and Simon Goldhill. Cambridge: Cambridge University Press.

Eagleton, Terry. 1984. *The Function of Criticism: From the Spectator to Post-structuralism*. London: Verso.

———. 2018. *Radical Sacrifice*. New Haven: Yale University Press.

———. 2020. *Tragedy*. New Haven: Yale University Press.

Edwards, James R. 1999. "What's in a Name: Why We Shouldn't Call the Old Testament the 'Hebrew Bible.'" *Christianity Today* 43.9:59–61.

Eliot, T. S. 1936. *Essays Ancient and Modern*. London: Faber & Faber.

Ellis, Heather. 2007. "Newman and Arnold: Classics, Christianity, and Manliness in Tractarian Oxford." Pages 53–69 in *Oxford Classics: Teaching and Learning 1800–2000*. Edited by Christopher Stray. London: Bloomsbury.

Elm, Susanna. 2020. "Julian the Emperor on Statues (of Himself)." Pages 126–48 in *Classical Philology and Theology: Entanglement, Disavowal, and the Godlike Scholar*. Edited by Catherine Conybeare and Simon Goldhill. Cambridge: Cambridge University Press.

Engberg-Pedersen, Troels, ed. 2001. *Paul beyond the Judaism-Hellenism Divide*. Louisville: Westminster John Knox.

Engel, A. J. 1983. *From Clergyman to Don: The Rise of the Academic Profession in Nineteenth-Century Oxford*. Oxford: Oxford University Press.
Euben, J. Peter. 1990. *The Tragedy of Political Theory: The Road Not Taken*. Princeton: Princeton University Press.
———. 1997. *Corrupting Youth: Political Education, Democratic Culture, and Political Theory*. Princeton: Princeton University Press.
———. 2003. *Platonic Noise*. Princeton: Princeton University Press.
Euben, J. Peter, John R. Wallach, and Josiah Ober, eds. 1994. *Athenian Political Thought and the Reconstruction of American Democracy*. Ithaca, NY: Cornell University Press.
Evans, Hubert. 1988. *Looking Back on India*. London: Totowa.
Fairweather, William. 1924. *Jesus and the Greeks, or Early Christianity in the Tideway of Hellenism*. Edinburgh: T&T Clark.
Finnis, John. 1994. "'Shameless Acts' in Colorado: Abuse of Scholarship in Constitutional Cases." *Academic Questions* 7:10–41.
Fitzmyer, Joseph A. 1970. "Languages of Palestine in the First Century A.D." *CBQ* 32:501–31.
Foucault, Michel. 1980. *The History of Sexuality: An Introduction*. Translated by Robert Hurley. New York: Vintage.
———. 1985. *The Use of Pleasure*. Vol. 2 of *The History of Sexuality*. Translated by Robert Hurley. New York: Vintage.
———. 1986. *The Care of the Self*. Vol. 3 of *The History of Sexuality*. Translated by Robert Hurley. New York: Vintage.
———. 1988. *Politics, Philosophy, Culture: Interviews and Other Writings, 1977–1984*. Translated by Alan Sheridan et al. Edited with an introduction by Lawrence D. Kritzman. New York: Routledge.
———. 2001. *Fearless Speech*. Edited by Joseph Pearson. Los Angeles: Semiotext(e).
———. 2002a. *The Order of Things: An Archaeology of the Human Sciences*. New York: Routledge.
———. 2002b. "What Is Critique?" Pages 191–211 in *The Political*. Edited by David Ingram. Malden, MA: Blackwell.
———. 2010. *The Government of Self and Others: Lectures at the Collège de France, 1982–1983*. Edited by Arnold I. Davidson. Translated by Graham Burchell. New York: Picador.
———. 2011. *The Courage of the Truth (The Government of Self and Others II): Lectures at the Collège de France, 1983–1984*. Edited by Arnold I. Davidson. Translated by Graham Burchell. New York: Palgrave Macmillan.

Fredriksen, Paula, and Adele Reinhartz, eds. 2002. *Jesus, Judaism, and Christian Anti-Judaism: Reading the New Testament after the Holocaust*. Louisville: Westminster John Knox.

Frye, Northrop. 1982. *The Great Code: Bible and Literature*. New York: Harcourt.

———. 2020. *Anatomy of Criticism: Four Essays*. Foreword by David Damrosch. Princeton: Princeton University Press.

Gager, John G. 1985. *The Origins of Anti-Semitism: Attitudes toward Judaism in Pagan and Christian Antiquity*. Oxford: Oxford University Press.

Gamwell, Lynn, and Richard Wells, eds. 1989. *Sigmund Freud and Art: His Personal Collection of Antiquities*. Introduction by Peter Gay. London: Thames & Hudson.

Garrison, Irene Peirano. 2020. "Source, Original, and Authenticity between Philology and Theology." Pages 87–109 in *Classical Philology and Theology: Entanglement, Disavowal, and the Godlike Scholar*. Edited by Catherine Conybeare and Simon Goldhill. Cambridge: Cambridge University Press.

Gerdmar, Anders. 2008. *Roots of Theological Anti-Semitism: German Biblical Interpretation and the Jews, from Herder and Semler to Kittel and Bultmann*. Leiden: Brill.

Godsey, William D. 2008. "Nation, Government, and 'Anti-Semitism' in Early Nineteenth-Century Austria." *The Historical Journal* 51:49–85.

Goldhill, Simon. 2002. *Who Needs Greek? Contests in Cultural History of Hellenism*. Cambridge: Cambridge University Press.

———. 2020a. Review of *Liddell and Scott: The History, Methodology, and Languages of the World's Leading Lexicon of Ancient Greek*, edited by Christopher Stray, Michael Clarke, and Joshua Katz. *Bryn Mawr Classical Review*. November 11, 2020. https://tinyurl.com/SBL06104b.

———. 2020b. "The Union and Divorce of Classical Philology and Theology." Pages 33–62 in *Classical Philology and Theology: Entanglement, Disavowal, and the Godlike Scholar*. Edited by Catherine Conybeare and Simon Goldhill. Cambridge: Cambridge University Press.

Grafton, Anthony, Glenn W. Most, and James E. G. Zetzel. 1985. "Introduction." Pages 3–35 in *Friedrich August Wolf's Prolegomena to Homer, 1795*. Translated with introduction and notes by Anthony Grafton, Glenn W. Most, and James E. G. Zetzel. Princeton: Princeton University Press.

Gruen, Erich. 2002. *Diaspora: Jews amidst Greeks and Romans*. Cambridge: Harvard University Press.

Gupta, Nijay K. 2014. "They Are Not Gods!" Jewish and Christian Idol Polemic and Greco-Roman use of Cult Statues." *CBQ* 76:704–19.
Hagerman, C. A. 2013. *Britain's Imperial Muse: The Classics, Imperialism, and the Indian Empire, 1784–1914*. New York: Palgrave Macmillan.
Hall, Edith. 2008. "Putting the Class into Classical Reception." Pages 386–98 in *A Companion to Classical Receptions*. Edited by Lorna Hardwick and Christopher Stray. Malden, MA: Wiley.
Hardt, Michael, and Antonio Negri. 2000. *Empire*. Cambridge: Harvard University Press.
Hardwick, Lorna, and Stephen Harrison, eds. 2013. *Classics in the Modern World: A Democratic Turn?* Oxford: Oxford University Press.
Harlow, Barbara, and Mia Carter, eds. 2003. *Scramble for Africa*. Vol. 2 of *Archives of Empire*. Durham, NC: Duke University Press.
Hattersley, Michael E. 2009. *Socrates and Jesus: The Argument That Shaped Western Civilization*. New York: Algora.
Hauser, Alan J., and Duane F. Watson. 2017. "Preface." Pages vii–ix in *The Enlightenment through the Nineteenth Century*. Vol. 3 of *A History of Biblical Interpretation*. Edited by Alan J. Hauser and Duane F. Watson. Grand Rapids: Eerdmans.
Heerink, M. A. J. 2011. "Ovid's Aeginetan Plague and the Metamorphosis of the *Georgics*." *Hermes* 139:464–72.
Hegel, Georg Wilhelm Friedrich. 2018. *The Phenomenology of Spirit*. Edited and translated by Terry P. Pinkard. Cambridge: Cambridge University Press.
Hengel, Martin. 1974. *Judaism and Hellenism: Studies in Their Encounter in Palestine during the Early Hellenistic Period*. 2 vols. Translated by John Bowden. Philadelphia: Fortress.
Higgins, Lesley. 1993. "Jowett and Pater: Trafficking in Platonic Wares." *Victorian Studies* 37:43–72.
Hilton, John. 2017. "Cecil John Rhodes, the Classics and Imperialism." Pages 88–113 in *South Africa, Greece, Rome: Classical Confrontations*. Edited by Grant Parker. Cambridge: Cambridge University Press.
Hinchliff, Peter. 1987. *Benjamin Jowett and the Christian Religion*. Oxford: Oxford University Press.
Honig, Bonnie H. 2013. *Antigone, Interrupted*. Cambridge: Cambridge University Press.
Horsley, Richard A. 2003. *Jesus and Empire: The Kingdom of God and the New World Disorder*. Minneapolis: Fortress.

Howard, Thomas Albert. 2009. *Religion and the Rise of Historicism: W. M. L. deWette, Jacob Burckhardt and the Theological Origins of Nineteenth-Century Historical Consciousness.* Cambridge: Cambridge University Press.

Huntington, Samuel P. 1996. *The Clash of Civilizations and the Remaking of World Order.* New York: Simon & Schuster.

Hurtado, Larry W. 2009. "New Testament Studies in the Twentieth Century." *Religion* 39:43–57.

Irigaray, Luce. 2017. *To Be Born: Genesis of a New Human Being.* New York: Palgrave Macmillan.

James, Patrick. 2019. "The Greek of the New Testament." Pages 151–80 in *Liddell and Scott: The History, Methodology, and Languages of the World's Leading Lexicon of Ancient Greek.* Edited by Christopher Stray, Michael Clarke, and Joshua Katz. Oxford: Oxford University Press.

Jensen, Uffa. 2007. "Into the Spiral of Problematic Perceptions: Modern Anti-Semitism and *gebildetes Bürgertum* in Nineteenth-Century Germany." *German History* 25:348–71.

Johnson, Luke Timothy. 2009. *Among the Gentiles: Greco-Roman Religion and Christianity.* New Haven: Yale University Press.

Johnston, Robert K. 1982. "Interpreting Scripture: Literary Criticism and Evangelical Hermeneutics." *ChrLit* 32:33–47.

Jones, Christopher P. 2014. *Between Pagan and Christian.* Cambridge: Harvard University Press.

———. 2015. "The 'Jesus' Wife' Papyrus in the History of Forgery." *NTS* 61:368–78.

Kearney, Richard. 2021. *Touch: Recovering Our Most Vital Sense.* New York: Columbia University Press.

Klein, Herbert S. 2018. "The 'Historical Turn' in the Social Sciences." *Journal of Interdisciplinary History* 48:295–312.

Kloppenborg, John S., and John W. Marshall, eds. 2005. *Apocalypticism, Anti-Semitism, and the Historical Jesus: Subtexts in Criticism.* New York: T&T Clark.

Kolstø, Pål. 2014. "Competing with Entrepreneurial Diasporians: Origins of Anti-Semitism in Nineteenth-Century Russia." *Nationalities Papers* 42:691–707.

Kraus, Thomas J. 2007. *Ad Fontes: Original Manuscripts and Their Significance for Studying Early Christianity—Selected Essays.* Leiden: Brill.

Lalitha, Jayachitra, and Mitzi J. Smith, eds. 2014. *Teaching All Nations: Interrogating the Matthean Great Commission.* Minneapolis: Fortress.

Lambert, Michael. 2011. *The Classics and South African Identities.* New York: Bloomsbury.

Langton, Daniel R. 2010. *The Apostle Paul in the Jewish Imagination: A Study in Modern Jewish-Christian Relations.* Cambridge: Cambridge University Press.

Leonard, Miriam, ed. 2010. *Derrida and Antiquity.* Oxford: Oxford University Press.

———. 2012. *Socrates and the Jews: Hellenism and Hebraism from Moses Mendelssohn to Sigmund Freud.* Chicago: Chicago University Press.

Leonard, Miriam, and James I. Porter. 2014. "Forum on Bonnie Honig's *Antigone, Interrupted.*" *International Journal of the Classical Tradition* 21:296–300.

Lepore, Jill. 2018. *These Truths: A History of the United States.* New York: Norton.

Levine, Amy-Jill. 2006. *The Misunderstood Jew: The Church and the Scandal of the Jewish Jesus.* San Francisco: HarperSanFrancisco.

Levine, Amy-Jill, and Marc Zvi Brettler, eds. 2017. *The Jewish Annotated New Testament.* 2nd ed. Oxford: Oxford University Press.

Lin, Yii-Jan. 2016. *The Erotic Life of Manuscripts: New Testament Textual Criticism and the Biological Sciences.* Oxford: Oxford University Press.

Livy. 1951. *History of Rome, Volume XIII: Books 43–45.* Translated by Alfred C. Schlesinger. LCL. Cambridge: Harvard University Press.

Longstaff, Thomas R. W., and Page A. Thomas. 1988. *The Synoptic Problem: A Bibliography, 1716–1988.* Macon, GA: Mercer University Press.

MacAskill, Ewen. 2005. "George Bush: 'God Told Me to End the Tyranny in Iraq.'" *The Guardian.* October 7, 2005. https://tinyurl.com/SBL06104c.

Macgregor, G. H. C. 1936. *Jew and Greek: Tutors unto Christ—The Jewish and Hellenistic Background of the New Testament.* London: Nicholson & Watson.

Malamud, Margaret. 2009. *Ancient Rome and Modern America.* Malden, MA: Wiley-Blackwell.

Mandela, Nelson. 1994. *Long Walk to Freedom.* New York: Little, Brown.

McCammon, Sarah. 2021. "'Love Your Neighbor' and Get the Shot: White Evangelical Leaders Push COVID Vaccines." *National Public Radio.* April 5, 2021. https://tinyurl.com/SBL06104h.

McKnight, Scot, and Joseph B. Modica, eds. 2013. *Jesus Is Lord, Caesar Is Not: Evaluating Empire in New Testament Studies.* Downers Grove, IL: InterVarsity Press.

Marchal, Joseph A. 2020. *Appalling Bodies: Queer Figures before and after Paul's Letters*. Oxford: Oxford University Press.

Mendonca, Megan. 2019. "Editor as Author: Q&A with Colin Whiting." *American School of Classical Studies at Athens*. April 8, 2019. https://www.ascsa.edu.gr/news/newsDetails/editor-as-author.

Michelakis, Pantelis. 2019. "Naming the Plague in Homer, Sophocles, and Thucydides." *AJP* 140:381–414.

Moore, Stephen D. 2012. "The Turn to "Empire" in Biblical Studies." *Search* 35:19–27.

Moore, Stephen D., and Yvonne Sherwood. 2011. *The Invention of the Biblical Scholar: A Critical Manifesto*. Minneapolis: Fortress.

Morgan, Robert. 2005. "Christian Faith and Historical Jesus Research: A Reply to James Dunn." *ExpTim* 116.7:217–23.

Morris, Jeremy. 2005. *F. D. Maurice and the Crisis of Christian Authority*. Oxford: Oxford University Press.

Morrison, Toni. 1993. "Nobel Lecture." *The Nobel Prize*. December 7, 1993. https://tinyurl.com/SBL06104d.

Most, Glenn W. 1985. *The Measures of Praise: Structure and Function in Pindar's Second Pythian and Seventh Nemean Odes*. Göttingen: Vandenhoeck & Ruprecht.

———. 2005. *Doubting Thomas*. Cambridge: Harvard University Press.

———. 2019. "Karl Lachmann (1793–1851): Reconstructing the Transmission of a Classical Latin Author." *History of Humanities* 4:269–73.

Mothoagae, Ithumeleng D. 2017. "The Transmutation of *Bogwera* in Luke 2:21 in the 1857 English-Setswana Bible." *HvTSt* 73.3:1–9.

———. 2018. "The Reordering of the Batswana Cosmology in the 1840 English-Setswana New Testament." *HvTSt* 74.1:1–12.

Moxnes, Halvor. 2003. "Asceticism and Christian Identity in Antiquity: A Dialogue with Foucault and Paul." *JSNT* 26:3–29.

Müller-Sievers, Helmut. 2001. "Reading Evidence: Textual Criticism as Science in the Nineteenth Century." *Germanic Review* 76:162–71.

Myles, Robert J. 2016. "The Fetish for a Subversive Jesus." *JSHJ* 14:52–70.

Naas, Michael. 2015. *The End of the World and Other Teachable Moments: Jacques Derrida's Final Seminar*. New York: Fordham University Press.

Nanos, Mark D. 2002. *The Irony of Galatians: Paul's Letter in First-Century Context*. Minneapolis: Fortress.

Nussbaum, Martha. 1994. "Platonic Love and Colorado Law: The Relevance of Ancient Greek Norms to Modern Sexual Controversies." *Virginia Law Review* 80:1515–651.

Oldson, William O. 1991. *A Providential Anti-Semitism: Nationalism and Polity in Nineteenth-Century Romania*. Philadelphia: American Philosophical Society.

Ong, Hughson T. 2015. *The Multilingual Jesus and the Sociolinguistic World of the New Testament*. Leiden: Brill.

Parchami, Ali. 2015. "The Echoes of Rome in British and American Hegemonic Ideology." Pages 105–122 in *Echoes of Empire: Memory, Identity and Colonial Legacies*. Edited by Kalypso Nicolaïdis, Berny Sèbe, and Gabrielle Maas. London: Tauris.

Parker, Grant. 2017. "The Azanian Muse: Classicism in Unexpected Places." Pages 3–52 in *South Africa, Greece, Rome: Classical Confrontations*. Edited by Grant Parker. Cambridge: Cambridge University Press.

Poirier, John C. 2009. "The Synoptic Problem and the Field of New Testament Introduction." *JSNT* 32:179–90.

Pormann, Peter E. 2009. "Classics and Islam: From Homer to al-Qā☒ida." *International Journal of the Classical Tradition* 16:197–233.

———. 2012. *Epidemics in Context: Greek Commentaries on Hippocrates in the Arabic Tradition*. Berlin: de Gruyter.

Punt, Jeremy. 2012. "Empire and New Testament Texts: Theorising the Imperial, in Subversion and Attraction." *HvTSt* 68.1:8–19.

Redondo, Jordi. 2000. "The Greek Literary Language of the Hebrew Historian Josephus." *Hermes* 128:420–34.

Reimarus, Hermann. (1879) 1970. *Fragments*. Translated by G. E. Lessing. Edited by Charles Voysey.. Repr., Philadelphia: Fortress.

Richmann, Christopher J. 2020. "America as New Jerusalem." *WW* 40:150–61.

Rosenthal, Franz. 1975. *The Classical Heritage in Islam*. Translated by Emile and Jenny Marmorstein. Berkeley: University of California Press.

———. 1990. *Greek Philosophy in the Arab World: A Collection of Essays*. Brookfield: Gower.

Rummel, Erika. 1985. *Erasmus as a Translator of the Classics*. Toronto: University of Toronto Press.

Sadler, Rodney S., Jr. 2007. "The Place and Role of Africa and African Imagery." Pages 23–30 in *True to Our Native Land: An African American New Testament Commentary*. Edited by Brian K. Blount. Minneapolis: Fortress.

Said, Edward W. 1983. *The World, the Text, and the Critic*. Cambridge: Harvard University Press.

Schäfer, Peter. 1998. *Judeophobia: Attitudes towards the Jews in the Ancient World.* Cambridge: Harvard University Press.

———. 2012. *The Jewish Jesus: How Judaism and Christianity Shaped Each Other.* Princeton: Princeton University Press.

Schein, Seth L. 2008. "'Our Debt to Greece and Rome': Canon, Class and Ideology." Pages 75–85 in *A Companion to Classical Receptions.* Edited by Lorna Hardwick and Christopher Stray. Malden, MA: Wiley.

Schüssler Fiorenza, Elisabeth. 1988. "The Ethics of Biblical Interpretation: Decentering Biblical Scholarship." *JBL* 107:3–17.

Scroggs, Robin. 1983. *The New Testament and Homosexuality: Contextual Background for Contemporary Debate.* Philadelphia: Fortress.

Segal, Alan F. 1990. *Paul the Convert: The Apostolate and Apostasy of Saul the Pharisee.* New Haven: Yale University Press.

Segovia, Fernando F. 2015. "Criticism in Critical Times: Reflections on Vision and Task." *JBL* 134:6–29.

Seitz, Christopher R. 1998. *Word without End: The Old Testament as Abiding Witness.* Grand Rapids: Eerdmans.

Sevenster, Jan Nicholaas. 1968. *Do You Know Greek? How Much Greek Could the First Jewish Christians Have Known?* Leiden: Brill.

Sick, David H. 2007. "When Socrates Met the Buddha: Greek and Indian Dialectic in Hellenistic Bactria and India." *JRAS* 17:253–78.

———. 2011. "The *Architriklinos* at Cana." *JBL* 130:513–26.

———. 2016. "Zacchaeus as the Rich Host of Classical Satire." *BibInt* 24:229–44.

———. 2017. "Alabamian Argonautica: Myth and Classical Education in *The Quest of the Silver Fleece.*" *CW* 110:373–97.

Sider, Robert D., ed. 2019. *The New Testament Scholarship of Erasmus.* Toronto: University of Toronto Press.

Smil, Vaclav. 2010. *Why America Is Not a New Rome.* Cambridge: MIT Press.

Sobrino, Jon. 1977–1978. "The Historical Jesus and the Christ of Faith: The Tension between Faith and Religion." Translated by John Drury. *CrossCurrents* 27:437–63.

Spivak, Gayatri Chakravorty. 1990. *The Post-colonial Critic: Interviews, Strategies, Dialogues.* Edited by Sarah Harasym. New York: Routledge.

Stover, Timothy J. 1999. "*Placata posse omnia mente tueri*: 'Demythologizing' the Plague in Lucretius." *Latomus* 58:69–76.

Stowers, Stanley K. 1998. "Paul and Slavery: A Response." *Semeia* 83/84:295–311.

Strauss, David Friedrich. 1892. *The Life of Jesus, Critically Examined.* Translated by George Eliot. 4th ed. New York: Macmillan.
Stray, Christopher. 1998. *Classics Transformed: Schools, Universities, and Society in England, 1830–1960.* Oxford: Oxford University Press.
Stray, Christopher, ed. 2003. *The Classical Association: The First Century, 1903–2003.* Oxford: Oxford University Press.
———, ed. 2007. *Oxford Classics: Teaching and Learning 1800–2000.* London: Bloomsbury.
Taylor, Charles. 1989. *Sources of the Self: The Making of the Modern Identity.* Cambridge: Harvard University Press.
Thatcher, Tom, and Catrin Williams, eds. 2013. *Engaging with C. H. Dodd on the Gospel of John: Sixty Years of Tradition and Interpretation.* Cambridge: Cambridge University Press.
Timpanaro, Sebastiano. 2005. *The Genesis of Lachmann's Method.* Translated by Glenn W. Most. Chicago: University of Chicago Press.
Tischendorf, Constantin von. 1896. *When Were Our Gospels Written? An Argument with a Narrative of the Discovery of the Sinaitic Manuscript.* London: Religious Tract Society.
Twomey, Jay. 2005. "Reading Derrida's New Testament: A Critical Appraisal." *BibInt* 13:374–403.
Underwood, Doug. 2006. "The Problem with Paul: Seeds of the Culture Wars and the Dilemma for Journalists." *Journal of Media and Religion* 5:71–90.
Vasunia, Phiroze. 2013. *The Classics and Colonial India.* Oxford: Oxford University Press.
Wake, Peter. 2014. *Tragedy in Hegel's Early Theological Writings.* Bloomington: Indiana University Press.
Wardle, David. 2017. "Cecil Rhodes as a Reader of the Classics: The Groote Schuur Collection." Pages 336–50 in *South Africa, Greece, Rome: Classical Confrontations.* Edited by Grant Parker. Cambridge: Cambridge University Press.
Whitehead, Alfred North. 1925. *Science and the Modern World.* New York: Free Press.
Wimbush, Vincent L. 2011. "Interpreters—Enslaving/Enslaved/Runagate." *JBL* 130:5–24.
Winterer, Caroline. 2002. *The Culture of Classicism: Ancient Greece and Rome in American Intellectual Life, 1780–1910.* Baltimore: Johns Hopkins University Press.

Yovel, Yirmiyahu. 1997. "Sublimity and Ressentiment: Hegel, Nietzsche, and the Jews." *Jewish Social Studies* 3.3:1–25.

Zuckerberg, Donna. 2018. *Not All Dead White Men: Classics and Misogyny in the Digital Age.* Cambridge: Harvard University Press.

An Argument for Being Less Disciplined

Denise Kimber Buell

The challenge for scholars, in the coming precious years, lies in the degree to which we choose to link our disciplinary explorations to urgent ethical responsibilities.
— Mark Levene, "Climate Blues"

How do we begin? First we classicists have to move away from the notion of discipline [that] evokes an image of narrow boundaries and rigid inflexibility and exclusion.
— Shelley Haley, "Black Feminist Thought and Classics"

We must now collectively undertake a rewriting of knowledge as we know it.
— Sylvia Wynter, "Unparalleled Catastrophe for Our Species?"

I read a lot of fiction. During the pandemic, I have been reading even more than usual. I have found the greatest solace in speculative fiction, especially works that imagine the transformation of the human into something else, such as Charlie Jane Anders's *The City in the Middle of the Night* (2019), Octavia Butler's classics *Clay's Ark* (1984) and her Xenogenesis series (1987–1989), Marlon James's *Black Leopard Red Wolf* (2019), N. K. Jemisin's Broken Earth trilogy (2015–2017) and *The City We Became* (2020), Liz Jensen's *The Uninvited* (2012), and Nnedi Okorafor's Binti

---

My thanks to Tat-siong Benny Liew and Caroline Johnson Hodge for organizing the stimulating conference for which this paper was initially developed and to my conference participants for their ideas, suggestions, and conversation, especially Timothy Joseph. I also am deeply grateful to the Williams College Archivists, Jessika Drmacich and Sylvia Kennick Brown, who steered me to many of the relevant institutional history sources.

trilogy (2015–2018). These works draw on and transmute stories of historical and persisting oppression, climate change, or both in the context of creating or adapting alternative stories of speciation, interspecies relationality, materiality, and power. This fiction gives me hope. These works make me think that we can and need to learn how to be human differently than those ways of being human complicit with valuing as superior what is white, Western, capitalist, consumerist, male, heteroreproductive, and individualistic. (You know the list goes on.) Thankfully, there are those who, today and in the past, offer precedents and possibilities for living, being, and doing otherwise.

If novelist, playwright, and critical theorist Sylvia Wynter (2015, 29) is correct that humans are hybrid beings, "that we are simultaneously storytelling and biological beings," we need to take our stories very seriously indeed; they make and can remake us. Scholars of the New Testament and classicists work with stories written long ago that are also deeply concerned with what it means to be human, stories that often also imagine, chart, or exhort the transformation of the human into something else in relation to or directly into materials and powers framed as nonhuman. We also have been raised and trained within larger embodied narratives, ones that we usually refer to as guiding epistemologies or interpretive frameworks. In what follows, I link stories and storytelling with epistemologies but also with institutional and disciplinary structures and practices.

Many of the contributors to this volume recount new stories or altered forms of storytelling that have in mind urgent issues of our present—including racial, ethnic, gendered, and economic injustices—and aim to assist us in continuing to grapple with epistemologies that perpetuate unjust structures, ideologies, and relations.

When we look to tell new stories, Abraham Smith cautions us in his essay that it is not enough to topple monuments to a white supremacist lost-cause ideology; Jennifer Glancy shows us that we cannot simply embrace relational ontologies and expect utopian and egalitarian intrahuman relations, let alone human and nonhuman ones, to ensue. The essay by Allen Callahan calls for a new algorithm as opposed to a new story, one that will do away with both rich and poor simultaneously so that the poor need not always be with us while the rich let themselves off the hook with voluntary pledges. To reorient how we approach the interpretation of antiquity, Joe Marchal draws upon Saidiya Hartman and Sara Ahmed, while Laura Nasrallah turns to contemporary Black artists and their practices to foreground aesthetics. Gay Byron offers us Nubia as an orienting device. Jorunn Økland and Candida Moss appeal to ancient evidence to alter the ways that *ekklēsia* and Paul's use of scribes, respectively, have been interpreted and thus can signify in the present. And Yii-Jan Lin reorients New Testament studies temporally by enacting it entirely within a modern set of intertexts that foreground questions of citizenship, ethnicity and race, and disease—very timely indeed. Thus, the colleagues contributing to this volume have already demonstrated commitments to tackle urgent contemporary ethical issues.

This particular essay is at once both more personal and more meta than the other studies in this volume. On the personal side, I reflect on my friendship and collaboration with classicist Denise McCoskey, on the history of the institution that employs me, and on three of the many scholars whose work inspires and challenges me: Shelley Haley, Bernadette Brooten, and Vincent Wimbush. These sections shuttle between my experience and institutional location and larger questions about academia and its relation to urgent ethical matters. I surface the specificity of the contexts in which we do our work and aim to push us to think more about New Testament studies and classics in relation to (1) the damaged world in which we are living; (2) the institutions that enable the existence of these and other disciplines; and (3) the ways that we do our work. My focus is not on what divides New Testament scholars from classicists but rather on how our different expertises, disciplinary histories, and institutional contexts, as well as our shared lot in the humanities, might serve us as prompts for the *rewriting of knowledge as we know it*. To this end, I join those who are asking about the roles that our disciplines have played and might play in defining what higher education (especially undergraduate education) is for, what ought it consist of, for whom does it exist, and what kinds of changes have we been making or might make in order to contribute better to the urgent need for racial justice within the larger context of planetary precarity. In what follows, I shall consider stories about New Testament studies, classics, their interrelations and embeddedness in higher education from four vantage points: (1) a snapshot of my own formative encounter with a classicist; (2) some reflections on how the institutional history of Williams College, where I work, illuminates ways that race and the study of antiquity have been interwoven into college education in the United States; (3) a brief look at an origin story about the humanities in higher education; and (4) a consideration of classicist Shelley Haley's outline for writing new, less disciplined, stories together with counterparts Bernadette Brooten and Vincent Wimbush in New Testament studies.

1. A Tale of Two Denises

I started my professional career in 1995 as an assistant professor at Miami University in its Religion Department. On my first humid day in southern Ohio, I met another twentysomething white woman named Denise, who had also newly arrived to join the university's Classics Department. Denise McCoskey and I hit it off right away. We swapped stories about hot button issues in each field and soon discovered a shared interest in antiracist, feminist scholarship, even as I knew nothing about Propertius and she had little interest in early Christianity. Galvanized, we designed and cotaught an honors seminar that brought critical theory on race and ethnicity into conversation with ancient materials from Ptolemaic and Roman-period Egypt; we presented papers at an annual meeting of the American Philological Association (now Society of Classical Literature) for a panel on ethnicity in antiquity; and eventually, we each published books focused on race in relation to the study of, respectively, early Christian history and classical antiquity (Buell 2005; McCoskey 2012).

I highlight this early career friendship and collaboration because it helped me discern the contours of my disciplinary training and realize that I was actually less interdisciplinary than I had imagined myself to be. We stretched each other, especially in the context of coteaching. That is not to say that I became a classicist or she became a scholar of early Christianity—rather, we benefited from one another's expertise, and we codeveloped ways of foregrounding the present stakes of historical interpretation and reconstruction with attention to racial formation and the racialization of interpretation. Working together attuned my sense of where some of my blind spots are and how to begin to hold myself accountable to them.

Unless or until doctoral training is itself radically overhauled, one way for scholars to speculate differently is to work more purposefully across disciplinary boundaries. I do not mean simply that we ought to read widely on our own (most of us do this already) but rather that we should act to bring ourselves into conversation and undertake shared work with those in other fields. This volume considers the relations of New Testament studies and classics; I see the need for cross-disciplinary work far beyond these proximate fields.

Denise McCoskey was and still is one of the few classicists I have met who is unapologetic, indeed insistent, about using the term *race* when interpreting materials of and about classical antiquity because she connects the need for racial justice in the present with the ancient past (see now McCoskey 2021). This commitment also informs how she structures her book *Race: Antiquity and Its Legacy*. While aiming "to document the fundamental role of race in the ancient world itself," she notes that

> I ultimately turn to the influence of ancient racial formations on the modern world as well, an influence mediated by the varied receptions and appropriations of classical antiquity. So unceasing has the use and abuse of the ancient world been that … it seems to have become central to the very constitution of modernity. (2012, 33)

Within New Testament studies and classics, *that* there are differences between the past and the present has the status of organizing principle. The feminist work that compelled me with its arguments for the present stakes of interpreting the past felt edgy and counterhegemonic; only over time did I realize how much New Testament studies has repressed the story of its reliance on the presentist significance of its work (for a different spin on this story see Moore and Sherwood 2011). The contemporary relevance of biblical texts and classical antiquity—as well as other ancient texts—was actually more visible in the nineteenth and early twentieth centuries than it was during my own upbringing and education. As Suzanne Marchand (2009, xxx) puts it, "we all too often fail to take seriously the nineteenth century's absorption in the ancient world and its range of knowledge about the past," an absorption that was fueled by convictions that the present was problematic and that the ancient past held keys to improving the present. Rather than being a gotcha for clever late twentieth- and early twenty-first-century scholars to discover, nineteenth- and early twentieth-century classicists and New Testament scholars (among others) were quite forthright about their sense that the study of the ancient past had present use value. The study of non-Christian literature in Greek, for example, functioned in part as a vehicle to articulate critiques of contemporary Christianity and to discover alternatives to it of equal or greater antiquity (as was also the case for the study of the materials bundled under the umbrella of oriental cultures and literatures) as well as to enact and demonstrate an educated subjectivity for minoritized persons such as African Americans (see Malamud 2019).

My friendship with Denise McCoskey allows me to introduce another important point, one that might seem obvious but is nonetheless worth stating: the significance of the contexts in which we do our work. In 1997, I left Miami University for a position at Williams College while Denise continued her career at Miami. A midsize public university, Miami relies on public funding and endures political oversight; Williams College is one of the most well-endowed private small liberal arts colleges in the United States. The Religion Department at Miami persists, in part on the strength of its master's program, but the Classics Department was recently dismantled and combined with French and Italian Studies (following the dismantling of Romance Languages). This kind of structural change raised concerns at Miami about "the future of the humanities." Even at Williams, while recently serving as dean of the faculty, I heard many faculty worry aloud about the future of the humanities, despite the fact that no department or program has been threatened with closure and that the college has added as many new faculty lines (tenure-track and tenured) in the humanities and humanistic social sciences as it has added in STEM+ fields in the last decade. These include additions in fields such as Africana studies, Arabic studies, American studies (with specializations in native and indigenous studies as well as in Asian American studies), environmental studies, and women's, gender, and sexuality studies.

Unfortunately, the metrics of attention to enrollments, majors, and minors used by boards of regents and many college and university administrators incentivize disciplines to treat one another as rivals for scarce resources rather than as partners. This territorialism distracts from attention to urgent ethical matters, both of local and global concern, and impedes the actions needed to address them. How will we learn to ask different questions or find new answers about how to be human while being committed to defending the intellectual territories or lines in our academic units? Moreover, this unit-centered culture has proven one of the biggest impediments to transforming the implicitly and explicitly racist structures and habits at Williams.

Most of the contributors to this volume have academic appointments, though some are also independent scholars. Our contexts shape and constrain us differently, as do many other factors. How large and well-resourced is our institution? What is its relationship (or lack thereof) to a religious tradition and to its national context? Is it private or public? When was it founded, with what kind of mission, and for what kind(s) of constituency? Do we work in a freestanding academic unit or a multidisciplinary one? Do we serve undergraduates, graduate students, or both? Can students earn degrees in our areas of specialization or not? New Testament studies and classics are thus located, practiced, and also potentially transformed in specific contexts—in institutions as well as through professional organizations and publishing apparatus, and in relation to broader forces.

Colleagues who work in seminaries, in divinity schools, and with doctoral students navigate different kinds of contexts, ones in which preprofessional training is paramount—different from my context in an institution that serves almost exclusively undergraduates. Faculty who work with doctoral students may feel pressure to perform and preserve the boundaries of what constitutes New Testament studies or classics. In contrast, at undergraduate-centered US institutions, students have to learn how knowledge is organized and of what a discipline consists. Few undergraduates arrive knowing what questions, methods, or topics are in or out of bounds in classics or the study of religion—let alone New Testament studies—even though they enter with their own lenses and presuppositions about religion, if not about Christianity or the Bible.

What I have experienced working in an undergraduate department of religion at a private liberal arts college differs not only from my experience at Miami but also from those who teach at other kinds of US colleges and universities or in seminaries and divinity or theological schools, as well as those who work outside of the United States. I shall now dive a little deeper into the specificity of my institutional home.

2. A New England Tale

The histories of our disciplines interact and intersect with the histories of the institutions for whom we work. In the United States, a number of historically or predominantly white colleges and universities, including Williams College, have recently begun to unearth "the relationship between slavery and universities—a relationship hiding in plain sight for the better part of two centuries" (Campbell, Harris, and Brophy 2019, 4) as well as the relationship of colleges and universities to the displacement of indigenous peoples and the production of white settler cultural and racial identities. The story of Williams College, for example, begins with the displacement of the Stockbridge-Munsee Band of the Mohican nation:

> During the summer of 1755, Colonel Ephraim Williams had looked to the future by designating funds in his will for a college.... In the following decades, hundreds of white families moved into western Massachusetts, where Williams had considerable property, and where the government

was actively eliminating Indian claims. In 1793 the residents of West Township (Williamstown), Massachusetts, requested that endowment for Williams College. (Wilder 2013, 159)

Williams was one of the eighteen colleges founded between the end of the Revolution and 1800 (Wilder 2019, 31), and one of twenty-five degree-granting institutions active in New England by 1800 (Baumgartner 2019, 182). As was the case for colleges and universities as well as secondary schools founded in colonial North America or in the decades after 1776, Williams College relied upon "families whose income came from the slave trade" (Wilder 2019, 24). During the late eighteenth and first two-thirds of the nineteenth centuries, "the American college trained the personnel and cultivated the ideas that accelerated and legitimated the dispossession of Native Americans and the enslavement of Africans" (10).

This orientation was not inevitable or uncontested, as illustrated by institutions such as Oberlin College (Morris 2019, 197–212), individual faculty members such as Charles Follen (1796–1840), a radical abolitionist and (briefly) professor of German at Harvard (Hansen 2012), and by student groups, especially for the abolition of slavery, including one established at Williams that sent petitions to abolish slavery to Congress in both 1809 and 1826 (Wilder 2013, 266). Nonetheless, Williams is among the majority of institutions of higher education in the United States whose track record is one of contributing to white supremacist, Christian, and androcentric modes of knowledge and citizen production rather than challenging them.

Williams College was the site of the 1806 Haystack Meeting, a prayer gathering of Williams students widely commemorated as catalyzing a global Christian missionary movement that included deep and controversial ties between Williams alums and the Kingdom of Hawai'i, a relation uncovered and examined in a recent exhibition at the Williams College Museum of Art (2018). The Haystack Meeting was also later credited with inspiring the creation of the American Colonization Society (or ACS, founded 1817), whose white supremacist goal was to create a colony on some part of Africa to send free blacks there (Wilder 2013, 247).

The ACS chose "colleges as a battlefield to defeat" what they called "our enemies—the abolitionists" (Wilder 2013, 266). Indeed, "by the 1830s ... colonizationists headed every college in New York State, New Jersey, Connecticut, and Massachusetts" (265). Among the members and champions of the American Colonization Society was Williams College president

Edward Dorr Griffin (1821–1836), whose name is featured on a historic college building in which many humanities courses are offered and who is celebrated for rescuing Williams from dissolution when the prior president defected along with most of the faculty and students to found Amherst College. He successfully countered the student antislavery group on the Williams campus during his presidency. Between 1831 and 1835, colonizationists helped to destroy or force the closure of three different institutions in New England aimed at offering higher education to free blacks or racially integrated groups (Wilder 2013, 271; Baumgartner 2019); by 1836, "African American and white abolitionists concluded that New England was inhospitable to Black institutions of higher education" (Baumgartner 2019, 191).

So what does all of this have to do with classics and New Testament studies? For classics, the answer is relatively straightforward: until the end of the nineteenth century, a Williams College education began with the study of Greek and Latin and culminated in Christian theology and natural philosophy. A liberal arts education was, foundationally, about learning Greek and Latin and acquiring the cultural legacy imbued in classical texts undertaken in a context in which Protestant Christian subject formation was most highly valued.

For New Testament studies, the answer is more oblique. Although the academic study of the Bible and the formation of New Testament studies began in Germany in the mid-nineteenth century, neither was formalized in the United States until the century's end. In the 1890s, Williams College briefly had a Department of Biblical Studies that offered an Introduction to the New Testament course, but it was not until the 1950s that the Department of Religion (created as a standalone department in 1911) offered courses on biblical literature.

Instead, the study of the New Testament matters primarily because of the college's orientation and commitment to a Christian-inflected education. Throughout most of the nineteenth century at Williams, the goal of a college education was expressly identified as training young white men to be Christian ministers and missionaries, as evidenced not only in the Haystack Meeting but also in the way that the college defined itself. For example, Mark Hopkins, the president of Williams for the middle third of the century (1836–1872), "saw Christianization of students as the principal mission of Williams. [He] … took special pride in the college's record of sending forth as many as a third of its graduates into church pulpits and mission fields" (Chandler 2015, 3–4). This goal of Christianization intertwined white supremacy, settler colonialism, and masculinity.

Williams was never formally linked with a Christian denomination, but its Protestant orientation is evident in the following requirement: from its founding in 1793 through 1934, daily attendance at chapel services as well as at the weekly Sunday service were compulsory for all matriculated students at Williams. In fact, in the late 1920s when the faculty agreed to permit students more leniency with the daily chapel requirement (allowing more missed services), they counterbalanced the attendant loss by implementing a new requirement for students. Between 1927 and 1934, all first-year students were required to pass an examination on the New Testament and all sophomores had to pass an examination on the Old Testament (Williams College 1926–1927, 8–11). These examinations were not linked with any coursework. Beginning in the 1935–1936 academic year (Williams College 1935, 12–13), the daily chapel requirement as well as these examinations were abolished, but attendance at the Sunday service (or an approved local Christian equivalent) remained mandatory until 1962. Despite the longevity of the daily chapel requirement, by the early twentieth century the purpose of a Williams education and its curriculum was redefined as the production of "good citizens" rather than good Christians (Chandler 2015, 19–21).

Until the beginning of the twentieth century, the college curriculum for students at Williams was entirely prescribed. The number of faculty members was very small and, as Elizabeth A. Clark (2011, 11, 12) has noted, "today, it is startling to realize that until the 1880s, … the few faculty employed by any institution taught whatever was necessary"; "most faculty were generalists" and not expected to advance original research as has become the benchmark for academic success. Being a generalist included proficiency in Latin and Greek.

Professionalization and specialization in the United States correlates with departmentalization and has been supported by the rise of professional societies with their corresponding journals (the American Philological Association in 1869; the Society of Biblical Literature in 1880); at the close of the nineteenth century, for the first time, faculty members were expected to undertake specialized research in their fields. Soon thereafter, university presses emerged as vehicles for producing and institutionalizing both disciplinary specialization and a distinction between academics and amateurs (Clark 2011, 13). (These structures to create professionalized academics in the United States also temporally overlap with the end of Reconstruction and the rise of aggressive white supremacist groups and violence and Jim Crow laws.)

In 1902–1903, the Williams curriculum became less fixed, moving to a curricular organization in which first-year students still took a fixed curriculum that included Latin, whereas in the latter three years students pursued a major while also taking courses across three broad curricular areas (a precursor to the distribution requirements of the present). With the 1902–1903 restructuring of the curriculum and a shift to departmentalization, students could take courses on specific New Testament texts as an optional part of second-year Greek within classics. Coursework in religious studies was located in the Philosophy Department until 1911, when Religion became a standalone department (though a major in religion was not offered until 1962).

In the United States, departments of classics and religious studies are thus really quite recent. At Williams, when the curriculum was structured into departments in the last decade of the nineteenth century, religion was one component of a department that also included philosophy and psychology. The establishment of departments of religion in private colleges and universities mostly occurred from the 1920s onward; only in 1962 did a religion department get constituted at a public university—at Miami University, in fact.

This brief overview illustrates some ways that these fields were complicit with the creation of white supremacist and Christian stories as well as structures that persist and need closer examination and reckoning. Thanks to many different individuals who work at Williams pushing the institution to take on this work, there have been efforts to better represent the college's part in missionary activities and the displacement of indigenous peoples. Yet the work of reckoning has not really begun. In summer of 2020, Williams College created a memorandum of understanding with the tribal leaders of the Stockbridge-Munsee Band, most of whose enrolled members now reside in Wisconsin as a result of dispossession and displacement. With a local tribal historical preservation office now in Williamstown, it remains to be seen what forms of restitution may result.

Classics and biblical studies now have a marginal place in the college's mission, in contrast with its first century. Within the current curricular structure (now about fifty years old), classics and religion (with course offerings included in early Christian history) are departments offering majors; students may take courses in these departments to fulfill college-wide distribution or skill requirements. At the same time, the reduced status of these fields opens up room for envisioning and enacting them differently.

3. An Origin Story about the Humanities

In the context of colleges and universities in the United States, both classics and New Testament studies are now considered part of the humanities. (New Testament studies as practiced in seminaries, divinity schools, and theological schools may have a different status as a form of professional training.) This shared location is noteworthy in part because a widely circulating origin story about the humanities might make this seem surprising. An online tool beloved by our students, Wikipedia, defines the humanities as follows:

> Humanities are academic disciplines that study aspects of human society and culture. In the Renaissance, the term contrasted with divinity and referred to what is now called classics, the main area of secular study in universities at the time. Today, the humanities are more frequently contrasted with natural, and sometimes social sciences, as well as professional training.
>
> The humanities use methods that are primarily critical, or speculative, and have a significant historical element—as distinguished from the mainly empirical approaches of the natural sciences, yet, unlike the sciences, it has no central discipline. The humanities include the study of ancient and modern languages, literature, philosophy, history, archaeology, anthropology, human geography, law, politics, religion, and art. (Wikipedia 2022)

Note especially the first two sentences: The humanities are defined as a secular, human-centered enterprise that emerged first in the form of classics in contrast to the study of theology. This story needs to be complicated in at least three ways.

First, one of the thinkers associated with the creation of the humanities, Erasmus, undertook his hotly contested advocacy for the study of Greek over the previously hegemonic study of Latin entirely within a Christian context. He published the first edition of the New Testament in Greek (1516), a challenge to the existing church dependence on the Vulgate. As Goldhill (2002, 24–25) points out, far from being a purely secular project, Erasmus's championing of the study of Greek, including of the New Testament, was closely associated with emerging Protestantism; a number of academics and students were burned at the stake for heresy as an outcome for promoting and participating in the study of Greek. In 1559, when Protestantism became the religion of England, learning Greek and learning

Protestant theology were explicitly combined such that "Greek knowledge and religious reform *did* go hand in hand, as the opponents of Greek had feared" (33). By no means was this linkage of humanism with Christianity a transitionary hangover. Classics and the study of Christian texts and history did eventually congeal as distinct professional fields, especially during the nineteenth century, but as Suzanne Marchand (2009, xxix) notes, the narrative of secularization in higher education runs roughshod over the "powerful shaping force of Christian humanism," a force she argues persists at least through the start of the First World War. Marchand's observation correlates well with the persistence of daily chapel requirements at Williams as well as the short-lived extracurricular compulsory exams on the Christian Bible.

Second, it would be fair to say that New Testament studies defines itself also as a secular enterprise in contrast to some former church-dominated form of theology, such that New Testament studies and classics emerge as contemporary disciplines. This secular orientation, however, has long been yoked with European Christianity, which brings us to the next point.

Third, we need to consider how this story of the emergence of the humanities relates to an understanding of what it is to be human. For Sylvia Wynter (2015, 15–16), Christian humanism, what she calls a "newly invented Renaissance humanist counterpoetics," changes the story about human relationship to divinity: "the relation was now renarrated as one between the traditional biblical Christian God and a mankind *for whose sake* (*propter nos homines*), rather than merely *for the sake* of his own glory (as the then nominalist orthodox theology held), he had indeed *created the Universe*" (emphasis in original). This shift, she proposes, opened up "a generalized *natural scientific* conceptual space," on the premise that

> as Copernicus was to centrally argue, as "the best and most systematic artisan of all," would *have had to have created* the universe's "world machine" according to rules that made it *law-likely* knowable by the human reason of those creatures *for whose sake* he had done so. (16, emphasis original)

She continues: "This conceptual space, then, was therefore to make possible Darwin's epistemological rupture or leap—that is, its far-reaching challenge to Christianity's biblical macro-origin story's theocosmogonically projected divinely created divide between an ostensibly generically Christian mankind, on the one hand, and all other species, on the other" (16).

Crucially, these shifting origin stories link the creation of the humanities not only with the rise of scientific authority but also with antiblack racism: "within the terms of the West's religious and secular chartering cosmogonies—[Africa] has been seen as either the site of the biblical Ham's cursed descendants or the site of the missing link between apes and fully evolved Western European humans" (31). Terence Keel's recent work (2018) powerfully charts the ways that Christian thought enabled and structured apparently and self-avowedly secular scientific theories of race in ways that confirm and elaborate upon Wynter's insights.

Reflecting on his academic training in New Testament studies, Vincent Wimbush (2017, 8) challenges us to think about how the humanities broadly and New Testament studies specifically are implicated in this story of "Man": "The practices of historical criticism (and related newer forms of criticism of biblical studies…) have, it needs to be said, reconstructed ancient worlds and ancient truths that seem remarkably reflective and affirming, even naturalizing/codifying, of modern white men's worlds." This congruence with white men's worlds saturates the humanities in a way that he traces to the dominant modes of New Testament practices:

> I was trained—as biblical exegete/historical critic—to be a good ideological "civil servant," tradent, interpreter of, apologist for, the Western regime that was centered around but extended far beyond "religion" and "the book," as these had come to be understood in the narrowest post-Enlightenment terms of modern-era high-protestant-inflected ascetical piety, intellectualism, and civility. Of course, my field is not the only one that functions in this way; almost all the traditional Western humanities fields are so constructed. Yet there is something quite poignant about being in a field that loans to others the very terms (canon, scripture, Bible, commentary, hermeneutics, exegesis) by which the chief interests and politics of the regime (construction and closure) are practiced and (mis-)identified. (13–14)

Even as we complicate origin stories about the humanities, what surfaces is a tale about the complicity of the humanities in the production of what it means to be Western, modern, white, and educated, a tale in which the interpretation of the Christian Bible and classical counterparts have been central even when elaborated in fields that appear to be distant, such as the natural sciences. Instead of clinging to the humanities as we look to the future, I want to ask how to write and embody different stories. Wimbush is among the leading visionaries in this process, so in the next section I return to his work and others who have begun this process in classics and New Testament studies.

4. Shelley Haley Meets New Testament Studies: Storyboarding and Enacting New Stories

One of the classicists Denise McCoskey and I both admire is Shelley Haley. Haley is the Edward North Chair of Classics and Professor of Africana Studies at Hamilton College and the 2021 president of the Society for Classical Studies. Haley's 1993 essay, "Black Feminist Thought and Classics," left a significant impression on my graduate school self, in part because of how much it resonated with the multiplicative, intersectional feminist approaches to biblical interpretation advanced by my mentors Bernadette Brooten and Elisabeth Schüssler Fiorenza. In advocating a move away from a narrow understanding of what constitutes the discipline of classics and further collaboration with Black feminist thought, Haley calls for three central changes to classics:

> (1) To assess the costs of forcing classics to be enacted as an "Anglo-Germanic construction" that privileges the standpoint of "white male privilege, or knowledge, or voice" (1993, 36–37).
> (2) "To recognize that classics was the educational foundation for our Black feminist foremothers. We need to analyze this and reclaim these feminists" (see 25, 37). In other words, reckoning with this racialized disciplinary history should not result erase the fact that Black women (and men) have studied and engaged with Greek, Latin, and classical materials; re-covering this history is vital to understanding the white racialization of classics in context for its stakes and alternatives.
> 3. To widen the parameters of what constitutes the scope of classics and thus alter the lenses for what it means to study classics: "We need to redefine our field so that it includes African languages, African history, African archaeology" (including Kush, Axum, Ethiopia broadly) (37) and to value the "standpoint of Black women" while also "acknowledg[ing] the silence of African women when we write books about ancient Africa from a Eurocentric viewpoint" (36–37).

In the more than a quarter century since the essay's publication, some classicists have taken up one or more of Haley's recommendations. Benjamin Isaac (2004), Denise McCoskey (2012), and Grant Parker (2017), for example, are among those who have tackled the first challenge. (Molly Myerowitz Levine's work also is an important contemporary voice; see especially Levine 1989 and 1990.) Emily Greenwood (2010, 2019, 2020), Grant Parker (2001), and Haley herself (1995) are among the classicists who have been recovering and analyzing the ways that Black women and men studied and engaged with Greek, Latin, and classical materials. *African Athena: New Agendas* (Orrells, Bhambra, and Roynon 2011) is an example of an anthology that tackles all three areas. Scholars trained outside of classics have also taken up this topic, such as Tracey Walters (2007; literary studies) and Margaret Malamud (2019; ancient history). I do not know of any graduate program in classics that has expanded its scope to include African languages, history, and archaeology as part of its requirements for demonstrating proficiency in classics; nonetheless more scholarship has been published that extends geographical consideration into Africa as well as India (see especially Parker 2008; Parker and Sinopoli 2008).

Some comparable exhortations and shifts have been taking place in New Testament studies. Haley's essay has its closest parallel in an important programmatic essay by fellow contributor Gay L. Byron (2009; see also her essay in this volume). As hinted earlier, part of what originally struck me about Haley's essay is its resonance with Schüssler Fiorenza's approach to feminist biblical interpretation (of her many works, see especially 1992) and Brooten's approach as she was writing *Love between Women* (1996). It also clearly resonates with Vincent Wimbush's work.

For those trained in New Testament studies, Brooten and Wimbush offer excellent models for how to forge new practices and stories, in part because of their success in building institutional structures for transformation that span disciplinary areas and also involve nonacademics (see also the *Journal of Feminist Studies in Religion*, cofounded by Schüssler Fiorenza). Brooten's Feminist Sexual Ethics Project (https://www.brandeis.edu/projects/fse/) embodies an alternative approach to the past that foregrounds the present of the interpreter-scholar and clarifies the issues and concerns that motivate engagement with the past. Through this multidisciplinary, multitemporal project, Brooten has built a collaborative network of scholars to document and to overcome the religious and sexual legacies of slavery, especially in the lives of women and girls (see also Brooten 2010). As soon as we begin to attend to the legacies of slavery, or even to the legacies of disciplinary norms such as historical criticism, we are asking questions about how the present is shaped by the past and, perhaps, if it could have been and how it could still be otherwise.

Wimbush's Institute for Signifying Scriptures (or ISS; see http://www.signifyingscriptures.org/) and his approach to scripturalizing and scripturalectics offers another kind of crucial intervention, one that is now independently run rather than located within a college or university structure. Instead of reflecting "and affirming, even naturalizing/codifying, of modern white men's worlds—that is, European or Euro-American worlds" (2017, 8; see also Wimbush 2012)—Wimbush's counterproject emphasizes instead "the meaning of complex engagements and uses of 'texts' on the part of a diverse people in an expansive history of fraught representations, performances, social-cultural-political efforts, gestures, reactions, and interests" (10). In the process, "Black Atlantic/African diaspora" and "Bible/scriptures" are

> analyzed in complex interrelationship and in terms of critical cultural historical and comparative analysis—as analytic windows for each other. None of the categories is to be accepted at face or for rhetorical/analytical value; each is to be excavated in order to determine its functions in relationship to others, within and against different historical frameworks and contexts. (2017, 11)

The work of the ISS includes a journal (*Abeng*), annual conferences, and a book series to support its goals and mission. And, fundamentally, it enacts in a radical manner the disciplinary undoing first prescribed by Haley.

5. Conclusion

> If we continue with our old way of thinking … we drift as a species toward an unparalleled catastrophe.
> —Sylvia Wynter, "Unparalleled Catastrophe for Our Species?"

> We must become undisciplined.
> —Christina Sharpe, *In the Wake: On Blackness and Being*

If, as Wynter (2015, 31) suggests, "we can trace [the first evidence of humans as storytelling beings] to the continent of Africa," this necessarily upends the place that the continent and its people have been situated within prior hegemonic human stories. We need new stories for being human, which, in turn, would require transformations to our disciplinary histories. And we also need new speculation. Even as we reckon with the troubled racialization of our fields and recover the counterhegemonic stories and practices that precede us, we might want to try writing more like Octavia Butler's time-traveling novel *Kindred* (1979), in which the present-day protagonist, after a head injury, keeps finding herself back in the nineteenth century as an enslaved woman. The brutal twist of the novel is that the protagonist discovers that she is both her own ancestor and descendant. To ensure her existence in the twentieth century, she must endure rape and the resulting pregnancy. Or try to write like Pauline Hopkins (1859–1930), whose 1902–1903 novel *Of One Blood, or, The Hidden Self* (1988) uses techniques of mesmerism and conjuring, as well as secrecy and historical disclosure, including the discovery of an underground hidden city in Ethiopia that had preserved esoteric knowledge and practices since antiquity that can now be used to restore an Afrocentric narrative to humanity with concomitant achievement of racial justice for African Americans.

Throughout, I have been foregrounding the importance of stories and storytelling, suggesting among other things that we need to keep making visible the stories that have been shaping us (even when we contest them) and to change our stories, and thus our disciplines, if we are to contribute to the urgent ethical issues of intrahuman injustices. Such efforts should seek new stories that both reckon with the damage that white Euro-American anthropocentric humanism has done to humans as well as nonhumans and not come at the expense of the nonhuman species that coinhabit this planet.

This goal raises larger questions about the purpose and future of higher education (not just the humanities). Instead of running around as if our house is on fire or attempting to defend our respective disciplinary hearths, I suggest we grasp the gift of classics and New Testament studies being less prominent academic fields to reframe our fields and speculate about how we can transform ourselves, which might mean undoing ourselves to make way to become differently.

In the United States we have had disciplinary specialization only for a few generations; PhD programs in the United States are even more recent. I am not promoting a nostalgia for a return to some nineteenth-century academic formation of fixed curricula to educate the elite young white men of the United States taught by generalists. But I am fueled by a metaquestion that has until now gone unstated: Is it even possible for elite, liberal arts colleges in the United States such as Williams to be anything other than engines of reproducing an elite class—even if that new elite is becoming racially and ethnically diverse and open to students of all economic backgrounds, nationalities, genders and sexualities, religions, and abilities? When we are anxiously seeking to defend the humanities or the tenure-track lines in our departments or seeking to attract more students to our classes or our majors, I think we are caught in a trap. Having seen how robustly resistant many senior colleagues are to real institutional transformation, I have become rather skeptical even as I am buoyed by evidence of instances of transformation both inside the academy—such as Brooten's Feminist Sexual Ethics project—and outside—such as Wimbush's Institute for Signifying Scriptures.

I conclude with some thoughts about the epistemological shifts I think should accompany this reorientation with reference to my title about "being less disciplined." By drawing on the calls by Haley, Sharpe, and other Black (often feminist/womanist) scholars to "become undisciplined," my position differs from Stephen D. Moore and Yvonne Sherwood's exhortation in their manifesto on biblical studies to return to universalisms and away from standpoint epistemologies.

As Haley has exhorted for classicists, and as many in New Testament studies (including those contributing to this volume) already practice, this reorientation needs to entail an embrace of *partial* knowing—knowing that is both avowedly perspectival and thus limited and also clear about the perspectives that its lens enables (or forecloses). This kind of knowing fits well with the study of ancient materials, given how fragmentary, fragmented, and incomplete are the materials with which classicists and New Testament studies scholars work (although we might connect those dots more explicitly). This reorientation also entails cultivating multidisciplinary practices that deliberately produce multiperspectival knowledge that makes possible what Maria Lugones (2003) has described as "fluency in more than one persistent logic" (see also Ortega 2006, 70), which might extend to nonhuman logics (ones that, admittedly, we imagine partly through the human form of storytelling).

These two steps of embracing partial knowing and multiperspectival knowledge forged through collaborative ventures might enable at least three things: (1) to make the most of the deep expertise that scholars gain in specific areas or techniques and that nonacademics gain through other experiential and professional pursuits; (2) to enable transformation of one's epistemic lenses through encounters with those holding differing epistemologies in a context in which all are needed and valued—including our students; and (3) especially for those who are majorized by embodiment or epistemology or both, to cultivate epistemic humility. All of this good work risks simply becoming an academic commodity unless it is grounded in an articulation of why this kind of work matters and to whom we will be held accountable.

I see the temptation, the lure, the good intentions of universalizing claims. Those who promote the notion of the Anthropocene, for example, may have excellent intentions to jolt us into a sense of collective responsibility for both climate disaster and for taking swift action to remediate it or mourn the imminent demise of the world as we have known it. But, as Katherine Yusoff has articulated so well, the humanism that wrought the planetary damage now commonly described as the Anthropocene is racialized and specific, contrary to its implied universalizing attribution. For Black and Brown people and for indigenous communities

> to be included in the "we" of the Anthropocene is to be silenced by a claim to a universalism that fails to notice its subjugations, taking part in a planetary condition in which no part was accorded in terms of subjectivity. The supposed "we" further legitimates and justifies the racialized inequalities that are bound up in social geologies. ... the end of this world has already happened for some subjects, and it is the prerequisite for the possibility of imagining "living and breathing again" for others. (Yusoff 2018, 12, 12–13, quoting Hartman 2008)

The end of the humanities, at least as it has been practiced and structured, *may be the prerequisite for the possibility of imagining living and breathing again* for those who have never been defined as fully human within the scope of the humanities.

Scholars and activists who are minoritized in one or more ways have long been calling for an undoing of conventional disciplines. Sharpe calls on Black academics to "become undisciplined" because

> despite knowing otherwise, we are often disciplined into thinking through and along lines that reinscribe our own annihilation, reinforcing and producing what Sylvia Wynter (1994, 70) has called our "narratively condemned status." We must become undisciplined. The work we do requires new modes and methods of research and teaching; new ways of entering and leaving the archives of slavery, of undoing the "racial calculus and ... political arithmetic that were entrenched centuries ago" (Hartman 2008, 6) and that live into the present. I think this is what Dionne Brand describes in *A Map to the Door of No Return* as a kind of blackened knowledge, an unscientific method, that comes from observing that where one stands is relative to the door of no return and that

moment of historical and ongoing rupture. A method along the lines of a sitting with, a gathering, and a tracking of phenomena that disproportionately and devastatingly affect Black people. (Sharpe 2016, 13)

The *new modes and methods of research and teaching*, the undisciplining she exhorts and enacts, finds its counterpart in creative revisioning that has already been happening in womanist, *mujerista*, Asian American women's, ecocritical, queer, and disability studies–informed New Testament scholarship, for example.

I want to be careful not to universalize the specific call Sharpe is issuing here. The stakes are different for me. The costs of becoming disciplined as a white woman masquerade as rewards. I cite Sharpe's injunction to underscore the embodied stakes of questioning the forms of knowledge production that have traveled, even in the humanities and definitely within biblical studies, as scientific (even social-scientific) and to identify and question the narratives that structure New Testament studies.

I opened by invoking the speculative fiction that has given me hope during the pandemic (though my love for it long predates it). In offering their version of the power of storytelling, Charlie Jane Anders (2021, 3) writes, "People will always try to control you by constraining your sense of what's possible. They want to tell you that reality consists of only the things that they are willing to recognize, and anything else is foolishness … the most powerful thing you can do is imagine how things could be different." Even after decades of working as a feminist scholar and teacher, I see the need now more than ever to center the power of storytelling as a means of shifting the epistemological frames that still constrain the fields of classics and New Testament studies. I want to close by acknowledging that this insight is by no means a new or original one. Nonetheless, it feels more urgent than ever to me now to tell stories about the value of stories and encourage my students and colleagues to weave new stories to remake not only our fields but our worlds.

Works Cited

Anders, Charlie Jane. 2019. *The City in the Middle of the Night*. New York: Tor.

———. 2021. *Never Say You Can't Survive: How to Get through Hard Times by Making Up Stories*. New York: Tom Doherty Associates.

Baumgartner, Kabria. 2019. "Towers of Intellect: The Struggle for African American Higher Education in Antebellum New England." Pages 179–96 in *Slavery and the University: Histories and Legacies*. Edited by Leslie M. Harris, James T. Campbell, and Alfred L. Brophy. Athens, GA: University of Georgia Press.

Brooten, Bernadette J. 1996. *Love between Women: Early Christian Responses to Female Homoeroticism*. Chicago: University of Chicago Press.

———. 2010. *Beyond Slavery: Overcoming Its Religious and Sexual Legacies*. New York: Palgrave.

Buell, Denise Kimber. 2005. *Why This New Race: Ethnic Reasoning in Early Christianity*. New York: Columbia University Press.

Butler, Octavia E. 1979. *Kindred*. Boston: Beacon.

———. 1984. *Clay's Ark*. New York: Warner.

———. 1987. *Dawn*. New York: Warner.

———. 1988. *Adulthood Rites*. New York: Warner.

———. 1989. *Imago*. New York: Warner.

Byron, Gay L. 2009. "Ancient Ethiopia and the New Testament: Ethnic (Con)Texts and Racialized (Sub)Texts." Pages 161–90 in *They Were All Together in One Place? Toward Minority Biblical Criticism*. Edited by Randall C. Bailey, Tat-siong Benny Liew, and Fernando F. Segovia. SemeiaSt 57. Atlanta: Society of Biblical Literature.

Campbell, James T., Leslie M. Harris, and Alfred L. Brophy. 2019. "Introduction." Pages 1–18 in *Slavery and the University: Histories and Legacies*. Edited by Leslie M. Harris, James T. Campbell, and Alfred L. Brophy. Athens: University of Georgia Press.

Chandler, John W. 2015. "The Williams Curriculum: Some History and Some Thoughts about the Present." Unpublished Paper.

Clark, Elizabeth A. 2011. *Founding the Fathers: Early Church History and Protestant Professors in Nineteenth-Century America*. Philadelphia: University of Pennsylvania Press.

Goldhill, Simon. 2002. *Who Needs Greek? Contests in the Cultural History of Hellenism*. Cambridge: Cambridge University Press.

Greenwood, Emily. 2010. *Afro-Greeks: Dialogues between Anglophone Caribbean Literature and Classics in the Twentieth Century*. Oxford: Oxford University Press.

———. 2019. "Subaltern Classics in Anti- and Post-colonial Literatures in English." Pages 576–607 in *1880–2000*. Vol. 5 of *The Oxford History of*

Classical Reception in English Literature. Edited by Kenneth Haynes. Oxford: Oxford University Press.

———. 2020. "Middle Passages: Mediating Classics and Radical Philology in Marlene Nourbese Philip and Derek Walcott." Pages 29–56 in *Classicisms in the Black Atlantic*. Edited by Ian Moyer, Adam Lecznar, and Heidi Morse. Oxford: Oxford University Press.

Haley, Shelley P. 1993. "Black Feminist Thought and Classics: Re-membering, Re-claiming, Re-empowering." Pages 23–43 in *Feminist Theory and the Classics*. Edited by Nancy Sorkin Rabinowitz and Amy Richlin. New York: Routledge.

———. 1995. *Fanny Jackson Coppin's, Reminiscences of School Life, and Hints on Teaching*. New York: Macmillan.

Hanson, Thomas S. 2012. "Charles Follen: Brief Life of a Vigorous Reformer." *Harvard Magazine*. https://tinyurl.com/SBL06104e.

Harris, Leslie M., James T. Campbell, and Alfred L. Brophy. 2019. *Slavery and the University: Histories and Legacies*. Athens, GA: University of Georgia Press.

Hartman, Saidiya. 2008. "Venus in Two Acts." *Small Axe* 26:1–14.

Hopkins, Pauline. 1988. "Of One Blood, or the Hidden Self." Pages 441–621 in *The Magazine Novels of Pauline Hopkins*. Introduction by Hazel V. Carby. Oxford: Oxford University Press.

Isaac, Benjamin. 2004. *The Invention of Racism in Classical Antiquity*. Princeton: Princeton University Press.

James, Marlon. 2019. *Black Leopard, Red Wolf*. New York: Riverhead.

Jemison, N. K. 2015. *The Fifth Season*. The Broken Earth 1. New York: Orbit.

———. 2016. *The Obelisk Gate*. The Broken Earth 2. New York: Orbit.

———. 2017. *The Stone Sky*. The Broken Earth 3. New York: Orbit.

———. 2020. *The City We Became*. New York: Orbit.

Jensen, Liz. 2012. *The Uninvited*. London: Bloomsbury.

Keel, Terence. 2018. *Divine Variations: How Christian Thought became Racial Science*. Stanford: Stanford University Press.

Levene, Mark. 2013. "Climate Blues: or How Awareness of the Human End might Re-instil Ethical Purpose to the Writing of History." *Environmental Humanities* 2:147–67.

Levine, Molly Myerowitz, ed. 1989. *The Challenge of "Black Athena"*. Special issue, *Arethusa* 22.1.

———. 1990. "Classical Scholarship: AntiBlack and AntiSemitic?" *Bible Review* 6.3:32–36, 40–41.

Lugones, María. 2003. *Pilgrimages/Peregrinages: Theorizing Coalition against Multiple Oppressions*. Lanham, MD: Rowman & Littlefield.

Malamud, Margaret. 2019. *African Americans and the Classics: Antiquity, Abolition, and Activism*. London: Tauris.

Marchand, Suzanne L. 2009. *German Orientalism in the Age of Empire: Religion, Race, and Scholarship*. Cambridge: Cambridge University Press.

McCoskey, Denise E. 2012. *Race: Antiquity and Its Legacy*. London: Tauris.

McCoskey, Denise E., ed. 2021. *A Cultural History of Race in Antiquity*. Vol. 1 of *A Cultural History of Race*. London: Bloomsbury.

Moore, Stephen D., and Yvonne Sherwood. 2011. *The Invention of the Biblical Scholar: A Critical Manifesto*. Minneapolis: Fortress.

Morris, J. Brent. 2019. "I Have at Last Found My 'Sphere': The Unintentional Development of a Female Abolitionist Stronghold at Oberlin College." Pages 197–212 in *Slavery and the University: Histories and Legacies*. Edited by Leslie M. Harris, James T. Campbell, and Alfred L. Brophy. Athens: University of Georgia Press.

Okorafor, Nnedi. 2015. *Binti*. New York: Tor.

———. 2017. *Home*. New York: Tor.

———. 2018. *The Night Masquerade*. New York: Tor.

Orrells, Daniel, Gurminder K. Bhambra, and Tessa Roynon, eds. 2011. *African Athena: New Agendas*. Oxford: Oxford University Press.

Ortega, Mariana. 2006. "Being Lovingly, Knowingly Ignorant: White Feminism and Women of Color." *Hypatia* 21.3:56–73.

Parker, Grant, ed. and trans. 2001. *The Agony of Asar: A Thesis on Slavery by the Former Slave, Jacobus Eliza Johannes Capitein, 1717–1747*. Princeton: Wiener.

———. 2008. *The Making of Roman India*. Cambridge: Cambridge University Press.

———, ed. 2017. *South Africa, Greece, Rome: Classical Confrontations*. Cambridge: Cambridge University Press.

Parker, Grant, and Carla M. Sinopoli, eds. 2008. *Ancient India in Its Wider World*. Ann Arbor: University of Michigan Press.

Schüssler Fiorenza, Elisabeth. 1992. *But She Said: Feminist Practices of Biblical Interpretation*. Boston: Beacon.

Sharpe, Christina. 2016. *In the Wake: On Blackness and Being*. Durham, NC: Duke University Press.

Walters, Tracey L. 2007. *African American Literatures and the Classicist Tradition: Black Women Writers from Wheatley to Morrison*. New York: Palgrave Macmillan.
Wikipedia. 2022. "Humanities." Wikimedia Foundation. Last modified August 22, 2022. https://tinyurl.com/SBL06104f.
Wilder, Craig Steven. 2013. *Ebony and Ivy: Race, Slavery, and the Troubled History of America's Universities*. New York: Bloomsbury.
———. 2019. "'Sons from the Southward and Some from the West Indies': The Academy and Slavery in Revolutionary America." Pages 21–45 in *Slavery and the University: Histories and Legacies*. Edited by Leslie M. Harris, James T. Campbell, and Alfred L. Brophy. Athens: University of Georgia Press.
Williams College. 1927. *Report of the President of Williams College Together with the Reports of Other Officers of Administration, 1926–27*. Williamstown, MA: Williams College Archives.
———. 1935. *The Administrative Report including Report of the Treasurer, 1934–35*. Williamstown, MA: Williams College Archives.
Williams College Museum of Art. 2018. "'The Field Is the World': Williams, Hawai'i, and Material Histories in the Making." https://tinyurl.com/SBL06104g.
Wimbush, Vincent L. 2012. *White Men's Magic: Scripturalization as Slavery*. Oxford: Oxford University Press.
———. 2017. *Scripturalectics: The Management of Meaning*. Oxford: Oxford University Press.
Wynter, Sylvia. 1994. "'No Humans Involved': An Open Letter to My Colleagues." Forum N.H.I.: Knowledge for the Twenty-First Century 1.1: 42–73.
———. 2015. *Sylvia Wynter: On Being Human as Praxis*. Edited by Katherine McKittrick. Durham, NC: Duke University Press.
Yusoff, Kathryn. 2018. *A Billion Black Anthropocenes or None*. Minneapolis: University of Minnesota Press.

The World of *Kandake*:
Foregrounding Ethiopian Queens and Empires

Gay L. Byron

> Until the lion has his own storyteller, the hunter will always have the best stories.
> —African proverb

#SayHerName

In Acts 8:26–40, Luke narrates a vivid story of the baptism of an Ethiopian eunuch. As the story goes, an angel speaks to Philip and summons him to go south along a wilderness road from Jerusalem to Gaza. While traveling, Philip runs into an Ethiopian court official of Candace (*kandake*), queen (*basilissēs*) of the Ethiopians. The official is returning home from Jerusalem, and while seated in his chariot he reads from the prophet Isaiah. The Spirit tells Philip to go over to the chariot and join it. When Philip runs up and hears the Ethiopian reading words from Isa 53:7–8, he asks, "Do you understand what you are reading?" The Ethiopian replies, "How can I, unless someone guides me?" (Acts 8:31). This question opens an *opportunity* for Philip to interpret the scripture and to proclaim to the Ethiopian "the good news about Jesus" (8:35). As they continue to travel down the road together, the Ethiopian spots some water and jumps out of the chariot, announcing: "What is to prevent me from being baptized?" So he commands the chariot to stop and both men go down into the water, and Philip baptizes the Ethiopian. After this, "the Spirit of the Lord snatched Philip away; the eunuch saw him no more and went on his way rejoicing" (8:39).

New Testament interpreters generally view this passage as a fulfillment of Acts 1:8, which declares that Christianity shall extend to the ends of the world. Yet after this dramatic baptism scene, the Ethiopian, the royal *kandake*, the kingdom of Nubia from which he traveled, and the other people who may have witnessed this encounter all disappear from the narrative as Philip is snatched away and the Ethiopian rides off rejoicing in his chariot.

Many New Testament critics focus on the Ethiopian in this narrative, his conversion, ethnic identity, and literary function in Luke's narrative (e.g., Felder 1993; Gaventa 1986; Martin 1989; A. Smith 1994). More recent studies have nuanced the Ethiopian's identity by calling attention to masculinity studies and Luke's use of *eunouchos* as a symbol of ambiguity, liminality, and effeminacy (Burke 2013; Wilson 2014, esp. 405–11). Brittany Wilson (2014, 418), in her analysis of this text, connects the "effeminate eunuch" with the "effeminate nation" Nubia, which was given this distinction by Greek and Roman authors because of its legacy of female rulers and queens. After a convincing argument about the gender ambiguity or "gender-liminal character" of the eunuch, *kandake*, who signifies that "Ethiopia has a long history of female rulers," is left in the background—hidden in plain sight (417–21, see esp. 418 n. 73).

I am concerned with this unnamed *kandake*. Given how womanist biblical critics have been highlighting experiences of Black women and finding creative ways to #SayHerName when it comes to reading biblical texts that are primarily centered on male characters and their preoccupations with power, social mobility, and survival (Byron and Lovelace 2016; Gafney 2016), the current social movement drawing attention to injustices against Black women (Crenshaw 2021) is the background for my writing of this essay and a fitting paradigm for foregrounding Nubian queens.

The baptism narrative about the Ethiopian eunuch and the *kandake* is not the only place where persons connected to Africa are hidden or disappear in Acts. John Mark (Acts 12:12, 25; 13:13; 15:36–39), known as the one who takes the gospel to Egypt (Eusebius, *Hist. eccl.* 2.16.1–2), also disappears from Luke's narrative after a dispute between Paul and Barnabas. After the disagreement over whether John Mark should continue with them in their travels (Acts 15:36–39), "Paul chose Silas" and "Barnabas took Mark with him and sailed away to Cyprus" (15:40). Nothing more is said about John Mark or the teachings he spread throughout Egypt. As a result, based on Luke's stories in Acts, readers are left with the journeys of Paul as the primary lens through which to understand the development of early Christian communities.

What are we to make of the vanishing of Ethiopians and other Africans from Acts? Marisa Parham (2009), in her book *Haunting and Dis-*

placement in African American Literature and Culture, develops the concept of "haunting," which "in its broadest sense is simultaneously a word for how knowledge comes together and also how it breaks apart, a term for an experience that emerges at the crossroads between what we know well and what we do not know easily."[1] The scant reference to *kandake* in the Ethiopian eunuch story hovers in the text and challenges the interpreter to investigate what has previously been inaccessible and not easily known. Ignoring or overlooking these lost pathways in early Christian literature invariably leads to relying on a single story, which in both classical and New Testament studies is de facto Greco-Roman, Western, and laden with Eurocentric worldviews and assumptions.

Novelist Chimamanda Ngozi Adichie, in her 2009 TED talk, calls attention to "The Danger of a Single Story." She recounts how she grew up reading British children's books, through which she unwittingly absorbed the patterns, symbols, and word choices reflecting European images and ideas. Years later, when she discovered African writers, she was able to find her own authentic, culturally rich voice and began writing stories that reflected the world she lived in and the people who nurtured her into being. Adichie claims that if we hear or read *only a single story* about another person or country, we risk a critical misunderstanding of the larger world and ourselves as unique individuals in it.

Indeed, this single-story phenomenon or single cultural perspective is what has characterized the way in which New Testament scholars have traditionally read sources from the ancient world, especially those of Africa (M. Smith and Kim 2018, 75). Even when there are efforts to study different trajectories of the New Testament or apply historical critical methods, these efforts are still pursued within a Western paradigm that privileges certain theological and cultural frameworks and leads to images, historical accounts, and geographical conceptualizations that marginalize the vast array of ethnic identities well represented in biblical and other sources documenting early Christianity.

So who is Candace (*kandake*) in Acts 8:27? How do we get to the *kandakes* and the world of Nubia, which was also a pivotal place of military

---

1. I want to thank Shelley P. Haley for raising this observation in her response to my conference paper on November 7, 2020. She was intrigued by Marisa Parham's (2002) concept of haunting and suggested this as a possible conceptual framework for interpreting disappeared Africans in Acts. Haley's own scholarship on gender, critical race theory, and classics also informs this essay on the *kandake* (Haley 1993, 2009).

battle and aesthetic beauty in the geographical and literary landscape of the early Christians? In this essay, I will introduce the lineage of queens (*kdke*) and rulers (*qora*) from Nubia, discuss the hellenization of Meroë, and suggest some possible ways that New Testament critics can interact more effectively with classicists to create an interpretive milieu of the ancient world that includes African and Greco-Roman sources and worldviews. Given the current cultural and political climate in the United States, I will also discuss recent efforts among biblical scholars who are reflecting on contemporary social justice movements and the ways in which these movements are reshaping their scholarship and impacting their vision for inclusive, collaborative scholarship.

Introducing the *Kandakes* (Ruling Queens of Ancient Meroë)

The *kandakes* of Meroë were queens from the kingdom of Kush who ruled from the city of Meroë from 284 BCE to 314 CE. The title "Candace" in Acts 8:27 is the Latinized version of the term *kentake* or *kandake* in Meroitic. Often confused as a name, it is more accurately translated as a title: "Queen Regent," "Queen Mother," or "Royal Woman" (Mark 2018; Hintze 1978, 98). The meaning of the title *kandake* (*kdke*), as well as the dates of their reigns, has been the subject of contradictory chronologies, timelines, and inconsistencies such as the conflation of their names and the impact of their sovereignty. Although some may have initially ruled with their husbands, a number of them ruled independently from 170 BCE to 314 CE (Mark 2018). Three of the *kandakes* are also recognized as rulers, as noted by the title *qore*, which will be discussed below. Given the limited scope of this essay, the following list of the *kandakes* is a starting point for identifying their lineage and highlighting their military and political achievements (Mark 2018):[2]

Shanakdakhete (r. ca. 177–155 BCE)
Amanirenas (r. ca. 40–10 BCE)
Amanishakheto (r. ca. 10 BCE–1 CE)
Amanitore (r. ca. 1–ca. 25 CE)
Amantitere (r. ca. 25–ca. 41 CE)

---

2. For more comprehensive surveys, see Török 1997b, 448–87; Phillips 2016; Welsby 1996. For a useful table of Meroitic queens, see also Fisher et al. 2012, xx; Ashby 2021, 28.

Amanikhatashan (r. ca. 62–ca. 85 CE)
Maleqorobar (r. ca. 266–ca. 283 CE)
Lahideamani (r. ca. 306–ca. 314 CE)

Shanakhdakheto (also known as Shanakdakhete) is the first *kandake* known to have ruled alone and whose tomb was inscribed with the first known Meroitic hieroglyphs. The British Museum has a gallery devoted to Nubia, which includes the reliefs from the funeral chapel of Queen Shanakdakheto (Fisher et al. 2012, 419). Although she was not given the title *qore*, she was buried with other rulers in the Northern Cemetery instead of in the Western Cemetery where the nonruling queens were buried (Haynes and Santini-Ritt 2012, 180–82).

Scholars generally agree that Amanirenas (ca. 40–10 BCE) was one of the most highly respected queens of Meroë who also had the title *qore* (Meroitic: "king"). Frank Snowden, in his seminal book *Blacks in Antiquity* (1971), documents the presence of an "Ethiopian Queen" in his chapter dealing with "Romans and Ethiopian Warriors." Snowden does not name this *kandake* since she is unnamed in his sources, which document the military and diplomatic encounters between the Romans and "the Ethiopians of the so-called Meroitic period south of Egypt" (131). Strabo describes how the Romans conquered Meroë, which was ruled by one of the *kandake*, most likely Amanirenas, the one-eyed *kandake* considered "a manly woman" (*Geogr.* 17.1.54).

Amanirenas is best known as the queen who won favorable terms with Augustus Caesar (r. 27 BCE–14 CE) following the conflict known as the Meroitic War between Kush and Rome (27–22 BCE). The war began in response to Kushite soldiers making incursions into Egypt, which at the time had been annexed as a Roman province after the Battle of Actium in 31 BCE. A chief supplier of grain, Egypt became one of the empire's most important territories. The Roman prefect of Egypt, Gaius Petronius, responded to the raids by invading Kush around 22 BCE and destroying the city of Napata. Amanirenas did not withdraw from this attack and retaliated with further aggression. She is depicted in the sources as a courageous queen, blind in one eye, and a skilled negotiator. Following the conflict, her control of the terms is evident in Rome's respect during the peace talks and an increase in trade between Rome and Meroë. Amanirenas captured a number of statues from Egypt, among them many of Augustus, which she returned following the peace, but the head of one statue she buried under the steps of her temple so that people would walk over Augustus on their daily visits! This is the famous Meroë Bronze Head now housed in the British Museum (Fisher et al. 2012, 419). Achebe (2020, 76) describes two portraits from the pyramid of Amanirenas. In the first, she is dressed in ceremonial clothes and is spearing captured prisoners. The second portrait shows the presence of three scars under her left eye, supporting the claim that she was the one-eyed *kandake* who fought the Romans.

Little is known about *qore* and *Kandake* Amanishakheto (ca. 10 BCE–1 CE) beyond her lavish jewelry and other artifacts found in her tomb by Giuseppe Ferlini, an Italian doctor and treasure hunter known for looting graves of Nubia in 1834 (Haynes and Santini-Ritt 2012, 183–84). Scholars have documented inscriptions and reliefs from her tomb that portray her as a powerful queen who ruled independently, but details of her reign have been lost.

Amanitore (ca. 1–25 CE) is considered the last of the well-known Meroitic ruling *kandakes*. She was a coregent (*qore*) with King Natakamani, and together they were responsible for the building and restoration of numerous temples in Napata, Meroë, Amara, and Wad ban Naqa (Haynes and Santini-Ritt 2012, 184). One of their most notable temples in Naqa has images of the king and queen side by side while smiting enemies whom they hold by their hair (Phillips 2016, 292).

Amantitere (ca. 25–41 CE), the *kandake* most likely referred to in Acts 8:27 (Achebe 2020, 76), is not as well documented as her predecessors (Phillips 2016, 291–92). Most sources agree that she is not identified as a *qore*; however, she is sometimes confused with Amanitore or even Amanirenas (Mark 2018). Likewise, Amanikhatashan (ca. 62–85 CE) who ruled after the golden age of Meroë—a peaceful time during which the kingdom made connections with India—is not as widely documented (Achebe 2020, 78). Phillips (2016, 292) claims that she is "not attested as *qore* or *kandake*, [and] she may have sat on the throne as 'Son of Re' and 'King of Upper and Lower Egypt, Lord of the Two Lands.'"

Nwando Achebe (2020, 77), in her book *Female Monarchs and Merchant Queens*, claims that the names of at least nine ruling *kandakes* of Kush at Meroë have survived, including Bartare (ca. 260–250 BCE), who was buried in one of the three pyramids in Meroë's south cemetery. Her chronology follows the one listed above, with the exception of the description "Amanirenas (ca. 1–20 CE)," which most likely is intended to be Amanitore (ca. 1–25 CE) (78).

According to Achebe (2020, 77–78), there are three more *kandakes* central to Ethiopian dynastic history: Makeda, queen of Sheba, who founded the Menelik or Solomonic dynasty; Queen Ahywa (or Sofya), who in 332 CE made Christianity the official religion of the kingdom (even before it became the official religion of the Roman Empire!); and Gudit (also referred to as Yodit, Judith, or Esato), a *kandake* of Jewish origin who invaded Axum and overthrew its king. This latter *kandake* ultimately caused the downfall of the empire and found the rival Zagwe dynasty (933–1253 CE). In this synopsis, Achebe, like other reputable scholars, is using the term *kandake* rather loosely to describe influential African queens and rulers from different historical periods and places. She is not alone in conflating stories about Nubian queens or exaggerating their accomplishments. Several other scholars have also incorrectly referred to the Queen of Sheba as a *kandake* (see e.g., Salés 2020; Houston 1985, 50)[3] or maintained outdated and inaccurate chronologies (Yamauchi 2004, 171–72).[4]

As much as I was hoping to garner some new information about Amantitere and confirm her identity as the unnamed *kandake* mentioned in Acts 8:27, it is best to conclude at this point that the *kandakes* were a known presence and threat in the Greco-Roman world who wielded influence through wealth, military victories, and strategic political alliances.[5] Given the inconclusive scholarship and the consensus that more archaeological and historical research is needed in this area (see e.g., Fisher et al. 2012; Phillips 2016 esp. 294; Ashby 2021), this preliminary outline of Nubian queens is a starting point for further discussion and refinement, not a final definitive statement.

---

3. Drusilla Dunjee Houston, in her 1926 book *Wonderful Ethiopians of the Ancient Cushite Empire*, discusses a "long line of queens called Candace" who "ruled over an Ethiopia that included Abyssinia, but their center was near Meroë, where they were buried" (see Houston 1985, 50). Houston does not name this queen but rather adds a reference to "a queen warrior of Ethiopia" mentioned by Strabo. This is most likely *Kandake* Amanirenas (or Candace the One-Eyed), mentioned above. More conflation continues as Houston claims that "the renowned queen of Sheba, queen of the south, who visited Solomon belonged to this line of queens" (50).

4. Yamauchi (2004, 171–72) includes only four of the *kandakes* in his summary: Amanirenas, Amanishakheto, Amanitare, and Nawidemak. More research is necessary to generate a comprehensive list of the *kandakes*, the years for their respective reigns, and their contributions.

5. Yamauchi (2004, 172) differs on this point. He claims that Queen Nawidemak is most likely the Candace mentioned in Acts 8. Houston (1985, 50) likewise confuses Amantitere with Amanirenas.

Historiography and the Hellenization of Meroë

European and American historians, classicists, and archaeologists all approach the study and engagement of Nubia (Kush/Ethiopia) with different goals and questions and are usually focused on a wide array of religious, cultural, political, economic, and military sources and artifacts. A common critique of their scholarship is that they invariably lift Nubia *out of Africa* and Europeanize it by creating a "false historiographical dichotomy that is supposed to separate the Classicist from the Africanist" (Keita 2011, 23). Historian Maghan Keita (2011, 24) argues that "this dichotomy is constructed on notions of race, a set of privileged epistemologies to which certain 'racial' and ethnic groups presumably have no access, and a historiography that posits that the peoples in question have neither histories nor historians."

In order to understand the place from which the *kandake* ruled, it is necessary to review the major kingdoms of Kush: Kerma, Napata, and Meroë. The nomenclature of these time periods and the fluid ways in which "Ethiopia" and "Nubia" are used to describe these different locales leaves interpreters mired in chronologies and details that are difficult to trace, without noting inconsistencies based on the academic discipline and ideological sensibilities of the interpreter.[6] This essay follows the chronology outlined by archaeologist Geoff Emberling in his review article on an exhibit featuring Nubia at the Boston Museum of Fine Arts.[7]

Emberling (2020) outlines four historical phases of Nubia: the kingdom of Kerma (2400–1550 BCE), the conquest and occupation of Nubia by the Egyptian empire of the New Kingdom (1550–1070 BCE), the resurgence of Kush during the Napatan (750–332 BCE), and the Meroitic period (332 BCE–364 CE). The collection at the Museum of Fine Arts largely comes from the series of excavations led by American archaeologist George Reisner and his teams, who excavated all the royal cemeteries of Kush from 1913 to 1932. These cemeteries were at Kerma, El-Kurru, Nuri, Gebel Barkal, and Meroë, as well as five Middle Kingdom era Egyptian

---

6. For example, see the entry on "Kush" in *The Encyclopedia of Black Studies* (Asante and Mazama, 2005).

7. For comprehensive historical and archaeological background on Kush and Nubia (esp. Meroë), see Török 1997a; Welsby 1996; Fisher 2012; Hintze 1997; Shinnie 1967; and Bonnet 2019.

fortresses: Semna, Kumma, Uronarti, Shalfak, and Mirgissa (Emberling 2020, 512).

Emberling notes the biased worldview of Reisner, who could not imagine that the site and its massive cemetery could have been the work of a "black African culture" (513). Reisner concludes that the settlement had been ruled by an Egyptian governor "gone native." This "clearly racist legacy of interpretation," as Emberling argues, is an ongoing challenge for the Boston Museum of Fine Arts. The museum recognizes the need to correct the story and attempted to do so by supplementing Reisner's interpretations with contemporary perspectives on ancient Nubia by scholars, artists, and community members (514).

Before Reisner excavated in Nubia, Giuseppe Ferlini also excavated several cultural sites of Nubia in 1834. Some scholars have identified the unethical practices of Ferlini, who was known for looting the treasures of Meroë. Ferlini could not find buyers for the looted artifacts, because the European market at the time refused to believe that a black African kingdom had produced such incredible works (Mark 2018; Markowitz and Lacovara 1996). As one scholar put it, "Egypt had long been 'whitewashed' and was considered distinct from the kingdoms to the south such as Kush which was associated with black Africa" (Mark 2018). Almost one hundred years later, when Reisner excavated Meroë, he concluded that the ruling class of Meroë were light-skinned people reigning over the "ignorant" black population who were elevated only by their monarchs exposing them to Egyptian culture. It was inconceivable to these early excavators that black people of Africa could have established such powerful kingdoms (Reisner 1923).

Unfortunately, Meroë and its environs continue to be interpreted primarily through the lens of Greek and Roman literary sources as well as archaeological approaches that privilege Greek and Roman perspectives— despite their inherent biases. For example, in his sourcebook, Stanley Burstein summarizes a document featuring Meroë based on descriptions by Diodorus and Strabo:

> Although Herodotus the father of History, had already heard of Meroë, the last and greatest capital of Kush, in the fifth century BCE, accurate knowledge concerning Meroë only became current in the Greek world in the third century BCE, when Ptolemaic explorers and diplomats visited the city and described it and its environs. From then until the end of antiquity, Meroë served as one of the fundamental reference points of

Greek world geography ... whose latitudes Greek geographers used to define the limits of the "oecumene": the civilized world (Burstein 2009, 53; see Diodorus, *Bib. hist.* 1.33; Strabo, *Geogr.* 17.2.2).

This framing of the civilized world around the narratives and perceptions of Greek and Roman geographers and historians is an inherently flawed byproduct of the sources and the interpreters who are limited by the contours of the ancient Greek world in presenting the material. Even when there is a focus on identifying race and ethnicity in the classical world, the orientation when it comes to Africa is still solely based on a hellenized litany of sources (Kennedy, Roy, and Goldman 2013; Burstein 2009). Despite these limitations, there is a well-documented tradition among African Americans to reclaim classics in its conventional Greek and Roman scope. Before addressing the implications of foregrounding the *kandakes* for bridging the divided worlds of New Testament and classical studies, a brief survey of the paradox associated with Meroë as witnessed in the black literary imagination is in order.

Excursus: Meroë and the Black Literary Imagination—A Paradox

The kingdom of Meroë, with its rich legacy of leaders, military might, architectural achievements (see esp. Garlake 2002, 59–71), and geographical splendor has been a source of educational superiority and racial pride and uplift among African Americans. Margaret Malamud (2019, 5) discusses the "paradox of appropriating the hegemonic discourse of American classicism in the struggle for abolition and equality." African Americans staked their own claims to the classical world by using texts, ideas, and images of ancient Greece and Rome in order to establish their authority in debates about slavery, race, education, and politics (Callahan 2006; McCoskey 2012, 194–97). Two examples serve as a springboard for further discussion.

First is a serialized novel written by Pauline Hopkins, the editor of the *Colored American Magazine* from 1902 to 1903. Hopkins's novel *Of One Blood, or, The Hidden Self* envisioned an African civilization living among the pyramids at Meroë. Allan Callahan (2006, 166) notes that *Of One Blood* is a combination of love story, mystery, and Ethiopianist legend. The protagonist Reuel Briggs, while on an expedition into Africa with a group of British scientists, is kidnapped by the local inhabitants, who believe that

Briggs is an heir to the Meroitic throne. The Meroites acclaim him king and arrange for him to be wed to their queen Candace.

The second example is from W. E. B. Du Bois, who in 1913 wrote a pageant titled *The Star of Ethiopia* in celebration of pan-African history and of the contributions of Africans to world history. In response to Hegel's claims that civilization originated in Greece and around the Mediterranean Sea, Du Bois intervened and refuted the negative images of Africa and Africans in the United States, as well as the claim that ancient Egypt did not belong to the "African spirit" (Malamud 2019, 188–89). In his *Lectures on the Philosophy of World History*, Hegel says,

> We shall therefore leave Africa at this point, and it need not be mentioned again. For it is an unhistorical continent, with no movement or development of its own.... Egypt will be considered as a stage in the movement of the human spirit from east to west, but it has no part in the spirit of Africa. What we understand as Africa proper is that unhistorical and undeveloped land which is still enmeshed in the natural spirit, and which had to be mentioned here before we cross the threshold of world history itself. (Malamud 2019, 189; Hegel 1975, 190)

Thus Du Bois, in his 1913 *The Star of Ethiopia*, countered this distorted view of history by tracing the history of Africa and Africans from prehistory right down to the present moment of African American history. Du Bois claimed that he created the pageant, which features the Queen of Sheba, to teach "the coloured people themselves the meaning of their history and their rich emotional life through a new theatre; and also 'to reveal the Negro to the white world as a human, feeling thing'" (Malamud 2019, 191; Du Bois 1996). As Malamud (2019, 193) observes in her study of *African Americans and the Classics*, Du Bois flips the script and chooses not to refer to Greece and Rome in the telling of his history. He did "nothing less than write classical civilization out of African American history."

Implications for New Testament and Classical Studies

In preparation for the Divided Worlds conference, I reached out to a few classicists to ascertain their perspectives on source material for the *kandake*, only to discover that they were not familiar with the name or title, nor could they refer me to any scholarship on the topic beyond Snowden's

Blacks in Antiquity.[8] This leads me to reflect on the question Emberling asks in his review article on the Nubia exhibit at the Boston Museum of Fine Arts: "Why is Nubia relatively little known to American and European scholars and public audiences?" (2020, 518). He concludes this is the case because the geographical area has been perceived as peripheral for several reasons:

> 1. "Its cultures developed on the southern border of Egypt, and it exists in a kind of intellectual and historical peripheral zone—not really a part of the greater Mediterranean, or the Middle East, but also not really part of Africa" (518).
> 2. "Nubia has been considered peripheral even to Egypt.… The perception by scholars in particular has been that Nubia was less wealthy and powerful than Egypt" (518).
> 3. "Nubian cultures have not generally been seen as a part of Western heritage, with the exception of African-American heritage narratives.… Nubia remains 'peripheral' in Western cultural imagination" (518).
> 4. "There has historically been a legacy of institutionalized racism in scholarly work on Nubia. Earlier generations of scholars tended to see Nubians as poor cousins of Egyptians, culturally dependent on Egyptian technology and religion, rather than as people who had agency in their own right. *And it must be said that covertly racist views are still present in the field*" (518–19, emphasis added).

I likewise ask: Why is it so difficult to bring to light the world of the *kandakes*? How does a biblical critic overcome the peripheral status of Nubia and Nubians and create a path for bringing this history, culture, and tradition into the interpretive purview of scholars and students? Is it possible for scholars specializing in New Testament studies and classical studies to find common ground within our divided worlds? These questions lead to naming what is most at stake in this essay about Nubian queens: How does one deal with "institutionalized racism" and expose the "covertly racist views" that are still present in our fields (Poser 2021), embedded in the biblical and classical sources (Byron 2009), and hover-

---

8. Molly Levine, who was a key respondent in the Martin Bernal, *Black Athena* debate, referred me to Frank Snowden's *Blacks in Antiquity*. She and other colleagues were excited to connect with someone who works with the same historical period and sources and look forward to future conversations and sharing of resources related to our respective fields of interest.

ing within the findings and conclusions of presumably reputable scholars? The *kandake* is more than a mere backdrop for signaling the geographical extent of early Christianity. Rather, the *kandakes* of Nubia illuminate the status and roles of African women in antiquity—indeed, roles of leadership, military savvy, diplomacy, and economic affluence. They also reveal the necessity for multiple stories and a polycentric interpretive framework that expands the literary and cultural imagination of the ancient world.

In his chapter on "Early Christian Attitudes toward Ethiopians" (1971), Snowden, a classicist, focuses on the conversion of Ethiopians and their "membership in the early Church" by citing passages such as Augustine's *Aethiopia credet Deo*, Gregory of Nyssa's *Commentarius in Canticum Canticorum*, which claims that "Christ came into the world to make blacks white and that in the Kingdom of Heaven Ethiopians become white," and the Ethiopian eunuch story in Acts 8:26–40 (1970, 205–6). In his discussion of this text, Snowden mentions the Queen of Ethiopia but does not provide any specific information about her. The central focus of this passage, according to Snowden, is on the baptism of the eunuch and his conversion as a foreshadowing of what was to be the practice of the early church (206). During his time, Snowden's conclusions were deemed transformative among classicists, who were challenged to recognize blacks in antiquity. Yet times have changed significantly since the 1960s and 1970s. Twenty-first-century classicists, such as Roman historian Dan-el Padilla Peralta, are calling into question the "Future of Classics" and are debating whether the discipline can be saved from whiteness (Poser 2021).

From another angle, Salim Faraji (2012, 185–86) argues in his critical study *The Roots of Nubian Christianity Uncovered* that merely focusing on the Ethiopian eunuch narrative as a basis for demonstrating the universal and inclusive scope of early Christian communities is insufficient. Citing the limitations of such trailblazing interpretations of Acts 8 by scholars such as Cain Hope Felder (1989, 37–48), Abraham Smith (1994), and others who emphasize Luke's inclusivity motif, Faraji (2012, 185) makes a convincing argument for the inclusion of "Kush as a significant player in Roman international relations." After briefly discussing the military prowess of "Queen Ameniras [*sic*]" during the Roman-Kushite war (29–20 BCE), Faraji raises the question, "how did this encounter impact Roman and early Christian views of the Kandake and the kingdom of Meroë?" (185). He further cites my earlier "ethno-political" reading of this text: "Byron suggests that Luke was writing to an audience that was familiar with the military conflict that had occurred between the Meroitic queen and the Roman emperor Augustus and therefore the mere mention of a *Kandake* would have signaled a political threat" (Faraji 2012, 186; cf. Byron 2002, 108–15, esp. 111).

Faraji's reading is accurate in terms of the Greco-Roman ethnopolitical rhetoric identified in the passage. Yet naming the *kandake* and even calling attention to the military conflicts and political threats that were obviously in Luke's literary purview (see, e.g., Acts 21:27–39) continues to privilege the hellenistic context of the passage and leaves the history of the *kandakes* dangling off the margins of the story, *vanishing* into the plot line of symbolic conversion (Gaventa 1986) or ethnic othering (Byron 2002). Or, as Parham (2009, 2) suggests, "haunting" the interpreter to acknowledge the "crossroads between what we know well and what we do not know easily." In this regard, foregrounding Ethiopian (Meroitic) queens and Kushite (Nubian) empires reveals what is not known easily. These additional people and places open up previously ignored pathways for interpreting the New Testament and early Christianity.

#BlackLivesMatter

The conference that prompted this essay is another opportunity to shine light on the world(s) of the Ethiopians who are located as far north as the Axumite Empire (modern Tigray Region of Ethiopia and Eritrea) (Byron 2009) and as far south as the Kushite kingdom of Nubia (modern Sudan). This essay takes another step in this direction by introducing the *kandakes* for the purpose of offering a framework for recentering, remapping, and reorienting the geographical landscape of classical antiquity and early Christianity toward Nubia. In an era of biblical interpretation that acknowledges marginal (minoritized) readers and affirms that Black Lives Matter,[9] it is imperative that marginal references to ancient Africans in general, and African women in particular, are pulled from footnotes, archaeological studies, and museum exhibits and given space in mainstream interpretive paradigms among biblical scholars and classicists.

The story of the Ethiopian eunuch has much more to offer than merely being a metaphor for conceptualizing the geographical reach of Luke's ver-

---

9. See recent programs and publications by the Society of Biblical Literature, such as https://tinyurl.com/SBLPress06104a0 and https://tinyurl.com/SBLPress06104a. Contributors to Reinhartz et al. (2017, 203–44) reflect on the Black Lives Matter movement and its impact on their scholarship. See also Byron and Page 2022.

sion of Christianity. The historiography of Nubia matters for the study of the New Testament and creates another center of social, cultural, and economic exchange that can no longer be ignored. Understanding how Nubia has been hellenized through the historical accounts of Greco-Roman writers and used to privilege Roman worldviews as opposed to cosmologies and worldviews of Kush challenges biblical scholars and classicists to move toward a polycentric view of antiquity that recognizes the subtle ways that gender, racism, and the institutional structures of our disciplines perpetuate a one-sided view of history.

Works Cited

Achebe, Nwando. 2020. *Female Monarchs and Merchant Queens in Africa*. Ohio Short Histories of Africa. Athens: Ohio University Press.

Adichie, Chimamanda Ngozi. 2009. "The Danger of a Single Story." TEDGlobal. https://www.ted.com/talks/chimamanda_ngozi_adichie_the_danger_of_a_single_story.

Asante, Molefi Kete, and Ama Mazama, eds. 2005. *The Encyclopedia of Black Studies*. Thousand Oaks, CA: Sage.

Ashby, Solange. 2021. "Priestess, Queen, Goddess: The Divine Feminine in the Kingdom of Kush." Pages 22–34 in *The Routledge Companion to Black Women's Cultural Histories*. Edited by Janell Hobson. London: Routledge.

Bonnet, Charles. 2019. *The Black Kingdom of Nubia*. Cambridge: Harvard University Press.

Burke, Sean D. 2013. *Queering the Ethiopian Eunuch: Strategies of Ambiguity in Acts*. Minneapolis: Fortress.

Burstein, Stanley M., ed. 2009. *Ancient African Civilizations: Kush and Axum*. Princeton: Wiener.

Byron, Gay L. 2002. *Symbolic Blackness and Ethnic Difference in Early Christian Literature*. New York: Routledge.

———. 2009. "Ancient Ethiopia and the New Testament: Ethnic (Con)Texts and Racialized (Sub)Texts." Pages 161–90 in *They Were All Together in One Place: Toward Minority Biblical Criticism*. Edited by Fernando Segovia, Randall Bailey, and Benny Liew. SemeiaSt 57. Atlanta: Society of Biblical Literature.

Byron, Gay L., and Vanessa Lovelace, eds. 2016. *Womanist Interpretations of the Bible: Expanding the Discourse*. SemeiaSt 85. Atlanta: SBL Press.

Byron, Gay L., and Hugh Page Jr., eds. 2022. *Black Scholars Matter*. RBS 100. Atlanta: SBL Press.

Callahan, Allan Dwight. 2006. *The Talking Book: African Americans and the Bible*. New Haven: Yale University Press.

Crenshaw, Kimberlé. 2021. *#SayHerName: Black Women's Stories on State Violence and Public Silence*. Chicago: Haymarket.

Du Bois, W. E. B. 1996. "The Star of Ethiopia." Pages 86–92 in *Black Theatre USA: Plays by African Americans 1847–1938*. Edited by James V. Hatch and Ted Shine. New York: Free Press.

Emberling, Geoff. 2020. "Exhibiting Ancient Africa at the Museum of Fine Arts, Boston: 'Ancient Nubia Now' and Its Audiences." *AJA* 124.3:511–19.

Faraji, Salim. 2012. *The Roots of Nubian Christianity Uncovered: The Triumph of the Last Pharaoh*. Trenton, NJ: Africa World.

Felder, Cain Hope. 1989. *Troubling Biblical Waters*. Maryknoll, NY: Orbis.

———. 1993. "Entry on the Ethiopian Finance Minister and the Kandake-Queen of Ethiopia." Page 1587 in *African Heritage Bible*. Edited by Cain Hope Felder. Iowa Falls, IA: World Bible.

Fisher, Marjorie M., Peter Lacovara, Salima Ikram, and Sue D'Auria, eds. 2012. *Ancient Nubia: African Kingdoms on the Nile*. Cairo: The American University in Cairo Press.

Gafney, Wil. 2016. "A Womanist Midrash of Delilah: Don't Hate the Playa Hate the Game." Pages 49–72 in *Womanist Interpretations of the Bible: Expanding the Discourse*. Edited by Gay L. Byron and Vanessa Lovelace. SemeiaSt 85. Atlanta: SBL Press.

Garlake, Peter. 2002. "'Nubia' and 'Axum.'" Pages 51–95 in *Early Art and Architecture of Africa*. Edited by Peter Garlake. Oxford: Oxford University Press.

Gaventa, Beverly R. 1986. *From Darkness to Light: Aspects of Conversion in the New Testament*. Philadelphia: Fortress.

Haley, Shelley P. 1993. "Black Feminist Thought and Classics: Re-Membering, Re-Claiming, Re-Empowering." Pages 23–43 in *Feminist Theory and the Classics*. Edited by N. S. Rabinowitz and A. Richlin. New York: Routledge.

———. 2009. "Be Not Afraid of the Dark: Critical Race Theory and Classical Studies." Pages 27–49 in *Prejudice and Christian Beginnings: Investigating Race, Gender, and Ethnicity in Early Christian Studies*. Edited by Laura Nasrallah and Elisabeth Schüssler Fiorenza. Minneapolis: Fortress.

Haynes, Joyce, and Mimi Santini-Ritt. 2012. "Women in Ancient Nubia." Pages 170–85 in *Ancient Nubia: African Kingdoms on the Nile*. Edited by Marjorie M. Fisher, Peter Lacovara, Salima Ikram, and Sue D'Auria. Cairo: The American University in Cairo Press.

Hegel, Georg Wilhelm Friedrich. 1975. *Lectures on the Philosophy of World History: Introduction*. Edited by Johannes Hoffmeister. Introduction by H. B. Nisbet, and Duncan Forbes. Cambridge: Cambridge University Press.

Hintze, F. 1978. "Kingdom of Kush: The Meroitic Period." Pages 89–105 in *Africa in Antiquity I: The Arts of Ancient Nubia and the Sudan*. Edited by Steffen Wenig. Brooklyn: Brooklyn Museum of Art.

Hopkins, Pauline. 1902–1903. "Of One Blood, Or, the Hidden Self. Parts 1–3." *Colored American Magazine*. November and December 1902, January 1903.

Houston, Drusilla Dunjee. [1926] 1985. *Wonderful Ethiopians of the Ancient Cushite Empire*. Baltimore: Black Classic.

Keita, Maghan. 2011. "Believing in Ethiopians." Pages 19–39 in *African Athena: New Agendas*. Oxford: Oxford University Press.

Kennedy, Rebecca F., C. Sydnor Roy, and Max L. Goldman, trans. 2013. *Race and Ethnicity in the Classical World: An Anthology of Primary Sources in Translation*. Indianapolis: Hackett.

Malamud, Margaret. 2019. *African Americans and the Classics: Antiquity, Abolition, and Activism*. London: Tauris.

Mark, Joshua J. 2018. "The Candaces of Meroë." *World History Encyclopedia*. March 19, 2018. https://tinyurl.com/SBL06104i.

Markowitz, Y. J., and P. Lacovara. 1996. "The Ferlini Treasure in Archaeological Perspective." *Journal of the American Research Center in Egypt* 33:1–9.

Martin, Clarice J. 1989. "A Chamberlain's Journey and the Challenge of Interpretation for Liberation." *Semeia* 47:105–35.

McCoskey, Denise M. 2012. *Race: Antiquity and Its Legacy*. London: Tauris.

Parham, Marisa. 2009. *Haunting and Displacement in African American Literature and Culture*. New York: Routledge.

Phillips, Jacke. 2016. "Women in Ancient Nubia." Pages 280–97 in *Women in Antiquity: Real Women across the Ancient World*. Edited by Stephanie Lynn Budin and Jean Macintosh Turfa. New York: Routledge.

Poser, Rachel. 2021. "He Wants to Save Classics from Whiteness: Can the Field Survive?" *New York Times Magazine*. February 2, 2021. https://

www.nytimes.com/2021/02/02/magazine/classics-greece-rome-whiteness.html?smid=em-share.

Reinhartz, Adele, et al. 2017. "The JBL Forum, an Occasional Exchange: Black Lives Matter for Critical Biblical Scholarship." *JBL* 136.1:203–44.

Reisner, George. 1923. *Excavations at Kerma*. 2 vols. Harvard African Studies 5–6. Cambridge: Peabody Museum of Harvard University.

Salés, Luis J. 2020. "To Kill a Matriarchy: Makədda, Queen of Ethiopia and the Specter of Pauline Androprimacy in the Kəbrä Nägäśt." *African Journal of Gender and Religion* 26.1:49–76.

Shinnie, P. L. 1967. *Meroë: A Civilization of the Sudan*. New York: Praeger.

Smith, Abraham. 1994. "'Do You Understand What You Are Reading?' A Literary Critical Reading of the Ethiopian (Kushite) Episode (Acts 8:26–40)." *Journal of the Interdenominational Theological Center* 22.1:48–70.

Smith, Mitzi J., and Yung Suk Kim. 2018. *Toward Decentering the New Testament: A Reintroduction*. Eugene, OR: Cascade.

Snowden, Frank M., Jr. 1971. *Blacks in Antiquity: Ethiopians in the Greco-Roman Experience*. Cambridge: Harvard University Press.

Strabo. 1932. *Geography*. Translated by C. L. Sherman. 8 vols. LCL. Cambridge: Harvard University Press.

Török, L. 1997a. *Meroë: An Ancient African Capital. John Garstang's Excavations in the Sudan*. Occasional Publication 12. London: Egypt Exploration Society.

———. 1997b. *The Kingdom of Kush: Handbook of the Napatan-Meroitic Civilization*. Leiden: Brill.

Welsby, Derek A. 1996. *The Kingdom of Kush: The Napatan and Meroitic Empires*. Princeton: Wiener.

Wilson, Brittaney E. 2014. "'Neither Male nor Female': The Ethiopian Eunuch in Acts 8.26–40." *NTS* 60:403–22.

Yamauchi, Edwin M. 2004. *Africa and the Bible*. Grand Rapids: Baker Academic.

An Apocalyptic Epidemiology of Foreignness: The Use of Revelation in American Associations of Immigrants with Disease

Yii-Jan Lin

> But let nothing unclean enter it, or anyone who practices abomination or falsehood, but only those who are written in the Lamb's book of life.
> —Rev 21:27

> When we see this fatal scourge of pagan, mahommedan, and anti-christian lands lighting upon our shores, and feel the first blow here at the heart of this aspiring nation, we may not forget that the moral influence of this city is felt to the extremity of the land.
> —Reverend Gardiner Spring, 1832 sermon

The language of disease is one of invasion. Viruses and bacteria, as described in textbooks and news stories alike, do not neutrally enter a body but infiltrate it through vulnerable points of entry on its periphery (e.g., mouth, nose, eyes, open wounds). Then the pathogen—literally, the "producer of suffering"—may breach the walls of individual cells, the myriad individuals constituting the defensive body. It takes no great leap of the imagination to view this indeed as an "attack," with enemies "marching" down windpipes and "hijacking" cell mechanisms, while white blood cells form a "front line" on the battlefield (e.g., Wadman et al. 2020). But, as Susan Sontag (1990, 183) notes, "the effect of the military thinking about sickness and health is far from inconsequential." The metaphor of war, in dramatizing—and narrativizing—disease, "overmobilizes" and "overdescribes," so that "it powerfully contributes to the excommunicating and stigmatizing of the ill."

War-themed dramatizations of disease cast survivors as heroes, but casualties who die or live on with disability consequently play the part of those not strong enough or not brave enough, so that they lose not only life or ability but also a moral contest. "Fighting" cancer or COVID-19 becomes a test of personal merit, a struggle to "dominate," rather than simply the experience of a disease within a nexus of economic, social, and cultural realities.[1] And if a person must "fight" a disease, the one who "loses the battle" easily becomes a "loser" and appears personally at fault because of their habits or lifestyle or, further down that road, their moral depravity. This is what Sontag and many others resist when they reject military language in epidemiology.

Alongside the stigmatization of those who suffer and die comes the categorization of these individuals into groups understood as especially susceptible to disease, socially and sexually deviant, disgusting in hygiene, or all of the above. In its first decades, AIDS, known as the "homosexual disease," was seen in the United States as belonging to a depraved community that deservedly suffered a divinely inflicted and apocalyptic plague (see Long 2004).

But in the full story of AIDS in America, the disease did not *originate* with homosexuals but came from *outside*. While at first the American public feared a group within their national borders, scientific discoveries of the virus's origins among West African primates drew attention to dangers lurking outside those borders (Clavel et al. 1986). The conjunction of *Africa, monkeys, plague,* and *sexually transmitted* easily coalesced in American public imagination into a new nightmare full of racist fear, playing on a "subliminal connection made to notions about a primitive past" that "cannot help but activate a familiar set of stereotypes about animality, sexual license, and blacks" (Sontag 1990, 140).

The equation of sickness with the Other is, of course, nothing new. During the Black Death, Rhineland city leaders targeted Jews for slaughter, accusing them of poisoning wells and spreading the plague (Cohn 2007). Further back in time, in the third century CE, the philosopher Porphyry blamed Christians and their neglect of Asclepius and the gods for causing the Cyprian Plague (Eusebius, *Praep. ev.* 5.1.9). But while these

---

1. For example, Donald Trump tweeted "I will be leaving the great Walter Reed Medical Center today at 6:30 P.M. Feeling really good! Don't be afraid of Covid. Don't let it dominate your life. We have developed, under the Trump Administration, some really great drugs & knowledge. I feel better than I did 20 years ago!" *Twitter*, October 5, 2020, https://twitter.com/realDonaldTrump/status/1313186529058136070 (account now suspended).

peoples constituted an Other, they were not groups delineated as outsiders or foreigners. Indeed, it was their integration in society that was part of the problem, so that the only way to appease the gods or safeguard society was the expulsion or destruction of the enemy already within it.

This essay, however, focuses on the fear of an enemy *outside* the city walls as the carriers of plague, on the perception of peoples wholly new and Other in the American context as the main cause of disease. The earliest immigrants to America, white Europeans, and later generations of white Anglo nativists viewed first indigenous peoples and then unwanted immigrant groups as especially prone to sickness. This essay shows how this belief was informed and influenced by the metaphors and theology of the book of Revelation, which depicts those outside the walls of the new Jerusalem as filthy, immoral, and barred from entry. White colonials and nativists, having imagined America as the shining new city of God, naturally produced—and continue to produce—a theologized anti-immigrant discourse that associates foreigners with plague.

It was after the European explorers happened upon the American continents that ideation of disease focused blame not only on the Other but particularly on the Other as an unknown outsider. Several new realities of the American context brought the figure of the diseased foreigner into sharper relief: the relative boundedness of the New World, lying between the Atlantic and Pacific Oceans; advances in nautical travel and, consequentially, the coming together of people groups heretofore separated by vast distances; and the speed by which these people groups could be mutually introduced. These factors have had similar effects on contemporaneous constructions of race (Brace 2005, 17–36).

When explorers and later colonists arrived in the Americas, they not only murdered indigenous populations by their own hand but also introduced tiny "colonizers." The actions of these first European immigrants mirrored simultaneously occurring microscopic events carried out by the pathogens they brought as they sought to "(1) colonize the host; (2) find a nutritionally compatible niche in the host body; (3) avoid, subvert, or circumvent the host's innate and adaptive immune response; (4) replicate, using host resources; and (5) exit and spread to a new host" (Alberts et al. 2002). This description was taken from a standard microbiology textbook describing the "successful" pathogen, one able to "maximally exploit" the host and multiply rapidly. Perhaps the metaphor of colonization more accurately describes the course of disease than the metaphor of warfare. In any case, new European immigrants, like the viruses they carried, exploited the native host and its resources and multiplied so that they decimated, by sword and disease, on average 90 to 95 percent of each native group they encountered (Spickard 2007, 43). In Jamestown, Virginia, the native population decreased from 25,000 to 2,000 between 1607 and 1700, while its colonist population grew from zero to around 100,000 (Thornton 1987, 60–90). To be sure, some colonists also suffered from disease strains new to them such as malaria (Kraut 1994, 22), but the pathogens they brought with them wrought far greater destruction on native populations.

Far from seeing themselves as the diseased Other and foreigner, however, the first European immigrants interpreted the death of the native population as part of a glorious destiny. In New England, epidemiology relied in large part on theology, framed by an apocalyptic mission to establish God's kingdom on earth. Puritan minister Increase Mather credited prayer and God's hand with the felling of the native "heathens" by disease. He wrote:

> How often have we prayed that the Lord would take those his Enemies into his own avenging hand … and send the destroying Angel amongst them. This Prayer hath been heard; For it is known that the Indians were distressed with famine, multitudes of them perishing for want of bread; and the Lord sent sicknesses amongst them, that Travellers have seen many dead Indians up and down in the woods that were by famine or sickness brought unto that untimely end. Yea the Indians themselves have testified, that more amongst them have been cut off by the sword of the Lord in those respects, then by the sword of the English. (1677, 5–6)

Colonist Daniel Denton (1670, 12) similarly saw divine will at work in the death of native populations in New York: "where the English come to settle, a Divine Hand makes way for them, by removing or cutting off the Indians, either by Wars one with the other, or by some raging mortal Disease."

Increase Mather's son Cotton Mather (1852, 51) further explained how this mortality made way for the establishment of God's people, ridding the land "of those pernicious creatures to make room for *better growth.*" In Puritan interpretations of the Bible and Revelation, the colonists were destined to reach a promised land on which to construct the New Jerusalem in the New World. Cotton Mather wrote, "This at last is the spot of *earth* which the God of heaven *spied out* for the seat of such *evangelical,* and *ecclesiastical,* and very remarkable transactions," where the Puritan fathers attempted "in the American hemisphere to anticipate the state of the New-Jerusalem" (45–46). Of course, God would clear the way for its foundations to be built.

Once established, however, New England colonists no longer played the part of those newly arrived and beginning God's work: in their own eyes they became natives, who were now responsible for the defense of God's city. Changing understandings of disease, along with the phenomenon of continuing immigration to their shores, shifted their perceptions of sickness. Most colonists during the eighteenth century believed toxic vapors arising from decay caused disease—and it made sense to them that the poor, living in dirtier and more dilapidated dwellings, would fall sick, since they had greater exposure to "miasma" (Kraut 1994, 21–23; see also Melosi 2000, 15–99). This belief that harmful environments are to blame for disease is called the localist position (since it pinpoints local environs as the root cause of sickness) or the anticontagionist position (when it argues for environment as the *only* cause of sickness, exclusive of contagion; for the waxing and waning of this theory in the nineteenth century, see Ackerknecht 2009).

But it soon became apparent to the colonists, as their populations gained immunities and lived to witness wave after wave of immigrants, that *newcomers* most often became ill. The idea of contagion from newcomers grew so that a "melding of miasmatic theory with a growing fear of contagia served to bind the cause of disease *directly to the sufferer*" (Kraut 1994, 23, emphasis added). In other words, both contagionist and localist theories of disease blamed the immigrants: they were either the spreader of disease or living in the squalor giving rise to miasma, or both. In either case, the sick and sick-making foreigner were to blame.

Disease stalked the land no longer as God's Angel of Death clearing the way, but as the filthy outsider threatening the now established city of God. Conceptions of immigrants as the unclean outside the walls of the New Jerusalem grew easily from existing theology and church order. John Davenport, according to Cotton Mather:

> did now at New-Haven make *church purity* to be one of his greatest concernments and endeavours.... He used a more than ordinary exactness in trying those that were admitted unto the communion of the church: indeed so very thoroughly, and, I had almost said, severely strict, were the terms of his communion ... that he did all that was possible to render the renowned church of New-Haven like the New-Jerusalem. (1852, 327–28)

Davenport guarded entry to the New Haven church *as if* it were the new Jerusalem, although he found it "impossible to see a *church* state, whereinto there 'enters nothing which defiles'" (Mather 1852, 328, quoting Rev 21:27).

On a civic level, the Massachusetts Colony likewise began to guard against those who might defile it. In 1700 it passed a law explicitly barring entry to the sick and disabled, declaring shipmasters liable for any passengers who were "impotent, lame, or otherwise infirm, or likely to be a charge [i.e., burden] to the place" and unable to provide security or procure a surety for their support (Massachusetts Colony 1869, 1:452). This law was strengthened in 1724 so that any town—not only port towns—could refuse entry to "poor, vicious, and infirm persons" (Massachusetts Colony 1874, 2:336; cf. Proper 1967, 29–30).

This last group of descriptors—poor, vicious, and infirm—exhibits the age-old combination and conflation of these characterizations, signaling the belief that if one is poor, one must be vicious or infirm, or if one is infirm, one must have been vicious and poor to deserve it, and so on. That these persons were dirty was obvious, as they embodied society's most unwanted elements, and dirt is a community's construction of what it wishes to expel (see, of course, Douglas 1966, but also Miller 1998 and Ashenburg 2008). This circle of association of filth, poverty, immorality, and sickness is evident in the continuing attitudes of nativists in colonial America and after independence.

In 1793, yellow fever struck Philadelphia and did so regularly until 1805 (see Apel 2016; Crosby 2006; and Powell 1949). The inhabitants blamed various foreign groups—Germans, French refugees escaping the slave revolution in Haiti, and immigrants from the British West Indies (Kraut 1994, 26–27). Regardless of who they blamed, Philadelphians in the main understood God to have inflicted this disease, its arrival indicating the imminence of the eschaton. "At length," states one Philadelphia pamphlet, "the sword of [God's] indignation, the two edged sword of wrath [Rev 1:16] is unsheathed" (*Earnest Call* 1793, 7; quoted in Apel 2016, 99). Presbyterian minister Ashbel Green told his congregation during the 1798 breakout of the fever, "It is predicted that 'in the last days perilous times shall come.' Those days it is our lot to behold" (Green 1799, 8; quoted in Apel 2016, 99).

While most clergymen and much of the general public viewed yellow fever as divinely inflicted, a minority of scholars turned to the history of plagues to determine the cause of disease. Viewing America as the heir to Greece and Rome, these academics naturally looked to Homer, Thucydides, Livy, Procopius, and even Edward Gibbon's *Decline and Fall of the Roman Empire* for clues (Apel 2016, 47–56). Perhaps the most prominent source—due to his literary stature, detailed description, and important historical context—was Thucydides and his recording of the Athenian Plague in the fifth century BCE. Thucydides notes that the sickness was reported to have first broken out in Ethiopia:

> It first originated, it is said, in Ethiopia above [i.e., upstream of] Egypt. Then, it descended on Egypt and Libya and most of the King's land. It struck the city of the Athenians suddenly, and at first it infected men in Piraeus, so that they said the Peloponnesians had put poison in the cisterns, since there were no wells there yet. Afterward it also reached the upper city, and now far more people died. Let every man, both doctor and layman, say what he thinks about it, about from where it is likely to have come, and for what reasons he thinks it had such power to produce so great a disaster: I will only say how it happened. (*P.W.* 2.48, my translation)

As Thucydides seems to foresee, doctors and laypersons have indeed debated and hypothesized the cause of the plague in Athens even up to the present (see Littman 2009). American scholars at the end of the eighteenth century were no exception.

Before the horrible outbreak of yellow fever in 1793, Philadelphian doctor Thomas Bond had already postulated that the sickness was the very same as that of Athens: "The yellow fever which I take to be exactly the same distemper as the plague of Athens, described by Thucidides [*sic*], has been five different times in this city since my residence in it" (Bond in 1766, quoted in Currie 1800, 40). Noted scholar and doctor William Currie (1800, 39–42), in detailing the 1793 outbreak, used Bond's argument to insist upon contagion as the way the disease spread, especially contagion imported from foreign places. He begins this treatise, *A Sketch of the Rise and Progress of the Yellow Fever*, by locating the first outbreaks at wharves receiving ships from the West Indies, including from Havana, Curaçao, and the Turks—places with predominant Black slave populations (5–9). Currie excerpts Bond's remarks on Thucydides above, and the ancient account of the Athenian Plague fits nicely into his argument of contagion by importation. Thucydides does, after all, note the claim that the disease traveled to Athens from far-off Ethiopia—a land in classical literature symbolic of remoteness, Black peoples, and the demonic (see Byron 2002, 29–51).

Anticontagionists (or localists), however, used Thucydides to argue the exact opposite—that both yellow fever and the Athenian Plague arose from the *environment*, not contagion. E. H. Smith (1797, 17), a young Yale

College graduate, argued that the way Thucydides referred to the report that the disease came from abroad shows that "he thought it entitled to very little credit." Via analysis of Thucydides's account, Smith concluded that it was the characteristics of ancient Athens's locale and urban atmosphere that gave rise to the disease as opposed to contagion from elsewhere (18). Because of Philadelphia's similarities to ancient Athens—its climate, position near the sea, crowdedness, and so forth—"a due consideration of every circumstance cannot but impress the mind with a deep conviction of the unity of cause" for both cities. Additionally, Smith stated: "If local causes originated a pestilence in Athens, local causes may generate a Yellow Fever in Philadelphia and New-York" (29).

In the sphere of medical debate, the localists won during the Philadelphia yellow fever pandemic: they published and publicized their arguments more aggressively, and they better appealed to the scientific rationale of the time (Apel 2016, 7–8). Prominent localists like Smith and Noah Webster (of dictionary fame) criticized contagionists effectively, including contagionist James Tytler (1799), who postulated that plagues—both Athenian and Philadelphian—were divinely inflicted, and who was therefore censured by medical professionals as a result (see Apel 2016, 36–37, 57–58).

But if the localists prevailed, did this mean an end to blaming epidemics on immigrants and foreigners? Did it curb the belief that God punished via plague? Did it stamp out the idea that disease was a sign of God's wrath and the end times? As the following pages show, for several connected reasons it absolutely did not. As illustrated above, in terms of blaming immigrants for disease, it did not matter whether they were the persons causing contagion or living in locales that did: as the dirty undesirable, they were a focus of blame either way. That they were blamed in apocalyptic terms, as we shall see, is tied to America's enduring identity as the New Jerusalem, the founding metaphor for American exceptionalism.

Therein lies the reason that localist scientific argument emphatically did not end belief in God's judgment of the United States by disease. Consider this: the localist argument likened American cities to others in world history during a time when narratives especially stressed American *exceptionalism* (Apel 2016, 36–37). To argue that "New-York, and some other cities and towns of North America, are beginning to suffer what other cities and towns in ancient and modern times have undergone before them" was to erode the hillside of the Shining City upon a Hill (Mitchill 1799, 16, quoted in Apel 2016, 63). "A New World, same as the Old World" is not the inspiring motto politicians wish to champion.

In contrast, to imagine God's punishment focused on a land via plague is to imagine its pride of place in a divine plan. American exceptionalism thus insists on God's wrath as centered not on Athens or Rome or London but on America—on Philadelphia, on New York, on San Francisco. This is not the divine wrath that obliterates evil cities, such as Sodom and Gomorrah, but the wrath that disciplines the holy beacon and example to the rest of the world, in order that it expels the sickness and evil that has infiltrated and defends against further disease threatening to invade. After all, God states in Revelation, "I reprove and discipline those whom I love" (3:19a).

Apocalyptic epidemiology, regardless of contemporaneous scientific understanding, heightens America's role as God's city while intensifying fears of the sick and filthy invader—the unwashed immigrant, the immoral, and the idolator at the gates. The logic of a bounded city—that it must be defended, that it excludes by borders, that it creates insider and outsider identities—comes with the metaphor of the New Jerusalem. And the book of Revelation itself emphasizes this logic throughout via the themes of plague and filth, playing with the circle of associations linking disease with dirt, poverty, and sin.

Throughout the book of Revelation those on the side of God, who ultimately dwell within the walls of the new Jerusalem, are depicted as wearing white robes, which both now and then symbolize cleanliness, purity, and wealth (Moss 2019, 100–9). White robes are given to the faithful who conquered, who did not "soil their clothes" (Rev 3:4) and who are "sealed" as God's chosen and virginally pure (14:4). These and all who live in the new Jerusalem have washed their robes in the "high powered detergent" blood of the Lamb (7:14, 22:14; terminology from Blount 2009, 135, 408). Having clean, washed robes is in fact a requirement for entering the New Jerusalem: "Blessed are those who wash their robes, so that they ... may enter the city by the gates" (Rev 22:14).

As for those outside, an angel in that same chapter pronounces them hopeless: "Let the evildoer still do evil, and the filthy still be filthy" (22:11). These are the worshipers of the beast who are diseased with "foul and painful sores" (16:2), who commit fornication, murder, and idolatry (22:15), who are not clothed in rich, white robes but are "wretched, pitiable, poor, blind, and naked" (3:17). These do not wash in the blood of the Lamb but rather imbibe, together with the drunken whore of Babylon, the blood of corpses (16:3–6), the blood of martyrs (17:6), and the wine of fornication (17:2). Those outside the New Jerusalem are both ritually and morally impure, poor, dirty, evil, and diseased (on overlap of ritual and moral impurity in ancient Judaism, see Klawans 2000; on Revelation as a text of purity and cleanliness, see Lin, forthcoming). These accursed, polluting dead stay eternally quarantined outside the city gates (22:3), out of reach of the purifying water of life and the healing leaves of the Tree of Life (22:1–2).

In the American context, this apocalyptic conflation of dirt, poverty, sin, and disease was easily aimed against immigrants. During the outbreak of cholera in New York City in 1832, Reverend Gardiner Spring of the Brick Church gave a sermon mimicking Revelation in identifying disease with idolatry. He argued the "fatal scourge" came from "pagan, mahommedan, and anti-christian lands" to arrive on American shores, and New York in particular, at the heart of the country and the center of its godly example to the rest of the world (Spring 1832, 30). Spring exhorted his audience to repentance and renewed righteousness, believing the last days had perhaps already begun when the righteous "shall be purified, and made white" and "the wicked are to be *shaken out of the earth*" (32). He implied that the epidemic and the turmoil in the city were the result of one of the end-time plagues, stating that the "*seven vials and the seven last plagues* are not yet all poured upon the earth." Thus, it was better for one to repent and be included in the heavenly city than to be grouped with the foreign diseased outside destined for destruction: "the righteous shall be received into the kingdom of their Father, and the wicked of every name shall be cast into the lake of fire," he concluded (32–33).

Irish immigrants were among the idolaters blamed for bringing disease, especially during the cholera epidemics that occurred from the 1830s to the 1860s, which seemed to afflict the Irish population disproportionately. As Catholics, they were suspected of "obey[ing] their priests as demigods," in the words of one xenophobic author (Morse 1969, 13, quoted in Kraut 1994, 34). The Irish, moreover, were supposedly lax in hygiene and thus also morality. And, because it had been their "lifelong habit" to bow down to the gods of Catholicism, pundits doubted their ability to assimilate to Protestant American ways (Morse 1969, 13; Kraut 1994, 34). This failure to assimilate became a litmus test for susceptibility to disease and led to the erection of further barriers at American points of entry. In 1855, New York's Emigration Landing Depot opened with quarantining procedures in place, and inspection, isolation, and detention procedures there were soon implemented across ports of the United States.

Cholera was also linked with other unwanted immigrants arriving in New York City. In an 1883 cartoon that ran in the magazine *Puck*, the figure of Death arrives by ship wearing caricatured Turkish dress, his belt

Fig. 1. F. Graetz, "The Kind of 'Assisted Emigrant' We Can Not Afford to Admit," *Puck* 13.332 (July 18, 1883): 326. Source: Yale University Library.

reading "Cholera" (fig. 1). On the shore, the New York Board of Health aims a bottle of carbolic acid at the ship, fighting disease and their carriers as they would invaders in battle with a front line of soldiers and a row of cannons. Though the cartoon points to changes in medical understanding of disease—it is carbolic acid and not prayer, for example, that is aimed at the ship—this does not mean that apocalyptic imagination and association ceased (pace, e.g., Rosenberg 1962, 229). Pragmatism and scientific knowledge may have gained ground, but the theological and apocalyptic rejection of the foreigner as unholy and diseased remained powerful. The Grim Reaper, after all, still prominently rides the bowsprit, ready to attack the brave, white city behind its battlements.

Other diseases were linked with different undesirable groups who were deemed unassimilable. Immigrants-by-force, those taken into slavery from Africa, had long been labeled unclean with so-called Negro diseases (see Kiple and Kiple 1980), and during the Great Northward Migration (1917–1970) African Americans were blamed for venereal diseases (see Tolnay 2003). And while blamed for venereal diseases such as syphilis, Black participants of the Tuskegee experiment suffered from the disease while white scientists lied and withheld the cure of penicillin. White scientists fixated on Black men as sexually impure and promiscuous while denying them life and healing (see Jones 1993, 22–23).

New York City officials blamed eastern European Jews for the spread of tuberculosis—the so-called White Plague—at the end of the nineteenth century. Immigrant Jews from eastern Europe were taken off incoming ships—and also from their homes in the city if they had settled—and were transported to quarantine islands (Markel 1997). Political and popular discourse argued against greater admittance of Jewish immigrants and groups from eastern and southern parts of Europe by associating them with disease and pests (see fig. 2).

Fig. 2. Samuel D. Ehrhart, "The Fool Pied Piper," *Puck* 65.1603 (June 2, 1909): centerfold. Source: Library of Congress.

Framing all these conceptions of disease, entry, and exclusion is the ideation of America as exceptional, as the New Jerusalem, from discovery to colonization, to nationhood and Manifest Destiny. The New Jerusalem in Revelation functions via ancient-city logic, with gates for defense, a purifying flow of water, and those who are sick and the polluting dead outside the walls. Immigration discourse, shaped by this city logic, trades in the fear of pestilence, of overcrowding, of miasma, and the figure of Death at the prow of incoming ships.

America as the New Jerusalem, as a unified, bounded, and crowded space (see fig. 3), marks absolute inclusion and exclusion. Inside the city there is one throne, one river, around which gather the saints—all with the Lamb's name written on their foreheads, all wearing white robes. Identity within is uniform, even if the inhabitants had once come "from every nation" (Rev 7:9).

The United States, when understood as a secure, bounded city, with a unified, uniform "native" population, must absolutely defend against the infiltration of disease, filth, and plague. And if their bearers are primarily the unassimilable, then by far the most unassimilable peoples in American imagination are the Chinese.

Fig. 3. The Cloisters Apocalypse, *Satan's Release from Prison*, f. 34v., ca. 1330. Source: The Metropolitan Museum of Art.

Figure 4 is an advertisement for pest poison to rid homes of rats and bugs. In the center is the caricatured Chinaman about to eat a rat—so disgusting an identity that he is both a pest that "must go" and a filthy eater of them guilty of the worst aberrations. This depiction captures the revulsion that white nativist Americans, who were already repulsed by foreigners from Europe, felt toward the Chinese.

The arrival of Chinese peoples during the 1850s triggered an even more ferocious rejection than unwanted European immigrants did. Why was this so? Mary Coolidge (1969, 401) observes that in 1909, "with physical and social characteristics so different from the rest of the population, it was perhaps inevitable that the Chinaman with his flowing trousers and queue should be a conspicuous mark for race persecution

Fig. 4. Forbes Co. Boston, "Rough on Rats" advertisement, ca. 1880s. Source: Learning for Justice, Southern Poverty Law Center.

in California at a time when the feeling against all foreigners was very strong." Doctors, politicians, and news media viewed Chinese people with horror. The September 29 edition of the *New York Daily Tribune* described Chinese peoples in 1854 as "unclean, filthy beyond all conception," so that "the Chinese quarter of the city [of San Francisco] is a by-word for filth and sin." The California State Board of Health pronounced that their entry into the country would cause national decay (see Stout 1862) and that intermixture with "a sensual and depraved people" would mean the transmission of "hereditary vices" (Stout 1870–71, 55).

The Chinese seemed so irredeemably foreign and corruptive that the passing of the Naturalization Act in 1870 formally barred them from naturalization. Speaking on the floor of Congress, Senator George Williams of Oregon argued that permitting the Chinese to naturalize would "sacrifice the pride and glory of American citizenship" to the *deities* of "ignorance, idolatry, immorality, vice, disease, and prostitution" (Gold 2012, 18). Blame of the Chinese for a variety of diseases, along with the alleged threat they posed to the virtue of the nation, grew to such a degree that the Chinese Exclusion Act of 1882 passed with overwhelming support from leaders throughout the country and not simply on the West Coast (Kraut 1994, 79–83).

San Francisco represented the holy city in the western United States and as such had to bravely resist the hordes of Chinese bringing sickness and depravity. Ironically, the city was also given a heavenly aura by Chinese immigrants, who named San Francisco, and California as a whole, *Jin Shan* (Mandarin) and *Gāmsāan* (Cantonese): "Gold Mountain." Even now, Chinese speakers refer to the city as *Jiu Jin Shan* or *Gauh Gāmsāan*: "Old Gold Mountain." Apocalyptic names dot the landscape—the Golden Gate Bridge, Angel Island, Gold Mountain, and the Golden State to name a few. While Chinese immigrants may initially have viewed their coming to California as approaching a golden realm, the white inhabitants of the city viewed the arrival of the Chinese in a decidedly different light.

"San Francisco's Three Graces," a cartoon from *The Wasp* in 1883, shows the specters of Malaria, Smallpox, and Leprosy looming over the city of San Francisco, with Leprosy literally pouring disease upon Chinatown from the bowl of God's wrath (fig. 5). All three figures are ghostly and demonic or bestial, and Leprosy in particular is identified as a Chinese coolie with a braid or "queue." Near the center bravely stands the tower of a church threatened by these plagues and representative of the pious who must guard against such corrupting invaders.

Fig. 5. George Frederick Keller, "San Francisco's Three Graces," *The Wasp* 8.304 (May 26, 1883): cover image. Source: the Billy Ireland Cartoon Library and Museum, Ohio State University.

In a cartoon from 1878 (fig. 6), it seems the circular association—poverty, filth, immorality, foreignness, sickness—has been compressed to such a level that the Chinese are not just poor, unclean, vile, and totally other and therefore susceptible to disease: they *are* the disease. Or rather, they are depicted *as* the plague itself. In the apocalyptic-diseased American imagination, the Chinese embody the horrors of Revelation visited upon the earth. Here, this swarm of locusts devouring the earth possesses "faces ... like human faces" (Rev 9:7)—Chinese faces, so it is revealed. Behind them looms the demonic figure of Famine (Rev 6:5–8; 18:8), driving the insects out of their own, plagued country toward the United States. Only a simple farm fence bars their way, a sign of weakness at the border.

Fig. 6. George Frederick Keller, "Uncle Sam's Farm in Danger," *The Wasp* 84 (March 9, 1878): 504–5. Source: Courtesy of the Bancroft Library, UC Berkeley.

Chinese people nevertheless still sought entry at San Francisco, and starting in 1910 they were received and detained at the Angel Island Immigration Station. There they found themselves herded into segregated quarters that divided men from women and Europeans from "Orientals," the most foreign of foreigners. They were subjected to humiliating physical examinations with no privacy: "The doctor told us to take off everything. Really, though it was humiliating," says Mr. Lee, who was detained there in 1930. "The Chinese never expose themselves like that. They checked you and checked you. We never got used to that kind of thing—and in front of whites" (Lee and Yung 2010, 39).

Throughout the twentieth century, even as scientific knowledge grew, Americans rejected foreigners on the basis of disease and the immorality they associated with it as well as a supposed incompatibility with Americanness and American patriotism, the yardstick measuring righteousness and ticket into the shining city. Jewish refugees fleeing Europe in the 1930s and 1940s were met with fear and denial of entry or internment. Congress debated their entry but was swayed by the sentiment that an explosion of the Jewish population would mean greater degeneracy and sickness for the nation (Kraut 1994, 256–58). The American perception of Asians as forever foreign, regardless of citizenship, revealed itself in the internment of Japanese Americans. As possible traitors to the nation, Japanese Americans were also feared to be disease prone, and so internees were subjected in the camps to physical examination, even though it was the environment they were forced into that fostered disease (258).

At the time of writing, the COVID-19 pandemic once again shows the association of the outsider with disease within an apocalyptic frame. As with any widespread disaster, but especially epidemics, end-times decoding of the event in terms of Revelation sprang up quickly across multiple media—one essay as early as January 30, 2020 was titled, "The Wuhan Coronavirus and the Bible's Prophesied Disease Pandemics" (Jacques 2020). Of course, just as many articles appeared debunking such claims and demonstrating the beliefs, questions, and fears of many congregants and readers (e.g., McMaster 2020; Bohlinger 2020; and Denison 2020). But the headline of this early essay proved to be prophetic of the identification of the virus with Chinese peoples and the apocalyptic offensive reaction against them, particularly in the United States where President Trump repeatedly referred to the virus as the "China virus," the "China plague," and "Kung Flu" (see Nakamura 2020; Bowden 2020; and Dwoskin 2020). From March 19, 2020, when shutdowns due to COVID-19 began in earnest in the United States, to June 30, 2021, Stop AAPI Hate received over 9,081 reports of hate incidents targeting Asian American Pacific Islander peoples (Yellow Horse et al. 2021). The forever foreigner, the Asian in America was again to blame for a plague.

This association of disease with the outsider, who can invade and strike even the office of the president, exists within the construct of America as God's country and the New Jerusalem, an association as old as Columbus's discovery and the Puritan colonies. Even in the rhetoric of the forty-fifth president, who knows neither the Bible nor belief in prophecy, the same key elements of Revelation and the heavenly city come to the fore: the supposed uniformity and righteousness of the true inhabitants; the threat of the filthy, diseased, and violent outside; and the necessity for walls—big, beautiful walls—demarking absolute inclusion and exclusion.

Works Cited

Ackerknecht, Erwin H. 2009. "Anticontagionism between 1821 and 1867." *International Journal of Epidemiology* 38:7–21.

Alberts, B., et al. 2002. "Introduction to Pathogens." In *Molecular Biology of the Cell*. 4th ed. New York: Garland Science.

Apel, Thomas A. 2016. *Feverish Bodies, Enlightened Minds: Science and the Yellow Fever Controversy in the Early American Republic*. Stanford, CA: Stanford University Press.

Ashenburg, Katherine. 2008. *The Dirt on Clean: An Unsanitized History*. New York: North Point.

Blount, Brian K. 2009. *Revelation: A Commentary*. Louisville: Westminster John Knox.

Bohlinger, Travis. 2020. "COVID-19 and the Mark of the Beast." *The Logos Academic Blog*. May 9, 2020. https://tinyurl.com/SBL06104j.

Bowden, John. 2020. "Use of 'China Virus' Led to Spike in Anti-Asian Bias: Study." *The Hill*. September 9, 2020. https://tinyurl.com/SBL06104k.

Brace, C. Loring. 2005. *Race Is a Four-Letter Word: The Genesis of the Concept*. Oxford: Oxford University Press.

Byron, Gay L. 2002. *Symbolic Blackness and Ethnic Difference in Early Christian Literature*. New York: Routledge.

Clavel, F., et al. 1986. "Isolation of a New Human Retrovirus from West African Patients with AIDS." *Science* 233.4761:343–46.

Cohn, Samuel. 2007. "The Black Death and the Burning of the Jews." *Past and Present* 196:3–36.

Coolidge, Mary Roberts. 1969. *Chinese Immigration*. New York: Arno.

Crosby, Molly Caldwell. 2006. *The American Plague: The Untold Story of Yellow Fever, the Epidemic that Shaped Our History*. New York: Berkley.

Currie, William. 1800. *A Sketch of the Rise and Progress of the Yellow Fever*. Philadelphia: Budd & Bartram.

Denison, Jim. 2020. "COVID-19 Is Not God's Judgment." *Christianity Today*. April 21, 2020. https://tinyurl.com/SBL06104m.

Denton, Daniel. 1670. *A Brief Description of New-York*. London: Hancock.

Douglas, Mary. 1966. *Purity and Danger*. London: Routledge.

Dwoskin, Elizabeth. 2020. "When Trump Gets Coronavirus, Chinese Americans Pay the Price." *Washington Post*. October 9, 2020. https://tinyurl.com/SBLPress06104b1.

An Earnest Call, Occasioned by the Alarming Pestilential Contagion. 1793. Philadelphia: Jones, Hoff, & Derrick.

Gold, Martin B. 2012. *Forbidden Citizens: Chinese Exclusion and the U.S. Congress: A Legislative History*. Alexandria, VA: TheCapitol.Net.

Green, Ashbel. 1799. *A Pastoral Letter from a Minister in the Country, to Those of His Flock Who Remained in Philadelphia during the Pestilence of 1798*. Philadelphia: Ormand.

Jacques, Jeremiah. 2020. "The Wuhan Coronavirus and the Bible's Prophesied Disease Pandemics." *The Trumpet*. January 30, 2020. https://tinyurl.com/SBL06104n.

Jones, James H. 1993. *Bad Blood: The Tuskegee Syphilis Experiment*. Exp. ed. New York: Fortress.

Kiple, Kenneth, and Virginia Kiple. 1980. "The African Connection: Slavery, Disease and Racism." *Phylon* 41:211–22.

Klawans, Jonathan. 2000. *Impurity and Sin in Ancient Judaism*. Oxford: Oxford University Press.

Kraut, Alan M. 1994. *Silent Travelers: Germs, Genes, and the "Immigrant Menace."* New York: HarperCollins.

Lee, Erika, and Judy Yung. 2010. *Angel Island: Immigrant Gateway to America*. Oxford: Oxford University Press.

Lin, Yii-Jan. Forthcoming. "'Let the Filthy Still Be Filthy': Revelation as a Test of Dirt and Danger."

Littman, Robert J. 2009. "The Plague of Athens: Epidemiology and Paleopathology." *Mount Sinai Journal of Medicine* 76:456–67.

Long, Thomas L. 2004. *AIDS and American Apocalypticism: The Cultural Semiotics of an Epidemic*. New York: State University of New York Press.

Markel, Howard. 1997. *Quarantine! East European Jewish Immigrants and the New York City Epidemics of 1892*. Baltimore: Johns Hopkins University Press.

Massachusetts Colony. 1869–1874. *The Acts and Resolves, Public and Private, of the Province of Massachusetts Bay*. 2 vols. Boston: Wright & Potter.

Mather, Cotton. 1852. *Magnalia Christi Americana*. 1702. Hartford, CT: Andrus & Son.

Mather, Increase. 1677. *An Historical Discourse Concerning the Prevalency of Prayer*. Boston: Foster.

McMaster, Geoff. 2020. "Why Some People Think COVID-19 Heralds the Apocalypse." *Folio*, April 24, 2020. https://tinyurl.com/SBL06104p.

Melosi, Martin V. 2000. *The Sanitary City: Urban Infrastructure in America from Colonial Times to the Present*. Baltimore: Johns Hopkins Press.

Miller, William I. 1998. *The Anatomy of Disgust*. Cambridge: Harvard University Press.

Mitchill, Samuel Latham. 1799. "Excerpted Letter to James Hardie." Pages 15–19 in *An Account of the Malignant Fever, Lalely [sic] Prevalent in the City of New York*. Edited by James Hardie. New York: Hurtin & M'Farlane.

Morse, Samuel F. B. 1969. *Imminent Dangers to the Free Institutions of the United States Through Foreign Immigration*. 1835. New York: Arno.

Moss, Candida R. 2019. *Divine Bodies: Resurrecting Perfection in the New Testament and Early Christianity*. New Haven: Yale University Press.

Nakamura, David. 2020. "With 'Kung Flu,' Trump Sparks Backlash over Racist Language—and a Rallying Cry for Supporters." *Washington Post*. June 24, 2020. https://tinyurl.com/SBLPress06104b2.

Powell, John H. 1949. *Bring Out Your Dead: The Great Plague of Yellow Fever in Philadelphia in 1793*. Philadelphia: University of Pennsylvania Press.

Proper, Emberson Edward. 1967. *Colonial Immigration Laws: A Study of the Regulations of Immigration by the English Colonies in America*. New York: AMS.

Rosenberg, Charles E. 1962. *The Cholera Years: The United States in 1832, 1849, and 1866*. Chicago: University of Chicago Press.

Smith, E. H. 1797. "The Plague of Athens." *Medical Repository* 1:3–29.

Sontag, Susan. 1990. *Illness as Metaphor and AIDS and Its Metaphors*. New York: Doubleday.

Spickard, Paul. 2007. *Almost All Aliens: Immigration, Race, and Colonialism in American History and Identity*. New York: Routledge.

Spring, Gardiner. 1832. *A Sermon Preached August 3, 1832: A Day Set apart in the City of New York for Public Fasting, Humiliation and Prayer on Account of the Malignant Cholera*. New York: Leavitt.

Stout, Arthur B. 1862. *Chinese Immigration and the Physiological Causes of the Decay of the Nation*. San Francisco: Agnew & Deffebach.

———. 1870–1871. *Biennial Report of the State Board of Health of California*. Sacramento: California State Board of Health.

Thornton, Russell. 1987. *American Indian Holocaust and Survival: A Population History since 1492*. Norman: University of Oklahoma Press.

Tolnay, Stewart E. 2003. "The African American 'Great Migration' and Beyond." *Annual Review of Sociology* 29:209–32.

Tytler, James. 1799. *Treatise on the Plague and Yellow Fever*. Salem, MA: Joshua Cushing for B. B. Macanulty.

Wadman, Meredith, Jennifer Couzin-Frankel, Jocelyn Kaiser, Catherine Matacic. 2020. "How Does Coronavirus Kill? Clinicians Trace a Ferocious Rampage through the Body, from Brain to Toes." *ScienceMag* April 17, 2020. https://tinyurl.com/SBL06104q.

Yellow Horse, Aggie J., et al. 2021. *Stop AAPI Hate National Report: 3/19/20–6/30/21*. https://tinyurl.com/SBLPress06104b3.

What Large Letters: Invisible Labor, Invisible Disabilities, and Paul's Use of Scribes

Candida R. Moss

I wrote this paper in the shadow of a pandemic that has revealed not only the frailty of twenty-first-century societies but also their pervasive ableism. As an immunocompromised transplantee and kidney patient who falls into the highest risk category for COVID-19 mortality (see Harrison 2020), I have been profoundly disappointed by the widespread failure of liberal academics and media commentators to notice the ableism. *The Journal of Biblical Literature* recently published a forum on the pandemic that did not include disability studies perspectives or contributors who explicitly identified themselves as disabled. I would like to recognize Jacqueline Hidalgo's contribution, which did reference ableism (Hidalgo 2020, 626), and note the irony that while this issue of the journal drew criticism from academics on social media for including only white men among the regular articles, nobody seemed to notice the absence of disability in a conversation about the deaths of hundreds of thousand people, most of whom had preexisting conditions.

This is illustrative of a larger problem: when we sick people have been invoked in the pandemic, it is to reassure those with normal bodies that they are safe. We are otherwise dispensable. Even as I smarted from this realization, I also struggled with and continue to wrestle with a harder truth: my survival depends on exploitation. I self-isolate because I can

---

I would like to thank organizers and attendees of the Divided Worlds conference for their helpful suggestions and comments. In addition, I am grateful to Jeremiah Coogan, Meghan Henning, Joe Howley, Shively Jackson Smith, Steve Reece, and Robyn Walsh for their help, conversation, and suggestions.

afford this particular luxury. I am an employed, wealthy white woman who works from home and lives in New York City, the center of delivery culture. My risk is lowered because other, less affluent people are placed in pharmacies, in grocery stores, in danger, and in my service. I am struck by the ways that the moralizing language of self-isolation and "having things delivered" replicates ancient Roman despotic discourse that erases the work of enslaved bodies. I think here, in particular, of the fantasies of "self-managing" olive trees in Virgil's *Georg.* 4 (Geue 2018, 120).

Thus, despite my dissatisfaction with the lack of public conversation about disability, I want to press ahead with a more intersectional project and think about disability and enslaved labor in the New Testament and, more precisely, Paul's reference to his large lettering in Galatians and his use of scribes elsewhere.[2]

Toward the end of his letter to the Galatians, Paul remarks on his penmanship, inviting his audience to "see what large letters I make when I am writing with my own hand" (Gal 6:11). This statement is what we might call an autograph, a section of text composed in his own hand that acknowledges that the preceding text was written by someone else and that what follows is written in the author's own hand (cf. 1 Cor 16:21; Col 4:18).[3] It draws attention both to something distinctive about his handwriting and also to his use of the hands of others or, as we might ordinarily put it, his use of a secretary. Paul's use of large lettering has received extended and, at times, imaginative treatment that attempts to explain why it is that Paul used a scribe. The purpose of this paper is both to examine the unspoken assumptions in scholarly analysis of this passage and to examine what it may tell us about invisible labor (the bodies and skills of enslaved or formerly enslaved workers) and effaced impairments (ordinary disability) in the production of Paul's letters. These subjects are rarely discussed among New Testament scholars as it is, but I hope to set them alongside one another and, in the process, bring to light some of

---

2. In thinking about intersectionality, disability, and ancient religion I am profoundly influenced by the important work of Candace Buckner (2019).

3. The phrase is used in 2 Thess 3:17, where it is followed by the authorizing statement that this is his mark (σημεῖον) in every letter that he writes. This is somewhat ironic, given that the majority of scholars do not think that Paul wrote 2 Thessalonians. The use of σημεῖον as an epistolary identifier is paralleled in a number of papyri (Youtie 1970, 105–16).

the unnoted intersections between enslaved workers and technologies of access in the ancient world.[4]

Paul's Body

Although a number of explanations for his inelegantly large lettering have been offered, the most common focus is on Paul's supposedly defunct body.[5] A number of scholars have argued that Paul suffered from some kind of impairment that affected his handwriting and, thus, necessitated the use of a scribe.[6] Writing around the turn of the twentieth century, Theodor Zahn (1905, 278) suggested that Paul's hands were deformed from the flogging he was subjected to in Philippi (Acts 16:22–23). Going several steps further, Nigel Turner hypothesized in the 1960s that Paul's description of himself as one who was "crucified with Christ" (Gal 2:19, 6:14) and bears the marks of Jesus on his body (Gal 6:17) is a literal reference to an attempted crucifixion in Pamphilia. On account of this oddly ineffective

---

4. There has been a tendency among scholars of early Christianity to overlook the presence of enslaved people in early Christian communities (Horsley 1998, 19–66). There is now a wealth of literature on slavery in general; in particular, see the important work of Harrill 1995, 2007; Glancy 2002; Brooten 2010; Shaner 2018; Parker, 2018, 35–37. With respects to disability, critically informed attentiveness to bodily difference in New Testament studies is an even more recent phenomenon (Avalos, Melcher, and Schipper 2007; Olyan 2008; Laes 2017; Yong, Melcher, and Parsons 2017).

5. Other arguments for Paul's use of large lettering here include (1) that he intends to flatter his scribe by highlighting his own literary inadequacies; (2) that he deliberately effaces his status; (3) that he is demonstrating, much as Cicero did, affection for his readers by writing sections of the letter himself; (4) that the larger letters were meant to be displayed to the audience; (5) that Paul uses large letters as a form of emphasis, much as we might use bold or underline portions of our own text; and finally (6) that Paul was poorly educated and perhaps illiterate. "Literacy" and "writing" in this context are terms that require substantial theorization and definition (Keith 2008, 39–58; Reece 2018).

6. In his recently published book, *Paul's Large Letters*, Steve Reece provides a thorough survey of explanations for Paul's handwriting in scholarship and concludes that, much like historical Jesus study, academic work in this area projects onto Paul those elements of his hypothetical biography that the individual scholar themselves find interesting. Unlike myself, Reece is not interested in the exceptionality of these arguments or what we might call incidental disability in the ancient world, but his book was indispensable to this study.

crucifixion, Paul subsequently acquired "ungainly handwriting" (Turner 1965, 93–94).[7]

Zahn and Turner are hardly alone in drawing upon other texts in the New Testament to provide an explanation for Paul's handwriting. A pantheon of scholarly titans has assembled to ask why it is Paul used scribes at all and have hypothesized that the answer might lie in his immoderate lettering and personal biography. These biographical explanations usually take their leave from Paul's reference to the "thorn in his flesh" in 2 Cor 12:7–10 and argue that Paul suffered from a physical disability that prevented him from writing his own letters.[8] As a result, those focused on the scribal issue almost always identify the thorn as either a visual impairment or a deformity involving his hands.

The association with vision loss is usually attributed to the blinding divine light that Paul experienced as he journeyed to Damascus (Acts 9:1–19) or from another physically overwhelming mystical experience such as the ascent to the third heaven mentioned in 2 Cor 12:1–6. As Steve Reece (2018, 86–87) shows in his book on the subject, recourse to impaired eyesight is a fairly recent explanation. The late nineteenth-century Scottish physician J. T. Brown (1858, 99–127) described Paul's eyes as "branded, half-quenched orbs" after the conversion experience, while his contemporary, G. J. Gwynne (1863, 313–314, 331–34), explains that "mortal orbs" are incapable of withstanding the power of "light inaccessible." What is distinctive about these diagnostic explanations is that they consistently tie Paul's use of large letters to impairments that arose from his missionary activity: either to the road to Damascus event described in Acts or his mistreatment by his "persecutors" (Farrar 1879, 652–61; Stott 1968; Hisey and Beck 1961, 125–29; Witherington 1998, 309–10, 441; Ponessa and Manhardt 2004, 64–66).

What is overlooked in such analyses is the possibility that Paul, like a large proportion of people in the ancient world, experienced what we might call mundane vision problems or a communicable eye disease.[9]

---

7. For possible examples, see Herodotus, *Hist.* 7.194.1–3; Chariton, *Chaer.* 8.8.4 (Samuelsson 2013, 44, 141).

8. The reception of the thorn in the flesh as impairment has its own lengthy history (Collins 2011, 165–83).

9. That the possibility is never considered reflects an ableist bias that overlays Paul's body with what critical disability theorists call the religious model of disability (Junior and Schipper 2013, 21–37). In this model, impairment is a negative bodily

Even those, like Ben Witherington III (1998, 309–10, 441), who use the ancient diagnostic category of ophthalmia to describe Paul's impairment, still connect it to an encounter on the road to Damascus. Given how common vision loss was in the ancient world, it is surprising that we have to make recourse to biographical details that Paul himself never explains.

Beyond what we might simply imagine from our own experience in the modern world, there is plenty of evidence that vision loss was remarkably common for those living in the Roman world.[10] The prevalence of visual impairments in the ancient world only contributed to the variegated ways in which these conditions were interpreted. As Martha Rose (2003, 79) has put it with respect to the Greeks, "the story of blind people in the ancient Greek world is neither glorious nor dismal and … blind people were far from exceptional" (see also Carter 2011, 89–114). A wide range of vocabulary was used to refer to a variety of experiences of sightedness, including total vision loss, partial vision loss, missing or damaged eyes, being one-eyed, having three eyes, dim-sighted, and poor eyesight. A number of cognomina refer to visual impairments including Strabo (cross-eyed) and Caecilius (blind). None of these conditions were uniformly understood: Horatius Cocles was a war hero, while Polyphemus was a monster (Moss 2019, 50–53, 61–63).

Evidence for visual impairments can be found in a variety of sources. Medical writers like Celsus discuss the subject at length (*De med.* 6). The popularity of anatomical votives of the eyes at healing shrines suggests that eye problems were a substantial problem, and more than three hundred collyrium stamps provide data about the ways in which those with means might seek out medical treatment (Hughes 2007; van Straten 1981, 109; Voinot 1999; Watson 1982, 75; Marganne 1994, 117–21; Rathbone 2006, 205–6). Numerous ancient authors narrate their personal struggles with the most common complaints: *lippitudo* and *aspritudo*.[11] Temporary

---

state caused by sin or a lack of faith and rectified by God. If ordinary bodily impairment is assumed to be a sign of spiritual deficiency and Paul is assumed to be in some way chosen or special, then it follows that Paul cannot suffer from any kind of run-of-the-mill disability.

10. For reasons of space, I am excluding from this brief survey the evidence for accidental eye loss and gouging (Trentin 2013, 98–104).

11. See Cicero, *Quint. fratr.* 2.2.1; Pliny the Younger, *Ep.* 7.21. Augustus was said to have lost vision in his left eye as he aged (Suetonius, *Aug.* 79.2) Medical writers do not comment at any length on age-related vision loss, though Celsus notes that eye

vision loss and spontaneous cure of blindness were well known to Pliny and Celsus, as were a number of reportedly effective cures.[12]

Just as they do today, the practical effects of an impairment on any given individual's life depended largely upon their socioeconomic status. In a world without spectacles the eyes and hands of literate enslaved workers became the technology by which the elite remained active in public life, read, wrote treatises, and corresponded with their peers. The praetor Gnaeus Aufidius wrote extensively on Greek history in his old age when he had gone blind (Cicero, *Tusc.* 5.112). The Stoic Diodotus, a houseguest of Cicero, devoted much of his time to studying philosophy even after he had gone blind (*Tusc.* 5.113). In both cases, their continued participation in political and intellectual life was facilitated by invisible laborers (de Libero 2002, 75–93; Rose 2003, 88; Trentin 2013, 110–11). For those with fewer resources, family members and friends likely served similar roles. Even though blindness was not generally thought to restrict a person's intellectual capacities, a number of stories suggest an association between blindness and poverty: blind beggars are something of a motif in ancient Greek literature (Trentin 2013, 109).

Despite all of this evidence for what we might call ordinary vision loss in antiquity, secondary literature that diagnoses Paul never seriously considers the possibility that he suffered from impairments unrelated to his call or missionary activity. Paul's body, like those described in Jewish and Christian martyrdom accounts, suffers only because of Christ.[13]

---

aches and declining eyesight are symptoms of aging (*De med.* 6.6.34; de Libero 2002, 75–93).

12. See Pliny the Elder, *Nat.* 11.149; Celsus, *De med.* 7. pr. 2. For a list of cures, see Celsus, *De med.* 6.6.3–8b. See also the occasion when Vespasian cured a blind man in Suetonius, *Vesp.* 7.2–3.

13. It is noteworthy that in 2 Macc 6 and the Martyrdom of Polycarp, Eleazar and Polycarp, respectively, are both described as reenergized and vivified prior to their trials and execution. Pain has been the subject of a number of key studies in martyrdom literature (Perkins 1995; Cobb 2016). Cobb's recent important analysis of pain in martyrdom literature has persuasively argued that martyrs do not feel pain in the accounts of their deaths. My own position, which agrees with Cobb but takes its leave from Audre Lorde's work, distinguishes between the suffering and the pain of the martyrs. While they do not feel pain, they are nevertheless portrayed and described as suffering like Christ. In Lorde's work, which responds to the oppressive theology of redemptive suffering, the language is reversed so that pain has transformative potential, whereas suffering is "the nightmare reliving of

The irony embedded in this protracted conversation is that large lettering demands no explanation. In his recent book, Steve Reece (2018, 111–97) surveys the papyrological evidence for the handwriting of epistolary subscriptions in Aramaic, Hebrew, Jewish, and Greek letters. Having studied manuscripts of thousands of letters, he concludes that "large handwriting is extremely common in autographic subscriptions on ancient letters that have survived in their original form, with dozens of extant examples, and it is nowhere associated with any visual impairment on the part of the writer" (90). Large lettering is more commonly associated with unpracticed hands, which could include both those with more rudimentary education and those whose wealth meant that they rarely transcribed their writing themselves. The association is hardly definitive, however. There is some evidence that handwriting grew ever worse over the course of a person's life as their vision (and other bodily abilities) declined. A sequence of autographic inscriptions to business contracts shows how the handwriting of a certain Hermas, son of Ptolemaios, transitioned from small semicursive letters to thicker, larger capitals between his forties and eighties (P.Mich. 10.583 [78 CE]; P.Mich. 10.584 [84 CE]; P.Mich. 11.605 [117 CE]; P.Mich. 3.188 [120 CE]; see Daniel 2008, 151–52). While we might connect the decline in handwriting to diminished vision, there are any number of explanations for this shift.

What Reece passes by in his consideration of this passage is the double duty that Paul's supposed infirmity does in scholarship on the epistles. Analysis of Paul's physical limitations not only accounts for his use of large letters but, more importantly, provides an explanation for his use of scribal workers at all. The presence of additional authors in the Pauline epistles constitutes an intrinsic threat to post-Romantic notions of the author as a solitary genius as well as to religious constructions of scripture as delivered through inspired, identifiable, saintly figures.[14] It is to this question, Paul's use of scribes in general, that we now turn.

---

unscrutinized and unmetabolized pain" (Lorde 1994, 159; Moss 2012, 110, 193 n. 35).

14. I am putting aside here the somewhat separate conversation about the inaccessibility and death of the author discussed by Barthes, Frye, and many others. On Romantic understandings of authorship, see Stillinger 1991. Many works that are believed to be the product of a single author (e.g., John Stuart Mill's *Autobiography*) are, in fact, the product of two or more authors. In an appendix to the book, Stillinger (1991, 208) notes that first-person narratives of the experience of enslavement were

The Bodies of Enslaved Scribes: Problems and Potentials

Scribes are a regular feature of Paul's writing process, and yet—even though we know some of their names—their identities, social status, and role in the composition of the Pauline epistles are often glossed over.[15] It is important to note at the outset, therefore, that there is nothing unusual about Paul's use of scribes. Just as we do not have to account for Paul's use of large letters, his use of scribes does not invite special commentary or justification. The vast majority of ancient writing involved the use of a *secretarius*, *librarius*, or *notarius*, just as the vast majority of elite reading was performed by a *lector* (Winsbury 2009, 79–85; Starr 1991, 33–43; Darnton 1982, 65–84; Habinek 2005, 38–93; Harris 1989, 249; Horsfall 1995, 49–56; McDonnell 1996, 46–91; Howley, 2020, 15–27).[16] If nothing else, writing by hand was a laborious and physically draining activity that people liked to avoid. In one letter from Oxyrhynchus, dictated by an Egyptian woman named Taesis, the scribe, a houseguest named Alexandros, complains that he has "worn himself out by writing the letter" (P.Oxy. 56.3860; Metzger and Ehrman 2005, 29–33). Others, like the author of the Rhetorica ad Herennium, seem to find writing by hand boring and laborious and discourage their audiences from doing it themselves. While elites could and did read and write, and reading (or being seen to read) often affirmed one's position in society, this did not mean that they regularly practiced it on a day-to-day basis (Johnson 2010; Howley 2018, 83). On the contrary, it

---

often rewritten by modern editors. The ancient world is not in his purview, but if it were one hopes he would have noted that enslaved laborers stirred the pot of the vast majority of ancient textual production, whether literary or documentary.

15. This is not merely an ancient phenomenon: we continue to erase the human labor that goes into producing textual artifacts. When academics thank esteemed colleagues for their advice on a piece of writing, we reproduce an elite Roman discourse in which the writer consults and acknowledges his friends rather than his enslaved scribes. It is rare that a published work thanks anyone other than the most senior editor and copyeditor; bought-and-paid-for labor, including that of the anonymous workers who hand keyed our footnotes, are erased from the process. This erasure of (Black and Brown) human labor is especially apparent in the production of digital texts (Goldsmith 2013).

16. Following Howley, I do not distinguish the work of the *secretarius* or *amanuensis* from the *notarius* because the work of these literary slaves often overlapped (2020, 15–27). For example, Cicero refers to Diphilus as the *scriptor et lector* of Crassus (Cicero, *De or.* 1.136).

seems that when it came to writing, in particular, the task was regularly delegated to enslaved or formerly enslaved workers (Hartmann 2020).

The vast majority of letters in antiquity, therefore, were dictated to trusted scribes, who often received special training in shorthand and were responsible for producing the longhand version of the correspondence. They were often also responsible for copyediting, expanding, and amending elements of the text. There is no reason to imagine that Paul, who follows a fairly standard epistolary format in writing his letters and references his use of scribes more than once, did anything different (see Rom 16:22; Richards 2004, 2019; Reece 2018).[17] Yet modern scholars tend to describe those performing these functions for him as scribes, associates, or secretaries.[18] This description obscures the reality that the vast majority of Roman scribes were enslaved workers or freedmen.

In addition, there is a tendency to diminish the contributions of scribes to the production of the text's meaning.[19] In discussing the function of Tertius, the named scribe of Romans, many New Testament scholars emphasize that he contributed little to the writing process of the content of this epistle. Deissmann (1912, 225), for example, writes that "St. Paul had dictated the little letter to his associate Tertius, and then gave him permission to add a line from himself." He sees in Tertius's greeting "the

---

17. Though our definition of writing is often undertheorized, I would not restrict my comments to the Pauline and Petrine epistles and suggest that there is no reason to think that any of the texts produced in the Jesus movement were produced without the assistance and skills of enslaved or formerly enslaved laborers. This much seems to have been assumed by some in the early church. On the construction of Mark as Peter's secretary, see Moss 2020.

18. In the context of a fledgling Jewish movement, the language of scribes denotes education and elevated social and religious status (Haines-Eitzen 2000, 79). See Laura Nasrallah's (2014, 432) description of the "crowded writing desk" of Paul.

19. This move is paralleled in classics, in which enslaved workers are presented as prostheses, critically important extensions of the slaveholder's body (Cicero, *Fam.* 16.10.2; Martial, *Ep.* 14.208). This argument follows ancient Roman slaveholder discourse about the role and function of slaves as useful but failing to fully grasp the meaning of the texts they read, transcribed, edited, and copied. See an anecdote about Plutarch beating an enslaved secretary in Aulus Gellius, *Noct. att.* 1.26.5–9. Aristocratic ideology about enslaved literate labor sees it as a bodily function, while the intellectual work is reserved for the elites (Reay 2005; Bodel 2012, 51). The discourse of prosthetic bodies intersects with conversation about technology and prosthetics in disability studies. This description is not, as Joe Howley has suggested to me, description: it is a form of despotics designed to demean and control enslaved people.

impress of the great man's creative soul on the soul which the great man had awakened in the insignificant brother" and "a type of the people who were elevated by Paul the missionary from their dull existence in the mass to the sphere of new-creative grace." Tertius here is neither an enslaved worker nor a person of note. More important, he has no command of the text itself, even the sentence that he wrote himself. Paul's control of Tertius's body and literary output is so pronounced that he seems even to shape and colonize his soul.[20] To some scholars Tertius was barely up to the task. Barclay (2002, 52) writes that Tertius "struggled to write down" Paul's words. Barclay rearranges Rom 16:13–16 on the basis of Tertius's presumed errors. Overall, there is a general consensus that Tertius was not an author but only took dictation, perhaps even syllable by syllable.

For some, however, Paul's use of secretaries does explanatory apologetic work that connects Paul to the narrative of his life provided in the Acts of the Apostles and smooths over authorial difficulties with the deutero-Pauline and Pastoral Epistles (Richards 2004; with criticisms in Ehrman 2012, 219–22). As early as 1933, Otto Roller hypothesized that the Pastoral Epistles, like other Pauline epistles, were entrusted to a secretary and that Paul later corrected and signed them. The use of secretaries could explain the substantive differences between the letters. Some go further and knit the canonical authors into a tidy web. C. F. D. Moule (1965, 430–52) speculated that Luke, the author of the eponymously named gospel and the Acts of the Apostles, authored the Pastorals at Paul's instruction (see also Strobel 1969, 191–210; de Lestapis 1976, 130–32; Feuillet 1978, 181–225). Others speak more generally and use the existence and use of secretaries in antiquity to support the notion that Paul may have authored Ephesians and Colossians (Murphy O'Connor 1995, 615; Reece 2018, 198–296).

What is striking is the sharp bifurcation between these two positions. On the one hand, there are those who argue that enslaved literate workers were mindless automatons who were responsible, at most, for the introduction of

---

20. Deissmann (presumably) inadvertently rehearses ancient slaveholder logic in which the elite shapes the habitus of enslaved workers. We might compare here Columella, who pictures himself manipulating the enslaved agrarian works on his estate (e.g., *Rust.* 1.9.8). Deissmann's spiritual elitism here is striking because of his political socialism. He was a member of the Nationalsozialer Verein, a turn-of-the-twentieth-century political party in the German empire that espoused the uniting of the working class and bourgeoise classes toward social and economic progress (Gerber 2010, 209–44). I am grateful to Steve Reece for drawing this to my attention.

errors into the text. On the other, there are those who speculate that these scribes had so much autonomy that their writing habits altogether eclipsed Paul's style, vocabulary, and even argument. The amorphous range of inextricably collaborative forms of literary production that lie between these two poles goes undiscussed, perhaps because these possibilities blur and confuse our ability to perform the usually cut-and-dried analysis that hinges on Romantic constructions of authorial genius (Walsh 2015). To unpack that somewhat, this is not merely about knowing our authors; acknowledging the very real contributions of literate enslaved workers to textual products complicates our ability to speak about sources and their redaction or use criteria like "consistency of thought" to evaluate authorial claims. Our methods of analysis would surely need review. It is easier either to rehearse Roman slaveholder logic that insists that enslaved workers were extensions of the bodies of their owners or to put enslaved workers to additional work in which they account for interpretive or authorial problems with our sources.

Conclusion

Thus far I have been driving toward a particularly unsatisfying point: scholarship on Paul's writings has somewhat relentlessly and unnecessarily pursued explanations for Paul's use of scribes and large lettering. These are features of his writing that, given the evidence, do not need special justification and only reveal ableist scholarly dis-ease with extraordinary bodies and ideologically loaded anxiety about collaborative textual production.

Given that it is decidedly unladylike to conclude a paper on a particular subject with the statement that we are simply asking the wrong questions, I shall instead make a humble proposal. What the scholarly conversation surrounding Paul's use of scribes and large letters unwittingly draws our attention to is the intersection of two significant categories of embodiment in the ancient world that are often treated separately: the status of those with impairments and the exploitation of the bodies of enslaved people.[21] In the ancient world, as in the modern, wealth can

---

21. I do not mean here to imply that those with disabilities and enslaved people are distinct groups of people. Beyond the use of atypical bodies as sources of entertainment (e.g., Hist. Aug., Hel. 29.3), we have references to the injuries and impairments of enslaved people (e.g., Stobaeus, *Flor.* 4.209), and there is some data that infants born with impairments were exposed and subsequently enslaved.

be used to purchase accommodations and technologies of access that not only mitigate the considerable disadvantages faced by those with disabilities but also complicate the legibility of some forms of disability in our sources.[22] Technologies of access are socioeconomically limited. The elite utilization of enslaved bodies to read and write could eliminate some of the ways that visual impairments and vision loss affected the lives of people living in an unspectacled world. Though Pliny and Cicero both complain of suffering from various intermittent eye-related complaints, their ability to read and write is unimpaired by these conditions as they could, as Horsfall (1995, 49–56) has observed, rely upon the skills and bodies of enslaved workers to accomplish these tasks. We have no idea whether a middle-aged Paul needed eyeglasses, though we might assume based on our own experiences that he did. The exploitation of enslaved bodies potentially erases some of the evidence for disability in our sources, just as the contributions of enslaved workers are themselves colonized and rendered invisible.

Works Cited

Avalos, Hector, Sarah Melcher, and Jeremy Schipper, eds. 2007. *This Abled Body: Rethinking Disability and Biblical Studies.* SemeiaSt 55. Atlanta: Society of Biblical Literature.

Barclay, William. 2002. *The Daily Study Bible: The Letter to the Romans.* 3rd ed. Louisville: Westminster John Knox.

Bodel, John. 2012. "Villaculture." Pages 45–60 in *Roman Republican Villas: Architecture, Context, and Ideology.* Edited by Jeffrey A. Becker and Nicola Terrenato. Ann Arbor: University of Michigan Press.

Brooten, Bernadette J., ed. 2010. *Beyond Slavery: Overcoming Its Religious and Sexual Legacies.* New York: Palgrave Macmillan.

Brown, John T. 1858. *Horae Subsecivae.* Edinburgh: Constable.

Buckner, Candace. 2019. "Made in an Imperfect Image: Race, Ethnicity, Disability, and Infirmity in the Life of Aphou." *JAAR* 87:483–511.

Carter, Warren. 2011. "'The Blind, the Lame and Paralyzed' (John 5:3): John's Gospel, Disability Studies, and Postcolonial Perspectives." Pages

---

22. We should be wary of conflating all forms of disability here, especially when the construction of disability and its meaning is always historically and culturally contingent (Strauss 2013, 462; Edwards 1997, 43).

129–50 in *Disability Studies and Biblical Literature*. Edited by Candida R. Moss and Jeremy Schipper. New York: Palgrave MacMillan.

Cobb, L. Stephanie. 2016. *Divine Deliverance: Pain and Painlessness in Early Christian Martyr Texts*. Berkeley: University of California Press.

Collins, Adela Yarbro. 2011. "Paul's Disability: The Thorn in His Flesh." Pages 165–83 in *Disability Studies and Biblical Literature*. Edited by Candida R. Moss and Jeremy Schipper. New York: Palgrave MacMillan.

Darnton, Robert. 1982. "What Is the History of Books?" *Daedalus* 111:65–84.

Daniel, Robert W. 2008. "Palaeography and Gerontology: The Subscriptions of Hermas Son of Ptolemaios." *ZPE* 167:151–52.

Deissmann, Adolf. 1912. *St Paul: A Study in Social and Religious History*. London: Hodder & Stoughton.

Edwards, Martha L. 1997. "Constructions of Physical Disability in the Ancient Greek World: The Community Concept." Pages 39–50 in *The Body and Physical Difference: Discourses of Disability*. Edited by David T. Mitchell and Sharon L. Snyder. Ann Arbor: University of Michigan Press.

Ehrman, Bart D. 2012. *Forgery and Counterforgery: The Use of Literary Deceit in Early Christian Polemics*. Oxford: Oxford University Press.

Farrar, Frederic W. 1879. *The Life and Work of St. Paul*. New York: Dutton.

Feuillet, André. 1978. "La doctrine des épîtres pastorales et leurs affinités avec l'oeuvre lucanienne." *RThom* 78:181–225.

Gerber, Albrecht. 2010. *Deissmann the Philologist*. Berlin: de Gruyter.

Geue, Tom. 2018. "Soft Hands, Hard Power: Sponging Off the Empire of Leisure (Virgil, *Georgics* 4)." *JRS* 108:115–40.

Glancy, Jennifer. 2002. *Slavery in Early Christianity*. Oxford: Oxford University Press.

Goldsmith, Kenneth. 2013. "The Artful Accidents of Google Books." *New Yorker*. December 4, 2013. https://tinyurl.com/SBL06104r.

Gwynne, George J. 1863. *A Commentary, Critical, Exegetical, and Doctrinal, on St. Paul's Epistle to the Galatians*. Dublin: Herbert.

Habinek, Thomas. 2005. "Slavery and Class." Pages 385–93 in *A Companion to Latin Literature*. Edited by Stephen Harrison. Oxford: Blackwell.

Haines-Eitzen, Kim. 2000. *Guardians of Letters: Literacy, Power, and the Transmission of Early Christian Literature*. Oxford: Oxford University Press.

Harrill, J. Albert. 1995. *The Manumission of Slaves in Early Christianity.* Tübingen: Mohr Siebeck.

———. 2007. *Slaves in the New Testament: Literary, Social, and Moral Dimensions.* Minneapolis: Fortress.

Harris, William V. 1989. *Ancient Literacy.* Cambridge: Harvard University Press.

Harrison, Pam. 2020. "COVID-19 Mortality Almost 30 Percent in Kidney Transplant Patients." *Medscape.* April 28, 2020. https://www.medscape.com/viewarticle/929585.

Hartmann, Benjamin. 2020. *The Scribes of Rome: A Cultural and Social History of the Scribae.* Cambridge: Cambridge University Press, 2020.

Hidalgo, Jacqueline M. 2020. "Scripturalizing the Pandemic." *JBL* 139:625–34.

Hisey, Alan J., and James S. P. Beck. 1961. "Paul's 'Thorn in the Flesh': A Paragnosis." *JBR* 29:125–29.

Horsfall, Nicholas. 1995. "Rome without Spectacles." *GR* 42:49–56.

Horsley, Richard A. 1998. "The Slave Systems of Classical Antiquity and Their Reluctant Recognition by Modern Scholars." *Semeia* 83/84:19–66.

Howley, Joseph A. 2018. *Aulus Gellius and Roman Reading Culture: Text, Presence, and Imperial Knowledge in the Noctes Atticae.* Cambridge: Cambridge University Press.

———. 2020. "In Ancient Rome." Pages 15–27 in *Further Reading.* Edited by Matthew Rubery and Leah Price. Oxford: Oxford University Press.

Hughes, Jessica. 2007. *Votive Body Parts in Greek and Roman Religion.* Cambridge: Cambridge University Press.

Jackson, Ralph P. 1996. "Eye Medicine in the Roman Empire." *ANRW* 37.3:2239–43.

Johnson, William A. 2010. *Readers and Reading Culture in the High Roman Empire: A Study of Elite Communities.* Oxford: Oxford University Press.

Junior, Nyasha, and Jeremy Schipper. 2013. "Disability Studies and the Bible." Pages 21–37 in *New Meaning for Ancient Texts.* Edited by Steven L. McKenzie and Jonathan Kaltner. Louisville: Westminster John Knox.

Keith, Chris. 2008. "'In My Own Hand': Grapho-Literacy and the Apostle Paul." *Bib* 89:39–58.

Laes, Christian, ed. 2017. *Disability in Antiquity.* London: Routledge.

Lestapis, Stanislas de. 1976. *L'énigme des pastorales de Saint Paul*. Paris: Libraire Lecoffre.

Libero, Lorentana de. 2002. "Dem Schicksal trotzen: Behinderte Aristokraten in Rom." *AHB* 16:75–93.

Lorde, Audre. 1994. "Eye to Eye: Black Women, Hatred, and Anger." Pages 145–75 in *Sister Outsider*. Crossing Press Feminist Series. Freedom, CA: Crossing.

Marganne, Marie-Hélène. 1994. "La collection médicale d'Antinoopolis." *ZPE* 56:117–21.

McDonnell, Myles. 1996. "Writing, Copying, and Autograph Manuscripts in Rome." *ClQ* 46:469–91.

Metzger, Bruce M., and Bart D. Ehrman. 2005. *The Text of the New Testament: Its Transmission, Corruption, and Restoration*. 4th ed. Oxford: Oxford University Press.

Moss, Candida R. 2012. *Ancient Christian Martyrdom: Diverse Practices, Theologies, and Traditions*. AYBRL. New Haven: Yale University Press.

———. 2019. *Divine Bodies: Resurrecting Perfection in the New Testament and Early Christianity*. New Haven: Yale University Press.

———. 2020. "Fashioning Mark: Early Christian Discussions about the Scribe and Status of the Second Gospel." *NTS* 67:181–204.

Moule, Charles F. D. 1965. "The Problem of the Pastoral Epistles: A Reappraisal." *BJRL* 47:430–52.

Murphy O'Connor, Jerome. 1995. *Paul the Letter-Writer: His World, His Options, His Skills*. Collegeville, MN: Liturgical Press.

Nasrallah, Laura. 2014. "1 Corinthians." Pages 427–72 in *Fortress Commentary on the Bible: New Testament*. Edited by Margaret Aymer, Cynthia Briggs Kettridge, and David A. Sánchez. Minneapolis: Fortress.

Olyan, Saul. 2008. *Disability in the Hebrew Bible: Interpreting Mental and Physical Differences*. Cambridge: Cambridge University Press.

Parker, Angela N. 2018. "One Womanist's View of Racial Reconciliation in Galatians." *JFSR* 34:23–40.

Perkins, Judith. 1995. *The Suffering Self: Pain and Narrative Representation in the Early Christian Era*. London: Routledge.

Ponessa, Joseph, and Laurie Watson Manhardt. 2004. *Prophets and Apostles*. Steubenville, OH: Emmaus Road.

Rathbone, Dominic. 2006. "Poverty and Population in Roman Egypt." Pages 100–114 in *Poverty in the Roman World*. Edited by M. Atkins and R. Osborne. Cambridge: Cambridge University Press.

Reece, Steve. 2018. *Paul's Large Letters: Paul's Autographic Subscriptions in the Light of Ancient Epistolary Conventions.* LSNT 561. London: T&T Clark.

Reay, Brendon. 2005. "Agriculture, Writing, and Cato's Aristocratic Self-Fashioning." *ClAnt* 24:331–61.

Richards, E. Randolph. 2004. *Paul and First-Century Letter Writing: Secretaries, Composition and Collection.* Downers Grove, IL: InterVarsity Press.

Richards, E. Randolph. 2019. *The Secretary in the Letters of Paul.* WUNT 2/42. Tübingen: Mohr Siebeck.

Roller, Otto. 1933. *Das Formular der paulinischen Briefe: Ein Beitrag zur Lehre vom antike Brief.* BWANT 58. Stuttgart: Kohlhammer.

Rose, Martha L. 2003. *The Staff of Oedipus. Transforming Disability in Ancient Greece.* Ann Arbor: University of Michigan Press.

Samuelsson, Gunnar. 2013. *Crucifixion in Antiquity.* 2nd ed. WUNT 2/310. Tübingen: Mohr Siebeck.

Shaner, Katherine A. 2018. *Enslaved Leadership in Early Christianity.* Oxford: Oxford University Press.

Starr, Raymond J. 1991. "Reading Aloud: *Lectores* and Roman Reading." *CJ* 86:337–43.

Stillinger, Jack. 1991. *Multiple Authorship and the Myth of Solitary Genius.* Oxford: Oxford University Press.

Stott, John R. W. 1968. *Only One Way: The Message of Galatians.* London: InterVarsity Press.

Straten, Folkert T. van. 1981. "Gifts for the Gods." Pages 65–151 in *Faith, Hope, and Worship: Aspects of Religious Mentality in the Ancient World.* Edited by H. S. Versnel. Leiden: Brill.

Strauss, Joseph N. 2013. "Autism as Culture." Pages 460–84 in *The Disability Studies Reader.* Edited by Lennard J. Davis. 4th ed. London: Routledge.

Strobel, A. 1969. "Schreiben des Lukas? Zum sprachlichen Problem der Pastoralbriefe." *NTS* 15:191–210.

Trentin, Lisa. 2013. "Exploring Visual Impairment in Ancient Rome." Pages 89–114 in *Disabilities in Roman Antiquity: Disparate Bodies A Capite ad Calcem.* Edited by Christian Laes, C. F. Goodey, and M. Lynn Rose. Leiden: Brill.

Turner, Nigel. 1965. *Grammatical Insights into the New Testament.* Edinburgh: T&T Clark.

Voinot, Jacques. 1999. *Les cachets à collyres dans le monde romain*. Montagnac: Mergoil.
Walsh, Robyn Faith. 2015. "The Influence of the Romantic Genius in Early Christian Studies." *Relegere* 5:31–60.
Watson, Patricia. 1982. "Martial's Fascination with the *Lusci*." *GR* 29.1:71–76.
Winsbury, Rex. 2009. *The Roman Book*. London: Duckworth.
Witherington, Ben, III. 1998. *Grace in Galatia: A Commentary on Paul's Letter to the Galatians*. Edinburgh: T&T Clark.
Yong, Amos, Sarah Melcher, and Mikeal C. Parsons, eds. 2017. *Disability and the Bible: A Commentary*. Waco, TX: Baylor University Press.
Youtie, Herbert C. 1970. "ΣΗΜΕΙΟΝ in the Papyri and Its Significance for Plato, Epistle 13 (360ab)." *ZPE* 6:105–16.
Zahn, Theodor. 1905. *Der Brief des Paulus an die Galater*. Leipzig: Deichert.

Wayward and Willful Members: Twisting Figures Past *Porneia* in Paul's Letters

Joseph A. Marchal

Strange Loves: Classics and New Testament Studies

How might New Testament studies and classics come together to inform and hopefully transform how we approach controversial issues in the present? At first, the answer might seem rather obvious to someone like me, who often feels interpellated to address the so-called biblical bashing passages that ostensibly condemn LGBTIQ people or practices—one of those issues that divide the world for at least some of us. If so moved, I could dutifully apply context from classical studies to properly situate two oft-cited passages from Paul's letters. In fact, this would seem like a pretty standard procedure, as classics has often been seen as providing one or even *the* necessary context for understanding New Testament texts like the ones we call Paul's letters. This Greco-Roman context, then, is itself a classic for biblical scholars looking for the proper background to these materials.

Indeed, a greater grasp of how ancient Greek and Roman materials sorted and structured dynamics of gender, sexuality, and embodiment partially accounts for my own strange loves, or at least how I learned to stop worrying about the bashing passages. Familiarity with what has been alternately called the Priapic protocol (Richlin 1983), the use of pleasure (Foucault 1990), an ethos of penetration and domination (Halperin 1990),

---

The research and writing of this essay were made possible by the generous support of the Louisville Institute's sabbatical grants for researchers program. Any views, findings, conclusions, or recommendations expressed in this essay do not necessarily represent those of the Louisville Institute.

the penetration paradigm (Kamen and Levin-Richardson 2015a), or simply Romosexuality (Ingleheart 2015) is appealing for a variety of queer uses of scripturalized texts (like Paul's letters), as they ostensibly provide stability and even certitude about the distance and difference reflected in ancient terms like *malakos* or *chrēsis* (in 1 Cor 6:9–10 and Rom 1:26–27). Modes of respectable expertise and sociohistorical accuracy operate in comforting ways by demonstrating that neither of the Pauline bashing passages are really about homosexuality, since the Roman imperial impenetrable penetrators sorted people and practices differently, casting the natural receptivity of those feminized as female, enslaved, youthful, non-elite, and/or foreign as coextensive with their sociopolitical inferiority and embodied degradation (Walters 1997). Scholars like Bernadette Brooten (1996) have magisterially demonstrated this correspondence between text and context.

But is that all there is?

To be sure, this turn to the Greco-Roman can function, commendably, to short-circuit the still too frequent exceptionalist projections of everything one does not like about Christian scriptures onto (ancient) Jews and/or Judaism(s). I suggest, however, that these dynamics of projection and protection can also alert us to biblical interpreters' appetites for purity and even (some) queer readers' desires for respectability. In turning to classics and inserting distance and difference between us and the bashing passages, such disciplinary techniques are also diversionary efforts to spare (one kind of) us any further stigma or shame, to avoid association with (targeted with notions of) perversion, degradation, or *porneia*. Yet, in doing so, these techniques preserve the ethnoracial dissociations and projections of these passages and their targeting rhetorics in ways quite compatible with white supremacy. As classical and biblical scholars such as Shelley Haley (1990, 1993, 2009) and Denise Kimber Buell (2005, 2009, 2018) have argued for decades now, efforts to decenter whiteness require assessing, disrupting, and transforming our disciplinary histories and internalized investments. Thus, feminist and queer approaches with antiracist commitments need to identify and alter this specific desire for distance, particularly since these letters are structured more by concerns for sexual exceptionalism than by sexual orientation. In the face of these biblical texts and traditions and a desire to do differently, wayward and willful can point elsewhere and otherwise.

My approach here then proceeds crookedly and waywardly, and willfully so, in refusing to straighten scriptures or any figures targeted by them, or even myself. (Perhaps this also indicates that everyone approaches these scriptures crookedly, even as too many might disavow this and their positionality.) This develops out of a certain kind of historical, ethical, and political commitment, which is really also a desire to read, think, see, and feel more beyond, beside, past, around, or maybe just alongside the prevailing perspectives of most of our available materials, particularly given their kyriarchal continuities, resonances, repetitions, or even extensions and reinforcements.[1] In what follows, then, I try to take cues from, draw inspiration from, or just get an alternative affective feel for people figured as wayward and willful from recent work by Saidiya Hartman (2019) and Sara Ahmed (2014). Hartman and Ahmed can show how to get around, past, beyond, or beside the standard procedures, usual suspects, and venerated uses of classics for New Testament interpretation. I direct my attention past the bashing passages to other figures in 1 Corinthians, Philippians, and Romans in an effort to resist kyriarchally racialized stereotyping without seeking people or practices of purification or perfection. This involves turning to different resources from classics, like the recent scholarship on graffiti that complicates and pushes back on totalizing visions of the past that obscure other possibilities for people and practices, both wayward and beautiful, disparaged and desired, including those individuals cast as sex laboring and, or *as*, receptive and, or *among*, the disreputable and often enslaved, members of these communities.

Wayward and Willful Assembly, with Hartman and Ahmed

Hartman's *Wayward Lives, Beautiful Experiments: Intimate Histories of Social Upheaval* (2019) critically summons and creatively renarrates the historical, ethical, and political significance of one set of wayward figures. Here she writes counterhistorically, crafting a counternarrative to institutionalized perspectives on the wayward or (supposedly) minor figures who migrated to and assembled in the urban spaces of the United States (between 1890 and 1935) by using case files, state archives, news clippings, and sociological studies.[2] As Hartman (2020) herself has reflected on her

---

1. Schüssler Fiorenza coined this term based on the Greek word for lord or master, *kyrios*, a title that would have also been used for a husband, father, enslaver, and/or an imperial authority. For introductory definitions of this neologism, see Schüssler Fiorenza 2001, 1, 118–24, 211; 1999, ix.

2. For previous examples of her creative, cross-genre writing, see Hartman 2007, 2008.

approach in this project, "I am not an archival sleuth, so my counternarratives have not been composed as a consequence of discovering new documents, but rather by engaging with extant archival materials critically and creatively. My aim has been to compose and reconstruct, to improvise and augment." Hartman's close narrations reimagine or simply re-create the lives of young Black women subject to moralizing reformist and carceral forces by attending to both their intimate spaces and the spaces they shared for performance, entertainment, escape, contact, and affiliation.

Refusing or simply redirecting the gaze of reformers intent upon finding and inculcating respectability, Hartman (2019, 4) instead traces "an urban commons where the poor assemble, improvise the forms of life, experiment with freedom, and refuse the menial existence scripted for them." The formal examinations that aimed to document Black social life missed that other spaces and often in-between places, like the hallways and stairwells of tenements, were places of assembly and intimate bodily contact (22). The presumed immorality and indecency of minoritized groups fits a politically and historically persistent rhetorical pattern, but such presumptions hardly tell the whole story. Thus redirected, Hartman finds waywardness takes form in both struggles and beautiful experiments (307; as the title indicates). People and practices that have been stigmatized and marginalized look alternatively yet recurrently like experiments in affiliation, sexuality, and conjugality. Flexible and shifting modes of kinship are not phenomena to be diagnosed and eliminated but resources for survival (91). The potential waywardness of (those classified and criminalized as) prostitutes, vagrants, and other deviants reflect refusals and negotiations, particularly in the face of the legally elastic and socially expanding categories of "wayward minors" and "vagrants" at the turn of (that) century (221–23, 241–51). Hartman, however, aims to improvise other angles on these figures through a reexamination of their own works, words, and actions, including the letters of imprisoned women and the remaining material traces of female and often gender-transgressive performers.[3] At several key points Hartman's poetically historical theorizations (or theoretically poetic historizations) also focus on times to come—the horizons, possibilities, and alternative futures of the past—as most clearly articulated in the "Wayward: A Short Entry on

---

3. For more on imprisonment and feminist interpretation of Paul's letters, see especially Fox 2017.

the Possible" and "The Chorus Opens the Way" sections (227–28 and 345–49, respectively).[4]

The entry on wayward, for instance, stresses the gaps and even gulfs between past, present, and the potentials for those "who inhabit the world in ways inimical to those deemed proper and respectable" (227). For Hartman, wayward names "the practice of the social otherwise, the insurgent ground that enables new possibilities and new vocabularies; it is the lived experience of enclosure and segregation, assembling and huddling together" (227–28). Wayward articulates and assembles alternative articulations and assemblies; it is their basis even within limits and constraints. It echoes, extends, and possibly reframes Judith Butler's (2004, 1, cf. 15) explanations of gender, sexuality, and embodiment as "improvisation within a scene of constraint" by historicizing and reimagining the limits and potentials of freedom after enslavement (which is not yet past):

> Waywardness is an ongoing exploration of what might be; it is an improvisation with the terms of social existence, when the terms have already been dictated, when there is little room to breathe, when you have been sentenced to a life of servitude, when the house of bondage looms in whatever direction you move. It is the untiring practice of trying to live when you were never meant to survive. (Hartman 2019, 228)

Because this waywardness is also "a *beautiful experiment* in how-to-live" (228), it is a feature of diffuse or decentered possible openings like those that proceed from the performers that comprise a chorus. The chorus is an electric and eccentric ensemble, as affective as it is apocalyptic.

Wayward's complications and uncertain evidences emerge not simply or only as a counter but as the strain beside and beyond reading against the grain, given the conditions for those subsisting by persisting in spite or because of their ascribed waywardness. The chorus serves as one such example for Hartman as a kind of movement within enclosure (347), just as waywardness "articulates the paradox of cramped creation, the entanglement of escape and confinement, flight and captivity" (227). For Hartman, as in previous projects (like her *Scenes of Subjection*, 1997), the paradox underscores the proximities of freedom and coercion, sex and violence,

---

4. For alternative futures of the past, including alternative apocalypses, within queer biblical studies, see Hidalgo 2016, 2018; Thomas 2018; Marchal 2018, 2021b.

intimacy and trauma.⁵ Yet the performers assembled in a chorus capture something of the collective possibility or the radical possibility of a collective even within such enclosures. It is "the vehicle for another kind of story, not of the great man or the tragic hero, but one in which all modalities play a part, where the headless group incites change.... The chorus propels transformation. It is an incubator of possibility, an assembly sustaining dreams of the otherwise" (2019, 348).

The chorus presents this possibility for Hartman and, in turn, links her wayward lives to Ahmed's (2014) willful subjects because they are embodied in particular ways. They assemble as a "headless group" with revelatory movements. Bodies and particularly the figurative uses of body parts in both philosophical and literary texts are a recurrent topic for Ahmed's characteristically dense, playful, and politically explosive reconsideration of will and willfulness.⁶ Such initial resonances between the wayward and the willful are hardly coincidental, as Hartman acknowledges the relations between the willful, the queer, and the wayward (2019, 392, citing Ahmed 2014), and Ahmed repeatedly links willfulness to waywardness and perversion (for instance, 2014, 13, 68, 113, 173, 177, 198).

As in her studies of happiness (2010) and use (2019), Ahmed (2014, 140, 143, 158) follows will around to assemble an alternative kind of archive or countermemory for feminist, antiracist, and queer purposes. Will initially appears to name dynamics of control: will is exercised through and valorized as a mode of self-control, but it is also recurrently deployed to legitimize the control of Others, those who (ostensibly) lack it, who are cast as willful. Will thus operates as a technique, "*a straightening device*" (7), a form of subjection but one with queer potential. For Ahmed, "Willfulness is the word used to describe the perverse potential of will and to contain that perversity in a figure" (12). It is clear from the start that will and desire share a historical itinerary (9), the histories of sexuality and of will treading some of the same ground. Ahmed tracks this back to Augustine's multiple or conflicted will(s) and his grappling with perversion, lust, or just desire (27–29), but with just a bit more will, or a

---

5. On such monstrous intimacies, see also Sharpe 2010.
6. Literary examples of willful hair appear on and off throughout Ahmed (2014), including the interrelation of hair, willfulness, and renunciation (227), suggesting other potential connections to the passages about hair and head covering in 1 Cor 11, women withdrawing from sex (with men) in 1 Cor 7, and approaches like those found in Matthews 2017; S. Smith 2019; and Marchal 2014, 2020.

slightly more wayward effort, she and we could turn in a more concentrated fashion to the letters attributed to Paul (something I will attempt shortly).[7] In delineating the itineraries of will, Ahmed shows how the willful (as an Other much like the wayward) is constructed as "one whose insistence on having her or his own way is presented as waywardness, as a perversion of the right path of the will" (68). These wayward, willful figures are then cast as occupying a certain kind of temporality: "willful subjects are *often given the past tense*: being willful as a way of being lodged in the past, unmoved by the willing embrace of the future" (215).

Thorough examinations of will and desire inevitably lead to reflections upon dynamics of consent and coercion. Indeed, one of Ahmed's stated aims is to "deepen the critiques of voluntarism by reflecting on the intimacy between freedom and force" (16). Here, she only briefly considers Hartman's (1997) previous work on slavery and subjection, a system that demanded willful submission from someone without will (Ahmed 2014, 201). Hartman (see esp. 1997, 80) demonstrates how slavery survives and even thrives in the confusion between person and thing, consent and coercion, and accompanying dynamics of reciprocity and submission, protection and violence, intimacy and oppression. Enslaved people, then, are alternately cast as willing or willful. A careful consideration of will then requires reckoning with force. These historical dynamics of a past that is not yet past gives new resonance to Ahmed's (2014, 18) description of willful as an affective and sweaty concept, "a trace of the laboring of bodies." It provides subtler texture to the ways willfulness works as "an attribution of negative affect" (152). This attribution might be crucial for the willful deployment of terms such as *wayward*, *queer*, or *willful*:

> As with other political acts of reclaiming negative terms, reclaiming willfulness is not necessarily premised on an affective conversion, that is, on converting a negative into a positive term. On the contrary, to claim willfulness might involve not only hearing the negativity of the charge but insisting on retaining that negativity: the charge after all is what keeps us proximate to scenes of violence. (Hartman 2014, 157–58)

---

7. Ahmed's consideration of Augustine's split or multiple will(s), in relation to desire or perverse lust, between body and mind, could also further relate to Paul's involuntary disgust-desire in Rom 6–7 (treated, in part, in Marchal 2019c).

Willful subjects, then, could be seen as taking on the technique that has been used to (try to) straighten or dismiss them without forgetting these histories.

In ways akin to Hartman's wayward lives, Ahmed aims to imagine willful as an alternative style of politics. She posits, "Feminist, queer, and antiracist histories can be thought of as histories of those who are willing to be willful, who are willing to turn a diagnosis into an act of self-description" (2014, 134). In doing so, she even highlights Alice Walker's (1983, xi) classic definition of womanist: "Usually referring to outrageous, audacious, courageous or willful behavior."[8] Willfulness can be valued for its creative audacity as a stand against, even as Ahmed (2014, 150) cautions "that we not reduce willfulness to againstness. It is this reduction, after all, that allows the willful subject to be dismissed," as if the willful are just being thoughtless contrarians. A willful subject negotiates the spaces shaped by these constraints, yet in unexpected fashion: "To accept a charge is not simply to agree with it. Acceptance can mean being *willing to receive*" (134). For Ahmed, this willed, willful receptivity operates differently. In assembling those who have received this charge, she construes a countermemory to will and willfulness.

> To become unwilling to obey (or willing not to obey) what is given as a command could be understood as a memory project: to discover a will of one's own is to recover a will that has not been fully eliminated.... Willfulness can be a trace left behind, a reopening of what might have been closed down, a modification of what seems reachable. (140)

Like Hartman's waywardness, Ahmed sees willfulness as a temporally revelatory project: "willfulness becomes what travels, as a relation to others, those who come before, those who come after" (143).

Flee *Porneia*: Constructions of Wayward and Willful Figures

So, I try to travel to Others, to reconsider particularly those targeted as wayward or willful in Paul's letters. Willfulness and waywardness are featured in a number of ancient arguments about various sets of constructed

---

8. For my other, recent, and partial attempts to sort this definition as one source of connection and collaboration between womanist and queer approaches, see Marchal 2019a, 2020, and 2021a. For two recent and helpful resources on womanist biblical interpretation, see M. Smith 2015 and Byron and Lovelace 2016.

Others, as one can find in several of Paul's letters (including Philippians, 1 Corinthians, and Romans). Ahmed only briefly touches upon the potential connection of will and willfulness to the rhetoric of body parts in Paul's First Letter to the Corinthians (see Ahmed 2014, 103–4, mostly via Bray 1999, 21). Here, Ahmed notes how the part and whole distinction of this classical social and political metaphor can address struggles and elicit (constrained) sympathies between parties cast as different body parts. Yet Ahmed does not consider how this argument is situated within and deployed in 1 Cor 11–14 to bring in those subjects Paul casts as willful and wayward, particularly the praying and prophesying women in the Corinthian assembly (see Wire 1990, to start).

Such efforts at control or containment are hardly isolated to those letters typically characterized by their contentious and conflicted rhetorics (like 1 Corinthians or Galatians). Even warm letters like Philippians look like (attempted) straightening devices. Cynthia Briggs Kittredge (1998, 37–51), for instance, presents a definitive case for the importance of obedience rhetorics in the letter, explicitly countering interpreters who want to dissociate a supposedly authentic Pauline kind of obedience from an obedience associated with submission and subordination. From another angle, however, these pale malestream interpreters' insistence on a kind of free obedience unwittingly demonstrates the degree to which freedom relies upon subjection, oppression, and coercion.[9] Paul's arguments about obedience are also intertwined with his anxieties about wayward or willful audiences like the assembly community at Philippi. His argument in the letter immediately connects the recitation of a likely precirculated hymn about Christ to the obedience he seeks from that assembly (Phil 2:12–13). This obedience should be marked by their "fear and trembling" (2:12), but also its alignment with divine "will" (*to thelein*) and work that brings God *eudokia* (2:13). The latter Greek term is alternately translated as approval or pleasure, connoting that, as in the verbal form of the word, (this) God consents to or is well pleased by their fearful obedience. These Philippians should neither question nor grumble (2:14), as they are seemingly surrounded by a "crooked and twisted" (NRSV; or "crooked and perverse," as in RSV) generation (2:15), whose influence could break in and ruin Paul's proud (boy) work before the imminent apocalypse (2:16).[10] In such

---

9. Kittredge in particular addresses Käsemann 1970, 1980, and Bultmann 1951.

10. For a related, womanist critique of how Paul deals with and perpetuates stigma in another letter (Galatians) in light of the devaluation of Black and Brown

a light, Paul urges a kind of willed submission from the Philippian assembly members partially derived from Christ's action of becoming slave(-like) in the hymn (2:7–8).[11]

But perhaps Philippians seems too far afield for the subjects of will and willfulness, particularly when passages from the Letter to the Romans have been central in the history of their construction. In this regard, Ahmed is right to note the impact of Augustine, but if she had lingered longer with him (something I do not necessarily recommend), she might have noticed the importance of his reading of Rom 7 for how he grappled with his own conflicted will.[12] To be sure, the "I" who appears in Rom 7:7–25 is riven by an inability to do what he wills (or wants, as various forms of *thelō* appear seven times in 7:15–21). This unwitting subject cannot will properly or cannot follow one kind of will: "For I do not do what I want, but I do the very things I hate.… Nothing good dwells within me, that is, in my flesh, I can will what is right, but I cannot do it. For I do not do the good I want, but the evil I do not want is what I do" (7:15, 18–19). This conflicted affective state leads then to the passage's rhetorical dissociation: "Now if I do what I do not want, it is no longer I that do it, but sin that dwells within me" (7:20). This sin figure prowls or simply preoccupies certain wayward body parts of this conflicted subject (who is now at least partially an object of sin's agency): "But I see in my members another law at war with the law of my mind, making me captive to the law of sin that dwells in my members" (7:23).[13]

---

bodies, see Parker 2018. On the operation of sexual slander, as particularly directed to outsiders, see Knust 2006.

11. For some of the potential complexities and ambivalences of this hymn in light of its slavery rhetorics and enslaved people, Briggs 1989 remains indispensable. For more on the (sexualized) violence in the first half of the hymn, see Shaner 2017. Given recent or, more accurately, ongoing events in the United States, a reconsideration of this hymn pivoting around the cross in light of the lynching tree (akin to Cone 2013) is much overdue. This reconsideration could, for instance, elaborate upon the brief consideration of the hymn as "a slave song of countercultural humanization," in M. Smith 2022 (particularly 57–59), as Marchal 2022 partially attempts. For another biblical scholar's effort to connect Cone's accounting to a scene at the cross in Luke, see Matthews 2019.

12. For a longer consideration of this passage in light of queer affects of disgust and desire, see Marchal 2019c. For a different, very promising engagement of this letter in light of queer affects, see Hoke 2021.

13. On sin (or "Sin") as the central figure or character in certain apocalyptic readings of Rom 7, see Gaventa 2013. On the double participation (that looks affectively conflicted to this reader) of this "I, yet not I, but sin" figuration, see Eastman 2013.

Though this passage is a crucial one in the development of notions of an introspective conscience (through Augustine and Luther, among others; see Stendahl 1963), more recent interpreters have resolved the conflicts for this subject with wayward members by identifying Rom 7 as an example of *prosopopoeia*, or "speech in character."[14] For some, the cue that this could not have been a truly Pauline "I" occurs slightly earlier in the passage's descriptions: "I was once living without law/Torah" (7:9), a time characterized even earlier as: "While we were living in the flesh, our sinful passions, aroused by the law/Torah, were at work in our members to bear fruit for death" (7:5). This is an important and classically informed distinction, pulling this apostolic "I" away from an anti-Jewish claim about the law or torah (see especially Eisenbaum 2009), even as it repeats the image of wayward and willful members, aroused body parts that have their own will and refuse to obey what the "I" wills. Paul, then, is not speaking for himself (or his own perverse members) but is speaking in the style of another character to present the topic at hand from a different angle. Though interpreters cannot settle on exactly what kind of character Paul is putting on, one of the more intriguing suggestions voiced by scholars like Stanley Stowers (1994, 1995) and Pamela Eisenbaum (2009) is that Paul is speaking as a gentile ... or at least how he imagines a gentile would speak.

This identification, however, throws us back to the persistent way Paul characterizes the people to whom (he claims) he was sent—the gentiles—as particularly prone to lapses and backsliding into their gender troubles, unchecked passions, and sexual sins. Paul deploys such ethnoracial stereotypes in both Romans and 1 Corinthians, the two letters that feature the infamous bashing passages.[15] The function of such sexualized scare-figures, of people from barbaric nations unable to control their bodies, their passions, themselves, or their subordinates, underscores that these letters are structured by concerns more for sexual exceptionalism than for sexual orientation. Still, will and desire are intertwined features of these arguments. The Letter to the Romans opens by stressing how it is God's and Paul's will (Rom 1:11, 13) for Paul to school both Greeks and barbarians in the Roman assembly community. Yet he claims that the members

---

14. See, for example, Stowers 1994, 258–84; 1995.

15. On such ethnoracial othering in these passages, see Kwok 2006; Ivarsson 2007; and Marchal 2015a, 2020; as well as the earlier insights of Bailey 1995. On the racialized dynamics that account for how Paul stigmatized and stereotyped others as a result of his own colonized consciousness, see Liew 2008, 75–97, 175–88.

from those foolish nations willfully turn away from what they know about (this) God (1:18–23) and thus receive a threefold divine punishment (1:24, 26, 28), characterized by excessive passions (1:24, 26, 27), improper use (1:26, 27), and unsuitably receptive bodies (1:27).

When Paul promotes a particular course of sexual (in)action in 1 Corinthians as the ideal, he wants (*thelō*, 1 Cor 7:7) everyone to be like him by exercising *enkrateia*, an exemplary self-control (7:7–9).[16] To Paul, this would be a strong sign of how he and any others who follow him are distinctly neither hot nor bothered by *porneia*—the persistent source of his concern in the two previous chapters of this letter (noted ten times in total: 5:1, 9, 10, 11; 6:9, 13, 15, 16, and twice in 18). This would be quite the feat, since Paul claims that one would actually have to leave this world to avoid mixing or associating (or possibly even having sex!?) with *pornoi* (5:9–10)! As in the brief consideration of Philippians, Paul envisions a vulnerable set of assembly members surrounded by a twisted generation (Phil 2:15). In this Corinthian case, though, Paul casts this as a particularly persistent problem, since he apparently felt the need to write a similar exhortation to avoid *pornoi* in a previous letter (1 Cor 5:9). This world is characterized by both *porneia* and idolatry, a characteristic combination in arguments about gentiles emphasized in both of the vice lists deployed in these middle chapters of the letter (5:10–11 and 6:9–10).[17] The latter is the second bashing passage, even as that list and its surroundings are hardly focused on either the *malakoi* or the *arsenokoitai* that have drawn so much contemporary attention. Such a focus misses the more continuous and concentrated concern with *porneia* among the Corinthian assembly members, including the gentiles whom Paul claims were once the very same people who engaged in such vices (6:11). They are not only surrounded, then, as "the call is coming from inside the house" (if you will)—these arguments reflect a Pauline anxiety about backsliding and

---

16. Intriguingly, in some cases this priority means that the consenting will resides *outside of* the body of the Corinthian assembly, if a member has a man/husband or woman/wife who does not belong to the assembly (yet) (1 Cor 7:12–13). See especially Johnson Hodge 2010. But Paul's will mostly prevails (7:32), wanting the Corinthians to be focused in the way he has prioritized (7:26–40), with exceptions to the engaged man or widowed woman who may do as they want (7:36, 39), even if it is a bit of a weaseled compromise to desire or secondary status.

17. For more extended consideration of these figurations, see Ivarsson 2007; Marchal 2019c, 2020.

inveterately perverse members who lack the proper will and are particularly prone to waywardness.

I have left these *porneia* terms untranslated so far, even as they are traditionally rendered as "prostitution," with the nouns *pornos* and *pornē* being the male and female versions of "prostitute." This choice is due not strictly to my willfulness but to the somewhat wayward uses of *porneia*, its elastic capacities, and shifting adaptations. Its broad association with sexual immorality remains, to be sure, but its uses can be reduced to neither prostitution nor fornication (contra Harper 2013). One recent survey of *porneia* shows how its use characterizes a range of illicit sexual acts or relationships (Wheeler-Reed, Knust, and Martin 2018; but see also Reno 2021), indicating that the word is increasingly associated with problems of desire and control. Under these shifting circumstances, to engage in sex as an expression of desire or for one's own pleasure is to be guilty of *porneia* (Wheeler-Reed, Knust, and Martin 2018, 398)! This elastic capacity is useful to bear in mind when considering this section of 1 Corinthians and the specific argument against assembly members joining closely with a *pornē*, a sex-laboring woman (or perhaps just some woman otherwise associated with sexual immorality) (1 Cor 6:15–18).[18] As Jennifer Glancy (see especially 2002, 65–67) has perceptively stressed, such sex-laboring women would have likely been enslaved, and their enslavement would have made adhering to the immediately following Pauline mandates for sexual control virtually impossible to observe (7:1–9).[19] To put the matter of their will plainly, "Slaves did not have the legal right nor cultural power to say 'no' to their owners' sexual demands" (Glancy 2002, 52).

Most proximately, Paul is apparently not speaking to these likely enslaved, perhaps sex-laboring females (and males [?], considering 5:9), but those who are making use of a *pornē*. His argument in 1 Corinthians

---

18. Some classical scholars like Witzke 2015 and Glazebrook 2015 have suggested using the term *sex laboring* to minimize the moralizing force of the term prostitute, in ways akin to contemporary movements for sex worker rights but have hesitated to adopt *sex working* for fear it obscures or minimizes the coercion and violence of enslavement as a significantly different factor for the ancient Roman imperial context. For a remarkable and under-cited study of sex labor in the Bible, undertaken with sex workers, see Ipsen 2009.

19. I do not mean to ignore the significance of this dynamic for those aiming to withdraw from sex (with men) in the Corinthian assembly (see especially Marchal 2018, 2020, and 2021b), even as my particular focus in this essay is the potential *pornoi* and *pornai* in Corinth.

can be partially summed up as "flee *porneia*" (6:18), even as he is the one who keeps bringing it up. The letter and the people targeted by its arguments cannot quite seem to escape the orbit of *porneia*. Yet this is apparently against the divine will for these wayward and willful subjects, since their bodies belong to (this) God who bought them (6:19–20).[20] This Pauline image for the Corinthian assembly members echoes the other letters, as when a fearful obedience is demanded in Philippians (Phil 2:12–16), or the choice must be made between remaining enslaved to sin or becoming enslaved to (this) God in Romans (Rom 6:6–7:25).

Disreputable and Desirable, Marginalized Yet Marking

To this point, I have followed (something akin to) will around a few of Paul's letters and noted how these letters cast other members of the assembly communities as willful and wayward or as too proximate to backsliding, disreputable, gender-troubled, perversely receptive, and sex-laboring figures. But, as decades of feminist biblical and classical scholarship and Hartman specifically remind us, canonized texts and institutionalized historical narrations are hardly the whole story.[21] Clarice Martin (2005, 224) reflects on these difficulties, compounded by the tendencies of both the Pauline letters and their interpreters: "The dim, ad hoc flashes of the lives of slaves in the assemblies of Christ remain shrouded in the concealed world of shadows on offer in standard scholarly reconstructions." If interested in the potential struggles and beautiful experiments of these wayward and willful figures, one must resist these tendencies and improvise and augment with other available materials. Some of these could be the Roman imperial-era materials of marginalized groups like sex-laboring females, receptive males, and performers, which could provide an alternative sense of the kinds of ancient urban spaces inhabited by those assemblies that sparked Paul's letters. The rhetorical, social, and political

---

20. For further discussion, see Glancy 2002, 65–70; Nasrallah 2013, 2019, 55–75.

21. None of the work I try to do would be possible without the insights and approaches generated by feminist scholars, as attuned to rhetorical dynamics as historical possibilities for those stereotyped and submerged. No note will properly and fully capture these debts, but the most direct influences on this approach are Wire 1990 and Schüssler Fiorenza 1999. See also Richlin's retrospective reflections on feminist strategies for dealing with silences and the variety of fragmentary evidence (particularly in 2014, 11–12).

subordination of women and (or among) the enslaved and (or among) the sex laboring does not equate to an absolute lack of creative negotiation of their conditions. Willfulness and waywardness are more complicated than the prevailing perspectives on them, suggesting that willful, wayward affects can also be techniques for approaching and archiving those figures targeted with such terms.

To be sure, the sources from mostly elite, free, Roman imperial males presume and project onto the various people they treat as receptacles of their (sexual) use. As Mira Green (2015, 155) has emphasized after a survey of the material and literary characterizations of enslaved participants and witnesses, free male users of these "wanted to imagine that slaves were willing participants in these relationships." Here, Green builds upon Hartman's earlier work (1997), noting that this presumed willingness of a person treated as property is analogous to North American slavery and subjection. Further, this limited or shadowy agency of the enslaved often worked as an alibi for the free male's excess or overindulgence (Green 2015, 155). As scholars such as Rebecca Flemming (1999) have long noted, slavery is crucial for describing the contours of Roman imperial sex labor, making historical comparisons difficult. Yet, to account for the sexual, social, and economic complexities of these enslaving institutions and enslaved experiences, Flemming proposes tracing forms of both victimization and agency (39), since "the precise combination of consent and coercion involved in such circumstances is not revealed" (42). The violence of such systems should not be evaded, but to insist that they are automatically or exclusively coercive is inadequate (58).[22] For Flemming, it is historically unsustainable "to discount issues of consent, coercion, and control completely; to create absolutes rather than a complex continuum of abuse and empowerment, degradation and achievement" (59).

The potential of this complex continuum for the negotiated subjectivity of marginalized and often stigmatized people animates other recent work on sex-laboring females, receptive males, and performers. Most intriguingly, the sexual graffiti that survives from Pompeii could offer rare access to these marginalized groups who likely wrote or certainly could have read, heard, and tried on their perspective (first suggested in

---

22. "Historically speaking, the view that the organization of prostitution is automatically coercive has little support" (Flemming 1999, 58). Note here that Flemming is also doing some crosscultural analysis of female sex labor, including in the contemporary context of sex worker activism. See also Ipsen 2009.

Levin-Richardson 2011, 2013).[23] Sarah Levin-Richardson (2011, 2013, 2015, and 2019) has focused on the material remains of the purpose-built brothel in Pompeii, and particularly the graffiti scratched into its hallways, doorways, and back entrances. These in-between spaces are affectively loaded sites for assembling "arenas for resistance, agency, and community that individuals carved out for themselves in the face of dire circumstances" (Levin-Richardson 2019, 10).[24] The material remains in these spaces underscore how female and male sex laborers were viewed as both disreputable and desirable (and how they negotiated that view).

More broadly, careful consideration of these materials alongside other literary representations qualifies prevailing perspectives of penetration as the exclusive axis for describing sexual contact. Amy Richlin (see 1993, 531) has long blanched at the reduction of penetrated people to the status of passive or inactive, but now Deborah Kamen and Levin-Richardson have highlighted how both females (Levin-Richardson 2013; Kamen and Levin-Richardson 2015b) and receptive males (Kamen and Levin-Richardson 2015a) are not only the subjects of the sexual verbs in this graffiti, but in many instances they select more active verbs to describe sex acts. In the case of penetrated males, the terminologies deployed imply an important difference in will. One Latin verb for fellatio, *irrumare* (or "face fucking"), often functions as a violent threat in both graffiti and literature, "its victim was conceptualized as an unwilling or inactive participant" (Kamen and Levin-Richardson 2015a, 450; cf. 451). While this aligns with the Priapic protocol, Kamen and Levin-Richardson (2015a, 452–53) note how the *fellator* and *fellare* (the noun and verb for "cock sucking," respectively) portrayed people and practices "willingly performed," and the *cinaedus* is "depicted as wanting to be penetrated." Likewise, any females who were objects of *irrumatio* were "likely to be an unwilling participant" (Kamen and Levin-Richardson 2015b, 242), but as the subject of the verb *fellare* she would have been seen as a "willing practitioner of fellatio" (239). Thus, while "the most salient axis for sexual acts remains penetration," Kamen and Levin-Richardson (2015b, 250; cf. 2015a) assert

---

23. For previous and better accounting of biblical interpretation in the light of the haunting agencies among subordinated groups, see Buell 2009, 2014.

24. On the kinds of emotional, care, or companionship work implied by the material remains of the brothel, and specifically as reflecting "affective communities," see Levin-Richardson 2019, 61–63.

the importance of adding an additional, if potentially subordinate, axis for the agency of the participants.[25]

In fact, graffiti play a key role in filling out ancient pictures of the actively moving, willed, or desired practices of otherwise subordinated or stigmatized females, preserving new or different vocabularies than literary remains. The agent noun *fellatrix* is used only in graffiti (Kamen and Levin-Richardson 2015b, 239), and the graffiti at Pompeii preserve the only known examples of *fututrix* ("fucker" in feminine form) as a title for a female who wants to engage in sexual activity (Levin-Richardson 2013, 333). The circumscribed appearance of these terms manages to both reflect and exceed the ambivalences and contradictions around proper female comportment (Kamen and Levin-Richardson 2015b, 235–236; 248): free, elite, Roman imperial males want cool, calm, and controllable wives but complain if she is not passionate or responsive. Within such double-binding constraints, it is no wonder that females who actively participated, moved during, and/or desired to be the receptive participant in vaginal or oral contact (*fututrices* and *fellatrices*) "are both disparaged and highly sought after" (2015b, 248). Levin-Richardson (2015) has also demonstrated that a larger yet overlapping range of marginalized practices and people were described by first-century residents of Pompeii as *calos*, the Latin transliteration of the Greek term for "beautiful." While previously it was

> used to hail the beauty of respectable citizen boys, at Pompeii, the word *calos* was associated with individuals and places on the margins of society: with prostitutes, tavern-boys, and actors; and with gates, taverns, inns, and whorehouses. That is, Pompeians found the word appropriate to describe those who willingly put themselves on display for the public—the *infames* of Roman society, whose position provoked desire and disparagement. (Levin-Richardson 2015, 280)

Graffiti was one practice that could mark a slightly different way of evaluating people and practices that were typically debased, a set of recognitions that these could be problematic *and* desirable. Levin-Richardson (2013,

---

25. In a note, they make an additional suggestion that could be potentially relevant for a discussion of Paul's Letters and the figures cast as wayward and willful: "Another possible axis (although one more relevant, arguably, to Greek sexuality) is relationship to one's passions. The two options on this axis could be called 'self-controlled' and 'lacking self-control'" (Kamen and Levin-Richardson 2015b, 450 n.74).

334–41) imagines the graffiti as not simply expressing the view of their creators, but also providing opportunities for passers-by to read, appropriate, try on, or redirect the colorful and direct exclamations, a fraught but potent experience for females both as or among other subordinated groups. Kamen and Levin-Richardson (2015b, 250) argue that these materials signal "the agency that subordinated groups (like women and slaves) could exercise within the constraints of Roman society."

Sensing the Enslaved/Receptive/Sex-Laboring

This graffiti provides a palpable if diffuse, a negotiated if still willful, receptivity to some of the most disparaged and marginalized groups in the Roman Empire who could be seen as wayward *and* beautiful. The materials they left behind reflect some of their constricted will and cramped creations, including otherwise lost titles and concepts.[26] An ancient brothel could be something akin to how Hartman (2019, 227–28) describes wayward as "the insurgent ground that enables new possibilities and new vocabularies." Creative and critical engagements of these materials alongside the letters of Paul could evoke similar if elusive dynamics among marginalized or submerged people, including the potentially sex-laboring (or just disreputable) members behind 1 Cor 5–6, the assembly of names foregrounded in Rom 16, or even the crooked and twisted generation of Phil 2.[27] Rather than using scholarship as a straightening device for scriptures, this affective approach senses the perverse potential of the wayward figures flittingly but willfully persisting across these letters and the centuries.

I am hardly treading on stable or respectable ground to suggest that *porneia* could be such a large subject precisely because the Corinthians were not fleeing it and that, on its own, need not have been a significant problem for an ancient assembly (since sex labor was a common and integrated part of urban life in the Roman Empire). Still, as Glancy has highlighted, it is quite possible that some of these members could not flee *porneia*, as ancient sex-laboring people lived lives riven by coercion, pressure, precarity, and violence. While it is utterly conventional to degrade sex laboring and, or as, receptive people (as echoed in Paul's arguments

---

26. For an alternative womanist treatment of agency in relation to New Testament interpretation, see S. Smith 2019.

27. For one of my own, initial attempts to engage these materials to shift our approaches to the targets of Pauline rhetorics, see Marchal 2019b.

here), such characterizations are hardly the whole story, particularly if one is interested in how wayward and willful people named and negotiated their conditions. Levin-Richardson's suggestions that many of these marginalized people would not only write but also read, hear, try on, and talk back to circulating verbal products could apply to letters as much as graffiti. How many Corinthian assembly members assembled in intimate, in-between spaces, like the crowded halls and doorways that connect Hartman's to Levin-Richardson's minoritized subjects and used their own means to talk back to the arguments of such letters, to write their own, or to voice or etch their own, if potentially complicated, replies? Such fuller, more energetic, or complex exchanges could have preceded the letter called 1 Corinthians, as apparently this was specifically not the first time Paul tried to advise against frequenting *pornoi* (1 Cor 5:9, 11). Some members may have been willing to receive others, given some of the formulas Paul appears to be quoting (6:12, 13), those that indicate that bodily appetites are not quite the same cause for consternation that Paul proclaims and projects. Despite Paul's efforts, this receptivity might not have been an adequate (if at all) cause for exclusion from this Corinthian assembly (5:4–5, 6:9), opening up the possibility that the ways sex laborers lived in Pompeii could be reflected in how *pornoi* and *pornai* negotiated assembling with or as these members. Whatever happened, it appears Paul's approach in this letter did not work out the way he wanted, as he felt compelled to write (at least) one more letter (2 Corinthians).[28] Such efforts underscore that sex-laboring and, or as, receptive (as or among other disreputable) members were possibly viewed as both wayward and beautiful, disparaged and desired.

Material remains might augment or help me to improvise a more willful and wayward approach to these people (cast likewise), but they cannot bestow authority, certainty, stability, or respectability (as some biblical interpreters might hope in their deployment of canonized texts or ancient artifacts). Still, I keep craning my neck to peer at all the people crammed into the closing chapter of the Letter to the Romans (16:1–16). Like many of the names that appear in the graffiti further down the Italian peninsula in Pompeii, many of these names are also Greek, reflecting the likely enslaved (or manumitted) or migrant status of people active in

---

28. For recent feminist reflections on this letter, the Corinthian women recipients and respondents, and the historical and rhetorical situations that would have prompted it, see Wire 2019 and Fox 2020.

the assembly community at Rome.[29] Further, two of the people hailed by Paul at Rome also share names with those featured in the graffiti at Pompeii: Ampliatus and Narcissus. Ampliatus is one of the numerous solitary names inscribed on the brothel's walls, making use of a communal sounding board quite possibly to boast or compete with other, likely lower-status (possibly enslaved) males (see Levin-Richardson 2011, 62–63; *CIL* 4.2271; cf. Levin-Richardson 2019, 102). Though Latin in origin, "Ampliatus" was a name created for enslaved people.[30] In his own attempt to reach an assembled community, Paul briefly if separately greets Ampliatus as "my beloved" (in Rom 16:8)—a fleeting reminder that (formerly) enslaved people could be degraded and valued. More explicitly, Narcissus is commended as a *fellator maximus* ("greatest cock sucker") in Pompeii (Kamen and Levin-Richardson 2015a, 452; *CIL* 4.1825a. Add. 212), another reminder that supposedly degraded and receptive parties could also be prized. The Narcissus mentioned by Paul is not directly addressed, only "those belonging to Narcissus" (16:11), presumably some of the enslaved members of his household. His name also indicates enslaved (or manumitted) status, but a group belonging to him suggests he would have been a slave-owning freed person. Several more likely enslaved people are named in these greetings (for instance: Herodion in 16:11, Hermes in 16:14, and Julia and Nereus, both in 16:15) and another circle belonging to Aristobulus (16:10). Like Ampliatus, there are other beloved enslaved (or freed) people like Epaenetus (16:5) and Persis (16:12).

One pair in this section that often stands out to me is Tryphaena and Tryphosa (Rom 16:12), described only as "workers in the lord." Mary Rose D'Angelo (1990) has considered them at greater length, in the context of recut funerary reliefs in the Augustan era. If these women were both freed women, they may have been *conlibertae*, freed together and bound together in this process (75, 83).[31] Their similar names could be a marker of the same owner-user, while the voluptuous or luxurious connotation of their names (derived from the same Greek verb, *tryphaō*) might also be a potential indicator of the sexual tasks they were given when enslaved, possibly even as prostitutes (D'Angelo 2000, 165–66). If this was how they

---

29. See the discussion in Lampe 2003, 171–83. On Greek names as one potential indicator of enslaved status in the graffiti, see Levin-Richardson 2013, 335. For another analysis of this letter in relation to remains from Pompeii, see Oakes 2009.

30. See the discussion in Lampe 2003, 173, 182–83.

31. See the discussion in Schüssler Fiorenza 1986, 428; and Lampe 2003, 179–80.

were "workers," whether enslaved or manumitted, sex labor is even more difficult to separate from the members of the assembly community "in the lord" at Rome. As several literary sources and manumission inscriptions attest, such labor for their (former) owner would have continued even if manumitted. Kamen (2014, 151), for instance, highlights a common condition enumerated in one inscription: it is only once the (former) enslaver dies that the freed people are able to "do whatever they want (*thelōnti*), and go wherever they want (*thelōnti*), and also be untouchable their whole lives."[32] It is not hard to imagine the conditions for these (enslaved or manumitted) females as akin to those sex laborers in Pompeii, who dealt with these conditions, talked back through the surviving graffiti, and assembled with many others in a range of confined but some contextually complicated spaces. They were among the many recipients of this letter, but it is Paul who pursues the approval of the assembly community by naming so many of these figures that he sought and perhaps even needed their approval to travel to this (new-to-him) site. Their names imply a tentative, unstable, even slippery similarity to those in another affective community, but they could have been more than how willful characterizations presume: wayward and working, disparaged and desired, with shifting, potentially complex relations of kinship, household, and intimate affiliation, within and beyond the assembly. My brief narrations—insufficiently conveying their messy, quotidian negotiations within such constraints—partially, waywardly, and willfully connect them to those who come before and after them.

Such connections twist and turn, waywardly, even unexpectedly (but finally) back around to Philippians, where Paul summoned the specter of an entire crooked and twisted generation surrounding those he calls to a willed submission. Seeking such slavish obedience is even more chilling if one glimpses Epaphroditus (Phil 2:25–30; cf. 4:18), appearing just a few beats after he sounds that specter in the time before the imminent apocalypse. This apocalypse is not yet now, but Paul aims for an apocalypse to which one cannot say no. His warm, if instrumental, rhetoric dispatches Epaphroditus back to the assembly community at Philippi for Paul's own purposes; even Epaphroditus's near-death experience is about (this) God's mercy to Paul (2:27), allaying Paul's anxieties (2:28)

---

32. This inscription could provide further nuance and texture to an interest elsewhere (within 1 Cor 7) in untouchability and withdrawal from sex (with males).

and fulfilling the Philippians' obligation to Paul (2:30). The name Epaphroditus also appears at Pompeii: Epaphroditus the *fellator* (in Kamen and Levin-Richardson 2015a, 452; *CIL* 4.10073c), one of those instances where a graffiti writer (possibly this Epaphroditus himself) briefly marks him(self) as willing and receptive. This name is also a common one for an enslaved person, appearing in other remains like this papyrus from Oxyrhynchus (and highlighted by Glancy 2002, 53): "Apion and Epimas proclaim to their best-loved Epaphroditus that if you allow us to bugger you it will go well for you, and we will not thrash you any longer" (P.Oxy. 42.3070).[33] This enslaved Epaphroditus is a commodified and threatened object, yet described affectionately by those who seek something like his acceptance or acquiescence.[34] Will is not entirely absent here, but the coercion of physical violence and, or as, penetrative acts is clear—another stark reminder of the complicated, compromising context for enslaved and, or as, receptive, and, or as, sex-laboring people.

As we have no letters nor replies from the Epaphroditus at Philippi, we can only wonder how this likely enslaved messenger (*apostolos*, 2:25) ended up in the middle of an exchange between another *apostolos*, Paul, and the assembly community at Philippi.[35] The brief arguments about him suggest another constrained combination: Pauline praise and the (potential) honorific applied to him, even as he is treated as an object. How willingly did Epaphroditus receive his tasks, bringing or simply being the Philippian support for Paul (2:25; 4:18) and being sent back with another object—the canonized letter itself? Epaphroditus would not have been the only person there intimately aware of life treated as an object, as the common economic modeling for the assembly at Philippi stresses a significant (if varying) proportion of enslaved or manumitted members.[36] Another female-female pair, Euodia and Syntyche, appears in the final chapter of this letter (4:2–3; also treated by D'Angelo 1990), with names

---

33. See Glancy 2002, 53; translating and discussing P.Oxy. 42.3070 (further discussed in Montserrat 1996, 136–38). For further reflections on Epaphroditus (in which I only briefly consider this papyrus), see Marchal 2015b. See also Nasrallah 2019, 125–26.

34. For an important meditation on the operation of Hagar as an enslaved person treated as a fungible object in Galatians (also in conversation with Hartman), see Armstrong 2017.

35. For more on enslaved leadership in these communities, see Shaner 2018.

36. Consider, for instance, De Vos 1999; Oakes 2001; Ascough 2003.

that similarly imply enslaved (or manumitted) status. Names with positive connotations of success or luck (like Euodia and Syntyche) can also reflect an instrumental view of other humans, not to mention the Roman predisposal to mock their social inferiors with names like "Lucky."[37] Such predisposal is also evident among the assembly members at Corinth, who sent Fortunatus to Paul (1 Cor 16:17).[38]

Fleeting, Not Fleeing: Cramped Creations instead of Conclusions

The Letter to the Philippians does not have the same abundance of named figures as Rom 16, or even 1 Corinthians, nor does it feature a concentrated series of arguments about *pornoi*, *pornai*, and the broader category of *porneia* (stalking and dragging Paul's [construction of the] gentile assembly members at Corinth backward). Yet these fleeting arguments still reflect the messy uncertainties and complicated ambivalences of these people's lives and my own wayward, willful (attempted) approach to them (see also Graybill 2019). Many in each of these assembly communities, at Rome, Corinth, and Philippi would have been enslaved and, or as, receptive and, or as, sex-laboring people—even as each of these letters reflect a mixed recognition among the assembly members, the necessity for Paul to reach out, cajole, appeal to, or simply just greet many of these named (and unnamed) figures. From within their urban assembled mess(es) these otherwise marginalized and stigmatized figures may have struggled and experimented, willing, refusing, and negotiating under the constraints of their embodied labors. They were among those who made these assemblies. They sent their own apostles, besides the one at the sainted center of Pauline studies. We are still reading their letters; they are not Paul's—he sent them to the Romans, to the Corinthians, to the Philippians.

---

37. Martin (2005, 228), for instance, stresses: "slaves bore only one name, often one that mocked his status (for example, Felix, meaning 'Lucky')." Thus, at the very least, names like Syntyche's can reveal an instrumental view of other humans: "either her parents or her owners wished the best for themselves in naming her" (Ascough 2003, 125). On the irony or just cruelty of these fictions of affective well-being, see also Levin-Richardson 2019, 118–19.

38. The feminine version of the name, Fortunata, also appears among the sex-laboring women who are female subjects performing fellatio. See the discussion in Levin-Richardson 2013, 328; *CIL* 4.2259, 2275. The possibility that this Fortunata could have written graffiti herself is discussed in Levin-Richardson 2013, 328, 331; and Kamen and Levin-Richardson 2015b, 241; *CIL* 4.8185; cf. *CIL* 4.2266.

But instead of seeing this as a bid for their, or our, or my respectability, stability, certainty, or authority, let us try to imagine them at the heart of the movements of these assemblies without presuming or projecting their recuperation and redemption.[39] So often, queer exercises in contextualizing or clarifying what these texts really mean are diversionary efforts to spare us any further stigma or shame, to avoid association with (those targeted with notions of) perversion, degradation, or *porneia*. Wayward and willful point elsewhere and otherwise. The point here is certainly that there were other people, that Paul's point of view is not the whole story. But also, in retraining our focus in a more wayward and willful fashion and toward wayward figures as, and, within, or among willful collectives, these other people and their practices were also disreputable and disparaged, but not only so. In countering prevailing perspectives on those cast as wayward or willful, the next option is not to save the receptive and, or as, the sex laboring from themselves, to turn them into respectable and settled sexual and ethnoracial minorities. Their and our approaches could do more than assent to either Roman imperial or corresponding, often accommodating, Pauline perspectives. Instead, these cities and these assemblies within them were occupied by many others, spaces suffused with mostly lost sensations, affectively bound by, with, or as people with constricted wills and cramped creations. Their settings should not be naively separated from intractable structures and scenes of violence woven into their intimacies and assemblies. But these many other figures engaged in messy negotiations of their complex quotidian and colonizing constraints. Those members so long marginalized could be stigmatized and recognized, wayward and beautiful, receptive and willing, problematic and desired, subordinated and sought after.

This is still uncertain, unsettling, perhaps intersectional, and certainly improvised.

Try, just for now, not to turn away from *porneia*.

---

39. Resonances from the graffiti might remind us that these may have persisted in those traditions associated, but distanced from authentic Pauline materials (like the disputed epistles and Acts). Nymphe (see also Col 4:15) is one of six instances of *fellatrix* at Pompeii (Levin-Richardson 2013, 332; Kamen and Levin-Richardson 2015b, 241; *CIL* 4.1389); and is the subject of *fututa* (in *CIL* 4.8897; see Levin-Richardson 2013, 327; Kamen and Levin-Richardson 2015a, 451). Secundus (see also Acts 20:4, for a Thessalonian named Secundus with Paul) is a *fellator rarus*, "cock sucker of rare talent" (Kamen and Levin-Richardson 2015a, 452; *CIL* 4.9027; translated by Varone 2002, 140).

Works Cited

Ahmed, Sara. 2010. *The Promise of Happiness*. Durham, NC: Duke University Press.

———. 2014. *Willful Subjects*. Durham, NC: Duke University Press.

———. 2019. *What's the Use: On the Uses of Use*. Durham, NC: Duke University Press.

Armstrong, Amaryah. 2017. "Of Flesh and Spirit: Race, Reproduction, and Sexual Difference in the Turn to Paul." *JCRT* 16.2:126–41.

Ascough, Richard S. 2003. *Paul's Macedonian Associations: The Social Context of Philippians and 1 Thessalonians*. WUNT 2/161. Tübingen: Mohr Siebeck.

Bailey, Randall C. 1995. "'They're Nothing but Incestuous Bastards': The Polemical Use of Sex and Sexuality in Hebrew Canon Narratives." Pages 121–38 in *Reading from This Place*. Vol. 1. of *Social Location and Biblical Interpretation in the United States*. Edited by Fernando F. Segovia and Mary A. Tolbert. Minneapolis: Fortress.

Bray, Gerald R., ed. 1999. *1–2 Corinthians*. Wheaton, IL: InterVarsity.

Briggs, Sheila. 1989. "Can an Enslaved God Liberate? Hermeneutical Reflections on Philippians 2:6–11." *Semeia* 47:137–53.

Brooten, Bernadette J. 1996. *Love between Women: Early Christian Responses to Female Homoeroticism*. Chicago: University of Chicago Press.

Buell, Denise Kimber. 2005. *Why This New Race: Ethnic Reasoning in Early Christianity*. New York: Columbia University Press.

———. 2009. "God's Own People: Specters of Race, Ethnicity, and Gender in Early Christian Studies." Pages 159–90 in *Prejudice and Christian Beginnings: Investigating Race, Gender, and Ethnicity in Early Christian Studies*. Edited by Elisabeth Schüssler Fiorenza and Laura Nasrallah. Minneapolis: Fortress.

———. 2014. "Hauntology Meets Post-humanism: Some Payoffs for Biblical Studies." Pages 29–56 in *The Bible and Posthumanism*. Edited by Jennifer L. Koosed. SemeiaSt 74. Atlanta: Society of Biblical Literature.

———. 2018. "Anachronistic Whiteness and the Ethics of Interpretation." Pages 149–67 in *Ethnicity, Race, Religion: Identities and Ideologies in Early Jewish and Christian Texts and in Modern Biblical Interpretation*. Edited by Katherine M. Hockney and David G. Horrell. London: T&T Clark.

Bultmann, Rudolf. 1951. *Theology of the New Testament*. 2 vols. Translated by Kendrick Grobel. New York: Scribner's.

Butler, Judith. 2004. *Undoing Gender*. New York: Routledge.

Byron, Gay L., and Vanessa Lovelace, eds. 2016. *Womanist Interpretations of the Bible: Expanding the Discourse*. SemeiaSt 85. Atlanta: SBL Press.

Cone, James H. 2013. *The Cross and the Lynching Tree*. Maryknoll, NY: Orbis.

D'Angelo, Mary Rose. 1990. "Women Partners in the New Testament." *JFSR* 6:65–86.

———. 2000. "Tryphosa." Pages 165–66 in *Women in Scripture: A Dictionary of Named and Unnamed Women in the Hebrew Bible, the Apocrypha/Deuterocanonical Books, and the New Testament*. Edited by Carol Meyers, Toni Craven, and Ross S. Kraemer. Grand Rapids: Eerdmans.

De Vos, Craig Steven. 1999. *Church and Community Conflicts: The Relationships of the Thessalonian, Corinthian, and Philippian Churches with Their Wider Civic Communities*. SBLDS 168. Atlanta: Scholars Press.

Eastman, Susan. 2013. "Double Participation and the Responsible Self in Romans 5–8." Pages 93–110 in *Apocalyptic Paul: Cosmos and Anthropos in Romans 5–8*. Edited by Beverly Roberts Gaventa. Waco, TX: Baylor University Press.

Eisenbaum, Pamela. 2009. *Paul Was Not a Christian: The Original Message of a Misunderstood Apostle*. New York: HarperOne.

Flemming, Rebecca. 1999. "*Quae Corpore Quaestum Facit*: The Sexual Economy of Female Prostitution in the Roman Empire." *JRS* 89:38–61.

Foucault, Michel. 1990. *The Use of Pleasure*. Vol. 2 of *The History of Sexuality*. Translated by Robert Hurley. New York: Vintage Books.

Fox, Arminta. 2017. "Decentering Paul, Contextualizing Crimes: Reading in Light of the Imprisoned." *JFSR* 33.2:37–54.

———. 2020. *Paul Decentered: Reading 2 Corinthians with the Corinthian Women*. Paul in Critical Contexts. Minneapolis: Fortress.

Gaventa, Beverly Roberts. 2013. "The Shape of the 'I': The Psalter, the Gospel, and the Speaker in Romans 7." Pages 77–91 in *Apocalyptic Paul: Cosmos and Anthropos in Romans 5–8*. Edited by Beverly Gaventa. Waco, TX: Baylor University Press.

Glancy, Jennifer A. 2002. *Slavery in Early Christianity*. Minneapolis: Fortress.

Glazebrook, Allison. 2015. "Beyond Courtesans and Whores: Sex and Labor in the Greco-Roman World." *Helios* 42.1:1–5.

Graybill, Rhiannon. 2019. "Fuzzy, Messy, Icky: The Edges of Consent in Hebrew Bible Rape Narratives and Rape Culture." *Bible and Critical Theory* 15.2:1–27.

Green, F. Mira. 2015. "Witnesses and Participants in the Shadows: The Sexual Lives of Enslaved Women and Boys." *Helios* 42.1:143–62.

Haley, Shelley P. 1990. "Livy, Passion, and Cultural Stereotypes." *Historia* 39:375–81.

———. 1993. "Black Feminist Thought and Classics: Re-membering, Re-claiming, Re-empowering." Pages 23–43 in *Feminist Theory and the Classics*. Edited by Nancy Sorkin Rabinowitz and Amy Richlin. New York: Routledge.

———. 2009. "Be Not Afraid of the Dark: Critical Race Theory and Classical Studies." Pages 27–49 in *Prejudice and Christian Beginnings: Investigating Race, Gender, and Ethnicity in Early Christian Studies*. Edited by Elisabeth Schüssler Fiorenza and Laura Nasrallah. Minneapolis: Fortress.

Halperin, David M. 1990. *One Hundred Years of Homosexuality: And Other Essays on Greek Love*. New York: Routledge.

Harper, Kyle. 2013. *From Shame to Sin: The Christian Transformation of Sexual Morality in Late Antiquity*. Cambridge: Harvard University Press.

Hartman, Saidiya. 1997. *Scenes of Subjection: Terror, Slavery, and Self-Making in Nineteenth-Century America*. Race and American Culture. Oxford: Oxford University Press.

———. 2007. *Lose Your Mother: A Journey along the Atlantic Slave Route*. New York: Farrar, Straus & Giroux.

———. 2008. "Venus in Two Acts." *Small Axe* 12.2:1–14.

———. 2019. *Wayward Lives, Beautiful Experiments: Intimate Histories of Social Upheaval*. New York: Norton.

———. 2020. "Intimate History, Radical Narrative." Joint online roundtable of African American Intellectual History Society with the *Journal of African American History*. May 22, 2020. https://www.aaihs.org/intimate-history-radical-narrative/.

Hidaglo, Jacqueline M. 2016. *Revelation in Aztlán: Scriptures, Utopias, and the Chicano Movement*. The Bible and Cultural Studies. New York: Palgrave Macmillan.

———. 2018. "'Our Book of Revelation ... Prescribes our Fate and Releases Us from It': Scriptural Disorientations in Cherríe Moraga's *The Last Generation*." Pages 113–32 in *Sexual Disorientations: Queer Tempo-

ralities, Affects, Theologies. Transdisciplinary Theological Colloquia. Edited by Kent L. Brintnall, Joseph A. Marchal, and Stephen D. Moore. New York: Fordham University Press.

Hoke, James N. 2021. *Feminism, Queerness, Affect, and Romans: Under God?* ECL 30. Atlanta: SBL Press.

Ingleheart, Jennifer. 2015. "Introduction: Romosexuality: Rome, Homosexuality, and Reception." Pages 1–35 in *Ancient Rome and the Construction of Modern Homosexual Identities*. Edited by Jennifer Ingleheart. Oxford: Oxford University Press.

Ipsen, Avaren, 2009. *Sex Working and the Bible*. London: Equinox.

Ivarsson, Fredrik. 2007. "Vice Lists and Deviant Masculinity: The Rhetorical Function of 1 Corinthians 5:10–11 and 6:9–10." Pages 163–84 in *Mapping Gender in Ancient Religious Discourses*. Edited by Todd Penner and Caroline Vander Stichele. BibInt 84. Leiden: Brill.

Johnson Hodge, Caroline. 2010. "Married to an Unbeliever: Households, Hierarchies, and Holiness in 1 Corinthians 7:12–16." *HTR* 103.1:1–25.

Kamen, Deborah. 2014. "Slave-Prostitutes and ἐργασία in the Delphic Manumission Inscriptions." *ZPE* 188:149–53.

Kamen, Deborah, and Sarah Levin-Richardson. 2015a. "Revisiting Roman Sexuality: Agency and the Conceptualization of Penetrated Males." Pages 449–60 in *Sex in Antiquity: Exploring Gender and Sexuality in the Ancient World*. Edited by Mark Masterson, Nancy Sorkin Rabinowitz, and James Robson. New York: Routledge.

———. 2015b. "Lusty Ladies in the Roman Imaginary." Pages 231–52 in *Ancient Sex: New Essays*. Edited by Ruby Blondell and Kirk Ormand. Columbus: Ohio State University Press.

Käsemann, Ernst. 1970. *Jesus Means Freedom*. Translated by Frank Clarke. Philadelphia: Fortress.

———. 1980. *Commentary on Romans*. Translated by Geoffrey W. Bromiley. Grand Rapids: Eerdmans.

Kittredge, Cynthia Briggs. 1998. *Community and Authority: The Rhetoric of Obedience in the Pauline Tradition*. HTS 45. Harrisburg, PA: Trinity Press International.

Knust, Jennifer Wright. 2006. *Abandoned to Lust: Sexual Slander and Ancient Christianity*. Gender, Theory, and Religion. New York: Columbia University Press.

Kwok Pui-lan. 2006. "A Postcolonial Reading: Sexual Morality and National Politics: Reading Biblical 'Loose Women.'" Pages 21–46 in *Engaging the*

Bible: Critical Readings from Contemporary Women. Edited by Choi Hee An and Katheryn Pfisterer Darr. Minneapolis: Fortress.

Lampe, Peter. 2003. *From Paul to Valentinus: Christians at Rome in the First Two Centuries*. Translated by Michael Steinhauser. Edited by Marshall D. Johnson. Minneapolis: Fortress.

Levin-Richardson, Sarah. 2011. "*Facilis hic futuit*: Graffiti and Masculinity in Pompeii's 'Purpose-Built' Brothel." *Helios* 38:1:59–78.

———. 2013. "*Fututa sum hic*: Female Subjectivity and Agency in Pompeian Sexual Graffiti." *CJ* 108.3:319–45.

———. 2015. "*Calos* graffiti and *infames* at Pompeii." *ZPE* 195:274–82.

———. 2019. *The Brothel of Pompeii: Sex, Class, and Gender at the Margins of Roman Society*. Cambridge: Cambridge University Press.

Liew, Tat-Siong Benny. 2008. *What Is Asian American Biblical Hermeneutics? Reading the New Testament*. Intersections: Asian and Pacific American Transcultural Studies. Honolulu: University of Hawai'i Press.

Marchal Joseph A. 2014. "Female Masculinity in Corinth? Bodily Citations and the Drag of History." *Neot* 48.1:93–113.

———. 2015a. "The Exceptional Proves Who Rules: Imperial Sexual Exceptionalism in and around Paul's Letters." *Journal of Early Christian History* 5.1:87–115.

———. 2015b. "Slaves as Wo/men and Unmen: Reflecting upon Euodia, Syntyche, and Epaphroditus in Philippi." Pages 141–76 in *The People beside Paul: The Philippian Assembly and History from Below*. Edited by Joseph A. Marchal. ECL 17. Atlanta: SBL Press.

———. 2018. "How Soon Is (This Apocalypse) Now? Queer Velocities after a Corinthian Already and a Pauline Not Yet." Pages 45–67 in *Sexual Disorientations: Queer Temporalities, Affects, Theologies*. Transdisciplinary Theological Colloquia. Edited by Kent L. Brintnall, Joseph A. Marchal, and Stephen D. Moore. New York: Fordham University Press.

———. 2019a. "On the Verge of an Introduction." Pages 1–61 in *Bodies on the Verge: Queering Pauline Epistles*. Edited by Joseph A. Marchal. SemeiaSt 93. Atlanta: SBL Press.

———. 2019b. "Bottoming Out: Rethinking the Reception of Receptivity." Pages 209–237 in *Bodies on the Verge: Queering Pauline Epistles*. Edited by Joseph A. Marchal. SemeiaSt 93. Atlanta: SBL Press.

———. 2019c. "The Disgusting Apostle and a Queer Affect between Epistles and Audiences." Pages 113–40 in *Reading with Feeling: Affect*

Theory and the Bible. Edited by Fiona C. Black and Jennifer L. Koosed. SemeiaSt 95. Atlanta: SBL Press.

———. 2020. *Appalling Bodies: Queer Figures before and after Paul's Letters*. New York: Oxford University Press.

———. 2021a. "Still After: Re-introducing the Corinthian Women Prophets at 30." Pages 1–46 in *After the Corinthian Women Prophets: Rhetoric, Power, and Possibilities*. Edited by Joseph A. Marchal. SemeiaSt 97. Atlanta: SBL Press.

———. 2021b. "Alternative Futures, Ephemeral Bodies: Untouching the Corinthian Women Prophets." Pages 123–44 in *After the Corinthian Women Prophets: Rhetoric, Power, and Possibilities*. Edited by Joseph A. Marchal. SemeiaSt 97. Atlanta: SBL Press.

———. 2022. "Toward Feeling Fragments: Melancholic Migrants and Other Affect Aliens in the Philippian and Corinthian Assemblies." *BibInt* 30:5:600–23.

Martin, Clarice J. 2005. "The Eyes Have It: Slaves in the Communities of Christ-Believers." Pages 221–39 in *Christian Origins*. Vol. 1 of *A People's History of Christianity*. Edited by Richard A. Horsley. Minneapolis: Fortress.

Matthews, Shelly. 2017. "'To Be One and the Same with the Woman Whose Head Is Shaven' (1 Cor 11:5b): Resisting the Violence of 1 Corinthians 11:2–16 from the Bottom of the Kyriarchal Pyramid." Pages 31–51 in *Sexual Violence and Sacred Texts*. Edited by Amy Kalmanofsky. Cambridge: Feminist Studies in Religion Books.

———. 2019. "The Lynching Tree and the Cross: James Cone, Historical Narrative, and the Ideology of Just Crucifixion (Lk 23:41)." Pages 147–70 of *The Narrative Self in Early Christianity: Essays in Honor of Judith Perkins*. Edited by Janet Spittler. WGRWSup 15. Atlanta: SBL Press.

Montserrat, Dominic. 1996. *Sex and Society in Greco-Roman Egypt*. New York: Kegan Paul.

Nasrallah, Laura Salah. 2013. "'You Were Bought with a Price': Freedpersons and Things in 1 Corinthians." Pages 54–73 in *Corinth in Contrast: Studies in Inequality*. Edited by Steven J. Friesen, Sarah A. James, and Daniel N. Schowaler. NovTSup 155. Leiden: Brill.

———. 2019. *Archaeology and the Letters of Paul*. Oxford: Oxford University Press.

Oakes, Peter. 2001. *Philippians: From People to Letter*. SNTSMS 110. Cambridge: Cambridge University Press.

———. 2009. *Reading Romans in Pompeii: Paul's Letter at Ground Level*. London: SPCK.
Parker, Angela N. 2018. "One Womanist's View of Racial Reconciliation in Galatians." *JFSR* 34.2:23–40.
Reno, Joshua M. 2021. "Pornographic Desire in the Pauline Corpus." *JBL* 140.1:163–85.
Richlin, Amy. 1983. *The Garden of Priapus: Sexuality and Aggression in Roman Humor*. New Haven: Yale University Press.
———. 1993. "Not before Homosexuality: The Materiality of the Cinaedus and the Roman Law against Love between Men." *Journal of the History of Sexuality* 3.4:523–73.
———. 2014. *Arguments with Silence: Writing the History of Roman Women*. Ann Arbor: University of Michigan Press.
Schüssler Fiorenza, Elisabeth. 1986. "Missionaries, Apostles, Coworkers: Romans 16 and the Reconstruction of Women's Early Christian History." *WW* 6:420–33.
———. 1999. *Rhetoric and Ethic: The Politics of Biblical Studies*. Minneapolis: Fortress.
———. 2001. *Wisdom Ways: Introducing Feminist Biblical Interpretation*. Maryknoll, NY: Orbis.
Shaner, Katherine A. 2017. "Seeing Rape and Robbery: ἁρπαγμός and the Philippians Christ Hymn (Phil. 2:5–11)." *BibInt* 25.3:342–63.
———. 2018. *Enslaved Leadership in Early Christianity*. Oxford: Oxford University Press.
Sharpe, Christina. 2010. *Monstrous Intimacies: Making Post-slavery Subjects*. Durham, NC: Duke University Press.
Smith, Mitzi J., ed. 2015. *I Found God in Me: A Womanist Biblical Hermeneutics Reader*. Eugene, OR: Cascade.
———. 2022. "Abolitionist Messiah: A Man Named Jesus Born of a *Doulē*." Pages 53–70 in *Bitter the Chastening Rod: Africana Biblical Interpretation after* Stony the Road We Trod *in the Age of BLM, SayHerName, and MeToo*. Edited by Mitzi J. Smith, Angela N. Parker, and Ericka S. Dunbar Hill. Lanham, MD: Lexington.
Smith, Shanell T. 2019. "'She Did That!': Female Agency in New Testament Texts—A Womanist Response." Pages 157–75 in *The Oxford Handbook of New Testament, Gender, and Sexuality*. Edited by Benjamin H. Dunning. Oxford: Oxford University Press.
Stendahl, Krister. 1963. "The Apostle Paul and the Introspective Conscience of the West." *HTR* 56:119–215.

Stowers, Stanley K. 1994. *A Rereading of Romans: Justice, Jews, and Gentiles.* New Haven: Yale University Press.

———. 1995. "Romans 7.7–25 as a Speech in Character (προσωποποεια)." Pages 180–202 in *Paul in His Hellenistic Context.* Edited by Troels Engberg-Pedersen. Minneapolis: Fortress.

Thomas, Eric A. 2018. "The Futures Outside: Apocalyptic Epilogue Unveiled as Africana Queer Prologue." Pages 90–112 in *Sexual Disorientations: Queer Temporalities, Affects, Theologies.* Transdisciplinary Theological Colloquia. Edited by Kent L. Brintnall, Joseph A. Marchal, and Stephen D. Moore. New York: Fordham University Press.

Varone, Antonio. 2002. *Erotica Pompeiana: Love Inscriptions on the Walls of Pompeii.* Translated by R. P. Berg. Rome: L'Erma di Bretschneider.

Walker, Alice. 1983. *In Search of Our Mothers' Gardens.* San Diego: Harcourt.

Walters, Jonathan. 1997. "Invading the Roman Body: Manliness and Impenetrability in Roman Thought." Pages 29–43 in *Roman Sexualities.* Edited by Judith P. Hallett and Marilyn B. Skinner. Princeton: Princeton University Press.

Wheeler-Reed, David, Jennifer W. Knust, and Dale B. Martin. 2018. "Can a Man Commit *Porneia* with His Wife?" *JBL* 137:383–98.

Wire, Antoinette Clark. 1990. *The Corinthian Women Prophets: A Reconstruction through Paul's Rhetoric.* Minneapolis: Fortress.

———. 2019. *2 Corinthians.* Wisdom Commentary 48. Collegeville, MN: Liturgical Press.

Witzke, Serena S. 2015. "Harlots, Tarts, and Hussies? A Problem of Terminology for Sexual Labor in Roman Comedy." *Helios* 42.1:7–27.

Master Jesus and the Enslaved Apostles

Jennifer A. Glancy

The apostle Paul described himself as a slave of the Master Christ, a formulation picked up by others throughout antiquity. I revisit these references in the context of twenty-first-century discourses about what it means to be human. Discussions of slavery and humanity have long been intertwined in Western thought. What might attention to this central trope of early Christian discourse contribute to contemporary theorizing, particularly to efforts to rethink the status of the human or, more broadly conceived, to discussions of ontology? In the introductory section of the essay, I draw on the work of two thinkers whose engagement with relational ontology takes seriously the impact of domination: New Testament scholar Denise Kimber Buell and cultural theorist Zakkiyah Iman Jackson. I also propose a succinct critique of contemporary philosopher Giorgio Agamben's analysis of what he calls anthropogenesis—the becoming human of the human being. Agamben's (2005, 28–29) discussion prominently features the figure of the slave in Aristotle and Paul, even contending that "the slave, as defined by Paul, is invested with a messianic vocation" (for fuller discussion, see Glancy 2020). However, unlike Buell and Jackson, Agamben does not acknowledge the constitutive force of domination. In dialogue with these theoretical perspectives, I turn my attention to the apocryphal Acts of Thomas and particularly to the relationship between Master Christ and the enslaved apostle Thomas.

I gratefully acknowledge the support of a 2018 ACLS Fellowship from the American Council of Learned Societies.

Introduction

First, though, let us briefly consider two theoretical takes on Paul's self-designation as slave, both relevant to larger issues raised in the essay. Underscoring the importance of ancient literary conventions, J. Albert Harrill (2006, 19, 31) argues that Paul relied on the literary convention of speech-in-character to construct "a recognizable stock voice of the slave self" as the "unlikely model of the *anthrōpos* in Romans 7:14–25." Paul's writerly construction of a slave persona accorded with the Roman ideal of the slave as one who had "accepted the master's wishes so fully that the slave's innermost self could anticipate the master's wishes" (21). Although agreeing with Harrill that the passage relies on literary convention, Giovanni Bazzana (2020, 163) nonetheless contends that there was "something more behind Paul's fondness for representing himself and his fellow Christ believers as enslaved persons." Bazzana proposes that Paul depended on "slavery images and idioms" to capture the experience of spirit possession (163), an experience of domination in which one's will was subsumed and one's body was not one's own. In particular, Bazzana argues that possession by the πνεῦμα χριστοῦ, the spirit of Christ, was a defining experience for Paul and other early Christ followers. Methodologically, Bazzana constructs a conversation between historical studies of the New Testament and contemporary ethnographic accounts of spirit possession. Grounded in history as well as anthropology, the stakes of the argument are both ontological and ethical.

Bazzana explicitly links the aims of his analysis to Denise Buell's exploration of writings produced by early Christ groups in light of relational ontologies and other posthumanist discourses, a project emphasizing what study of these ancient texts might bring to contemporary theory (Bazzana 2020, 206–7). In a series of articles challenging the notion of the sovereign, self-governing self that is foundational to modern liberalism, Buell proposes (2014, 63–64) that attention to the function of *pneuma* in early Christian discourse might foster an understanding of "the meaning and place of the human that is radically relational and radically vulnerable." And yet, Buell is clear, this shared and radical vulnerability does not inoculate us against persistent and death-dealing hierarchies. Elsewhere, she observes, "A relational, permeable notion of the self cannot simply be embraced as a good; the toxic legacies of sexism and slavery demonstrate that those relational ontologies are very bad indeed for wo/men produced and prescribed to be the instruments of and for others" (Buell 2017, 468).

As an example of pneumatic interaction, Buell (2014, 70) cites Paul's suggestion that those who receive in their hearts the *pneuma* of God's son at baptism undergo a transformation "at once material and symbolic," simultaneously effecting the adoption of the baptized as God's sons and their liberation from slavery to the elements (Gal 4:3, 6–7). Although the logic of Gal 4:1–7 is predicated on distinguishing (adopted) sonship from slavery—and the association of freedom with *pneuma* is presumed in the Sarah-Hagar allegory (4:29)—Paul gives a somewhat different account of the material and symbolic transformation of baptism in Rom 6–7. There, he tells a story in which the baptized are bought out from slavery to sin so that they might be slaves of righteousness enslaved to God. Paul acknowledges the limitations of the analogy. "I am speaking on human terms" (ἀνθρώπινον λέγω; Rom 6:19a), he says, thus calling attention to what cultural theorist Zakkiyah Jackson (2020, 121) terms "the material histories of our categories, as they are given shape and vitality by way of, and inside of, organismic bodies."

Homing in on the tired distinction between human and animal, Jackson is centrally concerned with disrupting standard Western ontology via engagement with the "unruly conceptions of being and materiality" that emerge in cultural productions from the African diaspora (1). Arguing that "the animalizations of humans and animals have contiguous and intersecting histories" in Western philosophy and science (23), Jackson proposes that global traditions of Black writing and visual art afford glimpses of alternate conceptions of being. For Buell, attention to premodern sources can serve a related purpose of helping us imagine relational ontologies that refuse the binary of human and nonhuman with implications for rethinking human relations of dominance and hierarchy. Taking a long view, the material history of ontological categories includes ancient conceptions of *pneuma*, spirit conceived as a kind of material stuff whose unruly capacity to disrupt ontology Buell helps us appreciate. "For Paul," Buell (2014, 70) writes, "pneuma rather than, say, oxygen … is the agential life-force humans need to make our embodied selves truly live."

What particularly interests me in the pneumatic discourses of Paul and other early Christ followers is the material entanglement of categories of slavery and the human, an entanglement confounding any sense of the self as sovereign or discrete. Paul writes in Romans that in baptism "our old human self [ἄνθρωπος] was crucified with Christ … so that we may no longer be enslaved to sin" (Rom 6:6). In a newness of spirit (ἐν καινότητι πνεύματος; 7:6), whoever is baptized belongs to another, to

Christ (7:4). Thus, when Paul writes in Galatians, "I have been crucified with Christ; it is no longer I who live, but Christ who lives in me" (Gal 2:19b–20a), I hear the voice of one who styles himself as a slave of Christ (e.g., Gal 1:10). For Paul, the pneumatic exchange of baptism effects a radical relationality. However, as Bazzana's ethnographic analysis suggests, this relationality is defined not by mutual reciprocity but by the hierarchical patterning of enslavement.

We might aptly use the Deleuzian term *assemblage* to characterize Paul's sense of his transcorporeal identification with Christ—but with the caveat that this is a despotic assemblage. We might also imagine Paul as a "sharer in the life" of Christ, recalling, in a disturbing way, a phrase Aristotle used to define the relationship of slave to master (κοινωνὸς ζωῆς; *Pol.* 1260a). Aristotle's theory of natural slavery does not seem to have been well known in the Roman Empire (Garnsey 1996, 11–16; de Wet 2015, 26–34). However, given its later impact on philosophical musing about what it means to be human, I would like to linger with the implications of Aristotle's phrasing, which has been problematically taken up by Giorgio Agamben in his account of what he calls anthropogenesis, the becoming human of the human being. Agamben (2016, 13) characterizes Aristotle's reference to the slave sharing the life of his master as "a 'community of life' between slave and master"—but Aristotle does not actually use the phrase "community of life" (i.e., κοινωνία ζωῆς). In the *Eudemian Ethics*, Aristotle insists that because the slave is part of the slaveholder, there can be no community or association (κοινωνία) between them. In Aristotle's view, slave and slaver are a unity—not two but one, the slave subsumed in the slaver (*Eth. eud.* 1241b). As Buell (2019, 209) writes about early Christian discourse, the radical sharing expressed in the term κοινωνία connotes "not a unity but a commingled new pluriform fabrication"—precisely what Aristotle denies in his contention that the slave is a sharer in the master's life. The trope of the enslaved apostle advances the pernicious fiction of the slave fully incorporated into the life of the master.

Drawing on both Aristotle and Paul, Agamben (2016, 78) contends that the "archaic nucleus of slavery" is a community of life defined by use rather than ownership, a zone of indifference between the body of the master and the body of the slave (for critique, see Glancy 2020). Agamben leaves no room to acknowledge the zone of difference between using and being used, the space of domination. In a pithy way, Mitzi Smith gets right what Agamben gets wrong about use. Observing that slavery relied on the "unbridled use of slave bodies," she writes, "When Paul returns … Onesimus to Philemon as one who was once 'useless' (*achrēston*) and is now 'useful' (*euchrēston*), the language of utility he employs reflects a shared language and culture regarding the expectations slave owners had of slaves" (M. Smith 2012, 48). Like Aristotle and Agamben, Smith recognizes that slavery is defined by the use of bodies, yet in her analysis it is clear that slavery compels the use of bodies: "Slave masters controlled slaves' bodies for their usefulness and productivity" (48).

This article explores what is ontologically at stake when we mistake domination for mutual use. Possessed by the *pneuma* of Christ, Paul claims that his will has been negated and overwritten by the will of his master. Such surrender or absence of will conforms to Aristotle's understanding of the slave—the two shall become one, and that one is the master. Paul's representation of himself as slave contributes to the material history of the category of slave, but the genre of letter writing does not allow us fully to trace the consequences of what it might mean to construe the life of an enslaved person as a sharing in the life of the master. I thus explore those consequences through analysis of a narrative about another enslaved apostle: the episodic third-century Acts of Thomas.

Slave of Master Jesus, Thomas is also the master's twin; the two at times are mistaken for each other in the Acts. Within the narrative, I argue, apprehension of Thomas as twin is ultimately indistinguishable from apprehension of Thomas as slave. Some scholars perceive censure of the institution of slavery in Acts of Thomas (Perkins 2005), but such disapproval is glancing and subordinated to the thoroughgoing logic of slavery that is the very fabric of the work (Glancy 2012; de Wet 2018, 13–21; Kartzow 2018, 125–44). Chris de Wet (2018, 8) has coined the useful neologism *doulology* to characterize the discourse of slavery and its impact on the most basic structures of ancient Christian thought, the degree to which Christians used "slavery and mastery to make sense of their own position in the world and society, and to better understand their relationship with God, the self, and others." Few texts employ doulology as central to a storyline as the Acts of Thomas. The transcorporeal but asymmetric identification of enslaved apostle with master underscores the urgency of accounting for the impact of inequality, coercion, and violence in our articulations of relational ontology. I understand that relational ontology typically places the human among nonhuman forces; my focus is rather on the distribution of power in human relationships that destabilize the sovereign self, leaving us radically open to each other.

On Being the Property of Master Christ

The opening scene of Acts of Thomas finds the apostles gathered in Jerusalem dividing the regions of the world into missionary districts.[2] Judas Thomas, also identified as Didymos (Δίδυμος), meaning Double or Twin, rejects his assignment of India. He argues that as a Hebrew he will not be effective in proclaiming the truth to the Indians. Even an apparition of the Savior fails to convince Thomas to accept his allotment. That is, until Thomas is sold to a traveling merchant by the Savior Jesus, who writes out a bill of sale. When the merchant asks Judas if Jesus is his master (δεσπότης), Judas affirms that Jesus is his master (κύριος; Acts Thom. 9–10).[3] This act of sale is key to the narrative, as the enslaved apostle surrenders his will and identity to the benignly despotic Jesus.

The Acts of Thomas is similar in style to other extracanonical works known collectively as the Apocryphal Acts of the Apostles, each of which focuses on the exploits, ascetic preaching, and travails of an apostle or other disciple of Jesus. Manuscripts divide Acts of Thomas into thirteen acts. Act 1 continues with Thomas traveling to India in the company of the merchant who arranges to purchase him on behalf of Gundafar, an Indian king. In act 2, Thomas endures imprisonment for embezzlement before Gundafar comes to understand that the enslaved carpenter has used the king's funds to build not an earthly but a heavenly palace. Acts 3 through 8 feature tales of exorcisms, wondrous deeds, and talking animals. Although acts 7 and 8 similarly focus on exorcism and talking animals, they also introduce the cast of characters who populate the rest of the work, including a military commander named Sifor who prevails on Thomas to help his demon-possessed wife and daughter. In acts 9 through 13, the apostle converts and baptizes a series of noblewomen and noblemen in the orbit of King Mizdai, whom Sifor serves. The most extended subplot revolves around a noblewoman named Mygdonia. The Acts of Thomas culminates with the martyrdom of the apostle.

By the end of act 2, the narrative largely loses interest in Thomas's enslavement to Gundafar, yet both those who are loyal to him and those

---

2. My translations are based on Bonnet's Greek text of the Acts of Thomas (Lipsius and Bonnett 1990, 2:99–291). I have consulted and at times adapted two standard English translations, Elliott 1993 and Attridge 2010. I have also consulted Klijn's commentary on the Syriac text (2003).

3. Attridge seems to read "my lord [κύριος]" (2010, 18).

who are suspicious of him continue to refer to him as a slave. In act 4 a talking ass emphasizes that Thomas had been sold as a slave (Acts Thom. 39); in act 5 a woman from whom Thomas expels a demon hails Thomas as both apostle and slave of God (42); and in act 6 those whom he has healed acknowledge him as Jesus's apostle and slave (59). The motif persists in the narrative's later acts. Carish, husband of the noblewoman Mygdonia, worries that his rival Thomas may be a fugitive slave (100). In an interrogation leading to his execution, Thomas responds to King Mizdai's question of whether he is free or slave by identifying himself as the slave of one over whom the king is powerless (163). Thomas repeatedly refers to himself as slave of God or of Christ (139, 141, 146, 160). In a gloss on Matt 25:31–46, he also seems to allude to his enslavement to King Gundafar, declaring that he had become poor and a stranger and a slave and a prisoner, hungry and thirsty and naked (145). Although episodes in the Acts of Thomas are often only loosely connected in terms of plot, recurring emphasis on Thomas as slave lends a thematic coherence to the work.

Jesus uses Thomas's body in a way that anticipates Agamben's speculation about the aboriginal nub of slavery in a community of life, to which we have already alluded. More fully, Agamben hypothesizes that:

> The master/slave relation as we know it represents the capture in its juridical order of the use of bodies as an originary prejudicial relation.... In use, the subjects whom we call master and slave are in such a "community of life" that the juridical definition of their relationship in terms of property is rendered necessary, almost as if otherwise they would slide into a confusion and *kononia tes zoes* [sic] that the juridical order cannot admit except in the striking and despotic intimacy between master and slave. (2016, 39)

Imagining mutual use rather than domination as the heart of slavery, Agamben denies the vector of brutality inherent to slavery. Although use in the Acts of Thomas is not represented as brutal, it is, I argue, largely unidirectional. Moreover, Thomas's willing subjugation of his own will to the will of Jesus glosses over the violence constitutive of the act of enslavement. It is thus helpful to keep in mind Aristotle's actual wording—not that there is a community of life between slaver and enslaved, but that the slave is a sharer in the life of the master. While Aristotle's formulation offers a grossly problematic take on historical relations of slaving, it nonetheless capsulizes the disturbing metaphor of enslaved apostle, which is developed into a narrative in the Acts of Thomas.

What, precisely, does it mean for a person to be the property of Christ or, for that matter, to be the property of a human master? A passage in which a crowd weeps and begs for forgiveness offers a clue. Confessing past misdeeds to Thomas, they say, "We dare not say that we are his [ὅτι αὐτοῦ ἐσμεν], (belonging) to that God you proclaim" (38). They aspire to become his property. If Jesus will only free them from the evils they have done, they promise, "we shall become his servants [θεράποντες] and we shall do his will to the end" (38). On the view of those who attend to the apostle's words, to be a servant or slave is implicitly to do the will of a master. Thomas is not Jesus's only possession, but the apostle's subordination of his own will qualifies him as a model asset, an ownable thing. What is at stake in the representation of Thomas as one who has "accepted the master's wishes so fully that the slave's innermost self could anticipate the master's wishes," to echo Harrill's (2006, 21) summation of Paul's self-representation as slave? I would argue that the slave's putative forfeiture of will is key to understanding what may be most peculiar in the notion of human property: the assimilation of human beings to things.[4]

Despite the categorization of slaves as property and thus as things by Roman law, the perception of humans as mere things is difficult to sustain on practical terms when, for example, assigning liability for criminal conduct or other perceived misconduct. In his taxonomy of Roman slave law, W. W. Buckland (1908, ix) includes sections on "The Slave as *Res* [Thing]" and "The Slave as Man," with "Criminal Slaves" being a subcategory of the latter. In parallel fashion, Ariela Gross (2006) examines courtroom scenes from the antebellum American South where courts reckoned with the independent wills of enslaved persons. An enslaved person's exertion of will had the potential to disrupt the smooth functioning of system of property predicated on the fantasy that a human being was a thing, the fantasy that a *homo* was a mere *res*. As literary and cultural critic Saidiya Hartman (1997, 82) concludes about slaving in the Americas, "The slave was recognized as a reasoning subject who possessed intent and rationality solely in the context of criminal liability; ironically, the slave's will was acknowledged only as it was prohibited or punished."

Scholars generally recognize Thomas's surrender of will as central to the text's depiction of the apostle as slave (Attridge 1997, 114; Pesthy 2001,

---

4. Thomas does not refer to himself in the singular as a possession of Jesus. However, as he returns to prison after an interlude away, he thanks God who "saved your possessions [τὰ σὰ κτήματα] from evil" (122).

69; Hartin 2006, 243–44; cf. Kartzow 2018, 127), yet with little attention to the troubling implications of defining slavery in terms of erasure of will. The enslaved Judas Thomas exemplifies the slaver's *fantasy* of slave as property, defined exclusively in terms of his relationship to his master, thing-like inasmuch as he lacks a will apart from that of his master. Within the narrative, the first words Thomas speaks in his persona as slave are addressed to his master, Jesus. Promising to go where Jesus sends him, he adds, "Your will be done" (3), repeated with variation multiple times in the narrative. The only hint that Thomas might be motivated by fear to submit to his master's will comes from a demon who likens his own situation to that of the apostle. The demon comments that Thomas will be disciplined if he fails to do the will of the one who sent him. In a similar vein, the demon suggests, he expects punishment if he ignores the will of the one who sent him (76). Whether the reader is supposed to accept this assessment is unclear—perhaps the demon fails to understand that Jesus is the kind of master who would never use force to achieve control, or perhaps the demon is willing to speak a truth about which the text is otherwise silent.

Not only does Thomas repeatedly speak the words, "Your will be done" (3, 30, 144), but he is also identified by the talkative ass as one "who does the will of him who sent him" (79). In a passage shortly before the account of his martyrdom, Thomas weaves together a number of allusions to Jesus's parables, comparing himself to the slaves represented there (146). Like the faithful slaves entrusted with talents, he has brought Jesus a good return on his investment (Matt 25:14–30; Luke 19:11–27). Unlike the slave who punished a fellow slave who neglected to pay a debt (Matt 18:21–35), Thomas has forgiven those in debt to him. Waiting for his master (δεσπότης) to return from a wedding banquet, he kept his lamp lit (Luke 12:35–40). "I have fulfilled your will," Thomas then declares, likening himself to the industrious slave who kept an all-night vigil against intruders (Acts Thom. 146). The apostle's will is thoroughly dominated by the master's, the radical relationality between Thomas and Jesus played out at the level of volition. Seeming to lack a will of his own, Thomas is thingified, a model slave ready to be used by Jesus at his pleasure.

Yet it is not so at the start of the narrative.

On Becoming Property

In the opening scene of the Acts of Thomas, we briefly glimpse a self-willed apostle. Rejecting his mission assignment, Thomas expresses an independent volition. When the Savior appears to him and orders him to go to India, Thomas disobeys (οὐκ ἐπείθετο)—*I am not going to the Indians!* (1). In a very different context, bioethicist Muireann Quigley (2018, 228) argues that "acting *as if* one lacks free will is not the same as actually lacking it." Quigley is not addressing the issue of slavery, but she is addressing the question of what it means to conceive oneself as property. Does Thomas lack his own will, or does he only behave as though he does? In several scenes, Jesus seems able to use Thomas without the apostle's cognizance, implying that the enslaved apostle has been conscripted as a unique embodiment of his master's will. The moment of sale marks Thomas's transformation into a biddable slave, his own will subsumed, a performance that plays out again and again throughout the narrative.

As the apostles congregate to parcel out mission territories in the very first scene, it is understood that each will "go to the nation to which the Master [Κύριος] had sent him" (1). If Christ is the Κύριος, then presumably all the apostles, including Thomas, could be understood as his δοῦλοι, his slaves. Yet it is not until the moment that his master sells him that the implications of that enslavement are felt for either Thomas or the reader. As the story unfolds, Thomas is identified by himself and by those he encounters as one who has been sold. He is not only a slave but also a slave who has been marketed (not all slaves were). On one level, of course, the sale of Thomas propels the plot, as the apostle embarks on his forced migration eastward. On another level, however, the moment of sale is an important juncture in enacting the relationship of Jesus and Thomas as despotic assemblage, for assemblage is a process rather than a state of being. The Acts of Thomas lingers on the sale with repetitive, emphatic references to buying and selling. The merchant who handles the transaction is introduced by noting he had been deputized by King Gundafar to buy and bring back a carpenter. Divining the merchant's purpose, Jesus initiates a conversation—does he wish to buy a carpenter? Because, Master Jesus explains, he has a slave he wishes to sell. A sale price is negotiated. Not only is the bill of sale mentioned, but its contents are spelled out: "I, Jesus, son of the carpenter Joseph, agree to sell my slave, Judas by name, to you, Chaban, a merchant of Gundafar, king of the Indians" (2). Deed of sale completed, the merchant approaches Judas Thomas.

Whatever the relationship between a slaveholder and an enslaved person might otherwise be, at the moment of sale the slave is commodified and treated as thing. At that point, it is clear that from the master's perspective there is no conceivable κοινωνία with the slave. Historians of

American slavery have identified the point of sale as a time when enslaved persons were forced to confront their classification as property, their worth itemized in dollars and rendered exchangeable for other material goods (Berry 2017; Gross 2006, 42, 51). Paradoxically, however, a sale might nonetheless depend on the active and even creative participation of the enslaved to personify the kind of merchandise sought by the potential purchaser. American historian Walter Johnson (1999, 16) contends that slave traders were ultimately "forced to rely on the slaves to sell themselves, to act as they had been advertised to be." As a result, Johnson explains, a slave might in some contexts exploit the situation to his or her own advantage: "In the way they answered questions, characterized their skills, and carried their bodies—in the way they performed their commodification—slaves could use the information unwittingly provided them by the traders' preparations and the buyers' examinations to select the best among the poisoned outcomes." Johnson quotes the formerly enslaved John Parker, "I made up my mind I was going to select my master" (179).

The sale of Judas Thomas by Master Jesus likewise turns on the apostle's willing performance of his own commodification. Thomas's buyer checks that the individual offered for sale is indeed a slave—the merchant confirms Thomas's eligibility for sale by asking, "Is this your master [δεσπότης]?" Thomas's confirmation that Jesus is his master (κύριος) is an avowal of faith made without insight into how the merchant would take that confession. However, when the merchant announces, "I have bought you from him," Thomas remains still (2). Confronted with commodification at point of sale, Thomas acquiesces, submissively performing his identity as obedient slave.

From beginning to end, the Acts of Thomas never loses sight of Jesus as slave (de Wet 2018, 16). Equally strikingly, having begun with a scene of sale, when the text meanders to a close it returns to identification of Thomas as a slave who has been sold, his commodification somehow integral to his identity, a moment of thing-ification that must be repeated to maintain the fiction of despotic assemblage. Just as Thomas is identified as one who is sold, Jesus is known as the one who sold him, as Thomas tells a crowd of believers as he heads to imprisonment before his execution: "I go up to my Master and God Jesus Christ, to the one who sold me" (Acts Thom. 159).[5] But who actually sold Thomas? On the way to prison while

---

5. Some manuscripts read, "I go up to my Master and God Jesus Christ, to the one who *sent* me" (rather than "to the one who *sold* me"); I am not concerned to establish the earlier reading.

King Mizdai considers his fate, Thomas pauses to praise Jesus, whom he calls "the manumitter of my soul," adding, "because I gave myself to be sold" (142).[6] The moment of Thomas's sale marks a turning point in his identity. Before the sale, Thomas is self-willed. All the self-possessed apostle needed do to derail the deal was identify himself as a legally free man. He does not do so. From that point in the narrative, he submits single-mindedly to the will of his master. Surrendering his will, the formerly strong-willed apostle comes to personify the archetype of slave as property. Lacking his own will, he is Jesus's second, his double—his twin.

Despotic Assemblage

The epithet used to introduced Judas Thomas in the Acts of Thomas— "Didymos" (Δίδυμος), Double or Twin—is a common appellation for the apostle in early Christian literature. The designation positions Thomas as confidante of Jesus and custodian of secret revelation. In the Acts of Thomas, the apostle is more frequently named as Jesus's slave than his twin. Monika Pesthy (2001, 72) suggests that "the twin motif emphasizes the identity of the two [Jesus and Judas Thomas], the slave motif emphasizes their difference." I disagree, holding instead with Harold Attridge (1997, 115), who writes, "The ways in which Thomas imitates Jesus as his twin and slave are manifold." This is in part because Christ himself could be understood as a slave. When the first of the verbal asses addresses Thomas as "Twin of Christ," he continues, "You who though free became a slave" (39), a parallel to the downward, self-emptying movement in the Philippians hymn where Jesus, though in the form of God, takes the form of a slave, in human likeness (Phil 2:6–7). Yet the connection between Thomas as slave and Thomas as twin is even more profound than the talky ass proposes.

As slave of Christ, Thomas is the slave of a slave, a role for which Latin has a specific term, *uicārius*, used specifically of a slave another slave purchases to do his work, used by extension of a substitute, a person who acts in the place of another. Thomas acts precisely in a vicarious role. The relationship is not reciprocal—the enslaved apostle is *used by* the Master Christ, who does not in turn act at Thomas's behest. Both as slave and as twin, Thomas is Jesus's double, his surrogate body, as Marianne Kartzow

---

6. "Manumitter of my soul" is de Wet's (2018, 17) translation.

(2018, 127) observes: "Thomas, as a real slave, is somehow identified with his master." That identification is extreme, their relationality being radical but asymmetric. The two serve as stand-ins for each other, at least in some contexts—each is reported to undergo changes in appearance, so presumably they do not always resemble each other.[7] As it happens, Thomas is the first to alter in visage (Acts Thom. 8), yet he does not seem able to reshape himself at will. The apostle's body is not his own; Jesus occupies the body and identity of the slave who is his understudy, his vicarious agent.

Along with the text's initial mention of Thomas as Δίδυμος, two other passages explicitly name him Christ's double. A demon refers to him as "twin [δίδυμος] of the Christ who always destroys our nature" (31). As twin, Thomas is also slave—a talking ass who greets him as "twin [δίδυμος] of Christ" elaborates, "who being free became a slave and was sold in order to lead many to freedom" (39). Thomas's own declaration that "I am not Jesus but his slave" (160) is elsewhere paralleled by Jesus's declaration: "I am not Judas Thomas; I am his brother" (11). Jesus makes this declaration to explain his presence in the nuptial chamber of the daughter of the king of Andrapolis, where Thomas had stopped en route to India. At the invitation of the king of Andrapolis, who has heard that Thomas is a prophet, the apostle blesses the bride and groom—no small challenge for one with negative views on marriage and reproduction! After he prays and departs the chamber, Jesus assumes his place. The groom sees Master Jesus, "having the semblance [τὴν ἀπεικασίαν] of Judas Thomas," talking to his bride (11). By the end of the scene, husband and wife swear to live in mutual celibacy.

Are Jesus and Thomas identical twins and therefore indistinguishable? Even within the scene of the nuptial chamber, the matter is more complicated. Jesus appears after Thomas's departure, having apparently materialized out of nowhere or walked through a wall, an ability akin to Jesus's capabilities in the resurrection accounts of the canonical gospels. Able to appear in the guise of Judas Thomas and in other guises as well, Jesus is polymorphous (πολύμορφος; 45, 153). As Gundafar and his brother Gad await full initiation—the sealing of the seal—they are able to hear the Master's voice but not yet see his visible aspect (τὸ εἶδος; 27). The linguistically gifted wild ass praises Jesus's divinity, "which appeared on our behalf

---

7. I argue elsewhere that in the Acts of Thomas both polymorphy and racial/ethnic mutability serve as vehicles for the construction of Christian identity, a peculiar identity with alterity at its heart (Glancy, 2019).

in the semblance of human beings" (δόξα τῇ θεότητί σου ἣ δι' ἡμᾶς εἰς ἀπεικασίαν ἀνθρώπων ὤφθη), then continues by praising Jesus's "humanity, which died on our behalf" (δόξα τῇ ἀνθρωπότητί σου, ἥτις δὶ ἡμᾶς ἀπεθανεν; 80). Despite being polymorphous himself, a demon complains that Jesus deceived demonic forces by appearing in a raggedy form (τῇ μορφῇ αὐτοῦ τῇ δυσειδεστάτῃ; 45). Recalling the transfiguration, Thomas comments, "His appearance [θέαν] we saw transformed before our eyes, but his heavenly archetype [τὸν δὲ τύπον αὐτοῦ τὸν οὐράνιον] we were unable to see on the mountain" (143). Jesus confuses even his twin when he appears as Thomas to usher the noblewoman Mygdonia and other women into the prison where Thomas is incarcerated, eliciting from the apostle the exclamation, "Glory to you, polymorphous Jesus!" (151–53).

To say that Jesus is able to pass himself off as Thomas because they are twins is thus insufficient; their relationality is hierarchically patterned. Thomas does not seem able to present himself as Jesus in a reciprocal way. An exception may be scene where Mygdonia fails to recognize Thomas because he is surrounded by a great light (118), light elsewhere associated with the presence of Jesus (27, 153). However, even this example is tenuous, as there is no indication that Thomas wills himself to be bathed in luminosity. In contrast, the polymorphous master appears in the guise of Thomas when it suits his purposes, his annexation of the apostle's persona a twist on a standard assumption of Roman law that a slaveholder is able to act through the body of his or her slave. Roman law recognized an enslaved person as a *persōna*, a person, but at the same time denied the slave certain aspects of *persōna* as legal personality—notably, the legal capability to own property (Nicholas 1962, 60–61; compare Patterson 1982, 28).

Roman law specified that the slaveholder could acquire a possession through his own intent (*animo*) and the body (*corpore*) of a slave (Dig. 41.2.3.12). Even when not visually doubled, Jesus operates in such a manner through Thomas, as the apostle tells a group of believers: "The Master wishes to accomplish something through me today. Let us pray … that his purpose and will may be realized through us" (κατὰ τὸ αὐτοῦ βούλημα καὶ θέλημα γένηται δι' ἡμῶν; Acts Thom. 29). These are the words, perhaps, of any Christian, but also quintessentially the words a master might hope to exact from a slave. What the master consistently intends to accomplish through Judas Thomas is to attract more believers, the master's dearly bought possessions (72). When Jesus appears as Thomas, he appropriates his slave's body in a more literal sense, treating that body as an extension of himself. Jesus uses the apostle's body. Judas Thomas does not use his master's body. The ongoing work of despotic assemblage requires the subordination of Thomas's being.

Although the demon who hails Thomas as slave of Jesus Christ demands to know why the apostle has become like (ἐξομοιοῦσαι) the son of God, the resemblance is not under Thomas's control (45). In a story in which Thomas is instrumental in restoring a woman to life, she asks him where his associate is—perhaps we could colloquially render it as his other half (ποῦ ἐστιν ἐκεῖνος ὁ ἄλλος ὁ συνών σοι; 54). When he in turn asks to hear her tale, she is confused as she perceives Thomas to have been present with her at the conclusion of a tour of hell. She explains that her odious guide expressed fear of the one who had instructed him both to lead the woman through hell and to restore her safely. The woman concludes the narrative of her tour of hell by stating that "the one like you" (ὁ δέ σοι ὅμοις) had given her into Thomas's care, even though Thomas seems to be learning of these events for the first time (57).

An episode about a young man whom Thomas restores to life affords parallel insight into the dynamics between Jesus and his doppelgänger. Claiming that Thomas has two forms (δύο μορφὰς ἔχων; 34), the youth insists that he saw another man by the apostle's side, an unnamed companion who explicitly claimed Thomas as his vicarious agent. According to the young man, the companion informed Thomas, "I have many wonders to make known through you and many great deeds to complete through you" (34). The anonymous confederate then directed Thomas to restore the youth to life. As in the episode with the woman returned from hell, Thomas seems to have completed a commission of which he was not even aware. The young man asserts that Thomas can be found where he wills to be, but he is mistaken. It is not the enslaved apostle who can appear at will, but his master, Jesus. Thomas is able to function as Jesus's double precisely because he is Jesus's slave, his master pursuing his own intent through the use of Thomas's body. Destabilizing any sense that the apostle might be a knowing sovereign subject, the doubling of Jesus and Judas Thomas confirms the sovereignty of his master.

Conclusions

Janet Spittler (2011, 207) argues that, although the Acts of Thomas stresses the corruptibility of bodies both physically and morally and anticipates the separation of body and soul at death, during a person's lifetime health of body is perceived to be closely aligned to health of soul, Jesus being the physician of bodies as well as souls. A body can be the habitation of a heavenly gift and the abode of God's *pneuma*. Preparing some followers for baptism, the apostle prays, "Make them your holy temples and let your holy spirit dwell in them" (Acts Thom. 156). This is one version of an assemblage, a pluriform sharing of a life that is not limited to a human plane. But heeding Jackson's (2020, 121) call for "the material histories of our categories, as they are given shape and vitality by way of, and inside of, organismic bodies," we cannot stop there. Given the centrality of slavery to the storyline of Acts of Thomas, we might also view the possession of body by spirit, by *pneuma*, as an aggressive occupation and a despotic assemblage. Drawing on Bazzana's work on spirit possession and the Pauline corpus, this is the lens I offered earlier in this essay to understand Paul's self-positioning as slave to Christ.

Buell's assessment of relational ontology in Ephesians offers an apt parallel. She draws attention to the ways that hierarchical intrahuman relationships and hierarchical human-divine relations of power mimic each other. "Each individual human is understood to be vulnerable to and instrumentally linked to a divine or demonic non-human power, whose agency gets expressed through the human. Each human seems to be accountable to their response to non-human powers but not as equal parties to the non-human parties" (Buell 2017, 470). For the purpose of extrapolation, a paraphrase: Thomas is understood to be vulnerable to and instrumentally linked to Master Jesus. Thomas is accountable in his response to a more than human power, but they are hardly equal parties.

In the Acts of Thomas, Master Jesus not only dominates Thomas's will. He also inhabits the enslaved apostle's body. In a number of episodes, it is unclear, sometimes even to Thomas, who is acting: master or slave or a despotic assemblage. This narrative construction of transcorporeality troubles distinctions between self and other, suggesting that selfhood is inevitably permeable. There is a sense of open potential with the realization of our porosity—we complete each other in ways that are expansive, that allow us to become more than we are (in a "we" that is not only human). Because I am concerned with the material entanglement of categories of slavery, however, I concentrate on the dynamics of domination within relational ontologies. An intense and asymmetric transcorporeality is exemplified in a troubling manner in the Acts of Thomas, where Thomas's body is available for his master's use.

Works Cited

Agamben, Giorgio. 2005. *The Time That Remains: A Commentary on the Letter to the Romans*. Translated by Patricia Dailey. Meridian: Crossing Aesthetics. Stanford: Stanford University Press.

———. 2016. *The Use of Bodies*. Vol. 4.2 of *Homo Sacer*. Translated by Adam Kotsko. Meridian: Crossing Boundaries. Stanford, CA: Stanford University Press.

Attridge, Harold A. 1997. "Intertextuality in the Acts of Thomas." *Semeia* 80:87–124.

———. 2010. *The Acts of Thomas*. Early Christian Apocrypha 3. Salem, OR: Polebridge.

Bazzana, Giovanni B. 2020. *Having the Spirit of Christ: Spirit Possession and Exorcism in the Early Christ Groups*. Synkrisis. New Haven: Yale University Press.

Berry, Daina Ramey. 2017. *The Price for Their Pound of Flesh: The Value of the Enslaved, from Womb to Grave, in the Building of a Nation*. Boston: Beacon.

Buckland, W. W. 1908. *The Roman Law of Slavery: The Condition of the Slave in Private Law from Augustine to Justinian*. Cambridge: Cambridge University Press.

Buell, Denise Kimber. 2014. "The Microbes and Pneuma That Therefore I Am." Pages 63–87 in *Divinanimality: Animal Theory, Creaturely Theology*. Edited by Stephen D. Moore. New York: Fordham University Press.

———. 2017. "Embodied Temporalities: Health, Illness, and the Matter of Feminist Biblical Interpretation." Pages 454–76 in *The Bible and Feminism: Remapping the Field*. Edited by Yvonne Sherwood with Anna Fisk. Oxford: Oxford University Press.

———. 2019. "Posthumanism." Pages 197–218 in *The Oxford Handbook of New Testament, Gender, and Sexuality*. Edited by Benjamin H. Dunning. Oxford: Oxford University Press.

Elliott, J. K. 1993. "The Acts of Thomas." Pages 439–511 in *The Apocryphal New Testament: A Collection of Apocryphal Christian Literature in an English Translation based on M. R. James*. Oxford: Clarendon.

Garnsey, Peter. 1996. *Ideas of Slavery from Augustine to Augustine*. W. B. Stanford Memorial Lectures. Cambridge: Cambridge University Press.

Glancy, Jennifer A. 2012. "Slavery in *Acts of Thomas*." *Journal of Early Christian History* 2:3–21.

———. 2019. "Alienated Identity in Acts of Thomas." Pages 73–90 in *The Narrative Self in Early Christianity: Essays in Honor of Judith Perkins*. Edited by Janet E. Spittler. WGRWSup 15. Atlanta: SBL Press.

———. 2020. "On Agamben's Slave without Slavery." *Diacritics* 48.4–26.

Gross, Ariela J. 2006. *Double Character: Slavery and Mastery in the Antebellum Southern Courtroom*. Studies in the Legal History of the South. Athens: University of Georgia Press.

Harrill, J. Albert. 2006. *Slaves in the New Testament: Literary, Social, and Moral Dimensions*. Minneapolis: Fortress.

Hartin, Patrick J. 2006. "The Character of Thomas in the *Acts of Thomas*." Pages 239–53 in *Thomasine Traditions in Antiquity: The Social and Cultural World of the Gospel of Thomas*. Edited by Jon Ma. Asgeirsson, April D. DeConick, and Risto Uro. Nag Hammadi & Manichaean Studies 59. Leiden: Brill.

Hartman, Saidiya. 1997. *Scenes of Subjection: Terror, Slavery, and Self-Making in Nineteenth-Century America*. Race and American Culture. Oxford: Oxford University Press.

Jackson, Zakkiyah Iman. 2020. *Becoming Human: Matter and Meaning in an Antiblack World*. Sexual Cultures. New York: New York University Press.

Johnson, Walter. 1999. *Soul by Soul: Life inside the Antebellum Slave Market*. Cambridge: Harvard University Press.

Kartzow, Marianne Bjelland. 2018. *The Slave Metaphor and Gendered Enslavement in Early Christian Literature: Double Trouble Embodied*. Routledge Studies in the Early Christian World. London: Routledge.

Klijn, A. F. J. 2003. *The Acts of Thomas: Introduction, Text, and Commentary*. 2nd rev. ed. Leiden: Brill.

Lipsius, Richard A., and Max Bonnett, eds. 1990. *Acta Apostolorum Apocrypha*. 2 parts in 3 vols. New York: Hildesheim.

Nicholas, Barry. 1962. *An Introduction to Roman Law*. Clarendon Law Series. Oxford: Clarendon.

Patterson, Orlando. 1982. *Slavery as Social Death: A Comparative Study*. Cambridge: Harvard University Press.

Perkins, Judith. 2005. "Animal Voices." *R&T* 12:385–96.

Pesthy, Monika. 2001. "Thomas, the Slave of the Lord." Pages 65–73 in *The Apocryphal Acts of Thomas*. Edited by Jan N. Bremmer. Studies in Early Christian Apocrypha 6. Leuven: Peeters.

Quigley, Muireann. 2018. *Self-Ownership, Property Rights, and the Human Body: A Legal and Philosophical Analysis*. Cambridge Bioethics and Law 43. Cambridge: Cambridge University Press.

Smith, Mitzi. 2012. "Utility, Fraternity, and Reconciliation: Ancient Slavery as a Context for the Return of Onesimus." Pages 47–58 in *Onesimus Our Brother: Reading Religion, Race, and Culture in Philemon*. Edited by Matthew V. Johnson, James A. Noel, and Demetrius K. Williams. Minneapolis: Fortress.

Spittler, Janet E. 2011. "The Anthropology of Acts of Thomas." Pages 203–16 in *Christian Body, Christian Self: Concepts of Early Christian Personhood*. Edited by Clare Rothschild and Trevor Thompson. WUNT 284. Tübingen: Mohr Siebeck.

Wet, Chris L. de. 2018. *The Unbound God: Slavery and the Formation of Early Christian Thought*. London: Routledge.

Visualizing Oppression: Slavery and the Arts of Domination

Abraham Smith

> Monuments to the "lost cause" will prove monuments of folly, both in the memories of a wicked rebellion which they must necessarily perpetuate, and in the failure to accomplish the particular purpose had in view by those who built them.
> —Frederick Douglass, "Monuments of Folly," 1870

In *Domination and the Arts of Resistance*, James C. Scott (1992, xii–xiii) argues that the public transcript—the relations of power operative in public—mask the hidden transcripts of both the weak, who strategically show deference in public though they are more defiant backstage, and the powerful, who also follow a performance script in public though they may actually suspect that the subordinates are putting on an act on the public stage. This essay, however, seeks to examine the arts of domination, especially the servile imagery and visual technologies of power that Roman elites deployed to complement literary affirmations of power in Roman public and private spaces. The objective, though, is not merely to document Rome's arts as yet another focal point in the history of scholarship on ancient slavery. Rather, the ultimate objective is to understand the weight even today of metaphors and monuments that visually divide the world into the binary trap of the conquerors and the conquered.

To make this argument about the visual productions of oppression, this essay will proceed in three steps. First, as grounding for yet another study of ancient Roman slavery, the essay offers an extended overview on the history of studies of ancient slavery and especially Roman slavery in antiquity. The history will examine the works of influential Roman classicists, comparative theorists (some of whom were also classicists), and

New Testament scholars for the contributions they have made to the study of Roman slavery.

As this study of Roman slavery will demonstrate, however, ancient Greek and Roman societies were both slave societies *and* patriarchies (Joshel and Murnaghan 1998, 2–3), and thus the construction of both slaves and women as inferior outgroups also played a role in constructing an elite masculinist ideal. According to Aristotle, whose moral postulates and stereotypes were not discursive outliers, both outgroups by nature were deficient supplements to a constructed masculine ideal and thus did not possess the ability to deliberate at all (as in the case of the enslaved) or sufficiently (as in the case of free women) to warrant their participation in political life (*Pol.* 1260a4–1260b8; 1277b33–1278a40; cf. Knust 2005, 27). Both outgroups were also stereotyped as morally inferior and deceitful, if not also dangerous, and therefore in need of constant surveillance and domination by the elite citizen (native) males of Greek or Roman societies (Joshel and Murnaghan 1998, 12–16).

In differing ways, based on the particularities of the intersecting markers of their assigned status, both were also sexually vulnerable and thus assigned in sexual liaisons the role of passive parties to be penetrated by the same elite citizen (native) males (Joshel and Murnaghan 1998, 4). By contrast, the self-construction of such elite males depended on their ability to dissociate themselves from any servile or feminine traces that might challenge the "social recognition" they otherwise publicly strove to gain through their deportment in ongoing contests of masculinity operative in their world (Burke 2013, 68, 71). Such elite males were inclined then to discipline the gait of their walk (Cicero, *Off.* 1.128–129; Seneca the Younger, *Ep.* 52.12), the intonations of their voices (Rhet. Her. 3.12.22; Seneca the Elder, *Contr.* 1, praef. 8–9, 10; Seneca the Younger, *Ep.* 52.12), the adornment of their hair (Seneca the Elder, *Contr.* 1, praef. 9), and the appearance of their attire (Ovid, *Ars* 1.509–522; Quintilian, *Inst.* 5.9.14; Cicero, *Cat.* 2.22) lest an actual deviation from the prevailing—even if contested—codes of masculinity or even an implied deviance wielded rhetorically through slander make them subject to condemnation for such slippage (Knust 2005, 35; Burke 2013, 71, 83).

Second, with a focus on visual technologies of power, the essay will note how Roman elites blended metaphorical remarks on Roman mastery (and gender) with visual imagery that appeared in arches and columns. Thus, Roman elites deployed what Davina Lopez (2016, 273–96) has called "monumental logics" or what may also be called "visual imperialism"

(Kuehnast 1992, 183-95). Such logics—with history monumentalized in places—were a part of the Roman collective memory, but such memory did not simply reflect reality (Cicero, *Fin.* 5.2.). Rather, it constructed a truth that was important to Roman elites as they assayed to promote or warrant imperialistic goals. What is also true is that the constructed truth is attached as much to texts as to monuments. As Andrew B. Gallia (2012, 7) has noted, "because cultural memory ... is inscribed in monuments and texts, it often presents the rememberer with certain fixed points that are difficult to tamper with or redefine, however inconvenient it may be."

Third, given that the elites of any age or place have access to their own brands of visual power technologies, the essay will examine one modern production of visual power technologies that might be compared to Rome's "monumental logics" (Lopez 2016, 273-96), namely, the making of Confederate monuments in the United States to memorialize the Confederate past. As the third section will suggest, moreover, visualized oppression works in tandem with discursive arts and thus the removal or toppling of demeaning iconography from public view does not always clear the ideology from public memory.

Inventing the Past: A History of Scholarship on Ancient Slavery

At least three branches of scholarship have contributed to the study of slavery in antiquity: classical studies, comparative studies, and biblical studies. Scholars in each branch have not operated as if confined to disciplinary silos. Instead, cross-pollination has contested ungrounded assumptions and provided a clearer view of slavery in general and of ancient slavery in particular.

The Contributions of Classicists

Not discounting the more recent cross-pollination between the so-called classical studies of ancient Greek and Roman slavery, on the one hand, and studies of the same systems of slavery in comparative studies and biblical studies, on the other, the turning point for much of the classicist work and the comparative work was marked by the scholarship of Moses I. Finley as he debated Johannes Vogt and the Mainz Akademie.

According to Jonathan S. Perry (2014, 221-24), before the arrival of Finley's scholarship, classical studies on slavery in the first few decades of the twentieth century largely focused on manumission (not slavery or enforced labor), as seen in the work of Arnold Mackay Duff and William Linn Westermann, though some of the latter's work was only translated into English decades later. Duff (1928) focused on the so-called social mobility of the new *liberti* (or freedpersons), accepted Roman elitist and ethnocentric notions against easterners (as found in "comedic genres"), and presumed that the *liberti* expedited Rome's decline (see McKeown 2011, 13–24). Westermann (1955, 113–14) presupposed that the presence of manumission procedures in both the Athenian and Roman periods (even when the number of enslaved persons trended upward in the Roman period) signaled either that the slaveowners were generally humane toward the enslaved or that any glut in the market was an aberration from the norm (cf. Perry 2014, 226).

Shortly after Westermann's key essay about the *liberti* appeared in the *Realencyclopädie der classischen Altertumswissenschaft* (also known as Pauly-Wissowa) in 1935, Moses Isaac Finley (née Moses Isaac Finkelstein, 1912–1986) critiqued the work of Westermann, his dissertation advisor at Columbia University, in a journal published by the Frankfurt School for Social Research (Perry 2014, 227; Thompkins 2006, 100). Although scholars debate whether all of Finley's critiques of his teacher were warranted, what seems compelling is that Finley—who preferred a macrohistorical approach as opposed to his teacher's microhistorical analysis, differed from Westermann in wanting to examine ancient slavery strictly as a sociological phenomenon without moralizing it—that is, without asking the apologetic question about whether or not it was viewed as humane in ancient times (Perry 2014, 229–36).

Finley's scholarship also contributed to a rift between German and Anglophone scholarship on slavery. At the center of that debate, Finley's scholarship clashed against the cultural productions of Joseph Vogt (1895–1986), a Tübingen classical historian and the founder of the Akademie der Wissenschaften und der Literatur at Mainz (Mainz Academy of Science and Literature, est. 1949). Using a multidisciplinary, microhistorical approach, Vogt and those who espoused the *Grundlagenforschung* (basic research) objective of the Akademie recognized the scourge of slavery, but they also looked for emotional ties of loyalty between masters and those enslaved by them. Vogt (1975, 104–9) presupposed a kind of intimacy between an ancient, enslaved child-nurse and a privileged child that he also assumed existed between the so-called Black Mammy and her charges in the antebellum South. Despite some good work that the Mainz Academy has produced recently, the research of its early years, which greatly influenced New Testament scholarship, viewed ancient slavery as humane when compared to modern slavery and even assumed that the infrequent mention of ancient slave revolts was evidence for the humaneness of ancient slavery (Harrill 2013, 507–8).

By contrast, Finley and many who espoused his macrostructural approach discredited Vogt and the Mainz Academy's early work for attempting to see the persisting value of humaneness in ancient Roman slavery (Wiedemann 2000, 155). Specifically, Finley (1980, 59–60) critiques Vogt for seeking to save classical humanism by arguing that the great achievement of the Athenian polis unfortunately had the attendant consequence of tolerating the inhumanity of slavery. Finley (1980, 67–92)—who had been influenced by Marx, Weber, and the neo-Marxist Frankfurt school—was, like Marx, committed to socially engaged criticism but shifted away from a teleological brand of Marxism that focused exclusively on class struggles to one that focused—in alignment with Weber—on status and relations of power.[1] Furthermore, Finley (1980, 67–92) would argue that Greece and Rome did not simply have slaves (which would mark them as slaveholding societies) but were genuine slave societies (which meant that these societies were dominated by slavery).

The Contributions of Comparative Studies of Slavery

With his 1968 encyclopedia article, "Slavery," which spoke of "slave societies" from the ancient past (e.g., Greece and Rome) to more contemporary times (e.g., the United States, the Caribbean, Brazil), Finley also played a role in the development of comparative studies of slavery. Likewise, Finley's *Ancient Slavery and Modern Ideology* (1980, 179–82) appealed to the same contemporary cases to show the brutality of slavery wherever it existed.

Sensing that the legal texts of the day were "legal fictions" that simplistically presented the slaveholder's view of the enslaved as property while obscuring the fundamental truth of the absolute power of the owners over the enslaved, the historical sociologist Orlando Patterson (1982, 31–32) made two contributions to the study of ancient slavery. First, Patterson deployed a comparative approach that examines slavery throughout the history of the world. Second, he produced a model to examine domination, the internal logic of slavery, wherever it may be found. Thus, for

---

1. On this reading of Finley, see Bodel 2019, 827. Cf. Horsley 1998a, 28.

Patterson, "there is nothing notably peculiar about the institution of slavery" (vii). Slavery existed in ancient *and* more complex modern societies. Furthermore, a study of slavery should not be limited to "slave societies," as Finley would call them, or to "large scale slave societies," as Patterson (1982, x) would render Finley's "slave societies."

As a historical sociologist, moreover, Patterson is fundamentally concerned with the internal dynamics of slavery. Thus, Patterson (1982, 13) famously states that slavery is "the permanent, violent domination of natally alienated and generally dishonored persons." Accordingly, slavery is, first, a brutal species of relations of domination such that it enduringly renders the enslaved powerless. Its use or even threat of violence is, in effect, a commutation of a social death for what could have been a physical one (1–5, 17–34).

Second, slavery also renders the enslaved natally alienated and cut off from any formally recognized genealogical rights from ancestors, communal attachments to a state, or genealogical obligations to descendants (5–10, 35–76). Cut off from such genealogical and communal connections, the ancient enslaved were simply a tool or extension of the master (7).

Third, given the enslaved person's absence of "independent social existence," the enslaved person can never have "public worth," while masters by contrast increase their honor by virtue of holding others in subjection (10–11, 77–104). Thus, ancient slavery brought a brand of "generalized dishonor" to the enslaved (or dishonor by default, as a part of a group) (11). As a group, the enslaved were not honored. Rather, they were rendered invisible and "stood outside the game of honor" (11–12).

Like Patterson, the Roman classicist Keith Bradley brought a comparative methodology to his reflections on ancient slavery. According to Neall McKeown (2011, 77), Bradley's work (e.g., *Slavery and Society at Rome* [1994] and *Slaves and Masters in the Roman Empire* [1984]) challenged the images of the enslaved that came from the elite writers of the Roman period or a few *liberti*. Instead, by examining Roman law *and* documentation from other literary sources, Bradley (1994, 100) widens the scope of resources from the period both to expose the brutality of slavery and to show resistance to slavery by those who were enslaved (Harrill 2013, 509; McKeown 2011, 85).

For Bradley (1994, 109), the absence of a sustained record of large-scale slave revolts in elite sources does not indicate the acceptance of slavery or acquiescence to it by the enslaved (McKeown 2011, 78). Rather, Bradley argues that scholars must consider the multiple ways in which resistance occurs. As Bradley (1994, 125) notes, "Beneath the surface calm which elitist writings evince, however, there was a constant ferment of defiant activity as slaves, of every description, ran away, stole, cheated, damaged property and shirked work, or as they directed violence against themselves or their owners, all in an effort to withstand the cruelty and deprivation heaped upon them." Furthermore, for comparative purposes, Bradley leans heavily but cautiously upon the world's history of slavery, especially the history of modern slavery, to fill in the data that we do not have from Rome because we lack—outside Epictetus—the direct testimony of a formerly enslaved person (9, 45). For example, Bradley compares the formation of communities and sanctuaries by Roman fugitives to the maroon societies in the more recent history of slavery in North America and in Brazil (67, 87–88).

Bradley also refuses to read the ancient debate on slavery—for example, Aristotle's view of slavery as natural/biological in *Pol.* 1255a versus the Roman legal presupposition that the enslaved are not born slaves but made that way by the fate of legal prescriptions—as a sign of evolving progress from Greece to Rome, which was endorsed by the early writings of the Mainz Academy. Rather, he reads the ancient debate as a sign of the horrific violence of Roman slavery, in that it needed no justification for animalizing people's lives (Bradley 1994, 1, 123). Where ancient writers paint the enslaved as cunning and as if cut from one cloth, Bradley (1989, 30–33) reads such caricatures—for example, in Plautus and Horace—as elitist representations of slaves (Hopkins 1978, 12; McKeown 2011, 82).

Sandra R. Joshel (1986, 5) also deploys a comparative approach. Refusing to accept Vogt's assumption of intimacy between an enslaved nurse-child and her charges, Joshel cautiously uses testimony from enslaved women of the American South to show that a privileged nursling's class-based and gender-based anecdotal commemoration of a compliant and loyal enslaved nurse-child might "distort the nurse and her lived reality."

The Contributions of New Testament Scholarship

A critical turn on the study of ancient slavery in biblical scholarship came with the early and later works of S. Scott Bartchy. The early Bartchy leaned heavily upon Westermann and Vogt, insofar as Finley's work was not yet known to Bartchy when he wrote his dissertation, and he was "insufficiently aware of the great significance of Bradley's scholarship back in 1989" (2013, 525–28) when writing his article on slavery for the *Anchor*

Bible Dictionary (1992, 58–73). Thus, the early work of Bartchy (1973, 30) viewed slavery as benign. By contrast, in a more recent work Bartchy (2013, 529) acknowledges how the works of Patterson and Bradley "challenged [him] to revisit and eventually change [his] mind about many aspects of the truly baleful and destructive consequences of ancient slavery, as well as about those early Christian writers who mention slavery."

In his revised dissertation *Slavery as Salvation*, Dale Martin (1990, 15–22) assumed that slavery could be salvation (or a mechanism for salvation) through an enslaved person's association with a highly respected owner or through the attainment of a managerial position. Several scholars have critiqued Martin's upward mobility thesis. Allen Dwight Callahan, Richard A. Horsley, and Abraham Smith (1998, 1–15), for example, argue that Martin discounts the "perennial dishonor" of the enslaved (a point made emphatically in Orlando Patterson's work), that he misreads the sources (such as Martin's reading of Petronius's *Satyricon* as a story about "upward mobility" instead of one that mocks Trimalchio's pretension), and that he anachronistically assumes a wide gap between the wealthy and the impoverished managers positioned in the middle rather than viewing them as a part of a wide base with others in the ranks of the impoverished.

Beyond his critique of Martin's work, Horsley, both on his own and with Callahan, has contributed correctives to New Testament scholarship on slavery and on Paul. For example, Horsley (1998a, 19–31) notes Bartchy's early dependence on Vogt (who was ideologically invested in saving the humanism of the classics), Finley's insistence on exploring ancient slavery with a methodology that interrelated multiple dimensions of ancient slavery, and Patterson's influential perspective on the totality of a master's power over the enslaved and the total alienation of the enslaved from any group except one chosen by the master. Horsley (1998b, 153–200) also shows how a careful, comprehensive reading of the horrors of ancient slavery reveals that Paul was not conservative toward slavery but counterimperial. In their article together, Callahan and Horsley (1998, 133–51) denounce the scholarship of earlier classicists who had wrongly reasoned that the paucity of slave revolts in the ancient period was a sign that slavery was benign or that the enslaved were contented. Rather, building on the more comparative work of Finley and Patterson as well as on Scott's expansive view of forms of resistance, Callahan and Horsley acknowledge acts such as dissembling, sabotaging, flight, guerilla warfare through marronage, and direct revolt as measures of resistance.

Accepting the reality of the horrific violence of ancient slavery, still other New Testament scholars have raised significant insights about ancient slavery, including the methodological mistake of assuming that the absence of slave rebellions indicates the contentedness of the enslaved with slavery (Harrill 1998, 97); the view of the enslaved as proxies for their masters (Glancy 2006); and the sexual vulnerability of the enslaved (Briggs 2000, 110–23; Glancy 2006, 50–57; Brooten 1996, 250–51; Marchal 2011, 749–70).

Some New Testament scholars also wonder whether it is even possible to appeal to early Christianity as a moral basis for contemporary problems because early Christianity either cultivated the dominant cultures' literary stereotypes about the enslaved (Harrill 2006; Charles 2019) or sanctified the cultural values underwriting the demeaning and dehumanizing treatment of the enslaved (Glancy 2006; Charles 2019). Recently, Katherine A. Shaner (2018, 3, 87–109), while conceding with Sandra Joshel and Lauren Hackworth Petersen (2014, 2) that ancient literary and archaeological evidence made the enslaved invisible, has uncovered evidence showing that some enslaved Christians actively resisted the domination of slaveholders by taking on the roles of bishops, deacons, and widows.

Thus, although passive voice constructions of the literature of the day often elided the work and agency of the enslaved and thus rendered them invisible (Joshel and Petersen 2014, 69, 165), this group that has been estimated to have made up "anywhere between from one-third or more of the total population" was ubiquitous in the Roman Empire (Byron 2008, 2). So, whether the enslaved were captured en masse in wars, produced as the offspring of those already enslaved, sold to owners in the markets, exposed as infants, or seized by pirates, they were present throughout the infrastructures of Greek and Roman societies (Kamen 2012, 174–94; Bradley 1994, 7, 29, 37, 43, 51). In the streets, the enslaved carried litters. On the seas, they were captains of ships. In the workshops, they were fullers and bakers. In urban houses and more remote villas, the enslaved were gardeners and doorkeepers, business managers and secretaries, child-nurses and attendants, cooks and musicians, and an assorted array of banquet personnel attending to the creature comforts of their masters and their masters' fellow diners (Bradley 1994, 57–80; Joshel and Petersen 2014, 172).

Still, in all cases, the enslaved were stripped of every vestige of social identity and honor (Joshel and Petersen 2014, 118). Their true names were replaced by ones given them by their masters. Also, the terms deployed to describe them demeaned them through animalization (when an enslaved one was called a *tetrapodōn* ["four-footed"]), commodification (when an enslaved one was called a *sōma* [body/thing] if not also a *mastigias* [something whipped]), or infantilization (when an enslaved one was called a *pais* [child]) (Kamen 2010, 96; 2012, 174–75; Bradley 1994, 110–25; Glancy 2010, 24–47).

They were also constantly subjected to physical and sexual violence—their backs scarred by whips, their skin chafed at the ankles by tight fetters, their faces branded (cauterized with marks) or tattooed (needle-pricked and dyed with ink to inscribe letters on their foreheads) (Kamen 2010, 95–110), and their whole bodies sexually dominated and exploited by masters who sold them into prostitution, paired them with others to breed more enslaved bodies, distributed them as sexual pawns to dinner guests, or used them to satisfy their own libidinal whims (Bradley 1994, 28; Harper 2016, 300–301; Saller 1994, 134–39).

Domination, Collective Memory, and Rome's Visual Technologies of Power

Given the cruel and brutal domination of ancient slavery (i.e., its violence, its production of the natal alienation of enslaved persons, and its rituals of dishonor), a second goal of this essay is to demonstrate how deeply embedded slavery was in Rome's cultural memories, as demonstrated by the ease with which its elites deployed servile metaphors in the lexical machinery of imperialistic propaganda and in Rome's visual depictions of its mastery of the world. Thus, in this section of the essay, I will first demonstrate the utility of examining Rome's visual technologies of power in alignment with Roman elites' discursive use of servile imagery to see how both types of arts enhanced Roman domination in the service of Rome's collective memory. Then, I will examine briefly how one early Christian writer may have resisted such discursive and aesthetic arts of domination only to fall short because of the traps of a binary, gendered discourse.

Collective Memory and Rome's Visual Technologies of Power

To understand how servile diction and Rome's visual technologies of power played a role in the construction of Rome's collective memory, one must first remember that Rome was a "spectacle-driven society" (S. Bell 2013, 2), one in which elites staged "ceremonial scripts" or commemorative practices to enhance the memory of themselves and their ancestors

(A. Bell 1997, 5). From the fourth century BCE until the Principate, the *nobilitas* controlled memory though the adornment of the city with statues, temples, and other public buildings that memorialized a war general's victory or his family's glory (Flower 1996, 70–71). Multiple inscriptions originally placed at the base of statues—and a few extant statues themselves—attest to the erection of ancestral statues, some of which were contiguous to temples and other civic or public buildings funded by their aristocratic families. Arches erected near the Roman forum also allowed aristocratic families to self-advertise their distinctive prominence in public spaces (71–72).

Beyond the city of Rome, the elites in the Roman Republic also participated in memory sanctioning as they encouraged or sponsored the toppling of the statues of provincial monarchs, the erasure of the names of such kings from the bases of their statues, or the appropriation of such statues and inscriptions with new or reconstructed monuments that lauded the Romans and thus transformed the collective memories of a province in accordance with the new political reality of Roman conquest and domination (Kousser 2017, 37–39).

Obviously, in the imperial period aristocrats had to adjust their quest for distinction. While triumphs were no longer celebrated outside of the emperor's household in the era of the Principate, the emperors deployed visual technologies of power to promote their right to rule or Rome's right to conquer (Hope 2000, 34).

Roman visual ceremonial scripts thus blended in with the prevailing discursive scripts by which Rome endorsed its hegemonic rule. Thus, on the one hand, Roman elites deployed *lexical* arts of domination. Whether Rome's armies were engaged in wars of conquests, strikes against revolts, or other ongoing acts of domination, Roman elites deployed servile metaphors to depict Rome discursively as the undisputed conqueror (*uictor*) or master (*dominus*) of the known world while those conquered were called slaves (*seruos*; Tacitus, *Ann.* 14.31–32) or persons captured (*capta*; Livy, *Ab ubre cond.* 39.9–10) (Lavan 2013, 33, 149).[2] As Myles Lavan (2013, 76) has noted, Roman elites deployed a consistent set of terms to highlight Rome's mastery of the world: "slavery (seruus, seruitus, seruitium, seruire), mastery (dominus, dominatio, dominatus, dominare), freedom (lib-

---

2. Unless otherwise specified, I am solely dependent on Lavan for all Latin translations. The translations for all the Greek expressions in Revelation are my own.

ertas, liber), the yoke (iugum, ceruices) and the causa liberalis (uindex, uindicatio, uindicare)."[3]

As can be seen by the use of the term *iugum* or "yoke," for example, such discursive servile imagery animalized conquered or revolting territories by referring to Rome as a yoke and to the dominated territories as needing to be tamed and broken or needing to have a yoke affixed to their neck (Lavan 2013, 83–88; cf. Cicero, *Rep.* 2.46; Livy, *Ab ubre cond.* 3.28; Tacitus, *Agr.* 15.3). Thus, remarking on the resistance of northern territories to Rome's generals much earlier in Roman history, the historian Lucius Annaeus Florus looks back and notes: "Peace was a new state of affairs and the proud and haughty necks of the nations, not yet accustomed to the reigns of servitude [*seruitutis*] revolted against the yoke [*iugo*] recently imposed upon them" (*Epit.* 2.33 [Forster, LCL]).

As another example, in response to taxation, land encroachment, and the brutality of Roman officials and soldiers, Queen Boudicca of Iceni—an area in Britain that now includes Norfolk and some of Suffolk—revolted against Rome in 61 CE during the reign of Nero. As Lavan (2013, 126–27) acknowledges, "In the short account of Boudicca's revolt, the Britons discuss the evils of slavery (mala seruitutis, 15.1), seek inspiration from German success in shaking off the yoke (sic Germanias excussisse iugum, 15.3) and attack Camulodunum [the capital of the province of Roman Britain] because it was the seat of slavery (sedem seruitutis, 16.1)."

That servile imagery could also depict captured territories in gendered ways is evident in Ovid's poetry. Imagining a triumph held in honor of Augustus's defeat of Germany (Germania), for example, Ovid writes:

> See! Even Germania is carried there, her hair in disarray. She sits despondent beneath the foot of the invincible leader. She offers her proud neck to the Roman axe and bears chains in the hand that once bore arms. (*Tris.* 4.2.43–46 [trans. Lavan 2018, 87–88])

On the other hand, Rome's arts of domination also deployed and exploited *visual* imagery—some servile (and some gendered)—to depict Rome as the undisputed master of the *oikumenē*. Accordingly, when we view the iconography of a theater, a coin, a map, or a monument, we see the arts of

---

3. Julius Caesar, for example, referred to himself as *dominus terrarum* and *dominus mundi*. See Weinstock 1971, 50–53. Cf. the Greek of Josephus, *B.J.* 2.379.

domination or the ceremonial replication of the lexical, servile, and gendered ideas that already were available in the elite discourses on Rome.

Thus, in the art of the period the empire is presented "as a set of feminized and/or familial subordinates surrounding a central, masculine figure of Roman authority" (Ramsby and Severy-Hoven 2007, 45). Pompey's theater in the Campus Martius (Mars Field), for example, used fourteen female characters to depict the fourteen nations that were Rome's subjects (Ramsby and Severy-Hoven 2007, 46–47). In an imperial temple at Aphrodisias, moreover, a frieze in the temple's south portico depicts the emperor Claudius holding up in subjection the head of Britannia (or Britain personified as a woman pinned and writhing underneath Claudius) while in the temple's north portico Rome is depicted as the ruler of many nations who are all represented as women (Gilbert 2002, 517; Lopez, 2006, 115–62).

Coins also communicated domination and often depict the goddess Roma either "holding a globe or with her foot upon the globe" (Ramsby and Severy-Hoven 2007, 86; Nicolet 1991, 34–38; cf. Mattern 1999, 196). According to Jane M. Cody (2003, 123), moreover, the most prominent coin type that represented Rome or Roman figures as conquerors in the republican, Augustan, and Flavian eras was the *capta* type with "the Roman [depicted] as absolute victor over a fallen barbarian foe." In the widely distributed *Iudaea capta* coinage, for example, the legend *Iudaea capta* (or something similar to it) appears with images of capture, such as a date-palm tree—a symbol for the Judean province—decorated with war spoils or the presence of a male captive and a personified female captive (i.e., Judea) with bound hands on the reverse. One of the three Flavian emperors (Vespasian or one of his sons, Titus or Domitian) appears on the obverse of the coins (Keddie 2018, 501–13).

Still, the *supplicatio* coin type (with the subjected figure[s] proffering a gift) and the *adoratio* coin type (with the subjected figure pleading for peace) also appeared during the same periods and likewise emphasized "the ideology of the Roman commander as all powerful conqueror" (Cody 2003, 123). The final two types—the *restitutio* coin, which communicated the restoration of a province, and the *fidelis* coin, which communicated a type of partnership between a Roman representative and a province—were infrequent in any of the aforementioned periods, but they also communicated "an ideology of Roman civic and military power reaching out to, restoring or co-operating with territories under Rome's sway" (105, 123).

Furthermore, visible symbols of world domination included maps that listed all of the nations conquered or controlled by Rome, "triumphal" monuments (e.g., the Arch of Titus or Trajan's Column) to commemorate victories or campaigns over foreign nations, and triumph celebrations in which "prisoners and spoils were paraded through the streets of the city" (Hope 2000, 83–85). For example, were one to look carefully at the visual imperialism of Trajan's Column (113 CE) beyond a simple positivistic documentary approach and beyond simply noting its artistic complexity as a spiraling helix, one might notice the gendered nature of the relief: its phallic symbolism, its "visual dominance of men" (because women appear in only eight of the 155 scenes despite the presence of a winged Victoria figure), and its virtual construction of Trajan and his soldiers as serene, self-controlled, and stoic (as a nod to the ever-fluid category of manliness in that day) in opposition to the depiction of writhing, groveling, fleeing, and defeated Dacians—not to mention the column's depictions of the severed heads of some Dacians (Kampen 1995, 46–73).

Other visual monuments of domination include the Ara Pacis, Augustus's Res Gestae, the reconstructed temple of Jupiter Capitolinus, and the Flavian Temple of Peace. The Ara Pacis (the Altar of Peace) includes relief sculptures that depict Roman propaganda about peace. If one faces the altar from the north, for example, one sees to the left a personified figure who presumably is Peace (*Pax*), while one also sees the goddess Roma (symbolizing Rome) sitting to the right. The first relief, on the southeast corner, depicts beasts at the feet of Peace as if she has domesticated them (Kraybill 2010, 59). The second relief, on the northeast corner, positions Roma so that she is sitting on top of the "armaments of defeated foes" even as she holds presumably a scepter (a symbol of ownership; de Souza 2011, 42) in her hand (Kraybill 2010, 59). The message is clear. She brings peace through war, through "pacification, compliance enforced by threat of arms" (Kraybill 2010, 59). In fact, the original location for this altar was on the Field of Mars, which was located "at the edge of Rome" and was "named for the god of war [Mars]" (59).

Augustus also visually supported Rome's imperial theology with his Res Gestae (Divi Augusti). Initially, this bronze inscription was placed "at the entrance to his new family mausoleum in Rome's Campus Martius [Mars Field]," but its remains were melted (Crossan 2007, 23). What was stated in the inscription, though, is known from a bilingual copy that is a part of a temple to Rome and to Augustus in the modern Turkish city of Ankara (formerly Ancyra, the capital of the Roman province of Galatia) (23). The Res Gestae speaks of Augustus's "political activity," his generosity, and his "conquests, victories, or diplomatic achievements" (trans. Lopez

2008, 24, 29). Noteworthy, moreover, is a summary that Augustus gives on the nations: "Wars, both civil and foreign, I undertook throughout the whole world, on sea and land, and when victorious [*neikēsas*] I spared all citizens who sued for (or requested) pardon" (Res Gestae 3 [trans. Lopez 2008, 89]; cf. Res Gestae 24, 29).

According to Josephus (*B.J.* 7.218), the *fiscus Iudaicus* tax that Vespasian exacted on Judeans, whether or not they lived in the province of Judea, helped to finance the reconstruction of the temple of Jupiter Capitolinus. The impression drawn from Vespasian's institution of the tax, therefore, is that money that the Judeans could have given to their own temple would now finance a new temple for the very dominant power that had destroyed the Jerusalem temple, treated the Judeans like slaves, in that many were whipped (*mastigoumenoi*) and then crucified (*B.J.* 5.446), and taken many other Judeans to be displayed in a triumph at Rome or traded as slaves in the markets (Keddie 2018, 513).

Beyond the imposition of a tax, Rome also used some of the spoils from the Jerusalem temple to finance the Flavians' own Temple of Peace, which itself harked back to Augustus's Ara Pacis. Therefore, in a different way, yet another Roman temple monument was supported by the Judeans, whose own temple had been destroyed, the spoils of which were also on display in the Flavian Temple of Peace (Keddie 2018, 513).

Thus, when Roman elites deployed servile imagery in their visual technologies of power, the visual imperialism matched Rome's discursive ideology. If it is the case that enslaved persons from the period resisted slavery in subtle and strategic ways, as several classicists and New Testament scholars have argued, the crassness of the metaphorical uses of servile diction served up with the visual arts of domination would have added yet another layer of brutality to the presence of slavery itself.

The Response That Replicates the Problems: The Case of the Apocalypse of John

Some persons—whether or not they were in the ranks of the enslaved among the early Christians—might have found in the Apocalypse of John a few rhetorical salvos that could have been directed at what was surely a visually ubiquitous imperial program of dominance (even if a given enslaved person or early Christian may not have been textually adept). For the remainder of this section of the essay, though, I suggest that a turn to the Apocalypse of John may not have been particularly helpful because it appears to replicate the problem of using servile and gendered metaphors and summons up visual imagery that revels in its own brand of binary "monumental logics" (Lopez 2016, 273–96).

Rescued from the serial abstractions of end-time prognostications, Revelation should not be read as though one were joining the latest wave of end-time pop fever first made fashionable in the modern period (Woodruff 2002, 1–45; Howard-Brook and Anthony Gwyther 2005, 1–45). Such end-time fixation may be a distraction from what Revelation's earliest auditors thought the writing was designed to do. In fact, the frenzy of late end-time speculation might deflect from the most recent, formal research on apocalypticism, which gives attention to the "cosmology" (or view of the world) and wisdom that apocalyptic thought reveals (Reynolds and Stuckenbruck 2017, xi). Given Revelation's references to "showing" (from the Greek word *deixai*, 1:1; 4:1; 17:1; 21:9–10; 22:1, 6, 8), attention should be given to what the seer is shown or to what is *made known* (*esēmanen*, 1:1) that the seer expects to happen *soon* (*en tachei*, 1:1) (Koester 2014, 211–12). Given that the first word in Revelation is the Greek word *apokalypsis*, which means an unveiling or uncovering, Benjamin E. Reynolds and Loren T. Stuckenbruck (2017, xi) assert that attention should be given to the link between apocalyptic texts and wisdom or to that which apocalyptic texts unveil or uncover.

What appears to me to be front and center in Revelation, then, is a moral movement's call for justice, its response to a worldwide political economy that produces suffering, and its affirmation that such suffering will not be eternal.[4] Revelation's clash of kingdoms tale, woven together with the fabric of multiple genres (an apocalypse, letters, and prophecy), is replete with diction about persecution (Rev 2:10, 13; 3:10; 6:9) and social alienation (*thlipsis*, 1:9; 2:9–10; 7:14; J. Collins 1979, 9). Its tale is

---

4. What distinguishes Revelation from other works that deploy apocalyptic thought—the uncovering of God's cataclysmic intervention into the world—is that it includes a narrative form. See Koester 2014, 104. In regarding Revelation as a tale of suffering, I am not suggesting that it gives an account of systematic, widespread persecution, for which there is no evidence. That is, if Nero persecuted Christians in the 60s CE, he did so in Rome only. Also, if Pliny knew about the persecution of Christians in the province of Bithynia (in modern Turkey) in the second century, he does not mention persecution in Roman Asia (which is also in modern Turkey). Still, I agree with Greg Carey (2018, 207), who argues that "the experience of—or the fear of—persecution" was "fundamental to resistance in Revelation." On Revelation as a response to Rome's political economy, see Callahan 1999, 46–65.

one in which the long list of cargo products sold on markets includes not just metals, precious woods, a variety of spices, and cattle but also *bodies* (*somatōn*, enslaved bodies) and even *human souls* (18:12–13; C. Martin 2005, 100). Its tale is one in which the precious *souls* of some of John's fellow believers may have been subject to severe alienation and even death for their refusal to acknowledge the Roman gods or to join others in Roman Asia who cultivated imperial beneficence through emperor worship. As John puts it, some souls have been slaughtered (or slain, 6:9; 18:24). No less so, though, from this apocalypse's vantage point, Jesus was victimized through the same slaughtering or butchering process (5:6, 9, 12; 13:8).[5]

Beyond the framing bookends, Revelation includes a series of interconnected visions that reveal how Jesus became "ruler of the kings of the earth" (1:5). Such a revelation, it may be argued, was necessary given the historical context of Roman Asia. Like other provinces, Roman Asia felt the weight of Rome's domination. Rome's citizens populated the cities; Rome's magistrates sat on tribunals, often with "a glint of legionary armor in the background" (Lintott 1993, 175); provincial coins, calendars, and inscriptions gave homage to Augustus and his successors (A. Collins 2000, 95 n. 53; Lintott 1993, 182–83); "hymns, encomia and plays" gave homage to Roman military commanders (Lintott 1993, 177); and the imperial cult, which the local elites initiated for themselves, proliferated itself through a variety of media and public spaces (temples, games, public festivals, statues, etc.) (Horsley 2003, 99–103; Lintott 1993, 183–84). In some instances, Greek cities in the east competed against each other for the title *neokoros*, which was a distinctive honor "by which … [a particular] city would take

---

5. Like Greg Carey and Steven J. Friesen, I presuppose that the suffering to which John gives note was neither expansive nor durative, and that it was more deadening than deadly. Like most scholars of Revelation, my essay also presupposes that, in accordance with church tradition, Revelation was written during the reign of Domitian, ca. 95–96 CE. That is, Irenaeus (*Haer.* 3.1.1–3; 4.20.11) asserted that what John saw happened in Domitian's time, but that John lived on even during the time of Trajan (98–117 CE) (Barr 2002, 444). Some scholars, though, argue for an earlier dating (68/69 CE) because of references to measurements of the temple in Jerusalem, as if the temple was still standing (Rev 11:1–2). See Gonzalo Rojas-Flores 2004, 377–78. Others presuppose stages of development in which an early form was written near the time of Nero and a final form during the reign of Domitian. See Aune 1997, lvi–lxix. For summaries of the debate, see Carey 2016, 117–22, and Friesen 2001, 136–51, who offers details on the problematic nature of Irenaeus's testimony.

on a position of primacy in the network of relationships with other cities" (Friedrich 2002, 194).

Thus, John's clash of kingdoms includes an inaugural vision (1:9–20), a throne-room vision that directs John's audience to worship God and the Lamb [or Christ] alone (chs. 4–5), and a series of three sets of judgments (6:1–16:21). Furthermore, in chapters 17–21, John's clash of kingdoms reveals to an audience of seven churches (cf. chs. 2–3) how the authorities behind the imperial cult (a dragon and a sea beast) are parodies of true and just rulers, God and the Lamb (deSilva, 2009, 112).

For the seer, moreover, the best way to resist Rome's seductive arts of domination was to challenge its notions of victory or conquering. To justify its imperial expansion, Rome had publicized the conquering power of its army. Victory arches, military triumphs, and acclamations on coins visibly celebrated Rome's power. Furthermore, as with the Greeks before them, the Romans embraced the idea of *Nike* (the Greek word for Victory) both as a god in her own right and as a benefit from other gods. Thus, to support its self-interests, Rome promoted the idea that *Nike* was on its side either with its individual generals or with Rome as a collective body.

Still, the seven churches of Roman Asia could not have contested a superpower with weapons of war. For the seer, though, the seven churches and the Lamb did not need to be viewed as totally passive. The seer simply needed to reconfigure victory. Thus, as Revelation's judgments roll out in three septets (the unsealing of seals, the blowing of trumpets, and the pouring forth of bowls in Rev 6–16), the audience learns about the principles of conquest.

According to Nestor Paulo Friedrich (2002, 207), cognates of the word "to conquer" occur twenty-eight times in the New Testament, with *fifteen* of those occurrences found in the Apocalypse of John. Yet, what does conquering mean for John the seer? Craig Koester (2008, 768) asserts that the Apocalypse speaks of two types of conquering. That is, on the one hand, "the Lamb and his followers 'conquer' (*nikaō*) evil by remaining faithful in and through the suffering that is inflicted on them (5:5–6; 12:11; 15:2)." On the other hand, "the Beast 'conquers' by inflicting suffering on others (11:7; 13:7)." Thus, the seer's use of *nikaō* subverts the ordinary view of "conquering." Most persons at the time would have associated conquest with arms and weapons. For the moral movement of which John was a part, however, conquering instead suggests winning through endurance (*hupomonē*, cf. 1:9: 2:2, 3, 19; 3:10; 13:10; 14:12). Given that Jesus conquers (3:21; cf. 5:5) even through his death and that the faithful conquer through

Jesus's blood (12:11), the seer's reconfiguration of *nikaō* demonstrates the agency of Jesus. Rome may have used each crucifixion as a microcosm of Rome's conquest of the *oikoumenē*, but Jesus's agency as a conqueror even in death changed the legacy of Jesus from a victim to a victor through his endurance.

While Revelation speaks against Rome's militaristic view of conquering, it yet upholds the binary between the conqueror and the conquered. Furthermore, it repeatedly relies on metaphorical servile diction (1:1; 2:20; 6:15; 7:3; 10:7; 11:18; 15:3; 19:2, 5; 22:3, 6) while it also denotes dominion through its description of a figure whose feet stand above that which is brought under dominion (10:2), as noted by Koester (2014, 477). Also, if Shanell T. Smith (2014, 127) along with Jennifer Glancy and Stephen Moore (2011, 543–62) are right to follow the lead of C. P. Jones (1987, 151) in viewing a forehead inscription as a type of tattoo for the enslaved, Revelation presupposes that the 144,000 are the enslaved (*douloi*) of God (7:3). Moreover, the roles of women in Revelation are limited to three options that reflect a male-centered culture. They "are caricatured as virgins, whores, or mothers" (Garrett 1998, 469). Such stereotypes, though, asserts Susan Garrett, "do not represent the full spectrum of authentic womanhood, either in John's day or in our own" (469). Furthermore, such stereotypes advocate passivity in women and marks men as protectors, as Tina Pippin (1992, 193–210) has noted.

Finally, if the seer actually drew on the commonplace of endurance that was associated with constructions of manliness, the seer's request of the audience would have drawn heavily on masculinist ideological logic. That is, endurance was seen as a virtue. Virtue itself, a philosophical ideal and a word etymologically linked to *vir* (the Latin word for "man"), was considered natural for men. On the other hand, if women achieved virtue they were described as acting like men (Quintilian, *Inst.* 5.11.10; cf. A. Smith 1995, 103; Satlow 1996, 21 n. 7). Thus, the ideological codes of Revelation continue a binary logic that categorizes others as both different and deficient. The net effect of the text, then, is to contribute to a collective memory that demeans women, just as the use of servile imagery also fails to catch the violence of slavery that the enslaved would have known in a bodily way.

Monuments, Memory, and Modern Binaristic Boundaries of Belonging

Debates about modern monuments did not begin exclusively after August 12, 2017, when white nationalists and counterprotesters clashed at the

Unite the Right rally in Charlottesville, Virginia—a space where alt-right groups protested the planned removal of a Robert E. Lee statue (Newson 2020, 1–2). The event proved violent and tragic because James Alex Fields Jr., a white nationalist, deployed his Dodge Challenger as a missile and injured nineteen anti-hate protestors while killing Heather Heyer.

Since the Daughters of the Confederacy created Confederate monuments to promote the so-called Lost Cause (the idea that the Civil War was fought not because of slavery but instead over the issue of states' rights), the debate over these statues has been ongoing, as manifested in the aforementioned 1870 epigraph from Frederick Douglass in W. E. B. Du Bois's (1931, 279) declaration that such monuments should be inscribed as "sacred to the memory of those who fought to perpetuate human slavery," and in the more recent protests to these symbols despite the so-called "heritage protection acts" passed by state legislators seeking to stem the tide of statue removal (Cox 2021, 1–11).

Across the globe, moreover, there have been clashes about monuments because of their connection to memory. Given the rape and genocidal destruction of South West Africa (now Namibia) by the Germans, a campaign was successful in 2013 in toppling the Reiterdenkmal (Equestrian) Monument that had been erected to honor German soldiers who died in the Herero and Namaqua War (1904–8) (Newson 2020, 5). Efforts to remove statues of the imperialist Cecil Rhodes from the University of Cape Town in South Africa were also successful, while a campaign to take a Rhodes statue down from Oriel College at Oxford University has met opposition from wealthy alumni and—although it was once recently scheduled to be brought down—has yet to be toppled at the time this essay was written (4–5). It may never be toppled.

What is at stake in each example of iconography is the politics of memory: who is authorized to narrate the past, how the visual technologies of power tie into other discursive technologies of power, what gets erased or saved in the collective memory, and how the arts participate in a narrative of belonging and othering through binary diction or images. Removing or toppling monuments that represent nations allegorically as women (as with Lawrence Tenney Stevens's 1936 series in the Esplanade at Fair Park in Dallas, Texas) or those that celebrate any ideas associated with the Lost Cause may provide a measure of healing that a prayer vigil could never muster. Yet the "triumphalist strain" (replete with arches, columns, and obelisks) landed on both sides of the Mason-Dixon divide (Brown 2019, 203). Furthermore, Thomas Ball's 1876 Emancipation Memorial sculpture (in Lincoln Park on Capitol Hill, Washington, DC), with a fully clothed President Abraham Lincoln holding the Emancipation Proclamation in his right hand and holding his left hand over a kneeling and shirtless slave, buys into the very logic of paternalism that the Confederacy supported (Savage 1997, 89–128). It is little wonder, then, that Frederick Douglass's guarded speech at the dedication of the Emancipation Memorial on April 14, 1876 was followed a few days later by his candid critique of the monument's design in a letter addressed to the editor of the *National Republican* newspaper: "What I want to see before I die is a monument representing the negro, not couchant on his knees like a four-footed animal, but erect on his feet like a man" (quoted by White and Sandage 2020).

Moreover, the reality is that Confederate iconographical works replicate other discursive technologies of power that certainly cannot all be banned, burned, or boycotted. Thus, the harder and larger work must be to expose and to extricate the dynamics of binaristic othering in *all* of its forms for the damage they do both in classifying people groups into taxonomies and in subordinating some over others by means of assumed universals that actually represent the interests of a dominant order in maintaining its hegemony.

Works Cited

Aune, David. 1997. *Revelation*. WBC 52. Dallas: Word.
Barr, David L. 2002. *New Testament Story: An Introduction*. Rev. ed. Belmont, CA: Wadsworth.
Bartchy, S. Scott. 1973. *Mallon Chresai: First-Century Slavery and the Interpretation of 1 Corinthians 7:21*. SBLDS 11. Missoula, MT: Scholars Press.
———. 1992. "Slavery (New Testament)." *ABD* 6:58–73.
———. 2013. "Response to Keith Bradley's Scholarship on Slavery." *BibInt* 21:524–32.
Bell, Andrew J. E. 1997. "Cicero and the Spectacle of Power." *JRS* 87:1–22.
Bell, Sinclair. 2013. "Roman Chariot Racing: Charioteers, Factions, Spectators." Pages 492–504 in *A Companion to Sport and Spectacle in Greek and Roman Antiquity*. Edited by Paul Christesen and Donald G. Kyle. Malden, MA: Wiley-Blackwell.
Bodel, John, 2019. "Ancient Slavery and Modern Ideologies: Orlando Patterson and M. I. Finley among the Dons." *Theory and Society* 48:823–33.

Bradley, Keith R. 1987. *Slaves and Masters in the Roman Empire: A Study in Social Control*. Oxford: Oxford University Press.

———. 1989. *Slavery and Rebellion in the Roman World, 140 B.C.–70 B.C.* Bloomington, IN: Indiana University Press.

———. 1994. *Slavery and Society at Rome*. Cambridge: Cambridge University Press.

Briggs, Sheila. 2000. "Paul on Bondage and Freedom in Imperial Roman Society." Pages 110–123 in *Paul and Politics: Ekklesia, Israel and Imperium*. Edited by Richard A. Horsley. Harrisburg, PA: Trinity Press International.

Brooten, Bernadette J. 1996. *Love between Women: Early Christian Responses to Female Homoeroticism*. Chicago: University of Chicago Press.

Brown, Thomas J. 2019. *Civil War Monuments and the Militarization of America*. Chapel Hill: University of North Carolina Press.

Burke, Sean D. 2013. *Queering the Eunuch: Strategies of Ambiguity in Acts*. Minneapolis: Fortress.

Byron, John. 2008. *Recent Research on Paul and Slavery*. Recent Research in Biblical Studies. Sheffield: Sheffield Phoenix.

Callahan, Allen Dwight. 1999. "Apocalypse as Critique of Political Economy: Some Notes on Revelation 18." *HBT* 21:46–85.

Callahan, Allen Dwight, and Richard A. Horsley. 1998. "Slave Resistance in Classical Antiquity." *Semeia* 83/84:133–51.

Callahan, Allen Dwight, Richard A. Horsley, and Abraham Smith. 1998. "Introduction: The Slavery of New Testament Studies." *Semeia* 83/84:1–15.

Carey, Greg. 2016. *Apocalyptic Literature in the New Testament*. Nashville: Abingdon.

———. 2018. "What Counts as 'Resistance' in Revelation?" *PRSt* 45:199–212.

Charles, Ronald. 2019. *The Silencing of Slaves in Early Jewish and Christian Texts*. Routledge Studies in the Early Christian World. London: Routledge.

Cody, Jane M. 2003. "Conquerors and Conquered on Flavian Coins." Pages 103–23 in *Flavian Rome: Culture, Image, Text*. Edited by Anthony Boyle and William J. Dominik. Leiden: Brill.

Collins, Adela Yarbro. 2000. "Mark and His Readers: The Son of God among Greeks and Romans." *HTR* 93:85–100.

Collins, John J. 1979. "Introduction: Towards the Morphology of a Genre." *Semeia* 14:1–20.
Crossan, John Dominic. 2007. *God and Empire: Jesus against Rome, Then and Now*. San Francisco: HarperSanFrancisco.
Cox, Karen L. 2021. *No Common Ground: Confederate Monuments and the Ongoing Fight for Racial Justice*. Chapel Hill, NC: University of North Carolina Press.
deSilva, David. 2009. *Seeing Things John's Way: The Rhetoric of the Book of Revelation*. Louisville: Westminster John Knox.
De Souza, Philip. 2011. "War, Slavery, and Empire in Roman Imperial Iconography." *Institute of Classical Studies* 54:31–62.
Du Bois, W. E. B. 1931. "The Perfect Vacation." *The Crisis* 40:279.
Duff, Arnold Mackay. 1928. *Freedmen in the Early Empire*. Oxford: Clarendon.
Finley, Moses I. 1968. "Slavery." Pages 307–13 in vol. 14 of *International Encyclopedia of the Social Sciences*. Edited by David L. Sills. New York: Macmillan.
———. 1980. *Ancient Slavery and Modern Ideology*. New York: Viking.
Flower, Harriet I. 1996. *Ancestor Masks and Aristocratic Power in Roman Culture*. Oxford: Clarendon.
Friedrich, Nestor Paulo. 2002. "Adapt or Resist? A Socio-political Reading of Revelation 2.18–29." *JSNT* 25:185–211.
Friesen, Steven J. 2001. *Imperial Cults and the Apocalypse of John: Reading Revelation in the Ruins*. Oxford: Oxford University Press.
Gallia, Andrew B. 2012. *Remembering the Roman Republic: Culture, Politics, and History under the Principate*. Cambridge: Cambridge University Press.
Garrett, Susan R. 1998. "Revelation." Pages 469–74 in *Women's Bible Commentary*. Exp. ed. Edited by Carol A. Newsom and Sharon H. Ringe. Louisville: Westminster John Knox.
Gilbert Gary A. 2002. "The List of Nations in Acts 2: Roman Propaganda and the Lukan Response." *JBL* 21:497–529.
Glancy, Jennifer A. 2006. *Slavery in Early Christianity*. Minneapolis: Fortress.
———. 2010. *Corporal Knowledge: Early Christian Bodies*. Oxford: Oxford University Press.
Glancy, Jennifer A., and Stephen D. Moore. 2011. "How Typical a Roman Prostitute Is Revelation's Great Whore?" *JBL* 130:543–62.

Harper, Kyle. 2016. *Slavery in the Late Roman World, AD 275–425*. Cambridge: Cambridge University Press.

Harrill, J. Albert. 1998. *The Manumission of Slaves in Early Christianity*. 2nd ed. Tübingen: Mohr Siebeck.

———. 2006. *Slaves in the New Testament: Literary, Social, and Moral Dimensions*. Minneapolis: Augsburg Fortress.

———. 2013. "Slavery and Humanity: Keith Bradley's Legacy on Slavery in New Testament Studies." *BibInt* 21:506–14.

Hope, Valerie. 2000. "The City of Rome: Capital and Symbol." Pages 63–94 in *Experiencing Rome: Culture, Identity and Power in the Roman Empire*. Edited by Janet Huskinson. London: Routledge.

Hopkins, Keith. 1978. *Conquerors and Slaves*. Cambridge: Cambridge University Press.

Horsley, Richard A. 1998a. "Paul and Slavery: A Critical Alternative to Recent Readings." *Semeia* 83/84:153–200.

———. 1998b. "The Slave Systems of Classical Antiquity and Their Reluctant Recognition by Modern Scholars." *Semeia* 83/84:19–66.

———. 2003. *Religion and Empire: People, Power, and the Life of the Spirit*. Minneapolis: Fortress.

Howard-Brook, Wes, and Anthony Gwyther. 2005. *Unveiling Empire: Reading Revelation Then and Now*. Maryknoll, NY: Orbis.

Jones, C. P. 1987. "Stigma: Tattooing and Branding in Graeco-Roman Antiquity." Pages 1023–54 in *Aufstieg und Niedergang der römischen Welt: Geschichte und Kultur Roms im Spiegel der neueren Forschung*. Edited by Hildegard Temporini and Wolfgang Haase. Berlin: De Gruyter.

Joshel, Sandra R. 1986. "Nurturing the Master's Child: Slavery and the Roman Child-Nurse." *Signs* 12:3–22.

Joshel, Sandra R., and Lauren Hackworth Petersen. 2014. *The Material Life of Roman Slave*. Cambridge: Cambridge University Press.

Joshel, Sandra R., and Sheila Murnaghan. 1998. "Introduction: Differential Equations." Pages 1–21 in *Women and Slaves in Greco-Roman Culture: Differential Equations*. London: Routledge.

Kamen, Deborah. 2010. "A Corpus of Inscriptions: Representing Slave Marks in Antiquity." *MAAR* 55:95–110.

———. 2012. "Manumission, Social Rebirth, and Healing Gods in Ancient Greece." Pages 174–94 in *Slaves and Religions in Graeco-Roman Antiquity and Modern Brazil*. Edited by D. Geary and S. Hodkinson. Newcastle upon Tyne: Cambridge Scholars.

Kampen, Natalie Boymel. 1995. "Looking at Gender: The Column of Trajan and Roman Historical Relief." Pages 46–73 in *Feminism in the Academy*. Edited by Domna C. Stanton and Abigail J. Stewart. Ann Arbor: University of Michigan Press.

Keddie, G. Anthony. 2018. "*Iudaea Capta* vs. Mother Zion: The Flavian Discourse on Judaeans and Its Delegitimation in 4 Ezra." *JSJ* 49:498–550.

Knust, Jennifer W. 2005. *Abandoned to Lust: Sexual Slander and Ancient Christianity*. New York: Columbia University Press,

Koester, Craig R. 2008. "Roman Slave Trade and the Critique of Babylon in Revelation 18." *CBQ* 70:766–86.

———. 2014. *Revelation: A New Translation with Introduction and Commentary*. New Haven: Yale University Press.

Kousser, Rachel. 2017. *The Afterlives of Greek Sculpture: Interaction, Transformation, and Destruction*. Cambridge: Cambridge University Press.

Kraybill, J. Nelson. 2010. *Apocalypse and Allegiance: Worship, Politics, and Devotion in the Book of Revelation*. Grand Rapids: Brazos.

Kuehnast, Kathleen. 1992. "Visual Imperialism and the Export of Prejudice: An Exploration of Ethnographic Film." Pages 183–95 in *Film as Ethnography*. Edited by Peter Crawford and David Turton. Granada Centre for Visual Anthropology. Manchester: Manchester University Press.

Lavan, Myles. 2013. *Slaves to Rome. Paradigms of Empire in Roman Culture*. Cambridge: Cambridge University Press.

Lintott, Andrew. 1993. *Imperium Romanum: Politics and Administration*. London: Routledge.

Lopez, Davina. 2006. "Before Your Very Eyes: Roman Imperial Ideology, Gender Constructs and Paul's Internationalism." Pages 115–62 in *Mapping Gender in Ancient Religious Discourses*. Edited by Todd Penner and Caroline Vander Stichele. BibInt 84. Leiden: Brill.

———. 2008. *Apostle to the Conquered: Reimagining Paul's Mission*. Minneapolis: Fortress.

———. 2016. "Victory and Visibility: Revelation's Imperial Textures and Monumental Logics." Pages 273–96 in *An Introduction to Empire in the New Testament*. Edited by Adam Winn. RBS 84. Atlanta: SBL Press.

Martin, Clarice. 2005. "Polishing the Unclouded Mirror: A Womanist Reading of Revelation 18:13." Pages 82–109 in *From Every People and Nation: The Book of Revelation in Intercultural Perspective*. Edited by David Rhoads. Minneapolis: Fortress.

Martin, Dale B. 1990. *Slavery as Salvation: The Metaphor of Slavery on Pauline Christianity*. New Haven: Yale University Press.

Mattern, Susan P. 1999. *Rome and the Enemy: Imperial Strategy in the Principate*. Berkeley: University of California Press.

McKeown. Niall. 2011. *The Invention of Ancient Slavery? Classical Essays*. London: Bristol Classical.

Newson, Ryan Andrew. 2020. *Cut in Stone: Confederate Monuments in Theological Discussion* Waco, TX: Baylor University Press.

Nicolet, Claude. 1991. *Space, Geography, and Politics in the Early Roman Empire*. Ann Arbor: University of Michigan Press.

Patterson, Orlando. 1982. *Slavery and Social Death: A Comparative Study*. Cambridge: Harvard University Press.

Perry, Jonathan S. 2014. "From Frankfurt to Westermann: Forced Labor and the Early Development of Finley's Thought." *AJP* 135:221–41.

Pippin, Tina. 1992. "Eros and the End: Reading for Gender in the Apocalypse of John." *Semeia* 59:193–210.

Ramsby, Teresa R., and Beth Severy-Hoven. 2007. "Gender, Sex, and the Domestication of the Empire in Art of the Augustan Age." *Arethusa* 40:43–71.

Reynolds, Benjamin E., and Loren T. Stuckenbruck. 2017. Preface in *The Jewish Apocalyptic Tradition and the Shaping of New Testament Thought*. Edited by Benjamin E. Reynolds and Loren T. Stuckenbruck. Minneapolis: Fortress.

Rojas-Flores, Gonzalo. 2004. "The Book of Revelation and the First Years of Nero's Reign." *Bib* 85:375–92.

Saller, Richard P. 1994. *Patriarch Property, and Death in the Roman Family*. Cambridge: Cambridge University Press.

Satlow, Michael L. 1996. "'Try to be a Man': The Rabbinic Construction of Masculinity." *HTR* 89:19–40.

Savage, Kirk. 1997. *Standing Soldiers, Kneeling Slaves: Race, War, and Monument in Nineteenth-Century America*. Princeton: Princeton University Press.

Scott, James C. 1992. *Domination and the Arts of Resistance: Hidden Transcripts*. New Haven: Yale University Press.

Shaner, Katherine A. 2018. *Enslaved Leadership in Early Christianity*. Oxford: Oxford University Press.

Smith, Abraham. 1995. *Comfort One Another: Reconstructing the Rhetoric and Audience of 1 Thessalonians*. Louisville: Westminster John Knox.

Smith, Shanell T. 2014. *The Woman Babylon and the Marks of Empire: Reading Revelation with a Postcolonial Womanist Hermeneutics of Ambiveilence*. Emerging Scholars. Minneapolis: Fortress.

Thompkins, Daniel P. 2006. "The World of Moses Finkelstein." Pages 95–125 in *Classical Antiquity and the Politics of America: From George Washington to George W. Bush*. Edited by Michael Meckler. Waco, TX: Baylor University Press.

Vogt, Josef. 1975. *Ancient Slavery and the Ideal of Man*. Translated by Thomas Wiedemann Cambridge: Harvard University Press.

Weinstock, Stefan. 1971. *Divus Julius*. Oxford: Oxford University Press, 1971.

Westermann, William Linn. 1955. *The Slave Systems of Greek and Roman Antiquity*. Memoirs of the American Philosophical Society 40. Philadelphia: American Philosophical Society.

White, Jonathan W., and Scott Sandage. 2020. "What Frederick Douglass Had to Say about Monuments." *Smithsonian*. June 30, 2020. https://tinyurl.com/SBL06104s.

Wiedemann, T. E. J. 2000. "Fifty Years of Research on Ancient Slavery: The Mainz Academy Project." *Slavery and Abolition* 21:152–58.

Woodruff, Archibald. 2002. "Thirty Years of Near Neglect: Apocalyptic in Brazil." *JSNT* 25:127–39.

$r > g$

Allen Dwight Callahan

The utter lack of any kind of real power below the highest class left even men of some property and local distinction helpless subjects of the great.... The screw, having already been tightened at the bottom of the social scale by landlords and tax collectors as far as it could safely go, and indeed farther, had from the second century onwards (as the situation became less favourable) and regularly during the third to be put on the curial class, as the only alternative for the increased taxation of the really rich, which they would never have endured.
—G. E. M. de Ste. Croix, *The Class Struggle in the Ancient Greek World*

Our government ought to secure the permanent interests of the country against innovation. Landholders ought to have a share in the government, to support these invaluable interests, and to balance and check the other. They ought to be so constituted as to protect the minority of the opulent against the majority.
—James Madison, Constitutional Convention, 1787

The inequality $r > g$ implies that wealth accumulated in the past grows more rapidly than output and wages. This inequality expresses a fundamental logical contradiction. The entrepreneur inevitably tends to become a rentier, more and more dominant over those who own nothing but their labor. Once constituted, capital reproduces itself faster than output increases. The past devours the future.
—Thomas Piketty, *Capital in the Twenty-First Century*

When some of his debtors whose default was clearly due to poverty took flight in fear of the fatal consequences of his vengeance, he carried off by force their womenfolk and children and parents and their other relatives and beat and subjected them to every kind of outrage and contumely in order to make them either tell him the whereabouts of the fugitive or discharge his debt themselves. As they could do neither the first for want

of knowledge nor the second because they were as penniless as the fugitive, he continued this treatment until while wringing their bodies with racks and instruments of torture he finally dispatched them by newly invented methods of execution.... And when there were no kinsmen left, the maltreatment was passed on to their neighbours and sometimes even to villages and cities which quickly became desolate and stripped of their inhabitants who left their homes and dispersed to places where they expected to remain unobserved.
—Philo of Alexandria, *Spec.* 3.159–162, writing of a Roman tax collector in Egypt

With the death of Marcus Aurelius, the 'golden age' of the Roman Empire was definitely finished.... The subsequent 120 years, which saw the struggle of the Roman state with Christianity, belong to a new period of Roman history. Traditional historiography considers the period as the time of the decline of Rome.... The pessimistic experience of the world, which became more common during the reign of Marcus Aurelius and was to dominate the following century, found its counterparts in the renewal of apocalyptic movements (Montanism), the expansion of Gnosticism, and in the beginnings of speculative philosophical theology; reactions to such developments include the creation of the canon of the New Testament scriptures, the codification of the early rabbinic traditions of the Mishnah, and the conclusion of ancient philosophy in Neoplatonism.
—Helmut Koester, *History, Culture, and Religion of the Hellenistic Age,* vol. 1 of *Introduction to the New Testament*

So at [the World Economic Forum in] Davos you've got all these people who earned their money through exploitation, rent-seeking, you name it, and then they do a little bit of philanthropy to distract from all of that.
—Rutger Bregman, Conversation with Dylan Matthews (2019)

Do away with the rich and you won't find any poor.
—The Sicilian Briton, *De divitiis* (*On Riches*) 12.2

Prologue

As contributors to this volume, we are, in the words of Thucydides, "those inquirers who desire an exact knowledge of the past as an aid to the interpretation of the future" (*P.W.* 1.1.22 [Crawley]). We are poised to read the era that Edward Gibbon (1994, 3:1084) called "the greatest, perhaps, and most awful scene in the history of mankind" to get some purchase on our own. We know a lot about the decline and fall of the Roman Empire. Our own decline and fall, apparently more rapid and precipitous as befits an era of capital transfer at the speed of light, is occurring right now. Unlike the Roman Empire, the future for us is not past: it is yet to be seen, because it is yet to be made.

As G. E. M. de Ste. Croix (1981) explains masterfully in *The Class Struggle in the Ancient Greek World*, the ruthless, relentless capital accumulation of wealthy elites under an imperial regime becomes a runaway freight train of kleptocracy, perilously bereft of a political apparatus adequate to the task of arresting its ongoing licit pillage. The people who make the economy work—that is, working people, people who provide goods and services, people who do things for other people with other people— are being collectively strangled by a regime that becomes more and more rapacious, brazen, and entitled with each passing market correction. The one measure that might under other circumstances afford some relief, that is, progressive taxation of the rich, has become impossible, because the rich can no longer be compelled to pay. It is this catastrophe that attended the birth of the New Testament.

De Ste. Croix reads the New Testament as a Marxist. His dialectical materialist reading of Roman imperial political economy describes in erudite detail a conjuncture congruent with our own. The Roman Empire after the sunset of the Julio-Claudia house, the period in which the New Testament had its gestation, and our own era are, at least in economic terms, homologous.

De Ste. Croix's account of the Roman ruling class may as well have been a description of the tax resistance of the very wealthy and merely wealthy of our own day. Ours is an era in which the inherited wealth of the minority of the opulent has triumphed. Now, an aristocracy—the rule of the *aristoi*, "the best of us"—is an interlocking directorate of high-level crooks, cronies, and clients committed to enriching themselves at everyone else's expense. This minority benefits from a winner-take-all political economy that siphons off more and more to fewer and fewer winners and produces a lot of losers, more and more of whom lose more and more. Meanwhile, the top decile just below that tiny ruling minority expends ever more time and energy servicing its betters, even as its own insecurity grows and its own cohort becomes marked by fewer and fewer winners and more and more losers. And beneath that cohort, impoverished citizens and denizens struggle to survive on short-term contracts, day work, and grifting, along with prostitution and other gig economies, their precarious means occasionally and inadequately supplemented by a dwindling, diminutive dole.

Thomas Piketty is the Stephen King of contemporary economists. Piketty knows how to write a big, best-selling horror story. The horror of Piketty's (2017) ponderous tome of dismal science, *Capital in the Twenty-First Century*, is summarized in one of his mathematical phrases, an expression describing capital accumulation: r (i.e., the private rate of return on capital) $> g$ (i.e., the rate of growth of income and output). Translation: taking becomes more lucrative than making, and so the takers overwhelm the makers. And yet it is the makers who make everything; they are the engine that drives the economy; they are its essential employees. Thus we arrive at what Piketty calls the "fundamental logical contradiction" (571): the takers themselves saw off the very limb upon which they are sitting and, driven by their own perverse compulsion, use their powers of expropriation to eat alive those who have produced their vast wealth. "The past devours the future" (571).

The phrase $r > g$ summarizes the condition that our era shares with the one that gave birth to the New Testament and killed late Roman antiquity. It is the preexisting condition that not only characterizes but constitutes both that era and our own, a season of catastrophe in which the Four Horsemen of the Apocalypse ride high with the best of us even as they run roughshod over the rest of us.

The Pledge

In 2010, less than two years after the most spectacular financial crash since the Great Depression, there were 404 billionaires in the United States. Three of the wealthiest among them, Bill and Melinda Gates and Warren Buffet, convened a confab of sixty other billionaires to take yet more matters into their own hands. Having been spectacularly successful at privatizing profit from the commons, sequestering obscene sums of capital, and pauperizing labor all over the world, they were now turning their attentions to philanthropy. What emerged from their deliberations was the Giving Pledge, the signatories' public promise to donate a considerable portion of their enormous wealth to "poverty alleviation, refugee aid, disaster relief" and "environmental sustainability," among other desperately urgent humanitarian challenges. The Giving Pledge's website describes it this way: "Created by Bill and Melinda Gates and Warren Buffett, the Giving Pledge came to life following a series of conversations with philanthropists around the world about how they could collectively set a new standard of generosity among the ultra-wealthy" (The Giving Pledge).

And Warren Buffett (n.d.) was clear from the start about what that new standard would be: "In 2006, I made a commitment to gradually give all of my Berkshire Hathaway stock to philanthropic foundations. I couldn't be happier with that decision. Now, Bill and Melinda Gates and I are asking hundreds of rich Americans to pledge at least 50% of their wealth to charity." The problem of financing worthy but woefully underfunded projects to save humanity, projects starved of the capital astronomically stockpiled by the minority of the opulent, would now be solved by a minority of that minority disposing of half of its wealth in philanthropic ventures.

Warren Buffett is not the first, however, to propose a philanthropic 50 percent solution in an era of catastrophe.

The Road

The nineteenth-century biblical scholar Ernst Renan (1877, 283) called it "the most beautiful book that ever was." The Gospel of Luke is the longest of the Bible's four gospels. With Acts, the second volume of this two-volume set, the Lukan contribution to the canon comprises more than one quarter of the entire New Testament.

The narrative of Jesus's death march on the Jericho road from Galilee to Jerusalem (Luke 9:51–19:28) is a florilegium of stories, sayings, and parables that we find nowhere else in the gospels. Here alone we learn that Jesus was rejected by a Samaritan village, worshiped by a Samaritan supplicant, and provoked to tell a tale about a Samaritan whom we now call good but whom he called neighbor. There are parables without parallel and with various protagonists—among them, some rising dough, some snooty socialites, a stunted tree, a robust weed, a cranky judge, a wayward son.

These stories told on the road, as it were, are marked if not by class struggle then by class stratification: the tales feature potentates (Luke 18:2, 19:12); the very wealthy (18:23); the merely wealthy (12:16, 14:12, 15:32, 16:1, 19:2, 21:1); their retainers (14:17, 16:2, 18:9–13); essential workers (10:35, 12:36, 13:7, 15:22, 16:13, 17:7); and the indigent (14:13, 16: 20–21, 18:35). The narrative point of view, however, is that of the propertied classes. In the Gospel of Luke, Jesus's stories are about people who have what Jesus does not have—money, property, servants, power—and do what Jesus does not do—raise families, erect buildings, throw parties, fire people. In the aggregate, the discourses and the narratives are alien to a bumpkin from Nazareth and his local audiences; the gospel trades up from homespun parables about the farmer and the fisherman to those about the magnate and the manager. Jesus even praises "the children of darkness" for being smarter with their money than "the children of light" (16:8–11) because the righteous would do well to do better in managing their portfolios. The writer of the Gospel of Luke, straddling the classes, knows something of the wealthy and the wretched and those in between; his view of the lower rungs, however, is from above. In the stories that Jesus tells and the stories told about him, the rich are accorded, as is befitting their station, special treatment.

The protagonists of these stories are at least well-to-do. The Good Samaritan can put a stranger up in a motel for several days without maxing out his line of credit (Luke 10:25–37). A wealthy fool lives, then dies, wealthy (12:13–21). The owner of a fig tree discusses its care with his private gardener (13:6–8). Jesus attends a toney dinner party, schooling his host on how to draw up a proper A-list (14:1–14) and telling an unflattering story about a dinner party snubbed by well-heeled invitees much like Jesus's audience (14:15–24). Jesus speaks of discipleship in terms of contracting (14:28–30) and kingship (14:31–33); of the huge herds owned by those in his audience (15:1–7); of a householder with ten days' wages of disposable income on hand (15:8–10); of a paterfamilias who celebrates the return of his errant son with a lot of bling and a lot of barbecue—a story about losing and finding a patrimony in a society in which inheritance is passed on from father to son, and so, a story exclusively about men (that is, a father and his two sons, with no mention of their mother). There is the story of a magnate and his hapless retainer, a mid-level manager capriciously fired on the grounds of hearsay (16:1–9), a parable which, the narrator tells us, provokes some jeering from Jesus's money-grubbing, Pharisaic audience (16:14). There is the story about a wealthy but clueless sybarite who dies and goes to hell (16:19–31). Jesus gives instruction on the customary management of servants (17:1–10), having spoken earlier in his journey of whipping slaves as standard operating procedure (14:47–48). He ends his road trip with a parable about investment banking (19:11–27)—but not before granting an audience to not one but two wealthy men who have come out to see him (18:18–30; 19:1–10). The first man, apparently a trust fund baby, departs crestfallen; the second, a tax collector, arrives overjoyed.

It is with that happy tax collector that we come to the giving pledge:

> He entered Jericho and was passing through it. A man was there named Zacchaeus; he was a chief tax collector and was rich. He was trying to

see who Jesus was, but on account of the crowd he could not, because he was short in stature. So he ran ahead and climbed a sycamore tree to see him, because he was going to pass that way. When Jesus came to the place, he looked up and said to him, "Zacchaeus, hurry and come down; for I must stay at your house today." So he hurried down and was happy to welcome him. All who saw it began to grumble and said, "He has gone to be the guest of one who is a sinner." Zacchaeus stood there and said to the Lord, "Look, half of my possessions, Lord, I will give to the poor; and if I have defrauded anyone of anything, I will pay back four times as much." Then Jesus said to him, "Today salvation has come to this house, because he too is a son of Abraham. For the Son of Man came to seek out and to save the lost." (Luke 19:1–10)

Zacchaeus is a chief tax collector, that is, a tax collector's tax collector. The Gospel of Luke allows—assumes, even—that tax collectors may continue in their odious profession while embracing and being embraced by the partisans of Jesus. Not so in the other gospels. Neither the Gospel of Mark nor the Gospel of Matthew represents Jesus as hanging out with tax collectors who were still "in the life." Jesus invites a tax collector named Levi to follow him, and, promptly forsaking his day job, Levi does so (Mark 2:14–15). Jesus eats with "tax collectors and sinners" at Levi's home (Mark 2:16), but otherwise has nothing to say to or about them. Twice in the Gospel of Matthew Jesus is confronted about paying taxes, and twice he dodges his confronters: in Capernaum tax collectors confront Jesus about his own tax bill, which Jesus dismisses with a gag (Matt 17:24), and in Jerusalem Jesus gives his famous nonanswer when questioned about paying imperial taxes (22:15–22). The Gospel of Matthew generally regards tax collectors as especially unsavory characters (see 5:46; 11:19; 21:31–32) and maintains an unquestioned zero-tolerance policy toward them (18:15–17). A former tax collector named Matthew is included among the Twelve (10:1), but clearly he has permanently closed up shop to follow Jesus (9:9–13). As for the Gospel of John—the work of an elite, nonpriestly clique with ties to Jerusalem—there nothing is said of taxes or tax collectors, presumably because taxes were a nonissue for the well-off, well-connected friends of Jesus whom that gospel features by name: Mary, Martha, and Lazarus, Nicodemus, and, later, Joseph of Arimathea.

The Gospel of Luke has more to say about taxes and tax collectors than do all the other gospels combined. The tax collector Levi not only has Jesus over for dinner but throws a big party in Jesus's honor (Luke 5:29). Tax collectors are tacitly expected to continue in their exactions. The interim ethic that John the Baptist enjoins upon tax collectors is a kinder, gentler parasitism, suggesting a naive ignorance of the tax collector's business model: "Even tax collectors came to be baptized, and they asked him, 'Teacher, what should we do?' He said to them, 'Collect no more than the amount prescribed for you'" (3:12–13). In the story known traditionally as the parable of the Pharisee and the publican (18:9–14), the tax collector is even represented as a paragon of humility. Unlike the pompous Pharisee, the publican knows what a poor excuse for a human being he is, and he is honest enough to admit it at the altar: beating his breast, he pleads for divine mercy. But he is, in fact, unrepentant. It is his honesty about his wickedness, not his forsaking of it, that makes him right with God, and he leaves the confessional to return to his dirty business with a clean conscience. As James Baldwin once put it, "People can cry much easier than they can change" (cited in Coles 1977).

Zacchaeus not only gives up 50 percent of his wealth but promises to make fourfold restitution for the damage he did amassing it: "And if I defrauded anyone by a false claim, I make fourfold restitution" (19:8). This is one of the most disingenuous conditional clauses in all of Greek literature, for Zacchaeus's enterprise requires a species of routine extortion; his profit margin was what he could wring from taxpayers above and beyond what they owed, his gain beginning precisely where their imperial tax bill ended.

There is no metric here: no implication of how much good was done, how many poor people were relieved, how much poverty was abated. There is no hard data on how much Zacchaeus paid, or when he paid it. Or if he paid anything at all. There is only one reported outcome: "Today salvation has come to this house," declares Jesus. The only beneficiaries mentioned are Zacchaeus and his household, precisely those who have benefited all along from his professional extortion. What Zacchaeus does, he does not for the poor but for himself.

According to the Gospel of Luke, rich people who do not share their wealth with the poor in this life, be they hoarders or hedonists, catch hell in the next. Elsewhere on the Jericho road, in the parable of Dives and Lazarus (Luke 16:19–31), Jesus sells philanthropy as a species of fire insurance. The beggar Lazarus finds eternal rest "in the bosom of Abraham" as compensation for his life of miserable poverty. Like most of the gospel's poor people, he says nothing; in the parable he makes a cameo appearance without any lines. The anonymous rich man, condemned to everlasting torment after having lived a life of sumptuous wealth while blithely oblivious to Lazarus's suffering, does all the talking. This is another parable about the administration of a patrimony, and so for men only. The anonymous protagonist pleads with Abraham on behalf of his father's house—that is, his five male siblings who are his father's heirs. Abraham's retort is at the same time a deft nod to Jesus's resurrection from the dead and an indictment that those who refuse to heed the words of Moses and the prophets may be expected to refuse to heed the words of Jesus.

But the afterlife, a grandiose wish—and it is nothing more than that—augurs the permanent sleep of justice, its death rattle as moral rigor mortis sets in. Future justice is an oxymoron; postponed as a reckoning in the hereafter, it is delayed and so denied. The grammar of justice has no future tense. Its only tense is the present; its only mood, the imperative.

The afterlife implies that God has been aware of injustices, dallying with tallying, merely counting all the outrages—that he knew better, but that he did not do better. Yet the Gospel of Luke implicitly concedes that, like the signatories of the Giving Pledge, Zacchaeus may indefinitely dally in his tallying, deciding in his own good time who gets what, when, and how.

The Algorithm

According to the *Forbes* annual list, there are now 2,153 billionaires in the world, 204 of whom have signed on to the Giving Pledge (Editorial 2019). Because the Giving Pledge neither requires nor reports donations, and because there are no mechanisms for enforcement or accountability for its philanthropy, we simply do not know how much the Giving Pledge signatories are giving.

But we do know how much they are making. And they are making a lot. A recent Inequality.org study entitled "Gilded Giving 2020: How Wealth Inequality Distorts Philanthropy and Imperils Democracy" (Collins and Flannery 2020), found that over the decade the combined wealth of the sixty-two billionaire signatories of the Giving Pledge in 2010 "has almost doubled—from $376 billion in 2010 to $734 billion as of July 18, 2020, in 2020 dollars." For nine of those sixty-two billionaires, the increase in wealth was well in excess of 200 percent over the decade. And between March and July 2020, months rocked by the COVID-19 pandemic, one hundred of the Giving Pledge billionaires saw their combined wealth jump from $758.3 billion to $971.9 billion—a 28 percent increase. Chafing at suggestions that there may be something amiss about all this, Bernard Marcus, the cofounder of Home Depot and a signatory of the Giving Pledge, told the *New York Times*, "All this money [of the Giving Pledge] is going for charity, to help people—what kind of numbskull would find something wrong with that?" (*Washington Life* 2019). Perhaps a numbskull concerned to have some idea of just how much all this money is; how much of it in fact is going to charity; how many people were, in fact, helped.

The Jericho road of philanthropic voluntarism turns out to be a dead end. The conviction of a few virtuous billionaires is no substitute for the consensus of a global commonwealth that to be a billionaire is itself a crime against humanity; that the wealthy, having so much, have too much; that wealth without work is wickedness; and that unearned income rightfully belongs to the commons whence it came. The rich will resist that rightful return, of course, for they seldom surrender their ill-gotten gains with the professed equanimity of Zacchaeus—or Bill Gates or Warren Buffett. Zacchaeus's promise of restitution is a conditional sentence, which suggests but does not require that he ever write the check. In effect, his Giving Pledge is more pledge than giving.

The Giving Pledge is entirely voluntary. It is Zacchaeus, not Jesus, who, unbidden, takes the initiative: it is the wealthy that take the Giving Pledge, promising to give what they want, when they want, how they want, and to whom they want. There is no obligation, no enforcement, no accountability. The Gospel of Luke at least claims the threat of eternal flames, though there is no evidence anywhere that such a threat caused wealthy would-be devotees to part with their money. And the Giving Pledge of Buffet and Gates, lacking even the vaguest whiff of brimstone, has persuaded relatively few multibillionaires to promise to surrender half their unrighteousness mammon.

The Fifty Percent Solution is itself a sign of the windfall of the wealthy; it is yet one more prerogative of their wealth—the great luxury of choice. Since they signed the fledgling Giving Pledge in 2010, the wealth of the Gateses has more than doubled, going from \$53 billion to \$111 billion today. Buffett is still the eighth-richest person in the world, with a net worth of \$69 billion. This, at the same time the United States Census Bureau reports that the gap between the have-nots and the have-mores is higher than it has ever been in the last half century (Best 2020).

The brute arithmetic implied in the phrase $r > g$ means that 50 percent is not enough to close the gaping chasm between the minority of the opulent and the rest of us. That minority unilaterally makes all the decisions indicated in the title of the twentieth-century political scientist Harold Lasswell's (1936) signal monograph, *Politics: Who Gets What, When, How.*

In this era of catastrophe, the wealthy have effectively become our politics. It is they who decide who gets what, when, and how. For it is their world, really. The rest of us just pay them rent to live in it.

The task of religion for the last ten thousand years has been to disguise class struggle. Religion is ideological conflict management. Religious leaders are at best reformers. But they are among the best. And the writer of the Gospel of Luke is one of the best of them, a pioneering reformer, and perhaps the first to propose a Fifty Pecent Solution—with restitution, a variable in the philanthropic formula that is lacking in the Fifty Percent Solution of Buffett. The promise of restitution, be it in the form of reparations or the universal franchise or land reform, has served as the incentive for militant working people to lay down their arms and sign on to charters and constitutions. Forswearing violence and abiding by the statutes that legalize in perpetuity the theft to date, working people are persuaded that one day they will get their due through due process. So the workers put down their pitchforks, only to plead their interminable cases in the courts. The law is now on their side, while justice is now, unbeknown to them, permanently out of reach. "The moral arc of the universe is long, but it bends toward justice," Martin Luther King Jr. majestically intoned (Craig 1964, 4). Perhaps. But it never gets there.

Postscript

"The absence of romance in my history will, I fear, detract somewhat from its interest," lamented Thucydides (P.W. 1.1.22). But the writer of the Gospel of Luke, the most beautiful book ever written, gives us romance. He maintains the bashful anonymity of the other gospel writers, but unlike any of them, he names his intended audience: "Since many have undertaken to set down an orderly account of the events that have been fulfilled among us, ... I too decided, after investigating everything carefully from the very first, to write an orderly account for you, most excellent Theophilus" (Luke 1:1, 3). It is for Theophilus's sake that the Jesus of the Gospel of Luke talks about things that a yokel from Nazareth could not have known anything about. Jesus opens his mouth, but it is the disguised voice of the gospel writer that Theophilus hears. So the writer is more than a propagandist. He is a ventriloquist, a spinmeister—one among many setting down orderly accounts of the failed messianism imputed to Jesus of Nazareth.

And there are other accounts, other romances. There are those who bewail the rot of the kleptocracy and impotently prophesy its demise:

the Cassandras who are murdered; the Jeremiahs who are driven out; the Nietzsches who are driven mad. There are the pampered Panglosses whose sunny cheerleading celebrates the great advances wrought by all the graft and greed. There are the strivers, touting in their desperate boosterism some new crumb-snatching scheme or a new and improved version of some old one. There are the embattled, déclassé nonelites with their embroidered doctrines of stoicism and other spiritualities of resignation. There are the preachers of apocalypse who stoke the resentment, entitlement, and disenchantment so congenial to the faith of an elect invariably comprised of the resentful, the entitled, and the disenchanted.

And there are those, like the gospel writer, who exhort some "most excellent Theophilus" to philanthropy, that fig leaf for all those outrages that the accommodation to power makes necessary and the accommodation to wealth makes inevitable—a pious call for the pledge of a minority of the minority of the opulent, with an algorithm in which salvation is 50 percent of taxable income plus a phantom variable of restitution.

All this, in a catastrophic age whose only real salvation is to be found in the righteous algorithm of the Sicilian Briton: zero rich = zero poor.

Works Cited

Best, Paul. 2020. "What Is the Giving Pledge?" July 10, 2020. https://tinyurl.com/SBL06104y.

Buffett, Warren. n.d. "Pledge Letter." The Giving Pledge. https://tinyurl.com/SBL06104v.

Coles, Robert. 1977. "James Baldwin Back Home." *New York Times*. July 31. https://archive.nytimes.com/www.nytimes.com/books/98/03/29/specials/baldwin-home.html.

Collins, Chuck, and Helen Flannery. 2020. "Gilded Giving 2020: How Wealth Inequality Distorts Philanthropy and Imperils Democracy." Inequality.org. https://tinyurl.com/SBL06104w.

Craig, John. 1964. "Wesleyan Baccalaureate Is Delivered by Dr. King." *Hartford Courant*. June 8.

Crawley, Richard. n.d. "Thucydides: History of the Peloponnesian War." https://tinyurl.com/SBL06104u.

De Ste. Croix, G. E. M. 1981. *The Class Struggle in the Ancient Greek World*. Ithaca: Cornell University Press.

Editorial. 2019. "Philanthropic 50: How Successful Is the Giving Pledge?" *Washington Magazine.* June 5. https://washingtonlife.com/2019/06/05/philanthropic-50-how-successful-is-the-giving-pledge/.

Gibbon, Edward. 1994. *The History of the Decline and Fall of the Roman Empire.* Edited by David Womersley. London: Penguin.

The Giving Pledge. https://givingpledge.org/About.aspx.

Matthews, Dylan. 2019. "Meet the Folk Hero of Davos: The Writer who Told the Rich to Stop Dodging Taxes." *Vox.* https://tinyurl.com/SBL06104t.

Piketty, Thomas. 2017. *Capital in the Twenty-First Century.* Translated by Arthur Goldhammer. Cambridge: Harvard University Press.

Renan, Ernst. 1877. *Les Évangiles et la seconde génération chrétienne.* Paris: Lévy.

Washington Life. 2019. "Philanthropic 50: How Successful Is the Giving Pledge?" https://tinyurl.com/SBL06104x.

Equality:
A Modern, Ancient Greek, and
Pauline History of the Concept

Jorunn Økland

It is often pointed out that the notion of citizenship in ancient Athenian democracy was one of radical inequality. By modern standards, the exclusion of women, slaves, and most foreigners from the assembly of citizens would be considered repulsive. Sometimes the Athenian assembly is contrasted with early Christian *ekklēsiai*, which were open to women and slaves and brought together people from different geographical areas. But with so many different notions of equality circulating in the present, by which notion should the ancient Athenian assembly be judged as radically unequal and the Christian assembly as equal? By *ancient* standards, the Athenian equality experiment with direct democracy was considered so radical and vulnerable that it ended up being rather short-lived for that reason. By contrast, the Christian *ekklēsia* developed a hierarchical structure that has survived the centuries.

To focus and proceed with this discussion, a clarification of basic terminology is necessary. I will present contemporary ways of discussing equality with special reference to gender (as concept, value, or practice). I will also discuss at which stage equality should be measured; the semantic fields of terminology relating to the concept of equality in a few key languages; and equality as quantity and quality. How is inclusion among a group of equals regulated today, and how are practices of equality discussed? In the second part I will trace the history of the concept back to the ancient world. Other terms could also in theory *imply* some level of what we today call equal worth between inhabitants or members of a group—for example, terms for unity and community such as the key Pauline term *ekklēsia*. In his use of *ekklēsia*, did Paul imply something overlapping with what we today call equality, or is such a reading better understood in terms of modern reception history?

In the conference call on which this volume is based, speakers were invited to reflect on "how to conceptualize our obligations to take positive moral stands on issues of our own time that are dividing our world." I recognize—across the divides of languages, political systems, and views regarding what generates social change—a shared frustration with the lack of connection between studies of the ancient Mediterranean (including the New Testament) and modern societies. I am rephrasing the concern regarding these divisions using what I see as the most effective concepts for engendering social transformation: social structure, material redistribution, social justice, and equality. Grounding these politically charged concepts are, of course, historically Marxist ideas that have fundamentally shaped the organization of European countries as welfare states. Less influential today, these ideas are still woven into the fabric of European national and international organizations, and there is still hope they may be revived for a new round of productive revolutions.

Conceptual History as Method

Equality is discussed along many different axes: as principles regarding the relation of justice and equality, asking what it governs (cf. Sen 1980), among whom it works, and how far it extends; as material requirements and quantitative measures; and as value with a certain status within a comprehensive (liberal) theory of justice (Gosepath 2021). Equality can be analyzed in a different, triangular setup as a *concept*, as a form of *social practice*, and as a social and political *value* or *principle*, as I will do here. The value of equality is taken for granted today but was further removed from the top of the value hierarchy in the ancient world. Today, equality as a value inspires people to think and talk conceptually about it and to try to put it into political and social practice.

In this essay, I make the *concept* of equality the main object of historical analysis. Conceptual history takes as its point of departure the idea that concepts are not stable and addresses the historical side of language rather than relying on stable meanings of terms and concepts that can be applied to historical data. Since equality is a concept that is also highly value-charged in the present, the value side cannot be excluded. With three adjustments, I borrow the approach developed in the "Arbeitskreis für Sozialgeschichte," formulated by Reinhart Koselleck (1989) and carried out in the multivolume *Geschichtliche Grundbegriffe: Historisches Lexikon zur politisch-sozialen Sprache in Deutschland* (Brunner et al. 1972–1997). This lexicon traces the development of politically charged concepts through different languages (hence the emphasis on *concept* rather than *term*, since a concept can be continuous across different terms in different languages) and historical periods on the European continent, culminating with modern Germany. The adjustments I will be making to this approach are as follows. First, the realization that it is the present that presents its exigencies and questions to us, rather than the past dictating the present, brings me to start in the present and move back in time genealogically. Second, I will not start or end my analysis in Germany but instead shall focus upon some recent Anglophone thinkers of gender equality and draw upon my own academic context in Norway, a country in which equality is still a stronger value than liberty (Hellevik 2008, 175–78). Norway and the United States are likely extremes in this respect, with most European countries located on the scale in between these extremes.[1] Third, given the current volume's academic context in biblical studies and classics, the classicist and scholar of religion Hubert Cancik's works on conceptual histories in religion and classics constitute an even more direct reference point than *Geschichtliche Grundbegriffe*.[2] Cancik's essay "Gleichheit und Freiheit" (1998) engages more broadly than Dann's (1975) entry on "Gleichheit" in Brunner and Koselleck's lexicon with the ancient world and addresses early Christianity throughout as the vehicle by which ancient concepts were transported and translated into medieval and even modern Europe. Although Cancik's *Handbuch religionswissenschaftlicher Grundbegriffe* (Cancik et al. 1988–2001) does not include an entry on Gleichheit, issues often discussed under the rubric of equality are instead discussed under that of Klassengesellschaft (Kippenberg 1993; cf also Cancik 1998). Kippenberg borrows the tools of Koselleck-style conceptual history, not least (like Müller-Wille 2014; see

---

1. "Inter-country variations, consistently observed in surveys, can be explained less by factors such as levels of economic development, levels of inequality, and the nature of active redistributive policies than by history and cultural beliefs. Using data from twenty-six countries, Lubker (2006) found that intolerance for inequality and public support for redistribution are not driven by the level of inequality, but instead by social justice norms" (Fukuda-Parr 2016, 263). For a broader picture, see the subchapter "Obedient-vs. Emancipative Values" in the "Inglehart-Welzel Cultural Map" in Inglehart et al. 2014.

2. Cancik is also editor of *Der Neue Pauly*.

below) the distinction between proposition and description: equality is a hope of a paradisiac condition that has either remained wishful thinking or inspired collective action (Kippenberg 1993, 366–67).

A final, important feature of the conceptual-historical method is that it analyzes the intertwining of conceptual categories and historical materialities. In the case of equality or equal rights, the question of the concept also implicates members of a concrete social corpus, their material resources, and their language. Thus, investigation must combine philology, philosophy, and material(-ist) history.[3] This intertwining means that the approach does not depend on the concept per se accurately summing up any existing fact on the ground. To quote Staffan Müller-Wille (2014, 599), who writes on the conceptual history of race:

> I believe that one can avoid this dilemma by basing the history of race on an understanding of concepts as mental tools, rather than mental representations. This corresponds to a continental understanding of propositions as judgments, that is, essentially social and political actions, rather than as descriptions of states of affairs as the majority of analytic philosophers would have it. A concept in this understanding does not somehow mirror its object, but rather serves as an anchoring point for evaluations and judgments.

Modern Exigencies

Modern exigencies challenge scholars of the ancient world to reflect on how their materials might contribute to burning issues in the present. For the current paper, the entry point to the ancient world is through the concept of *isotēs*, equality: How inclusive was it? What characterized the social corpus within which the members should be equal? Foregrounding gender equality, analyses of gender, sexuality, and feminism relating to equality will be presented first.

The current exigency of gender equality is radically formulated in a series of publications by British journalist and self-declared "Communist feminist" Beatrix Campbell (Campbell 2013, 2014a, 2014b). Even as patriarchy had been on the wane and losing legitimacy through the last quarter

---

3. E.g., Dann 1980, 21. His basic question is "What role has the issue of—and discourse on—equality played in the context of the modernization of European societies?" (my trans.).

of the twentieth century, new inequalities are emerging in the twenty-first century. Working mainly from British and European evidence with some global outlooks, Campbell argues that the "cultural journey toward equality" has ground to a halt and even in some respects reversed. Gender-based violence, pay inequality, body anxieties, and sex trafficking have combined into a picture of neopatriarchy. This had happened after "the world's institutions reached a consensus: they came together to hail the goal of gender equality. Ironically, this was at the very moment when we were witnessing the limits, the exhaustion, of the equality paradigm" (Campbell 2013). In other words, the liberal, optimistic belief that we are on a journey toward equality—in the workplace, on the street, and in the home—must be immediately interrupted and reality-checked. This chapter is a contribution to her project. Campbell will not give up equality as *value* and *goal*. She criticizes liberal practices of inequality, patriarchy dressed up as equality, and calls for a restorative equality revolution.

At first look, Nancy Fraser could represent the optimistic belief Campbell explodes. Fraser stated in 2009 that "feminist ideals of gender equality, so contentious in the preceding decades, now sit squarely in the social mainstream; on the other hand, they have yet to be realized in practice" (2009, 98). But on a closer look, Fraser also worries about the cooption of gender equality politics in a neoliberal era:

> the fate of feminism in the neoliberal era presents a paradox. On the one hand, the relatively small countercultural movement of the previous period has expanded exponentially.... On the other hand, feminist ideas have undergone a subtle shift in valence in the altered context. Unambiguously emancipatory in the era of state-organized capitalism, critiques of economism, androcentrism, étatism, and Westphalianism now appear fraught with ambiguity, susceptible to serving the legitimation needs of a new form of capitalism. After all, this capitalism would much prefer to confront claims for recognition over claims for redistribution. (113)

Since Fraser wrote this, there has been increased global pressure against legislation protecting women's and LGBT rights (even in some European countries); misogynist hate and harassment campaigns have been waged against female politicians (even in Scandinavia).[4] Campbell's sinister

---

4. Including the assassination attempt on former Prime Minister Gro Harlem Brundtland; see Økland 2017, 18–19.

analyses and Fraser's uneasiness are confirmed. Could it be that the concept of equality itself, with its ancient configuration in the term *isotēs*, is a Trojan horse?

Many activists write off equality as a helpful aim due to its modern association with liberal democracy, an increasingly negative term in parts of the world due to the inability of this political system to deliver equality in practice. The question is which system would currently represent a better alternative. Behind the necessary parading of its shortcomings follow those governments who coopt the criticism as license to withdraw previously enjoyed democratic freedoms and rights: voting rights, inviolable bodily rights, press freedom, and so forth. In Europe, COVID-19 has given more space to governments who want to restrict the rights of its citizens.

Fraser (2013) discusses this dilemma in her book *Fortunes of Feminism*. Analyzing the shift from the politics of equality of the mainstream social democracies to the politics of identity in the new social movements (mainly in her US context), she points out that the shift coincides with rising neoliberalism and a feminist neglect of economy and issues of redistribution. Fraser still supports liberal and equality values, but from within a Marxist framework.[5]

These examples must suffice to show that (gender) equality is the sort of exigency for which the current volume searches. But for further discussion, Judith Butler's recent analysis of radical equality helps us better grasp how equality as a multifaceted concept needs specification, which in turn awakens appreciation for how the concept of equality itself has changed over time:

> Equality cannot be reduced to a calculus that accords each abstract person the same value, since the *equality of persons has now to be thought precisely in terms of social interdependency*. So, though it is true that each person should be treated equally, *equal treatment is not possible outside of a social organization of life in which material resources, food distribution, housing, work, and infrastructure* seek to achieve equal conditions of livability. Reference to such equal conditions of *livability is therefore essential to the determination of "equality" in any substantive sense of the term*. (Butler 2020, 40, emphasis added)

---

5. For the nuances of liberal/liberty/liberation in relation to Marxism, see Økland and Boer 2008, 16–18.

Butler's three important qualifications prepare the ground for the rest of this essay. The term *equality* is used in different ways, and Butler argues for one, ethical-political, material understanding of it: not so-called formal equality, nor equality of opportunity, but equality of result—livability for all. A concept of equality contingent on Butler's list of conditions for livability was most certainly not at work in ancient Greece, much less in most countries in the modern world. But biblical sources may also have something to bring to this discussion. Butler's equality-of-result approach finds deep resonance in Pauline ecclesiology and his concern for the weak (1 Cor 8; 9:22) and those without knowledge (1 Cor 1:17–25) or food (1 Cor 11:21–22), although he uses hierarchical rather than equality language to deal with these cases (weak vs. strong, fools vs. wise, haves vs. have-nots). Thus, strictly speaking, he confirms hierarchy reversal rather than equality. But his aim, too, seems to be livability for all, as we shall see in what follows.

A Conceptual History of *Isotēs*

Terminology

Equality is a concept with a long history of constant recharging. Its definition, uses, relationship to other concepts, and translation into other cultural and linguistic domains have varied over time. In fact, the term *equality* is itself a late translation developed from the Latin root *aequ-* documented in ancient Latin inscriptions and literature.[6]

Since this essay is written in English, I will use the English term(s) for the concept. Over the last generation, it has also become more common to use the term *equity* in gender-critical contexts. To distinguish between equality and equity, *equality* refers to the qualitative side of *isotēs* and *equity* to its quantitative and arithmetic side. Since the mid-nineteenth century, my mother tongue, Norwegian, has distinguished between *likhet* (equality)[7] and *likestilling*. The latter term can be translated "equity."[8] *Like-*

---

6. *Oxford Latin Dictionary*, s.v. "aequalitas, aequalis, aequo, etc." Philosophical and nonphilosophical authors listed in the entry include Virgil, Catull, Ovid, Cato, Pliny, Seneca, and Cicero.

7. The term is also used to express the concept of sameness, and is therefore useless in political contexts.

8. Kari E. Børresen (1968), the first Norwegian to complete a PhD on a feminist-

stilling means to put separate entities side by side to create a level surface across their differences. The term was originally coined to prescribe shared legal status of two Norwegian languages: they should be *likestilt* and have the same official status. Soon the term was adopted by the feminists and operationalized politically to prescribe a new relation between women and men. Today, the term refers to the leveling of all sorts of differences, whether language, gender, sexuality, ethnicity, ability, and so on, in order to achieve equality of result.

Since there is no terminological distinction in ancient Greek—the distinction of quantitative and qualitative is itself a matter of philosophical discussion, as we shall see[9]—I use equality as the English translation with the ancient Greek ambiguity intact.

Isotēs in Early Modern Europe

In the early modern period, antiquity's radical notions of thinking *isotēs*/equality were resuscitated and developed further under the new influence of the science of mathematics. In their eagerness to be scientific, early modern philosophers borrowed concepts from the booming natural sciences, as Ingeborg Owesen (2021, 28–29, 46 and 66; cf. Hajdin 2018, xi–xiv) has recently shown. Owesen demonstrates how "the route from one discipline to another was shorter then than now" (28), resulting in an advance for the more quantitative understanding of equality, which in turn paved the way for the modern understanding of gender equality according to which women and men can be equal even if they are not the same. Robert Record, the inventor of the equals sign in mathematics, was also a physician; similarly Descartes and John Locke were both scientists and philosophers. As Owesen states, "The present 'Berlin wall' between the humanities and the natural sciences did not exist in the 17th century. Thus, the shift in collective consciousness that gave rise to feminism and the liberation of women originates perhaps from mathematics" (29). Owesen goes on to corroborate her observation with statistics and etymol-

---

theological topic, proposed the term *equivalence* as an English translation of *likestilling*. At the time, *equity* was not used much outside of arithmetic/fiscal contexts. Her main concern was to avoid the problematic connotations of (qualitative) equality in the direction of sameness, an extremely problematic notion on all sides of the philosophical debates in difference-consumed 1960s Paris where she wrote her thesis.

9. This is still the case in analytical philosophy, as reflected in Gosepath 2021.

ogy: the use of the terms equality/égalité increases from the fifteenth century onward, and the Latin *aequalis* becomes anglicized. The equals sign (=) travelled during early modernity into social and political philosophy, where it influenced French language, in which the Enlightenment democratic ideals were most poignantly formulated as "liberté, égalité, fraternité." Since then, equality has been a progressive social ideal.[10] That being said, women were not considered citizens by Rousseau, whose thought was one of the revolution's inspirations, nor did they become citizens in the revolution's aftermath (Scott 1996; Stuurman 2005).[11] This demonstrates how the value of equality usually operates within a closer defined group, as I shall explore more fully below.

Isotēs in Ancient Greece

Terms and concepts of equality also existed in pre-Hellenistic Greece.[12] A database search (e.g., TLG, Perseus)[13] reveals that the term *isotēs* occurs most frequently in Plutarch, who was a near contemporary to Paul. It also occurs in some writings by Stoic philosophers and in the corpora of Plato and Aristotle.

Here I go back to the latter texts rather than to writings more contemporary with Paul, since in the history of a concept the earlier period must also be represented.[14] I emphasize again that I include Paul in this longer

---

10. "At least since the French Revolution, equality has served as one of the leading ideals of the body politic" (Gosepath 2021). More recently, other terms have been introduced in French, such as *parité*, to denote the more quantitative aspect of equality (Scott 2005).

11. The preface of Rousseau's (1754) *Discours sur l'origine de l'inégalité parmi les hommes*, should suffice: "Could I forget that precious half of the republic that assures the happiness of the other and whose sweetness and goodness maintain its peace and good morals? Amiable and virtuous women of Geneva, the destiny of your sex will always be to govern our destiny. Happy are we when your chaste power, exercised solely within the marriage bond, makes itself felt only for the glory of the state and the wellbeing of the public. Thus it is that in Sparta the women were in command, and thus it is that you deserve to be in command in Geneva" (see Rousseau 2009, 11).

12. The following summary is based on research that will be published in *Hierarchy and Equality: Representations of Sex/Gender in the Ancient World* (Økland et al. forthcoming).

13. Translations are taken from these sources unless otherwise stated.

14. Doing this, I carry with me the important caution expressed in Lopes 2017.

history of a modern, politically charged concept that many find in the Pauline texts themselves. In the context of this interdisciplinary volume, neither Paul nor Plato and Aristotle are fixed reference points; they are just episodes in a longer history that is important from a modern perspective. However, it is my conviction that we might understand Paul's take on terms such as *isotēs* and *ekklēsia* better when he is allowed to occupy this modest place within a long history.

The most common terminology (and thus today given an aura of originality) is derived from the Greek root *isos/ē/on*. I will survey several representative uses of *isotēs* before turning to the concept's reception in the body of literature through which ancient Greek terms and concepts were most widely disseminated in Europe (evident through the number of manuscript copies of each writing): the earliest Christian literature. The representative cases are drawn from Pauline literature.

First, within a discussion of imitative art and how it produces likenesses to a charming original, Plato has an Athenian say: "the correctness of these things would primarily be brought about by equality, both quantitatively and qualitatively speaking, not by pleasure" (*Leg.* 2.667d [my trans.]). I mentioned above that there is no terminological distinction in ancient Greek between qualitative and quantitative equality; rather, the quantitative/qualitative distinction is a matter of philosophical discussion of the concept *isotēs* itself. This quote illustrates this point, thus proving the continuity between the modern, comprehensive, liberal-philosophical theory of justice (on which modern theories of gender equality and other equalities are also based)[15] and the ancient, slightly unsystematic materials, which is approximately similar to the continuity between modern religious dogmas and ancient, slightly unsystematic biblical materials. The ancients were not analytic philosophers in the modern sense.

Note also the abstract notion of sameness in quality so prevalent in ancient Greek thought on conditions for equality. Among the criteria for evaluating imitative arts are both correctness (*orthotēs*) and pleasure (*hēdonē*). It is *isotēs*, equality with the original in both quantity and qual-

---

Part of the rationale for focusing on the concept is that it is impossible to extrapolate a view of women, slaves, or other groups in a short chapter like this, as Lopes shows.

15. Gosepath (2021) demonstrates how the distinction has continued in philosophical discourse up until the present, even if in the realms of practical politics and gender mainstreaming it has become easier to translate the philosophical distinction into a terminological distinction (e.g., equality versus equity/equivalence).

ity, that produces correctness—that is, in the relation between the object of art and what it represents. An object that produces neither usefulness nor truth nor *homoiotēs* can still be judged by the criterion of pleasure.

It is interesting that the term *homoiotēs* occurs in this context. This conglomerate of closely related words (we also have *technai eikastikai* here) is reminiscent of both the creation story of the human in the Greek version of Genesis (*eikōn* and *homoiotēs*) and Paul's reference to it in 1 Cor 11:7–9. It is also interesting that *isotēs* turns up in the same context, and just as the fine distinctions between the terms occurring in Gen 1:26 have been discussed since antiquity, the distinctions between *isotēs* and *homoiotēs* continue to fascinate modern thinkers. What is clear within this aesthetic theory, however, is that the equality the Athenian talks about here has little to do with human rights or legal and social status, which are the contexts in which we often discuss equality today. A modern human rights lawyer would answer no if asked whether equality is dependent on identity and likeness with a normative original. In this sample, only equality regarding quantity *and* quality can produce a correct likeness.

Another interesting example is found in Plato's *Phaedrus*: "I think that equality of age leads them to similar pleasures and through likeness produces friendship" (240c [my trans.]). The passage addresses the connection between sexual-erotic pleasure and friendship between men who are similar in age (quantity) and sex (quality). Again, the criteria of quantity and quality plays a role. Likeness (*homoiotēs*) engenders filial love and proximity in age ensures common preferences regarding pleasure. The various layers of friendship between men is what *Phaedrus* is about; women are out of the picture in its vision of equality, likeness, and love.

Next, Aristotle's work Πολιτικά is usually translated *Politics*, but it could also be translated "civil society," since the society in which he formed his theories had no real distinctions between politics, culture, and civil society.[16] The central topic is how a social community should be run and governed:

> the good in the political field is justice, that means the common good. It is therefore thought by all that justice is some sort of equality, up to a certain point at all events they agree with the philosophical discourses in which it has been established regarding the ethical questions what justice is and for whom: they say that it is to give to the equals what is equal. But

---

16. Even the modern Greek term for "culture" is *politismos*.

equality in which characteristics/respects, and inequality in which? It is important not to forget this question. (1282b [my trans.])

This long and dense quote from an important passage contains many issues that are relevant in our context. First, it demonstrates the same preoccupation as the above quote from *Laws* by Plato, in that the *quality and quantity* of likeness/identity are the basis for equality. Second, Aristotle brings another element into the discussion: promoting his own political philosophy, he ties equality closely up to *to dikaion* "the just," which I, following mainstream translations, have translated "justice." Third, the statement "it is therefore thought by all that justice is some sort of equality" gives an important ancient precedent of the modern, secular idea that gender equality and gender justice are intimately connected, and if there is no structure securing justice, it is difficult to ascertain equality.

Rackham's (1932) Loeb Classical Library translation has "all men" rather than just "all" in the line I just quoted, which spells out the gendered implication of the text, although the dative plural *pasi* could in theory also be feminine. It was as obvious to translators in 1932 as it is to modern gender scholars that the group Aristotle addresses—who partake in the active philosophizing over politics, can practice citizenship, and take on public offices—are indeed all men.

In the politics-culture-civil society organism Aristotle imagines, there is a cycle between ethical and political issues, philosophy, lawmaking, and the running of the city-state. These were not the developed academic disciplines they are today but rather topics for common reflection and discussion among citizen-peers. Equality is discussed within this context and thus always predefined by the laws regulating issues of gender, country of origin, self-ownership (slave/free), and economy.

Aristotle goes on to present a hypothetical counterexample, in which someone suggests that state offices should be distributed unequally (ἀνίσως) on the basis of superior merits, qualities, and so on: "even if the candidates in all other respects did not differ at all but happened to be exactly alike [ὅμοιοι], for those (men) who are different (i.e., different in quality) have different rights and merits ... the just is something else than what is according to worth [τοῖς γὰρ διαφέρουσιν ἕτερον εἶναι τὸ δίκαιον καὶ τὸ κατ'ἀξίαν]" (*Pol.* 1282b).

Aristotle rejects this hypothetical scenario resembling the meritocracy that our current world holds up as ideal (Markovits 2019), since it means that those who have a superior quality of some kind will be able to take political advantage of it. He concludes brutally through the use of several comparative examples, particularly one regarding flute players. It would make as little sense to give the highest political offices to those who have accumulated wealth, come from good families, or have good stature, just as it would make little sense to give the best flute to the best-looking flutist rather than to the superior performers (*Pol.* 1283a).

The basis on which Aristotle can present this example as ridiculous is the democratic template where offices are distributed through ballot. Incompetent citizens will inevitably hold high offices, but they can only stay for a year (or two). And the citizens will inevitably be free men anyway.

Next we turn to Plutarch, the late first-century philosopher who wrote many books as commentaries or reflections on previously published works. In his *Praecepta gerendae reipublicae*, he comments on Euripides, who "chanted" (the tragedies are written in rhythmic prose) approvingly regarding the man who spent sleepless nights restlessly hanging around another (mightier) man's court and subjecting himself to sexual intercourse with the mightier head of tribe or land (*hēgemonikē synētheia*). This might be "the most noble way to proceed for the sake of [his] native land, but otherwise to welcome and preserve the friendships based on equality and justice?" (*Praec. ger. rei publ.* 18.6 [Fowler, LCL]).

Plutarch finds that, in general, Euripides's tragedy too primarily recommends friendships based on equality and justice. But in contrast to the tragedy, Plutarch does not find it recommendable to make this exception for a statesman submitting to a mightier one. There is no reason to further humble his native state by subjecting "the neck to the yoke, as some do." Friendship is different from networking and statesmanship. In the latter case it may be good advice to "lie back and think of England," to use a modern colloquialism. Friendship, equality, and justice are constitutive elements. Thus, for Plutarch friendship can only occur between people on the same level.

Thus, we may begin to approach why there cannot be gender equality within this ancient Greek political system (cf. Blair 2017): wives would as a rule have to "lie back and think of Athens." The *hetairai* could *at best* be viewed as women running their own business—still without the rights and material resources to manifest themselves as equal with property-owning, free male Athenians. There was no legal-material structure for a genuinely equal friendship between a man and a woman in the way we today understand equality as something that is level, be it the playing field or the result.

One final example to discuss is recognizable, content-wise, from Plato, but quoted from Pseudo-Plutarch's "On Monarchy, Democracy, and Oligarchy" because it confirms knowledge of Plato's views on equality closer to early Christianity in time: "A kingdom gives birth to hybris/violence and to the irresponsible (behavior). Oligarchy (breeds) arrogance and stubbornness; democracy (breeds) anarchy, equality, and out of bounds behavior. In sum, all of them breed folly" (*Mon.* 3.1 [my trans.]).

In the presentation of the three main forms of government and their respective pitfalls, the problem with democracy is that it breeds equality, anarchy, and leveling. Equality is a danger and part of the chaos that ensues when you give citizens the power in a true democracy. It is interesting that this chart is repeated as authoritative in a later period, when the type of direct democracy Athens once had no longer existed.[17]

To summarize, this short survey makes clear that there was a concept of equality in ancient Athens between free men who were already eligible to hold offices in the city-state. In Plutarch's period of emperors and kings, it was relevant to discuss whether a statesman would have to submit sexually to a mighty king or head of state. He recommends not to put the neck under the yoke, while wives and slaves had to do so even if they might be seen as equal inside their own respective groups. But we cannot know for certain, for the male citizens who wrote were less interested in them.

Solon (sixth century BCE) organized courts so that jurors and judges were chosen from all Athenian free men. The courts had the final decision over disputes brought to them. Cleisthenes's reform (ca. 507 BCE) assigned all Athenians to *phylai* (tribes) in control of citizenship with its military, political, and social implications. This new notion of *politeia*, "citizenship," created a semblance of equality among the free men who belonged to the *phylē* and was foundational for *ekklēsia* in a Greek civic context.

In spite of the semblance of equality, differences in wealth had the implication that some were more equal than others, that is, had more

---

17. Pseudo-Plutarch goes into further detail (*Mon.* 3.1): "Of these forms of government, which have achieved the widest and greatest power in their periods of dominion, the Persians received as their lot royalty absolute and irresponsible, the Spartans oligarchy aristocratic and uncontrolled, the Athenians democracy self-governing and undiluted. When these forms are not hit exactly, their perversions and exaggerations are what are called (1) tyranny, (2) the predominance of great families, (3) or mob-rule: that is, (1) when royalty breeds violence and irresponsible action; (2) oligarchy, arrogance and presumptuousness; (3) democracy breeds anarchy, equality, excess, and all of them folly" (trans. Fowler [LCL]).

opportunities to exercise their citizen rights and opportunities, while poorer citizens were in practice barred from participation, even if they had the same rights in theory. Since this was seen as weakening the strength of the democracy in its military, political, and social implications, the Periclean reform of the fifth century BCE ensured that citizens were paid to serve the public in the council, assembly, and juries.

In addition to these male citizens, there were the "wives of the Athenians." The Athenians proper were the male citizens who had wives, children, and slaves.[18] Finally, there were the metics (resident foreigners) filling a middle category between foreigner and citizen.[19]

Paul and *Isotēs*?

The term *isotēs* and the related word *isos* figure in Pauline literature only on a few occasions. As in the quotes above, the terms for justice and equality are linked:

> Not so that there should be relief for others while for you pressure, but out of equality between your present abundance and their deprivation, so that also their abundance may be there for your deprivation, in order that there may be equality. As it is written, "The one who had much did not have too much, and the one who had little did not have too little. (2 Cor 8:13–15)

Expressing similar ideas as the Butler quote above, the official Norwegian translation has *likhet* for *isotēs* here, which corresponds to English "equality." However, given the built-in ambiguity of these translations, denoting both equilibrium *and* similarity, the NRSV has "fair balance," which grasps the nuance of *isotēs* here well. The text is about a quantitative *equality of*

---

18. This summary is based on the already brief Lang and Camp 2004.

19. Both Athenian metics and denizens of the modern world have less than full membership in a political community. Nonetheless, the identity of these groups of noncitizens was firmly linked to exclusive nodes of belonging we today know as states. What does it mean to be a noncitizen—historically, legally, and politically? What similarities and differences can we find between ancient and contemporary forms of belonging? The place and status of the Greek metics, today's denizens, and women as a category in the makeup of political belonging—these topics are highly relevant for the current essay, but I have treated them separately at a conference at the Norwegian Institute at Athens.

result—that is, between economic and social classes, rich and poor, *inside* the *ekklēsia*. This confirms the issue raised in the introduction that a concept of *isotēs*, some sort of equality-making, was operative in the Pseudo-Pauline Letter to the Colossians: "You Masters, provide justice and equality to your slaves, knowing that also you have a Master in heaven" (Col. 4:1). As in Aristotle, justice and equality are linked. The text further uses the same expression, *to dikaion*, "the just" (rather than the noun) as we saw in Aristotle.

For both of these biblical examples, the older or more tradition-bound translations use the English "equal" for *isotēs*, whereas the usually more progressive NRSV has "fair."[20] In the case of Col 4:1, treating slaves with justice and equality would have been far more progressive in the ancient world. Although it is not clear how the author understands the justice-related basis for the equality of slaves, the verse does go much further than just postulating a form of equality "in Christ." Again, since this is written to an *ekklēsia*, there are different rules about the relationships between masters and slaves than those outside of the *ekklēsia*. But since a slave remains a slave (there is nothing here indicating that the slaves should be given freedom), *the masters* should provide for the slaves so that the masters can expect fair treatment by their master in heaven.

Paul uses the adjective form *isos* for equal (quantitative) value or qualitatively of being equal/identical to God, as in Phil 2:6: "he who was in the form of God, did not regard equality with God as something to be exploited." Maybe "identical" or "likeness to" would offer a more precise translation? *Isos* may mean qualitatively "like" or just "equal to." I have pointed out the problematic ambiguity between "similar" and "same" already, which directly affects our approach to Paul's understanding of the relationship between humans and God—including how he understands the creation of the human in God's image. I included this last example to complement the two occurrences of *isotēs* in Pauline literature. A full treatment of the use of *isos/ē/on* in earlier Greek literature would have been far too large a project for this chapter.

---

20. Thus the phrase ἀλλ' ἐξ ἰσότητος in 2 Cor 8:13 is rendered as "but by way of equality" in NASB and "but by an equality" in the KJV (cf. the NIV "equality") and ὅπως γένηται ἰσότης in v. 14 is rendered as "that there may be equality" (NASB) and "but by an equality" (KJV; cf. NIV "equality"). The phrase καὶ τὴν ἰσότητα τοῖς δούλοις in Col 4:1 is rendered as "justice and fairness" (NASB), "just and equal" (KJV), and "right and fair" (NIV).

The above examples show that many of the same ambiguities in the ancient Greek understandings of the term *isotēs* are also present in Pauline literature. *Isos* terminology is not charged with respect to gender difference but occurs in the context of redistribution of wealth and privileges (quantity and equilibrium). Paul, who like Plutarch draws women into discussions where the older philosophers would never mention them, never draws terms derived from *isos* into any discussion of male and female, and their mutual relations.

Still, the Pauline texts present some interesting developments. First, Col 4:1 stands out since it encourages slave masters to treat their slaves with equality and links this to justice, although the author uses hierarchical language to deal with these cases (weak vs. strong, fools vs. wise).

Second, the main Pauline use of the term *isotēs* is to denote equality of result (quantitative equality). Material differences between rich and poor (2 Cor 8:13–15) and masters and slaves (Col 4) should be leveled in Christ—an idea that resonates in traditional social democracies and in the Butler quote above. Second Corinthians 8:13–15 is a call for redistribution that might have been taken straight out of the program of a modern, socialist or social democrat party, and much in line with what has been emphasized by Fraser.

This interpretation is strengthened by further passages expressing the same idea, although without using *isos*-derived terminology. Paul's dismissal of *gnosis* in 1 Cor 1:17–25 is another way of leveling advantages that education (which used to follow a wealthy background) might bring. In 1 Cor 8 and 9:22, he highlights the virtue of solidarity of the strong with the weak. First Corinthians 11:17–22 admonishes those who *have* to wait for and share with those who *have not*. Finally, his insistence on manual labor (1 Cor 9:3–18) alongside his teaching parallels modern self-proletarization and disturbs any easy connection between the Pauline concept of equality and the already-presented concept of equality among the ancient Athenian citizen class.

Gender Equality without the Concept and before the Name?

So a concept of equality not only existed in the linguistic world of ancient Greek but also had a designated term and was continuously discussed. But, surprisingly from a modern perspective, notions of equality and notions of gender were unconnected except when it came to sex and friendship relations between men and not between women or between the sexes.

Authors such as Pseudo-Plutarch and Plato describe the *filia* and sexual intimacy between men of the same age and equal rank as the clearest example of equality. These texts in my opinion challenge the view that, in antiquity, sex had to involve hierarchy and that any sex that did not involve hierarchy (i.e., between women) was seen as unnatural and punishable, as Bernadette Brooten (1996, 186) has argued most persuasively. In her view, the fundamental active-passive dichotomy within the sexual semantics of antiquity combined with a negative view of women in general and led to the condemnation of love and sex between women (103, 253–58). The material presented here calls for a nuancing of this view. Not all sex between men was normatively hierarchical, and there was a designated, positive term for describing sexual mutuality based on equality between male partners.

The volume *Feminism and Ancient Philosophy* (Ward 1997) discusses which, if any, of the ancient philosophers introduces topics of gender equality and justice. Most of its contributors discuss and qualify notions of equality and then go on to answer in the negative along a very wide, sliding scale. Catherine Gardner (2006, 79–80) points to Plato's *Republic* as the *first* systematic account of sex equality, "where he argues that equal work and education for women are part of the requirements of the ideal state." But among the occurrences of *isotēs* in Plato's writings, none of them occur in book 5 of the *Republic* where he writes on the Guardians. Julia Annas (1976, 315) who had studied this part of the *Republic* in detail, argues that any education and relief of women from reproductive tasks there is due to a purely utilitarian approach to the state and not due to a concern for women's rights. Furthermore, it is a utopian text: "there is nothing in *Republic* 5 which would commit Plato to the view that it was unjust for fourth-century Athenian women to be treated as they were" (315). In her discussion of Paul, Plato's *Republic*, and Annas's interpretation, Karin Neutel (2013, 44) adds: "While there are some women who are better at some things than some men, as a group, women are weaker and far surpassed by men. The rationale for having both male and female guardians is thus not based on gender equality, but rather on inequality."

Gender equality in a modern sense—supported by formal justice, women's rights, citizenship, and so on—was not part of the discussions of equality in ancient Greece, as we have seen. At the same time, there are traces, not least in the early Christian materials, of *values* and ethics of mutual care, of women running their own businesses and leading, sponsoring and speaking in Christian assemblies. None of these phenomena presuppose equality, and Paul does not use the *isos* terminology much either. As Stanley Stowers (2011, 241–42) reminds us, no one is served with confused concepts and terminologies, and the current paper's strict focus on the *concept*, but with side glances toward traces of values, ethics, and practices of care that might diminish hierarchical divides, is greatly helped by Stowers's precisions. To those heuristic side glances I will now turn, starting with the notion that the Christians are *hen*: one.

Foundational for *ekklēsia* in a Greek civic context is the concept of the citizen, *politēs*, clearly defined in legal terms (Conze et al., 1972, 833–35). Like *isotēs*, *politēs* is not a central concept in Pauline discourse on *ekklēsia*. Still, notions surrounding both *isotēs* and *politēs* might be *implied* in other expressions in Pauline literature, such as expressions of unity:

> Now a mediator is not mediator of just one; but God is one.... As many of you as were baptized into Christ have clothed yourselves with Christ. There is not Jew or Greek, there is no longer slave or free, there is no longer male and female; for all of you are one in Christ Jesus. (Gal 3:20, 27–28)

Galatians 3:20 implies that two parties need a mediator who is responsible toward both of them. But God, who is above all differences and does not need a higher arbiter, can be one in and of oneself. In 3:27–28 this higher arbiter is Christ Jesus. But even so, the baptismal formula, as it is often taken to be, is remarkable in its alleviation of differences but not of hierarchy as such. It is superior to be male, Jewish, and free both in the formula Paul quotes and when considering other issues he tends to write about.

Searching for possible *practices* of equality, the term *ekklēsia* may yield more than statements of unity. Miller (2015, 5; see further below) demonstrates that "locating the origin of the Christian title *ekklēsia* in select aspects of its Septuagint usage obscures the full application of the term in the Septuagint ... [and] also neglects the widest and most persistent use of the word from the classical period into the first century: the designation for the civic, political assembly of citizens." In the Septuagint, *ekklēsia* with various determining attributes, such as *kyriou, tou hypsistou, hagion, huiōn Israel*, and others, denoted the assembly of Israelites and the bearers of the covenant. As a technical term, then, *ekklēsia* denoted in both the Septuagint and broader Greek culture primarily male gatherings. Since the term *ekklēsia* had gone out of use as main designation on Jewish religious assemblies by the time of Paul, it was a vacant term from the Jewish side, without any need to overlook the term's heavy baggage.[21] *Ekklēsia* already had positive connotations designating the organization of citizens, and public life more in general, in two different geographical-cultural realms. Maybe the term's transgressiveness was perceived as giving space for utopian ideas of unity and equality within the limited and limiting confines outlined in the above examples extended across ethnic, class, and material divisions? It is the limitations within which expressions of equality operate and make sense that are sometimes overlooked in New Testament research (cf. Dann 1975, 997–98). Belonging to the in-groups of Greek citizens or Israelites was an exclusive form of equality with narrow confines. Paul tries to negotiate categories and practices that produce hierarchies by inviting everyone into the *ekklēsia* while reproducing social inequalities in other ways between men and women, slaves and freeborn (Økland 2004).

It is also relevant regarding *ekklēsia* and citizenship that Paul does use the expression *basileia theou* on six occasions, in an eschatological sense (Rom 14:17; 1 Cor 4:20; 6:9; 15:24, 50; Gal 5:21). One is subject, not citizen, under a king or emperor, but John Kloppenborg (2019, 347) suggests that the Pauline collection, when viewed alongside the practice of *epidosis*—the collection of funds for a project—could be seen as a form of ritual action, a way "for contributors to perform citizenship." This is a good example of how Christian *ekklēsia* membership—for members who were already free and financially in charge of their own means—could be seen as a kind of citizenship.[22]

I have thus far alluded to women with an apparent level of autonomy. Roman era authors refer to women in positions of leadership and business. Paul mentions Prisca, Phoebe, Chloe, Junia, and others. They provided funding for his activity; led households, house churches, and businesses; and were missionaries, teachers, apostles, and prophets (see Osiek and MacDonald 2006). The fact that Paul mentions them and their

---

21. The term is used by Philo and Josephus, though most of the time in a nontechnical sense (Rengstorf 1975). For example, in Josephus, *A.J.* 19.332 Simon, a native of Jerusalem, assembles the crowd for a "public meeting" (*ekklēsia*; trans. Feldman [LCL]). Miller (2015) devotes a full chapter to Josephus and shows how previous research understanding the Christian *ekklēsia* as continuous with the Septuagint usage of the term (only), overlooks the contemporaneous usage of the term, e.g., in Josephus.

22. This would clearly not apply to those members who did not own themselves, such as women who were under a husband or slaves.

contributions matter-of-factly while at the same time limiting women's religious authority in some respects might indicate a division between theory and practice or something else. Conceptual history traces primarily theory, although it is kept in check by material practices (cf. the introduction to this chapter). Theoretically, Paul does not speak of equality in relation to gender. But he is more explicit than the other ancient authors surveyed about different arrangements in practice, which may have to do with the practical limits of politics and legislation. Recently Anna Miller (2015) has explored exactly this space. In her *Corinthian Democracy*, she shows how discourses of *ekklēsia* had not disappeared even in the Roman imperial times, and she situates equality as a natural part of these discourses. She devotes two chapters to Josephus, Dio Chrysostom, and Plutarch, all of whom are roughly contemporaneous with Paul.

Miller takes the rhetorical genre of 1 Corinthians as her point of departure, like Antoinette Wire (1990) and Elisabeth Schüssler Fiorenza (1987) before her and emphasizes that Paul writes to persuade. For Wire, this betrays that he was not in any position of authority from the outset; he could not command the Corinthians. Miller builds on Schüssler Fiorenza and uses the same observation to draw our attention to the ancient Greek *ekklēsia* context in which deliberate rhetoric had its *Sitz im Leben*. When Paul borrows the term for the ancient democratic civic assembly to designate the groups of Christ-believers, this must have some significance. Miller argues that even though the institutions were gone, the *ekklēsia* model of running a city was still inspiring for social organization, particularly in Rome's eastern provinces. This engendered debates on authority, gender, and speech and created space for political-democratic intervention.

Miller's suggestion seems plausible, not least considering Fergus Millar's (1981) descriptions of the wild crowds described in the novel *The Golden Ass*: they break Roman law then step in for the court in a formally recognized court's absence. *Lex Romana* was only as strong as the strength and number of the legal representatives in any given town, which could be none. Perhaps this power vacuum might have engendered a historical space for women to carve out some kind of equality of opportunity as Miller seems to imply? Paul, living in that world and not particularly in its upper classes, would relate to the situation on the ground better than to lawyers and high-ranked slaves in the imperial hierarchy in Rome. Plutarch, for his part, dedicated a whole volume to brave women. But as Jill Marshall (2017, 102) has argued, despite being attributed bravery in war, in this moral-philosophical work the women come across as idealized but still separate and different from men.²³ Moreover, bravery does not presuppose equality.

Miller (2015, 13) seems to qualify her notion of equality very much down to "equality of speech." This is apt given the sources and brings her onto the "qualified equality scale" of Ward (1997). But then it should be noted that in any case, like the Stoic women of Asmis (Ward 1997, 69 and 75), Miller's women's speech is not transmitted in writing either.²⁴ Kloppenborg (2019) reasons along the same lines regarding *ekklēsiai*, mainly that although the institution of the ancient Greek city state was gone, voluntary associations, funerary societies, collegia, and the like perpetuated its democratic ideals but also extended participation to slaves, women, and foreigners. Jews, who had their own ownership of the term through the Septuagint, must have been among these foreigners too. Kloppenborg's point is that the Christian *ekklēsia* as a historical entity fits a larger pattern following a more general cultural logic. In contrast to Miller, who considers the Pauline *ekklēsia* more in terms of an authoritative democratic assembly from the perspective of the members themselves, Kloppenborg coins the term "playing with democracy" (2019, 284–86, 346) for the broader phenomenon of voluntary associations, in order to emphasize the following: (1) that this game is still ongoing and at stake in the period of the founding of the first Christian *ekklēsiai* (a term he avoids); (2) that *deme* and private association, *ekklēsia*, funerary society, and the like—all played a role to negotiate, perpetuate, and expand democratic ideals (including equality) to groups that were excluded in the initial Athenian setup: slaves, women, and mostly the metics, the Pauline *ekklēsia* was not unique in doing so; and (3) that the democratic fabric thus created, was still far from the radical ideals embedded in the setup of the independent Athenian city-state. Also, early Christian concepts and values, including those of equality and oneness, were bound to be conditioned on class systems and inequality on the material level. Since Kloppenborg and his colleagues (Rollens,

---

23. Marshall shows how Plutarch gives more restrictive advice in the social practice-oriented *conjugalia praecepta* than in *mulierum virtutes* (98–107). The assignment of the latter (from the priestess Klea) was to argue that men and women's virtues are the same, but Marshall shows how women end up as exemplars of bravery with little first-person discourse (101).

24. See Ward 1997 regarding women's equality and authorship in Stoic circles. Access to writing is part of freedom of speech and expression.

Ascough, Harland, and others) engage more with the material aspects and limitations of the social history of associations (see Kloppenborg 2019), their work can more precisely gauge the extent of equality as *social practice* and not just as *value*. The conceptual history that I have tried to pursue in this chapter is based exactly on the conviction that concepts change content when political *and* material conditions change, hence the necessity to study the intertwining of the two, although the material history has been outside the scope of this chapter.

Bridling the Trojan Horse

Dann (1975, 997–98) starts his entry on equality by stating:

> "Equality" is a relational concept … and this relationship is produced solely through the judging mind. 3. Equality is always only equality in a certain respect. Every comparison presupposes a *tertium comparationis*.… Equality is therefor never a general, but always a partial statement about the compared objects. 4. A judgment about equality presupposes the difference of what is compared. "Complete'" or 'absolute' equality are self-contradictory statements. (my trans.)

In short, this means that those who maintain that certain ancient social units were equal must qualify what concept of equality, what *tertium comparationis*, these historical incidents are measured against.

I mentioned equality as a possible Trojan horse, and perhaps this *tertium comparationis* is it: the ancient examples examined above show that *isotēs* was never without qualification. Equality functioned as an ideal value within and between clearly defined groups—as Dann suggests and as Butler also presupposes—in the Athenian council, in Christ under eschatological circumstances, and under capitalism in the present. Fraser (2013, 164) quite rightly perceives the qualifications as "ideological boundaries that delimit 'separate spheres' and thereby rationalize inequality." But as Dann and more recently Gosepath (2021) have pointed out, "'Equality' and 'equal' are incomplete predicates that necessarily generate one question: equal in what respect?… Equality essentially consists of a tripartite relation between two (or several) objects or persons and one (or several) qualities." Failing to realize this sobering, uncomfortable aspect as part of the modus operandi of the *concept* equality has perhaps made the equality *value* we strive to put into practice more elusive. Part of the point with this brief conceptual history has been to display the many ways of discussing and understanding the concept's complexity. Acknowledging the limitations at the roots of the concept, might also make it clearer as a current concept and political goal.

Equality is not a frequently invoked ideal in Pauline literature, and in a conceptual study the scarcity of evidence is significant. On the other hand, the semantic fields of *isotēs* and *ekklēsia* share some connotations, as I have highlighted. How the recipient communities of Paul's letters might have understood their mutual relations is not clear; we cannot presuppose that Pauline rhetoric represents their understanding in a transparent way, as Wire (1990) has clearly shown. Social history can teach us more about general material limitations and parameters, but since we do not have Paul's recipients' version of the story, we can only keep in mind that they probably did see things differently (hence Paul's need to write).

In the ancient literature surveyed, there has been little conceptual controversy around *isotēs*; there is an intimate relation between justice and equality but less so between gender and equality. Some texts explicate qualitative requirements for equality, for example, the Philippians text where Paul talks about being equal to or like God, whereas others consider equality more in quantitative terms. Also, the conceptual history developed in this study has made clear that equality has meant different things in different periods. In the modern world, we tend to think of equality as a universal value, but a short dip into conceptual history shows us that this is a modern development. Further, the concept is far more central to our way of thinking today than it was two thousand years ago.

While the Pauline *ekklēsia* set the frame for this exploration of terms and concepts relating to equality in ancient and modern contexts, confusion may still arise in the present. If gender equality slips away again as Campbell (2014) and Fraser (2013) fear, it may partly be because we have failed to grasp clearly what it could be in the first place. In my Norwegian context, policies are all about achieving equality as if it were an achievable situation. This arithmetic, quantitative way of thinking about equality has brought us far, but it fails the continuous discussion on equality across vast qualitative difference, as value and ideal. Can a value be achieved? In that case, it would no longer be an ideal but a fact.

For equality to work in social practice, not just as a value or an ideal, it requires—and produces—support structures such as legislation, distribution of resources, and so forth. Where structures are missing, one can only take those in power's word for equality in practice. In my opinion, the Pauline *ekklēsia* would fit Butler's (2020, 40; cf. above) definition of radical equality of result, "a social organization of life in which material resources, food distribution, housing, work, and infrastructure seek to achieve equal conditions of livability." But those members of the *ekklēsia* who had no formal support to claim equality in the larger community would have no recourse.

Pauline *ekklēsiai* practiced neither the Platonic-Aristotelian nor the modern liberal understanding of equality. Even if gender hierarchy was still the default mode of relations between the sexes in the first century, including in the Pauline *ekklēsiai*, it does not follow that there was no concept or ideal of equality, no notion of women's authority and right to speak, no notion of mutuality, and no way to express it (Økland 1998).

Works Cited

Annas, Julia. 1976. "Plato's "Republic" and Feminism." *Philosophy* 51:307–21.
Aristotle. 1932. *Politics*. Translated by Harris Rackham. LCL. Cambridge: Harvard University Press.
Asmis, Elizabeth. 1997. "The Stoics on Women." Pages 68–92 in *Feminism and Ancient Philosophy*. Edited by Julie K. Ward. New York: Routledge.
Blair, Elena Duvergès. 2017. *Plato's Dialectic on Woman: Equal, Therefore Inferior*. Routledge Monographs in Classical Studies. London: Routledge.
Børresen, Kari E. 1968. *Subordination et equivalence: Nature et rôle de la femme d´après Augustin et Thomas d'Aquin*. Oslo: Universitetsforlaget.
Brooten, Bernadette. 1996. *Love between Women: Early Christian Responses to Female Homoeroticism*. The Chicago Series on Sexuality, History, and Society. Chicago: University of Chicago Press.
Brunner, O., R. Koselleck, W. Conze, eds. 1972–1997. *Geschichtliche Grundbegriffe: Historisches Lexikon zur politisch-sozialen Sprache in Deutschland*. 8 vols. Stuttgart: Klett.
Butler, Judith. 2020. *The Force of Nonviolence: An Ethico-Political Bind*. London: Verso.
Campbell, Beatrix. 2013. "The End of the Equality Paradigm—The Kilburn Manifesto." openDemocracy. https://tinyurl.com/SBL06104z.
———. 2014a. "After Neoliberalism: The Need for a Gender Revolution." *Soundings* 56:10–26.
———. 2014b. *End of Equality*. London: Seagull.

Cancik, Hubert. 1998. "Gleichheit und Freiheit. Die antiken Grundlagen der Menschenrechte." Pages 293–315 in *Antik—Modern: Beiträge zur römischen und deutschen Kulturgeschichte*. Edited by Richard Faber, Barbara von Reibnitz, Jörg Rüpke, and Hubert Cancik. Stuttgart: Metzler.

Cancik, Hubert, Burkhard Gladigow, Matthias Samuel Laubscher, Karl-Heinz Kohl, eds. 1988–2001. *Handbuch religionswissenschaftlicher Grundbegriffe*. 5 vols. Stuttgart: Kohlhammer.

Conze, Werner, C. Meier, R. Koselleck, H. Maier, and H. L. Reimann. 1972. "Demokratie." Pages 821–99 in *A–D*. Vol. 1 in *Geschichtliche Grundbegriffe: Historisches Lexikon zur politisch-sozialen Sprache in Deutschland*. Edited by O. Brunner, R. Koselleck, and W. Conze. Stuttgart: Klett.

Dann, Otto. 1975. "Gleichheit." Pages 997–1046 in *E–G*. Vol. 2 of *Geschichtliche Grundbegriffe: Historisches Lexikon zur politisch-sozialen Sprache in Deutschland*. Edited by O. Brunner, R. Koselleck, and W. Conze. Stuttgart: Klett.

———. 1980. *Gleichheit und Gleichberechtigung. Das Gleichheitspostulat in der alteuropäischen Tradition und in Deutschland bis zum ausgehenden 19. Jahrhundert*. Berlin: Duncker and Humblot.

Fraser, Nancy. 2009. "Feminism, Capitalism, and the Cunning of History." *New Left Review* 56:97–117.

———. 2013. *Fortunes of Feminism: From State-Managed Capitalism to Neoliberal Crisis*. New York: Verso.

Gardner, Catherine Villanueva. 2006. *Historical Dictionary of Feminist Philosophy*. Historical Dictionaries of Religions, Philosophies, and Movements 64. Plymouth: Scarecrow.

Glare, P. G. W., ed. 1996. *Oxford Latin Dictionary*. Oxford: Clarendon.

Gosepath, Stefan. 2021. "Equality." In *Stanford Encyclopedia of Philosophy*. Edited by Edward N. Zalta. https://tinyurl.com/SBL06104a1.

Hajdin, Mane. 2001. "Introduction." Pages xi–xxiii in *The Notion of Equality*. Edited by Mane Hajdin. The International Research Library of Philosophy. Burlington: Ashgate.

Hellevik, Ottar. 2008. *Jakten på den norske lykken: Norsk Monitor 1985–2007*. Oslo: Universitetsforlaget.

Inglehart, R., C. Haerpfer, A. Moreno, C. Welzel, K. Kizilova, J. Diez-Medrano, M. Lagos, P. Norris, E. Ponarin, B. Puranen, et al., eds. 2014. *World Values Survey Wave 6*. Madrid: JD Systems Institute. https://www.worldvaluessurvey.org/WVSDocumentationWV6.jsp.

Josephus. 1981. *Jewish Antiquities in Ten Volumes*. Vol. 9: *Books XVIII–XIX*. Translated by L. H. Feldman. LCL. Cambridge: Harvard University Press.

Kippenberg, Hans G. 1993. "Klassengesellschaft." Pages 362–71 in *Gesetz–Kult*. Vol. 3 of *Handbuch religionswissenschaftlicher Grundbegriffe*. Edited by Hubert Cancik, B. Gladigow, M. Laubscher, and K. H. Kohl. Stuttgart: Kohlhammer.

Kloppenborg, John S. 2019. *Christ's Associations: Connecting and Belonging in the Ancient City*. New Haven: Yale University Press.

Koselleck, Reinhard. 1989. *Vergangene Zukunft: Zur Semantik geschichtlicher Zeiten*. Frankfurt: Suhrkamp.

Lang, Mabel, and John McK. Camp. 2004. *The Athenian Citizen: Democracy in the Athenian Agora*. Rev. ed. Athens: ASCSA.

Lopes, Rodolfo. 2019. Review of Plato's Dialectic on Woman: Equal, Therefore Inferior, by Elena Duvergès Blair. *Bryn Mawr Classical Review*. https://tinyurl.com/SBL06104b1.

Markovits, Daniel. 2019. *The Meritocracy Trap*. London: Lane.

Marshall, Jill E. 2017. *Women Praying and Prophesying in Corinth*. WUNT 2/448. Tübingen: Mohr Siebeck.

Millar, Fergus. 1981. "The World of the Golden Ass." *JRS* 71:63–75.

Miller, Anna C. 2015. *Corinthian Democracy: Democratic Discourse in 1 Corinthians*. Princeton Theological Monograph Series 220. Eugene, OR: Pickwick.

Müller-Wille, Staffan. 2014. "Race and History: Comments from an Epistemological Point of View." *Science, Technology, & Human Values* 39:597–606.

Neutel, Karin. 2013. "A Cosmopolitan Ideal: Paul's Declaration "Neither Jew nor Greek, Neither Slave nor Free, nor Male and Female" in the Context of First-Century Thought." PhD. diss., Rijksuniversiteit Groningen.

Økland, Jorunn. 1998. "'In publicum procurrendi': Women in the Public Space of Roman Greece." Pages 127–41 in *Aspects of Women in Antiquity: Proceedings of the First Nordic Symposium on Women's Lives in Antiquity*. Edited by Lena Larsson Lovén and Agneta Strömberg. Studies in Mediterranean Archaeology and Literature. Jonsered: Åström.

———. 2004. *Women in Their Place: Paul and the Corinthian Discourse of Gender and Sanctuary Space*. LNTS 269. London: T&T Clark.

———. 2017. "Death and the Maiden: Manifestos, Gender, Self-Canonisation, and Violence." Pages 15–44 in *The Bible and Feminism: Re-Map-*

ping the Field. Edited by Yvonne Sherwood with Anna Fisk. Oxford: Oxford University Press.

Økland, Jorunn, and Roland Boer. 2008. "Towards Marxist Feminist Biblical Criticism." Pages 1–25 in *Marxist Feminist Criticism of the Bible*. Edited by Roland Boer and Jorunn Økland. The Bible in the Modern World 14. Sheffield: Sheffield Phoenix.

Økland, Jorunn, et al., eds. Forthcoming. *Hierarchy and Equality: Representations of Sex/Gender in the Ancient World*. Papers and Monographs of the Norwegian Institute at Athens. Athens: Norwegian Institute at Athens.

Osiek, Carolyn, and Margaret MacDonald, with Janet H. Tulloch. 2006. *A Woman's Place: House Churches in Earliest Christianity*. Minneapolis: Augsburg Fortress.

Owesen, Ingeborg W. 2021. *The Genealogy of Modern Feminist Thinking: Feminist Thought as Historical Present*. Routledge Research in Gender and Society. London: Routledge.

Perseus Digital Library. Edited by Gregory R. Crane. Tufts University. http://www.perseus.tufts.edu.

Philo. 1927–1953. *Philo in Ten Volumes*. Translated by F. H. Colson and G. H. Whitaker. LCL. Cambridge: Harvard University Press.

Plato. 1914. *Euthyphro. Apology. Crito. Phaedo. Phaedrus*. Translated by H. N. Fowler. LCL. New York: Macmillan.

———. 1926. *Laws: Books 1–6*. Translated by R. G. Bury. LCL. Cambridge: Harvard University Press.

Plutarch. 1960a. "Precepts of Statecraft." Pages 155–300 in vol. 10 of *Moralia in Fifteen Volumes*. Translated by H. N. Fowler. LCL. Cambridge: Harvard University Press.

———. 1960b. "On Monarchy, Democracy, Oligarchy." Pages 301–12 in vol. 10 of *Moralia in Fifteen Volumes*. Translated by H. N. Fowler. LCL. Cambridge: Harvard University Press.

Rengstorf, Karl H. 1975. *E–K*. Vol. 2 of *A Complete Concordance to Flavius Josephus*. Leiden: Brill.

Rousseau, Jean J. 1948. *Discours sur l'origine de l'inégalité parmi les hommes*. Paris: Hatier.

———. 2009. *Discourse on the Origin of Inequality*. Translated by Franklin Philip. Edited with an Introduction by Patrick Coleman. Oxford: Oxford University Press.

Schüssler Fiorenza, Elisabeth. 1987. "Rhetorical Situation and Historical Reconstruction in 1 Corinthians." *NTS* 33:386–403.

Scott, Joan W. 1996. *Only Paradoxes to Offer: French Feminists and the Rights of Man*. Cambridge: Harvard University Press.

———. 2005. *Parité: Sexual Equality and the Crisis of French Universalism*. Chicago: University of Chicago Press.

Sen, Amartya. 1980. "Equality of What?" Pages 197–220 in vol. 1 of *Tanner Lectures on Human Values*. Edited by Sterlin M. McMurrin. Cambridge: Cambridge University Press.

Stowers, Stanley. 2011. "The Concept of 'Community' and the History of Early Christianity." *MTSR* 23:238–56.

Stuurman, Siep. 2005. "François Poulain de la Barre and the Invention of Modern Equality." *Journal of Modern History* 77:1055–57.

Thesaurus Linguae Graecae Digital Library. Edited by Maria C. Pantelia. Irvine: University of California. http://www.tlg.uci.edu.ezproxy.uio.no.

Ward, Julie K., ed. 1997. *Feminism and Ancient Philosophy*. New York: Routledge.

Wire, Antoinette C. 1990. *The Corinthian Women Prophets: A Reconstruction through Paul's Rhetoric*. Minneapolis: Fortress.

Aesthetics: New Testament, the Classics, and a Case Study in 1 Corinthians

Laura Salah Nasrallah

Look. It's embarrassing to write about aesthetics because it reminds you of the clunkiness of your prose as you try to stretch toward something more, something beautiful, something inspired by others' thoughts of the sublime. But perhaps it's acceptable to plod, knowing how the covert aesthetics of your academic field also conceal an ugliness: assumptions about what is beautiful that are driven by prejudicial racial and gendered logics, calls to the beautiful or to completeness or perfection (*teleion*) both ancient and recent that do not disclose—or that actively obfuscate—their underpinnings.

The conversations that drew this volume together explored how New Testament studies and the field of classics have sometimes stood at odds with each other. The texts that happen to be collected in the canon of the New Testament do not often attain to the sophistication of the Greek in what have come to be considered the classics—Homer, Hesiod, Herodotus—or the feints and dips of the writers of the so-called Second Sophistic as they imitated the Attic greats and sometimes mocked them at the same time. This is both a fact and an aesthetic judgment. My essay explores a case study in this problem: interpretations of 1 Cor 13:1, a small portion from a letter of Paul and Sosthenes to those in Christ at Corinth, a text so

---

I am grateful to Noreen Khawaja for initial rescue/bibliographical help regarding eighteenth- and nineteenth-century aesthetics, to Denise Buell for conversations about an early draft, and to research assistants Rikki Liu and Joseph Lee for editing suggestions. I am grateful for support from the Beyond Canon project of the University of Regensburg. Portions of this essay appear in various forms in the forthcoming *Ancient Christians and the Power of Curses: "Magic," Aesthetics, and Justice.*

often beautifully intoned at weddings and here quoted in the familiar, not-yet-gender-neutral RSV: "If I speak in the tongues of men and of angels, but have not love, I am a noisy gong or a clanging cymbal." As we shall see, the idea of speaking in tongues raises an aesthetic ruckus.

Maybe it is safest to begin an essay on aesthetics by means of a beautiful object that also offers a critique of aesthetic assumptions. Artist Emma Amos's *Measuring, Measuring* (fig. 1) offers a theory-driven rejoinder to aesthetics grounded in whiteness, a kind of response to the aesthetic taxonomy of nineteenth-century German scholar Johannes Winckelmann and its ongoing effects. A laser transfer photograph on the left side of Amos's work depicts a nude bronze female body which seems to be appropriated from Aristide Maillot; at the same time, this armless sculpture reminds us of the Venus de Milo (see Farrington 2005, 161), puzzlingly held or propped up by an invisible figure with a hat. (What man carries the fragmented female body?) The middle figure is a colonial-era photo of an African woman crisscrossed with seamstress-style measuring tape in the yellows of yardsticks. These recall measuring rods or canons. These measuring tapes sever her at her neck, pudenda, and knees. She alone is affixed atop a printed essay about Greek art that includes words, some clear and some obscured, including at the outlined point of her severed legs, "male body in action at gymnasiums … experience, and sculptors had … observe its proportions." It is as if Amos is quoting from an art historical text (indeed, she likely is) about what was considered perfect and worth replicating in sculpture: the nude male form, duly trained as ephebe or athlete in the gymnasia of the ancient world. The rightmost image presents one of the canonical objects of art history: the fifth-century BCE Greek "Kritios Boy." The image is framed by Kente cloth and allusions to Kente cloth in the form of modern legs abstracted and stacked into what look like parallel lines, an excess and remainder of the severed or missing limbs of the three central images. Amos engages the classics and its aesthetics.

How the Disciplines Discipline

The conference that occasioned this volume was based on the premise that there is a divide between New Testament studies and the classics. This can be true; often, there is a kind of down-nose snobbery in classics departments about the philological weaknesses of New Testament scholars and the bad Greek of the Christian Testament. In turn, *neutestamentliche* philological interest in terms like *charis* (grace? gift?) or *hamartia* (sin?)

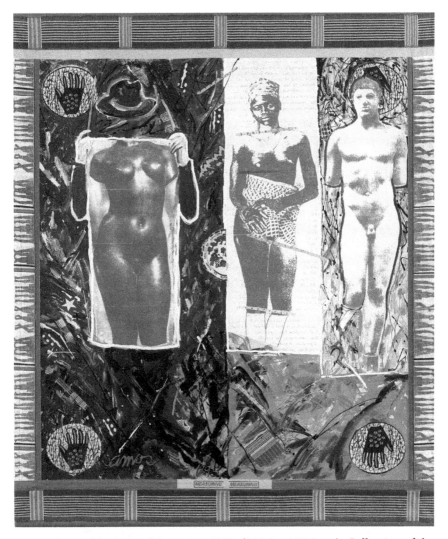

Emma Amos, *Measuring, Measuring*, 1995. (213.4 × 177.8 cm). Collection of the Birmingham Museum of Art; Museum purchase with funds provided by the Collectors Circle for Contemporary Art and the Traditional Arts Acquisition Fund. Photo by Sean Pathasema.

is sometimes so overwhelming that the magnification of a small word blocks from view the social, political, economic contexts of its surrounding world. Moreover, New Testament scholars sometimes use ancient texts as a quarry, not caring if we pluck a comparand from Homer, Herodotus, Aelius Aristides, Dio Chrysostom, or Philo, flattening out meaning across time and place and genre without taking into account the social and rhetorical contexts in which a word's meanings emerge more clearly. There has also been a divide within classics departments. A strongly philological-aesthetic-literary side in the classics can sometimes conflict with another side that also embraces Hellenistic or Roman history, on the one hand, and a classics that is aware of how the very history of the field is intertwined with race, imperialisms, and power, on the other. These divides sometimes depend upon which intellectual-racial inheritances one claims, upon one's (mal)formations from the *askēseis* or disciplines of the discipline, and upon whom one considers as ancestor or paterfamilias.[2]

Whether within classics or between it and New Testament studies, the disciplinary walls that have been constructed by the processes of forming the disciplines in Anglo-European contexts still exist.[3] But they are also under siege.[4] Such boundaries are sometimes loosened because of this exigent moment, at least in the United States, when and where anyone who cares about antiquity had better link arms with anyone else in the savage Red Rover game that is the shrinking of the humanities. Some scholars are loosening the boundaries between New Testament studies and the classics as well as between the classics as the study of ancient languages and the classics as an investigation of reception history for exciting intellectual reasons. There is no love for Cicero's prose that does not also benefit from an understanding of the janky politics of his time. There is no honoring of Seneca or the apostle Paul that does not also need to speak to white supremacist uses of such figures. There is no attention to Homer

---

2. For racial inheritances and disciplinary formations, see Jennings 2020, 103: "We cannot simply think our way into discerning the racial paterfamilias and its seductive cultivating power. We must feel and think it.... The racial paterfamilias, however, wove itself into the institutional unconscious of educational institutions, and especially theological institutions, inviting us to sense through the cultivation logics of the plantation and whiteness the way the world actually is and to imagine how we could function efficiently and effectively in it." On Homer as ancestor and rethinking genealogical ties in the field of classics, see Greenwood and Gratiosi 2007, 1–24.

3. Consider the *Black Athena* struggle of the 1990s. For the larger principle from which I draw, see Jennings 2020; Ferguson 2012.

4. See Haley 2009; Bond 2019; Padilla Peralta 2015, 2018; and Future of Classics Panel: Society for Classical Studies 2019. For an ongoing documentation of white supremacist appropriations of the classics, see https://pharos.vassarspaces.net/category/documenting-appropriations/. See also Arthurs 2012; Kallis 2014; and Kotrosits 2020, 146–54.

that does not benefit from the study of the bright collages of Romare Bearden's *Black Odyssey*.

In the field of classics, Shelley Haley (2009) has made us aware of how translators of ancient Greek and Latin texts have erased the beauty of brown and black skin or found its beauty befuddling.[5] James I. Porter (2000, 181–91, 257–59) has also outlined debates over scholarly aestheticizing of the ancient Greeks in the late eighteenth and early nineteenth centuries and the subsequent influences of the likes of Johannes Winckelmann, Friedrich Nietzsche, and Ulrich von Wilamowitz in our own perceptions of beauty and the classics. Scholars in the fields of New Testament and classics could benefit by investigating again, together with one another, these aesthetic prejudices and conceptual underpinnings rather than taking them as common sense or natural.

(Re)defining Aesthetics

Aesthetics—sometimes defined in relation to good or beautiful things—is a key, if covert, basis for ongoing tensions within the field of classics, divisions between the fields of classics and the New Testament, and interpretive judgments of texts from the Christian or New Testament. What was and is considered good or beautiful is often implicitly defined within ethnic-racial hierarchies (not to mention the able, masculine body): the speech or body of the barbarous barbarian, such as the burnt Ethiopian, as counterpoint to the beauty of the Greek or Roman (Byron 2002; see also Konstan 2014). The history of aesthetics is generally traced from Aristotle's definition of aesthetics, which considered aesthetics less in terms of beauty and more in relation to *aisthēseis*, that is, to sense perceptions and their trustworthiness and utility. As Birgit Meyer and Jojada Verrips (2008, 21) put it, "Aisthesis then refers to our total sensorial experience of the world and to our sensitive knowledge of it" (see also Grieser and Johnston 2017, 8–11).

Modern conversations about aesthetics are informed by this Aristotelian definition, but also by a more modern definition of aesthetics in terms of beauty. As Jacques Rancière (2013, ix) states at the start of his *Aisthesis*, "For two centuries in the West, 'aesthetics' has been the name for

---

5. On debates over race and translating Song 1:51 "black and beautiful" or "black, but comely/but," and for a new interpretation of this verse, see Bellis 2021.

the category designating the sensible fabric and intelligible form of what we call 'Art.'" What interests Rancière is how aesthetics is one "[regime] of the identification of art" built from the "sensible fabric of experience" and "material conditions—performance and exhibition spaces, forms of circulation and reproduction" (x–xi); that is, how valuations of "Art" are produced by the idea of aesthetics and how both occur within political, economic, and social conditions of power.

Alexander Gottlieb Baumgarten's (1750–1758) *Aesthetica* is often cited as the foundational text for our current genealogy of aesthetics, a book that bridged ancient Greek philosophical discussions of sense perception (often via commentaries on Aristotle's *De anima*) and later discussion of aesthetics (Grieser and Johnston 2017, 9–13). Baumgarten wrote: "aesthetics is taken very literally as a defense of the relevance of sensual perception," in opposition to the work of Descartes's "rationalization of cognition" and a worldview that understood aesthetic judgments as connected with the emotions, on the one hand, and beauty as a "by-product of flawed human cognition," on the other (Hammermeister 2002, 4).[6] This connection of aesthetics with emotion is not surprising.[7] It is part of the larger Romantic philosophical landscape at the time, and it is linked to the ancient philosophical debate about how the *aisthēseis* are conduits for *pathē*, which can be defined as passions, what one experiences, or what one suffers.

In the modern period, discussions of aesthetics were tied not only to ancient philosophical conversations about the *aisthēseis* but also to ancient Greek objects in the second primary definition of aesthetics: beauty. For example, Johann Christian Friedrich Hölderin (or perhaps Friedrich Wilhelm Joseph Schelling) wrote:

> The idea that unites everyone [is] the idea of beauty.... I am now convinced that the highest act of reason, by encompassing all ideas, is an

---

6. Baumgarten writes in Latin, his ideas popularized by his student G. F. Meier's *Anfangsgründe aller schönen Wissenschaften*. Baumgarten's own *Aesthetica* offers the definition: "Aesthetics (as the theory of the liberal arts, as interior cognition, as the art of beautiful thinking and as the art of thinking analogous to reason) is the science of sensual cognition" (quoted in Hammermeister 2002, 11).

7. "[Baumgarten's] notion of 'aesthetic enthusiasm' reunites artistic emotionality and cognitive achievements that had been opposed to each other since Plato's criticism of artistic interpretation (*mania*) as interference with rationality" (Hammermeister 2002, 12). See the discussion of emotion and Moses Mendelssohn in the same chapter, and Crawley 2020, 22.

aesthetic act, and that truth and goodness are siblings only in beauty. (Gorodeisky 2016)

John Keats manifests this theory in his 1820 poem "Ode on a Grecian Urn" (lines 49–50).[8] It is not incidental that the beautiful urn that speaks truth, that *is* truth, is a Grecian urn: this is part of the neoclassicizing aesthetics of the Romantic period that led to an intense identification with (a particular understanding of) Greece. Keats's contemporary, Romantic poet Lord Byron, would even lead forces for Greek independence against the Ottomans. That is, these ideas of what is the good, the true, the beautiful are grounded in notions of ethnic-racial identification (Buell 2005), on the one hand, and have real political and social effects, on the other.

Even as Baumgarten famously presented a theory of aesthetics, even as Keats opined on an ancient Greek object, Johann Joachim Winckelmann offered his own development of a theory of aesthetics based in a taxonomy of ancient art (Hammermeister 2002, 15); Rancière (2013, xiii) points to "the historical moment, in Winckelmann's Germany, when Art begins to be named as such." Winckelmann's 1764 *History of Ancient Art* defined a taxonomy of ancient art that haunts our disciplines, setting forth four stages of art, with Greekness represented as the height of aesthetics (see 2006, 232–38). In Winckelmann's third or "beautiful" phase, commenced by Praxiteles, the remaining angularity of the high style came to flow (234; see Nasrallah 2009, 51–78) with "grace" being its main characteristic. Winckelmann links this grace to Ionian artists (Parrhasios and Apelles) and thus ethnically situates this style in the Greek East and in colonies of Athens. The fourth phase is characterized by imitation. With the rise of the Romans, the genius of the past "cramp[ed] the spirit" and led to a mechanistic and derivative art. This imitation was characterized not only by timidity and diligence, but also by a "[decline] into the effeminate" (Winckelmann 2006, 238). Roman "copies" of earlier sculptures were seen as inferior, mechanical, and not embodying the "Greek" spirit (232). Ethnicity—race—and aesthetics are intertwined (Buell 2005, 1–34).

Roman art historians have rejected Winckelmann's characterization of Roman art as the mere copying of Greek art (e.g., Gadza 2002). Scholars use terms like *emulation* or *repetition* to avoid the derogatory implications of *copying* or *imitation*, evaluative terms which arose from Winckelmann's

---

8. Cited in Gorodeisky 2016. Keats is often invoked in conversations regarding the classics and aesthetics; e.g., Gurd 2016, 5; Butler 2015, 89.

hierarchical temporalization and ethnic periodization of ancient art. Nonetheless, Winckelmann's work continues to haunt: it was one foundation for the debate over German aesthetics in the Romantic period.[9]

The fault was not Winckelmann's alone; he expresses a larger aesthetic discourse of his age found also in the work of painters and sculptors who selected certain ancient art as worthy of replication and imaginative engagement (Nasrallah 2009). And Winckelmann himself was perhaps misunderstood.[10] Winckelmann had a complex understanding of Greek art, as found in his interpretation of the Apollo Belvedere or the Laocoön; he admits that in works such as these, disdain and beauty, agony and gorgeousness combine (Porter 2000, 258–59). Yet Friedrich Nietzsche, a critic of Winckelmann, "shows what classicism already knows—namely, that its idealism is a product of modern German idealism and its yearnings" (Porter 2000, 185). These "advocates of the classical ideal knew full well that they were misreading antiquity." To take one example, Friedrich Schlegel, who wrote *On the Study of Greek Poetry*, "could repeat, rather than divulge, the open secret that 'everyone has found in the ancients what he needed or wished to find: *chiefly, himself*'" (Porter 2000, 193).

For New Testament scholars, the phrase "everyone has found in the ancient what he needed or wished to find: *chiefly, himself*" may startle, echoing as it does the saying that scholarly quests for the historical Jesus are similar to looking into a deep well: the face of Jesus reflected back looks startlingly like those of the authors of those quests (usually attributed to Schweitzer's *The Quest of the Historical Jesus*; this image is from Tyrrell 1909, 44). That this reflection is marked by the gender, race, geography, and status of the interpreter, and that this quest is a bourgeois, masculinist, usually European project, has been well discussed (Kelley 2002; Georgi 1992; Schüssler Fiorenza 2000; Kotrosits 2020, 156–57; see also Blum and Harvey 2012).

The fields of classics and New Testament studies are haunted by a racialized aesthetic that both constructs and elevates the (putative whiteness of the) Greeks as translated through German neoclassical valuations

---

9. One can visit the Staatliche Antikensammlungen und Glyptotek in Munich to see Winckelmann's theory still in action. See also Nasrallah 2010, 5–6.

10. For example, by someone like Nietzsche, whose own difficult-to-understand arguments (Porter 2000, 227–28) include notebook entries with lecture content of "Weeks 7 and 8. *Classical* antiquity (against Wolf, Winckelmann, Goethe)" (quoted in Porter 2000, 184); see also Konstan, 2014, 182–86.

and the putative whiteness of the "author and the perfector" of *pistis*, Jesus, and his first followers (Haley 2009; Buell 2009, 159–90; 2008; Kelley 2002; Douglas 1994). This racialized aesthetic, which is grounded in racism and produces racism, has done all sorts of deep damage, constraining our definitions of our fields in ways that have excluded the insights and participation of persons of color.[11]

How, then, might we do aesthetics differently? The production of art can be understood as a set of practices that are themselves also research/ theorizing or "research-creation" (Loveless 2019; Nelson 2013; see also Sorett 2016, 3–4; Crawley 2020, 32–33 on the Hammond organist as a theorist). Emma Amos's *Measuring, Measuring* crystallizes such a critical inquiry and prompts questions such as: What bodies are beautiful? What is the art historical conversation about humanness and beauty over time, and how is this discourse undergirded by gendered and racialized ideas of beauty as well as assumptions regarding wholeness and ability? It also calls into question a racialized aesthetic that has defined as quintessentially beautiful some of the once-painted, now-white marble male sculptures of the classical Greek period. It also asserts the beauty of the central body in Amos's artwork. Even if the woman of African descent is cut by the yellow yardsticks, the other aesthetic options of the Maillot-type female body and the Kritikos boy, to her left and right, are ultimately framed by allusions to Kente cloth on the top and bottom, and to the left and right by a joking and abstracted allusion to the lost or severed legs of the three primary figures.

Measuring, Measuring critiques existing aesthetic paradigms. A critique of aesthetics is found in different form in Kandice Chuh's (2019, 3, 18) *The Difference Aesthetics Makes: On the Humanities "After Man"*, which defines aesthetics both as "sensibility as a crucial domain of knowledge and politics" and as "the beautiful and the sublime" as constructed by "Western modernity." Chuh begins with a quotation from Black critical theorist Sylvia Wynter about "accelerat[ing] the conceptual 'erasing' of

---

11. These aesthetic prejudices undergird scholarly preferences regarding not only visual art but also prose. For example, Marco Formisano has argued that "aestheticization processes exercise a marked impact on historiographical perspective." In conversation with Averil Cameron and Henri Marrou, he argues for a more expansive, "polyphonic" definition of the literature of late antiquity, taking a cue from art historians who have more frontally engaged spoliation and adaptation of a "classical" past as aesthetic moves (Formisano 2007, 278, 281–82). For different approaches to late antique/Byzantine aesthetics, see also Peers 2004; Mariev and Stock 2013.

the figure of Man"[12]—that is, Wynter's project and Chuh's inheritance is to expose how concepts of whiteness, masculinity, and colonizing power define the category of Man over and against other humans. Or, to borrow from theology, the sort of aesthetic critique materialized in Amos's *Measuring, Measuring* exposes, to use Willie Jennings's (2020, 63) words, "a white aesthetic regime that circulated and still circulates ideas of the true, the good, the beautiful, the noble, ... the transcendent, and the full range of human existence around the white body."

1 Corinthians 13:1: A Case Study in What Can Be Heard

Implicit and explicit ideas of aesthetics have shaped the disciplines of New Testament studies and the classics. I turn now to sound in the ancient world, with a focus on *glōssai* (tongues) in 1 Corinthians, a letter sent around 54 CE from Paul and Sosthenes to the *ekklēsia* (assembly) at Corinth. We can think about sound both in terms of how its beauty is judged and in terms of *aisthēsis*: how a person experiences sound. In 1 Cor 12:28, tongues are evidently downgraded and listed last among the *charismata* or spiritual gifts; 1 Cor 14 even points to *glōssai* as potentially dangerous, as a phenomenon that might make an outsider think that the *ekklēsia* is crazy (14:23). This interest in tongues, prophecy, and *pneumatika* (spiritual things) at the *ekklēsia* at Corinth developed in relation to women's speech (1 Cor 11) and in relation to a larger debate about *pneuma*, or spirit, and whether the Corinthians had attained to the status of "spiritual people" (1 Cor 1–4).[13] We cannot know what sounds were being produced at Corinth or fully reconstruct what is at stake in the controversy over *glōssai*. But we can point to debates about ancient sound and to the limitations of some strands of New Testament interpretation and their implicit aesthetic judgments of tongues.

Ashon Crawley's *Blackpentecostal Breath: The Aesthetics of Possibility* focuses on aesthetics as it manifests in the "choreosonic" (2017, 23):[14]

---

12. Chuh 2019, 1, citing Wynter 1987. Sianne Ngai (2012, 13) exposes the aesthetic tendencies of late capitalism and their imbrication with affect and emotion, language and communication, and intimacy and care.

13. On multilingualism and struggles with a dominant language, see also Tupamahu 2020, esp. 79.

14. With this turn to insights gleaned from a critical engagement with Blackpentecostalism, I reject scholars who have dismissed charismatic religion(s) or Pentecostalism as relevant for the study of *genē glōssai*. At the same time, I do not think there

During the antebellum era, both clergy and scholars alike levied incessant injunctions against loud singing and frenzied dancing in religion and popular culture. Calling for the relinquishment of these sensual spiritual experiences, I argue that these injunctions led to a condition where Blackpentecostal aesthetics were and are considered to be excessive performances, unnecessary because of their purported lack of refinement, discardable because of their seeming lack of intellectual rationality and rigor. And this because the flesh performing such aesthetic practices, the intellectual capacity, the capacity for thought and imagination, came to be racialized and gendered, and such racializing and gendering meant the denigration of black flesh. (2017, 7)

Crawley's analysis focuses on flesh and sensation, the *aisthēseis* that manifest in shouting, tarrying, whooping, and tongues.[15] While I might say that aesthetics allows the development of a theoretical frame by which to analyze ancient texts and objects, Crawley uses the term "hermeneutics" or "otherwise possibility" (24; see "transformative possibility" in Crawley 2020, 30–31). Crawley is interested in an "aesthetics of belief" that include "the performative behaviors and gestures that accompany collective modes of intellection and knowledge of divine, otherworldly worlds" (2017, 25; see also Sorett 2016, esp. 3–4).[16]

---

is a historical connection or a phenomenological, cross-temporal basis for connecting whatever was happening in Roman Corinth to the varieties of speaking in tongues today.

15. "The practices I analyze are a range of sensual, affective, material experiences: 'shouting' as dance; 'tarrying' as stilled intensity and waiting, as well as raucous praise noise; 'whooping' (ecstatic, eclipsed breath) during praying and preaching; as well as, finally, speaking in tongues" (Crawley 2017, 4). Crawley continues: "they also yield a general hermeneutics, a methodology for reading culture. What I am arguing throughout is that the disruptive capacities found in the otherwise world of Blackpentecostalism is but one example of how to produce a break with the known, the normative, the violent world of western thought and material condition. Black aesthetics are Blackpentecostal; they are unbounded and found in the celebration of the flesh." See also Crawley 2020, esp. 5, 19–20; Moten 2003. See Appadurai's (2021) review of Mbembe's *Out of the Dark Night*: "Mbembe's Africa is where the newest technologies (digital, mediatic, and fiscal), in concert with its new forms of language, art, and philosophy, are being experimented with and innovated upon in ways that prepare this emerging Africa to be a model for the decolonization of the planet, without having to abandon or forget the colonial encounter."

16. Crawley 2017, 250: "Blackpentecostal aesthetic practice 'ruins' the normative, neoliberal university, 'ruins' such a zone of inhabitation in the service of producing otherwise possibilities. As carriers of such an aesthetic practice, black

Braxton Shelley's (2019) "Analyzing Gospel" focuses on sound and song, offering a formal exegesis of gospel songs, attending to the use of vowels and to how a performer "visualizes what is audibly apparent" by gesturing during song. He shows how a simple, ubiquitous, and usually ignored element, the vamp (or repetitive musical cycle), is "a sonic resource used by many African American Christians to experience with their bodies what they believe in their hearts" (185). Shelley (2021, 2) analyzes a song tradition that embeds within itself scripture, thus developing an "interworldly motivation." Shelley brings together the *aisthēseis*—sense perceptions, and emotions—to note how the sonic produces epistemological effects within the body (through the vamp, one knows something different) and without (the collapsing of human and extrahuman realms). What Crawley calls an "aesthetics of possibility" resonates with Shelley's (2021, 30) analysis of the formal aspects of gospel music that have epistemological effects both for the singer-preacher and for those who participate in the sonic environment produced by Black church traditions. Both Crawley and Shelley fit within a larger scholarly attempt to make sense of aesthetics (particularly the experience/emotion of sound) not only as the beautiful but also as "sensational forms [that] organize encounters with an invisible beyond, the realm of spirits or the transcendental" (Meyer and Verrips 2008, 27).

Crawley and Shelley offer sonic insights that are helpful theoretical frameworks for an analysis of antiquity, offering comparanda from another time and place that shed light on how commentators are "measuring, measuring" this text. First Corinthians 13 begins:

Ἐὰν ταῖς γλώσσαις τῶν ἀνθρώπων λαλῶ καὶ τῶν ἀγγέλων, ἀγάπην δὲ μὴ ἔχω, γέγονα χαλκὸς ἠχῶν ἢ κύμβαλον ἀλαλάζον

---

objects are ruinous. We must look to, travel to, journey below surfaces, dig deep in the expanse of capacious blackness, go beyond and look askance. It is there, in the otherwise zones of possibility, where a critical practice of pedagogy is enacted." In the midst of debates about how race is displayed in secular contexts, Josef Sorett (2016, 4) insists that religion, too, funds this aesthetics. He uses Aretha Franklin (e.g., her album *Spirit in the Dark*) to demonstrate that music and ideas are impossible without religion; they are predicated upon both scripture and gospel music. For Sorett, an aesthetic is "a philosophy of art and culture"; "I show religion to be a consistent and vital—yet always contested—ingredient in efforts to define (as well as debunk) the idea of a distinctive black literature and culture. *Spirit in the Dark* is in short, a religious history of racial aesthetics."

If I speak in the tongues of mortals and of angels, but do not have love, I am a noisy gong or a clanging cymbal. (1 Cor 13:1; NRSV)

The translation and meaning of this verse are hardly clear. They are, moreover, more fighting words than words of love: this verse follows a passage that ranks tongues last among the *charismata* (1 Cor 12:28). Thus the emphasis upon love is also a mechanism for suppressing tongues, which in the larger context of 1 Corinthians are understood as a manifestation of *pneuma* (Wire 1991; Schüssler Fiorenza 1999; Nasrallah 2014; Fox 2019). Even if Paul boasts that he speaks in tongues more than anyone else, he also calls into question the significance of *glōssai*: "I thank God that I speak in tongues more than all of you; nevertheless, in church I would rather speak five words with my mind, in order to instruct others also, than ten thousand words in a tongue" (1 Cor 14:18–19; NRSV).

The many library shelves of articles and commentaries on this verse alone indicate a good deal of anxiety about glossolalia in ancient Corinth and thus sometimes also reveal a good deal of anxiety on the part of interpreters regarding whether this authoritative text matches their own aesthetics. An article titled "The Nature of Pauline Glossolalia and Its Early Reception" (Eurell 2019, 182) begins: "With the emergence and growth of charismatic Christianity during the last century, the essence and place of glossolalia in the early church has become an increasingly important area of biblical interpretation." The article uses the historical-critical method and explicitly claims to "consciously [avoid] the production of anachronistic interpretations of the texts through associations with phenomena from our time or analogies to texts from other cultures and religions" (182). This interpretive move bars some explicitly contemporary insights, such as those of the charismatic Christianity to which the article refers, and makes invisible other forms of contemporary interpretations, including the article's own. The article's arguments imitate 1 Corinthians, minimizing tongues and arguing they were not a significant or widespread phenomenon.[17]

---

17. The article concludes: "Although it is not possible to discern exactly what Paul means here, it appears that he is not referring to unintelligible ecstatic utterances, but rather to real languages not previously known to the speaker that can be interpreted by someone with the gift of interpreting tongues" (Eurell 2019, 183). The article argues that references to speaking in tongues in ancient Christian texts (Acts, the longer ending of Mark, and Irenaeus) are all derived from Paul's writing in 1 Corinthians. He concludes

Aesthetic concerns are revealed even in debates over the translation of this passage. The NRSV translates the phrase γέγονα χαλκὸς ἠχῶν ἢ κύμβαλον ἀλαλάζον as "I am a noisy gong or a clanging cymbal." Todd Sanders (1990, esp. 618) presses heavily on the ἢ between the phrases, usually translated "or." He argues that the verse should instead be translated "I have become only a resonating acoustic jar rather than a flourish of cymbals." This judgment is in part informed by aesthetics: "the interpretation of κύμβαλον ἀλαλάζον as discordant cacophony is inconsistent with the discriminating tastes of antiquity"; the phrase regarding the cymbal instead denotes a cry of enthusiasm. Anthony C. Thiselton (2000, 1038) argues that Sanders does not adequately take into account how wisdom, rhetoric, and speech were prized elements by "Graeco-Roman converts" who would have been "unlikely to regard the crash of cymbals as the height of their ambition." Thiselton asserts: "but to build the rhetorical focus of a carefully designed didactic poem on an introductory contrast between acoustic bronze and reverberating cymbals, even celebratory, festal, 'good' cymbals, hardly accords with the rhetorical and lyric weight of all the other images and contrasts" (1038).

Thiselton's characterization of 1 Cor 13 as a "carefully designed didactic poem" (1038) is an implicitly aesthetic claim rather than something demonstrated through analysis of meter or language.[18] The scare quotes of "'good' cymbals" indicate a weighing of value: does resonating bronze sound *good* to folk? And to what sort of folk?[19] Thiselton himself elevates 1 Corinthians 13 as generally characterized by "rhetorical and lyrical weight," while implying that whatever sounds are evoked by the phrase χαλκὸς ἠχῶν ἢ κύμβαλον ἀλαλάζον are not. The commentary erupts with revelatory aesthetics at the point of discussion of this verse: "When the Queen opens the

---

(oddly) by stating that that the longer ending of Mark and Irenaeus may "speak of glossolalia as a legitimate expression of apostolic Christianity" but do not suggest "that the writer had personal acquaintance with the phenomenon." While it seems right to me that 1 Corinthians drives later reception of the idea of tongues, including Acts and Mark, Eurell's analysis sounds like an apologia for a tongues-free Christianity. See also the classic Castelli 1991 on the power of Pauline injunctions to imitate him.

18. On 1 Cor 13 as poetry, including metrical analysis and comparisons with Pindar and other quite ancient Greek poets, see e.g., Hitchcock 1933, 63–75. For a critique of New Testament scholars' tendencies to find poems and hymns where there may have been none, see Peppard 2008.

19. On the meaning of χαλκὸς ἠχῶν in relation to Vitruvius's mention of echoing jars for acoustic purposes, see Harris 1982, supported and developed in Klein 1986.

Church of England General Synod in Westminster Abbey, one's spirit may soar with the decibels of the organ's thunder, while the same level of decibels would for some be sheer torture coming from a local amateur music group" (1038–39). The organ of Westminster Abbey, thundering under the queen and vibrating the mitres of bishops, is presented as the apex of a soaring aesthetics—an aesthetics of elitism, of crown and church hierarchy, compared to the local and amateur.[20]

Thiselton's and Sanders's attention to these five Greek words opens the aesthetic possibilities of the phrase and the lost sonic experiences of antiquity. What their writings also reveal are aesthetic prejudices and the theological-ideological anxieties that attend 1 Corinthians. How might we read 1 Cor 13:1 differently in light of aesthetics like Crawley's Blackpentecostal aesthetics or Shelley's emphasis on the vamp?[21]

I suggest that we place this passage within the language play and the discussions of language, voice, resonance, beauty, and ugliness that were going on more broadly in antiquity. Such work is not easy. An incantation on a *defixio*, a hint of tongues in 1 Corinthians, instructions regarding the sound passing the teeth as the rhetor speaks—these can fruitfully be seen as fragments of sound (chant, voice, poetry, song) or as stray evidence of it: the winding windblown black-gray tapes of the disintegrating cassette of antiquity. As Sarah Nooter and Shane Butler (2018, 2) write, evidence from Mediterranean antiquity indicates that sound was everywhere—cacophonous in the insulae, ringing through the heavenly spheres. Yet "sound leaves behind no directly accessible ruins or residues." Nonetheless, sound in antiquity has been on the minds of many. Sean Gurd (2016, 1–4) trawls ancient literature for a range of sounds from the belly to the streetscape. Butler (2015, 13) asks us to consider whether we can overcome our mental divide between the "linguistic voice, which writing has long recorded, and the extralinguistic voice, which had to wait for

---

20. Thiselton (2000, 1038) also writes: "Empty, noisy reverberations go on and on. In Yorkshire idiom in the north of England, they are 'now't but wind and rattle.'" This comment succinctly and implicitly does many things: it establishes as normative Paul's perspective that tongues are an inferior *charisma* or gift, and it offers an aesthetic judgment at two levels: at the level of beauty or euphony and at the level of sense perception, namely, hearing. Aesthetics undergird contemporary analyses of *glōssai* in 1 Corinthians.

21. There are different interpretive possibilities within New Testament studies; even in the 1970s Krister Stendahl (1975b, 56; see also 1975a), in conversation with charismatic Christians, discussed glossolalia as "high-voltage religion," to give one example.

the phonograph." He points out that "centuries of literary texts are filled with—and at least partially defined by—phonic features that cannot be reduced to a function that is, strictly speaking, linguistic" (13). This is the very theme of Pauline LeVen's (2018, 230) *Music and Metamorphosis* and her writing on the "erogenous ear." She points not only to ancient language but also to its impact: "the power of sounds is not a function of language itself, and the power of poetry or special language does not reside ... in the stoicheia of the language, but in the attunement of the ear, ... in its willingness and desire to be played with."[22] Thomas Denecker (2017, 49) traces early Christian ideas about whether voice and writing are the same thing, about the impossibility of expressing ideas about God in language, and about the way in which the human body is shaped by God for the purpose of hearing as well as speaking: truly the person as instrument, ears like cymbals and tongue like plectrum.[23] James I. Porter (2010b, 93), speaking of Pythagoras as depicted by Iamblichus, points to the possibility of a blur between voice and word: "The emergence of the voice in the guise of disembodied logos represents the triumph of the voice as an aesthetic phenomenon in its own right, its liberation from the constraints of sight, though not from the body per se. The voice when it is heard has a body of its own: it has pitches, melodiousness, timbre, rhythms, and other euphonic qualities."

To understand better the phrase "kinds of tongues" in 1 Corinthians, I take a cue from the approaches to sound and aesthetics of scholars such as Crawley, Shelley, Butler, and LeVen. I also turn to contextualize this passage within ancient sonic practices, reading the reference to *glōssai* in 1 Corinthians in light of a highfaluting theory of composition developed by Dionysius of Halicarnassus, on the one hand, and a curse tablet from Roman Corinth that employs *voces magicae* (streams of letters which form no known words), on the other.

---

22. Pentcheva 2017 takes a different tack, attempting to reconstruct the sonics of Hagia Sophia.

23. Denecker 2017 notes that "the author of the pseudo-Clementine *Recognitiones* (in Rufinus' translation) at 8.29.3–4 praises the functionality of the parts of the human body as it was shaped by the divine *artifex*. In doing so, he refers to the ears, which were shaped as cymbals in order to amplify the 'reverberated sound of the received word' and thus to transmit it to the heart. The author subsequently mentions the tongue, which is shaped in such a way 'that it performs the task of a plectrum (*plectri reddat officium*) for speaking, by being beaten against the teeth (*illisa dentibus*)'. A very similar description occurs in Jerome's *Ep.* 108.24.1."

Defixiones or curse tablets from Corinth, which postdate the writing of 1 Corinthians by perhaps a century, provide evidence of a long-standing practice. These were discovered *in situ* at the Acrocorinth in the Sanctuary of Demeter and Kore near several bases, which were perhaps used as altars, in a layer of dirt mixed with the residue of burnt materials (Bookidis and Stroud 1997, 277–91). One such curse tablet, aimed against a garland weaver named Karpime Babbia, includes this sentence: "I adjure you and I implore you and I pray to you, Hermes of the Underworld, that the mighty names of Ananke, Nebezapadaieisen[.]geibebeohera, make me fertile" (Stroud 2013, nos. 125/6). Here we find evidence of adjoining Greek letters that seem to make no sense—*voces magicae*—at Corinth. These may be one context for understanding *glōssai* in 1 Corinthians. This curse tablet or the larger phenomenon of *voces magicae* does not explain or fix the meaning of 1 Corinthians' discussion of *genē glōssōn* or "kinds of tongues." Rather, it demonstrates the larger context of ancient play with and theorizing about sound and language, evidence found both in ritual and philosophical-theological-rhetorical speculation. We must take seriously the aesthetics (including the materiality) of ritual objects from antiquity, no matter how ugly they seem to be to us, including rolled-up lead, pierced through with nails, with scratched letters and odd phrasings (Nasrallah 2022). These aesthetics would have included not only the ritual objects themselves but also a sonic world lost to us: the incantations of the letters and words on the curse tablet. Scholars like David Frankfurter (2019, esp. 615–16), Henk Versnel (2002), and Esther Eidinow (2019) seek in their study of ancient magic to understand as much as possible about ritual and poetics, not just the scratched words on a curse tablet but also how that object would have been used—the chant, the song, the gesture.[24] In the case of ancient Corinth, similar linguistic practices occurred at different sites: the one at the Sanctuary of Demeter and Kore at Corinth, the other among Christ-followers likely somewhere in the lower city, folk who lacked a sanctuary or *temenos* for their practices. Nonetheless, both the curse tablet and 1 Corinthians remain as data for ritual practices that involved play with language.

In the *defixio*, we find materialized a theory of how language works ritually: an incantation to be said, *voces magicae* perhaps to be uttered, the object to be left on one of the bases in what archaeologists have called the

---

24. Also, on incantation, see D. Collins 2008, 104–31.

"Building of the Tablets" within the precinct of Demeter and Kore at the Acrocorinth. We find another theorization of smoothness of speech, about beauty and sound in human language, of the mouth and resonance in Dionysius of Halicarnassus's *On Composition*. Written in the Augustan period, this discussion of rhetoric is also a discussion of voice and sound. Voice and sound are elements that arise as significant in *defixiones* and amulets as well as in their recipe books, where vowels spill out, *voces magicae* emerge, and *charaktēres* (symbols that look like letters) defy vocalization, at least to our knowledge (Gordon 2014).

Dionysius of Halicarnassus's σύνθεσις ("putting together" or "composition") is lush with a vocabulary of aesthetics, focusing on and differentiating attractiveness (ἡδονή) and beauty (τὸ καλόν). The stated purpose of *On Composition* is to give young people direction, to teach them so that they do not utter "whatever word has sprung to an ill-timed tongue nor ... put together at random any chance combinations, but ... select words which are both pure and refined and to arrange them in a combination which unites grace and dignity" (*Comp.* 1 [Usher, LCL]).[25] Yet this little book does so much more, discussing as it does what is rough or problematic in language and how this too can be used to aesthetic effect, albeit from an elite and educated point of view.

Dionysius begins with the Homeric passage in which Odysseus stays in the swineherd's hut. Its lowly theme and vocabulary allow Dionysius to demonstrate that even what is base can be composed so as to "allure and enchant the hearing, and not at all be deemed lesser than the most pleasure-producing poems" (*Comp.* 3, μὲν ἐπάγεται καὶ κηλεῖ τὰς ἀκοὰς ποιημάτων τε τῶν πάνυ ἡδίστων οὐδενὸς ἧττω μοῖραν ἔχει). What is rough or everyday can become beautiful. As Dionysius puts it:

> the whole passage is woven together from the most commonplace, humble words, such as might have come readily to the tongue of a farmer, seaman or artisan, or anyone else who takes no trouble to speak well. Indeed, if the metre is broken up, these very same lines will appear ordinary and unworthy of admiration.... What alternative, therefore, is left but to attribute the beauty of the style to the composition? (*Comp.* 3)

Dionysius also goes on to explain that arrangement and meter have power to change "the structure, the colors, the customs, the feelings, and all the

---

25. All translations of Dionysius, unless otherwise noted, are from Usher.

poetics" (*Comp.* 37, τὰ σχήματα, τὰ χρώματα, τὰ ἤθη, τὰ πάθη, τὴν ὅλην τῶν ποιημάτων). This phrase points out the entanglement of the customary and affective with synthesis or composition—*ta ēthē, ta pathē*—and the synesthesia of Dionysius's vision (on Dionysius and the sublime, see Porter 2016, 3–7; De Jonge 2013).

Dionysius's *On Composition* creates a taxonomy of kinds of composition and appropriate styles, demonstrating how these work in both poetry and prose and arguing that the human voice should be understood in light of song and music (*Comp.* 11). In this he participates in a broader, elite tradition, which includes Demosthenes, Quintilian, Longinus, and others, who frequently discuss "the three styles" (the sublime or grand, *megaloprepeia*; the middle, *glaphuros* or *apheleia*; and the low, *tapeinos*) (Porter 2016, 14). Yet Dionysius, even in his discussions of what is disruptive to pleasure or beauty (see e.g., *Comp.* 11), hints at the *power* of disrupting what is expected.

Dionysius's discussion of composition and its performance tilts us toward a synesthetic ritual that includes gender and the very mechanisms of the human body and *pneuma* producing speech. He argues that composition in its "beautiful and attractive unified effect" (*Comp.* 6, καλὴν καὶ ἡδεῖαν ... συζυγίαν) must guard against gendered degeneration; the arrangement of words in the composition can also be "precious, degenerate, effeminate" (*Comp.* 4, μικρόκομψον, ἀγεννές, μαλθακόν) (see also Gleason 1994). The rhetorically adept, masculinized body produces particular kinds of sound. Dionysius talks about the beauty of the seven vowels and how they are "produced from the windpipe, which resounds to the breath" (*Comp.* 14, παρὰ τῆς ἀρτηρίας συνηχούσης τῷ πνεύματι) with the tongue at rest. The vowels are measured by breath: the long vowels (η ω) and sometimes the common vowels (α ι υ) "take an extended and continuous column of breath [τὸν αὐλὸν τοῦ πνεύματος], while the short vowels [ε ο] and those which are pronounced short are uttered abruptly, with one burst of breath and only a brief movement of the windpipe" (*Comp.* 14). The most powerful and most attractive in sound are long vowels and long-uttered common vowels because they do not "arrest the flow of the breath" (*Comp.* 14, ὅτι πολὺν ἠχεῖται χρόνον καὶ τὸν τοῦ πνεύματος οὐκ ἀποκόπτει τόνον). I want to pause here on this topic of breath, *pneuma*.[26] In this technical section of the treatise we find concerns with the

---

26. There is no time in this essay for a detailed discussion of *pneuma*, a very important term in 1 Corinthians (esp. chs. 1–4), indicating that Paul participates in a conversation dominated by Corinthian interest in *pneuma*, whether this interest is

windpipe, breath, the mouth, and the teeth. This treatise brings together exquisite details regarding the aesthetic value of letters or *grammata* with the human body and its performance of these sonics. For example, Dionysius states that some semivowels (*hemiphōnōn*) that are doubled "are ampler than the others and seem nearer to perfect letters" (*Comp.* 14, ἐπειδὴ μείζονά ἐστι τῶν ἑτέρων καὶ μᾶλλον ἐγγίζειν δοκεῖ τοῖς τελείοις καὶ μᾶλλον ἐγγίζειν δοκεῖ τοῖς τελείοις). Yet even Dionysius, in his discussion of the "austere style," knows that ugliness has its uses and its own aesthetics. Dionysius offers:

> When men are being dashed against rocks, and he is portraying the noise and their pitiable fate, he will dwell on the most unpleasant and ill-sounding letters, nowhere attempting to make the arrangement smooth or attractive:
> A pair of them he snatched and dashed, like puppies on the ground. Their brains flowed freely on the floor and incarnadined the rocks.

> ἀραττομένων δὲ περὶ πέτρας ἀνθρώπων ψόφον τε καὶ μόρον οἰκτρὸν ἐπιδεικνύμενος ἐπὶ τῶν ἀηδεστάτων τε καὶ κακοφωνοτάτων χρονιεῖ γραμμάτων οὐδαμῇ λεαίνων τὴν κατασκευὴν οὐδὲ ἡδύνων·
> σύν τε δύω μάρψας ὥστε σκύλακας προτὶ γαίῃκόπτ᾽·
> ἐκ δ᾽ ἐγκέφαλος χαμάδις ῥέε, δεῦε δὲ γαῖαν. (*Comp.* 16)

Dionysius's discussion of letters, syllables, and rhythms that *do the work* of bringing the hearer into violence and war stand in conversation with others, and even in tension.

Dionysius is part of an elite discourse, while 1 Corinthians is not. Dionysius not only throws in references to Plato and Theophrastus but also in his very prose embodies the tone and talents of a wordsmith. Dionysius is part of a larger movement in the Augustan period in which writers were interested in what was *hypsos*, high or sublime, with relation to rhetoric.[27] As Casper de Jonge (2012, 271–300) has argued, Dionysius should be understood as part of this larger conversation on the sublime and God or divinities and their sublimity, a conversation most

---

grounded mainly in spirit possession (e.g., Bazzana 2020; Eyl 2019) or Stoic philosophical engagements with *pneuma* (e.g., Engberg-Pedersen 2010). For a study of *pneuma* and its importance in producing charismatic Catholic Christian bodies in Brazil via "Jesus aerobics," see de Abreu 2021.

27. I should add that the sublime is a key component of nineteenth-century European discussions of aesthetics; see Porter 2016, 1–56.

associated with Longinus. Nonetheless, his prose resonates (!) with some of the terminology and implicit conflict of 1 Corinthians. Dionysius borrows from the beauty of low status prose, from the glories of Homer's everyday phrasings, even as Dionysius worries about the corrupting influence of the effeminate and analyzes the human body's own mechanics of *pneuma* and sound. First Corinthians contains a preponderance of language of *pneuma*, or spirit; tongues are in fact one of the *pneumatika* or spiritual things or spiritual gifts at stake, particularly in 1 Cor 11–14. The issue of who speaks and how they can speak is found in the letter's insistence that women be veiled as they pray or prophesy; the gendered prejudices of Dionysius might remind us of this passage or of 1 Cor 14:33a–36, which argues for women's silence in the *ekklēsia*. The low prose of 1 Corinthians and the likely common language of its recipients may be fuel for a different kind of beauty.

Dionysius of Halicarnassus offers assessments of sound and composition that help us to extrapolate to the aesthetics of "kinds of tongues" (*genē glōssōn*) or curse tablets: How are these, in a ritual context, deliberately playing with the consonants (the frictive, the plosive; see e.g., *Comp.* 9), along with the vowels and other sounds that were considered so beautiful by Dionysius and others, to produce a particular aesthetic (see Porter 2010a, 5)?[28] Language's so-called vices (see Galen, *De capt.* 2.90) can also be exploited positively, aesthetically, as word play or as a deliberately mystifying element on a *defixio*. *Voces magicae* obscure normal human realms of language for a ritual purpose. The use of vowels in recipes for ritual opens up voice and sound to a deliberately breath-filled mode of embodied utterance that has no evident purpose of communication in normal human realms. Perhaps they also open up a possible understanding of what was going on with *genē glōssōn* at the assembly in Christ in Roman Corinth. What some might label as ugly or a *hamartia* (flaw) are the poetic modes deployed in *defixiones* to short-circuit normal modes of communication, to act, in the words of Patricia Cox Miller (1986), "in praise of nonsense." But these are precisely *not* nonsense, insofar as *voces magicae* both perform as signs and were likely vocalized in ritual. Curse tablets adopt multiple forms of signs: strings of known letters that make no sense to us but sometimes sound vaguely like the names of gods; *charaktēres* that are

---

28. Note that Dionysius used to be thought of as a hack, someone whose primary utility was thought to lie in the preservation of earlier sources (de Jonge 2008, 3–6).

signs that have no evident human alphabetical meaning; vowel sequences that sustain the breath.

These ancient materials and contemporary theorists enable a historical reconstruction of the *glōssai* mentioned in 1 Corinthians as a sonic counterpoint to ancient conversations about breath, sound, and beauty (see also Fotopoulos 2014). That is, *glōssai* may be understood as an alternative means of expressing sound and manifesting beauty. Insofar as curse tablets in antiquity often worked as "prayers for justice" (*inter alia*, Versnel 2013) or alternative judicial documents aimed at disempowering others in a judicial setting (Nasrallah 2021), and insofar as texts like 1 Corinthians use curse formulae (A. Collins 1980; Fotopoulos 2014, among others), we can also wonder whether tongues were an alternative expression of language in conditions of injustice. Curse tablets precisely use the faults of language to do their own work at the border of human and nonhuman comprehensibility. Perhaps so too the kinds of tongues heard at Corinth.

Conclusions

We cannot know fully how *glōssai* sounded at Corinth; we know that by the time that tongues are discussed in the Acts of the Apostles, they are rationalized as heteroglossia, as speaking in other languages.[29] By the time that *glōssai* are again interpreted at Azusa Street in Los Angeles in the early twentieth century, as blacks and whites together spoke in tongues no doubt in a way very different from the Roman Corinthians, they function to bridge (however briefly) racial barriers.

This essay seeks to remind us of the racial and racist inheritances of the fields of New Testament and the classics and their implicit and explicit definitions of beauty: their work of "measuring, measuring," to remind us of Emma Amos's theorization of aesthetics. I have used 1 Cor 13:1 as a case study, contextualizing it among the phenomenon of *voces magicae* on a curse tablet from Corinth and amid the discussion of rhetoric, beauty, and sublimity in antiquity in order to trace a context for tongues. I interpret these as offering their own aesthetics. Such a reconsideration of aesthetics can open up our disciplines and can push us to continue in the work of

---

29. On Hebrew and foreign languages as an "esoteric alterity" that parallels magical language, see Thomson forthcoming.

making central objects and texts previously marginalized by disciplinary prejudices regarding beauty and truth.

First Corinthians 13:1 downgrades the practice of tongues and prophecy in favor of love, downgrading the significance of the Corinthians' *charismata* and spiritual gifts. It does so with a sonic argument, one that is difficult to understand: γέγονα χαλκὸς ἠχῶν ἢ κύμβαλον ἀλαλάζον "I am a noisy gong or a clanging cymbal" (NRSV). With the phrase *kymbalon alalazon* we have a firm musical resonance and a cognate in the form of the English word "cymbal," although scholars still debate the exact look of this instrument (castanets? a thin metal strip to be struck?) especially since the word is a *hapax legomenon* within New Testament texts (Thiselton 2000, 1037). Here, too the, modifying adjective *alalazon* has special force as an onomatopoetic term reverberating with near ululation or cry (1037). The phrase brings the hearer not only to practices of tongues that span humans or angels but also to acoustic strategies and to instruments that reverberate. We are in the sonic world of the first century. Even if we cannot hear this world, we can reasonably reconstruct that Paul and Sosthenes, the writers of 1 Corinthians, found such tongues problematic, even if Paul boasts that he speaks in tongues (1 Cor 14:18–19). Some women and others of Corinth prophesied, and we can reasonably reconstruct that they also spoke in tongues, engaging in forms of linguistic effervescence and play that were current in ritual practice elsewhere in Corinth and that are hinted at in rhetorical and compositional theorizing at the time, such as that found in Dionysius of Halicarnassus.

While those of us who study antiquity have no recourse to some of these sonic aspects of our sources, Shelley's attention to such details reminds us that incantations in antiquity were performed, that sound is part of the ritual, and that the smallest detail of evidence—the clash of two consonants, the meter that emerges briefly into a *defixio*—are significant data for our understanding of how such ancient rituals were produced and how they hit the ear. Shelley and Crawley remind the historian of antiquity to consider the larger aesthetic context: that people making music, sounds, and moans do so in a larger aesthetic context—a larger context of beauty, on the one hand, and of *aistheseis*, or sense perception, on the other.

This essay reveals that theorization of language and sound does not happen only among elites, instantiated in treatises, but also among those of lower status. It does not only happen in the philosophical conversation in the villa garden, but also in the everyday rituals of the making of curse tablets. And ancient ritual is more than words on the printed page of an edition. Ancient ritual involved air pushed through the trachea, the scratching of letters onto a lead or papyrus surface that is folded or rolled, the sound—whatever that sound was—of tongues.

Works Cited

Abreu, Maria José de. 2021. *The Charismatic Gymnasium*. Durham, NC: Duke University Press.

Appadurai, Arjun. 2021. "Beyond Domination: The Future and Past of Decolonization." *The Nation*. March 9.

Arthurs, Joshua. 2012. *Excavating Modernity: The Roman Past in Fascist Italy*. Ithaca, NY: Cornell University Press.

Bazzana, Giovanni B. 2020. *Having the Spirit of Christ: Spirit Possession and Exorcism in the Early Christ Groups*. New Haven: Yale University Press.

Bellis, Alice Ogden. 2021. "I Am Burnt but Beautiful: Translating Song 1:5a." *JBL* 140:91–111.

Blum, Edward, and Paul Harvey. 2012. *The Color of Christ: The Son of God and the Saga of Race in America*. Chapel Hill: University of North Carolina Press.

Bond, Sarah. 2019. "Blog: Addressing the Divide between Biblical Studies and Classics." *Society for Classical Studies*. https://tinyurl.com/SBL06104c1.

Bookidis, Nancy, and Ronald S. Stroud. 1997. *The Sanctuary of Demeter and Kore: Topography and Architecture*. Corinth 18.3. Princeton: American School of Classical Studies at Athens.

Buell, Denise Kimber. 2005. *Why This New Race: Ethnic Reasoning in Early Christianity*. New York: Columbia University Press.

———. 2009. "God's Own People: Specters of Race, Ethnicity, and Gender in Early Christian Studies." Pages 159–90 in *Prejudice and Christian Beginnings*. Edited by Laura Nasrallah and Elisabeth Schüssler Fiorenza. Philadelphia: Fortress.

Butler, Shane. 2015. *The Ancient Phonograph*. Boston: Zone.

Butler, Shane, and Sarah Nooter. 2018. "Sounding Hearing." Pages 1–11 in *Sound and the Ancient Senses*. Edited by Shane Butler and Sarah Nooter. New York: Routledge.

Byron, Gay. 2002. *Symbolic Blackness and Ethnic Difference in Early Christian Literature*. New York: Routledge.

Castelli, Elizabeth. 1991. *Imitating Paul*. Louisville: Westminster John Knox.
Chuh, Kandice. 2019. *The Difference Aesthetics Makes: On the Humanities "After Man."* Durham, NC: Duke University Press.
Collins, Adela Yarbro. 1980. "The Function of "Excommunication" in Paul." *HTR* 72:251–65.
Collins, Derek. 2008. *Magic in the Ancient Greek World*. Malden, MA: Blackwell.
Crawley, Ashon T. 2017. *Blackpentecostal Breath: The Aesthetics of Possibility*. New York: Fordham University Press.
———. 2020. *The Lonely Letters*. Durham, NC: Duke University Press.
Denecker, Tim. 2017. *Ideas on Language in Early Latin Christianity: From Tertullian to Isidore of Seville*. Leiden: Brill.
Dionysius of Halicarnassus. 1985. *On Literary Composition*. Volume 2 of *Critical Essays*. Translated by Stephen Usher. LCL. Cambridge: Harvard University Press.
Douglas, Kelly Brown. 1994. *The Black Christ*. Maryknoll, NY: Orbis Books.
Edlow, Robert Blair. 1977. *Galen on Language and Ambiguity*. Leiden: Brill.
Eidinow, Esther. 2019. "Binding Spells on Tablets and Papyri." Pages 351–87 in *Guide to the Study of Ancient Magic*. Edited by David Frankfurter. Leiden: Brill.
Engberg-Pedersen, Troels. 2010. *Cosmology and Self in the Apostle Paul: The Material Spirit*. Oxford: Oxford University Press.
Eurell, John-Christian. 2019. *The Nature of Pauline Glossolalia and Its Early Reception*. Cambridge: Cambridge University Press.
Eyl, Jennifer. 2019. *Signs, Wonders, and Gifts: Divination in the Letters of Paul*. Oxford: Oxford University Press.
Farrington, Lisa. 2005. *Creating Their Own Image: The History of African American Women Artists*. Oxford: Oxford University Press.
Ferguson, Roderick. 2012. *The Reorder of Things: The University and Its Pedagogies of Minority Difference*. Minneapolis: University of Minnesota Press.
Formisano, Marco. 2007. "Toward an Aesthetic Paradigm of Late Antiquity." *Antiquité Tardive* 15:278, 281–82.
Fotopoulos, John. 2014. "Paul's Curse of Corinthians: Restraining Rivals with Fear and Voces Mysticae (1 Cor 16:22)." *NovT* 56:275–309.
Fox, Arminta. 2019. *Paul Decentered: Reading 2 Corinthians with the Corinthian Women*. Paul in Critical Contexts. Minneapolis: Fortress.

Frankfurter, David. 2019. "Spell and Speech Act: The Magic of the Spoken Word." Pages 608–25 in *Guide to the Study of Ancient Magic*. Edited by David Frankfurter. Leiden: Brill.

"The Future of Classics: Racial Equity and the Production of Knowledge: Future of Classics Panel." 2019. Society for Classical Studies. San Diego, CA.

Gadza, Elaine, ed. 2002. *The Ancient Art of Emulation: Studies in Artistic Originality and Tradition from the Present to Classical Antiquity*. Ann Arbor: University of Michigan Press.

Georgi, Dieter. 1992. "The Interest in Life of Jesus Theology as a Paradigm for the Social History of Biblical Criticism." *HTR* 85:51–83.

Gleason, Maud W. 1994. *Making Men: Sophists and Self-Preservation in Ancient Rome*. Princeton: Princeton University Press.

Gordon, Richard. 2014. "Charaktêres between Antiquity and Renaissance: Transmission and Re-Invention." *Micrologus Library* 60:253–300.

Gorodeisky, Keren. 2016. "Nineteenth Century Romantic Aesthetics." *The Stanford Encyclopedia of Philosophy*. Edited by Edward N. Zalta. https://tinyurl.com/SBL06104d1 /.

Grieser, Alexandra, and Jay Johnston, eds. 2017. *Aesthetics of Religion: A Connective Concept*. Berlin: de Gruyter.

Greenwood, Emily, and Barbara Gratiosi. 2007. *Homer in the Twentieth Century: Between World Literature and the Western Canon*. Oxford: Oxford University Press.

Gurd, Sean Alexander. 2016. *Dissonance: Auditory Aesthetics in Ancient Greece*. New York: Fordham University Press.

Haley, Shelly. 2009. "Be Not Afraid of the Dark: Critical Race Theory and Classical Studies." Pages 27–50 in *Prejudice and Christian Beginnings: Investigating Race, Gender, and Ethnicity in Early Christianity*. Edited by Laura Nasrallah and Elisabeth Schüssler Fiorenza. Philadelphia: Fortress.

Hammermeister, Kai. 2002. *The German Aesthetic Tradition*. Cambridge: Cambridge University Press.

Harris, William. 1982. "Ancient Musical Instruments: "Sounding Brass" and Hellenistic Technology." *BAR* 8.1:38–41.

Hitchcock, F. R. M. 1933. "St. Paul's Hymn of Love." *Theol* 26:65–75.

Jennings, Willie James. 2020. *After Whiteness: An Education in Belonging*. Grand Rapids: Eerdmans.

Jonge, Casper C. de. 2012. "Dionysius and Longinus on the Sublime: Rhetoric and Religious Language." *AJP* 133:271–300.

Kallis, Aristotle. 2014. *Third Rome, 1922–43: The Making of the Fascist Capital*. London: Palgrave Macmillan.

Kelley, Shawn. 2002. *Racializing Jesus: Race, Ideology and the Formation of Modern Biblical Scholarship*. London: Routledge.

Klein, William. 1986. "Noisy Gong or Acoustic Vase? A Note on I Corinthians 13.1." *NTS* 32:286–89.

Konstan, David. 2014. *Beauty: The Fortunes of an Ancient Greek Ideal*. Oxford: Oxford University Press.

Kotrosits, Maia. 2020. *The Lives of Objects: Material Culture, Experience, and the Real in the History of Early Christianity*. Class 200. Chicago: University of Chicago Press.

LeVen, Pauline. 2018. "The Erogenous Ear." Pages 212–32 in *Sound and the Ancient Senses*. Edited by Shane Butler and Sarah Nooter. London: Routledge.

Loveless, Natalie. 2019. *How to Make Art at the End of the World: A Manifesto for Research-Creation*. Durham, NC: Duke University Press.

Mariev, Sergei, and Wiebke-Marie Stock, eds. 2013. *Aesthetics and Theurgy in Byzantium*. Berlin: de Gruyter.

Meyer, Birgit, and Jojada Verrips. 2008. "Aesthetics." Pages 20–31 in *Key Words in Religion, Media, and Culture*. Edited by David Morgan. London: Routledge.

Moten, Fred. 2003. *In the Break: The Aesthetics of the Black Radical Tradition*. Minneapolis: University of Minnesota Press.

Nasrallah, Laura Salah. 2009. "The Knidian Aphrodite in the Roman Empire and Hiram Powers's *Greek Slave*: On Ethnicity, Gender, and Desire." Pages 51–78 in *Prejudice and Christian Beginnings*. Edited by Laura Nasrallah and Elisabeth Schüssler Fiorenza. Philadelphia: Fortress.

———. 2010. *Christian Responses to Roman Art and Architecture: The Second-Century Church amid the Spaces of Empire*. Cambridge: Cambridge University Press.

———. 2014. "1 Corinthians." Pages 427–71 in *Fortress Commentary on the Bible: The New Testament*. Edited by Margaret Aymer, Cynthia Briggs Kittredge, and David A. Sanchez. Minneapolis: Fortress.

———. 2021. "Judgment, Justice, and Destruction: *Defixiones* and 1 Corinthians." *JBL* 140:347–67.

———. 2022. "The Work of Nails: Religion, Mediterranean Antiquity, and Contemporary Black Art." *JAAR* 90.2:1–21.

Nelson, R., ed. 2013. *Practice as Research in the Arts: Principles, Protocols, Pedagogies, and Resistances*. London: Palgrave Macmillan.

Ngai, Sianne. 2012. *Our Aesthetic Categories: Zany, Cute, Interesting*. Cambridge: Harvard University Press.

Padilla Peralta, Dan-El. 2015. "Barbarians Inside the Gate, Part 1." *Eidolon*. https://tinyurl.com/SBL06104e1.

———. 2018. "Hammer Time: The Publicii Malleoli between Cult and Cultural History." *ClAnt* 37.2:267–320.

Peers, Glenn. 2004. *Sacred Shock: Framing Visual Experience in Byzantium*. University Park: Pennsylvania State University Press.

Pentcheva, Bissera V. 2017. *Hagia Sophia: Sound, Space, and Spirit in Byzantium*. University Park: Pennsylvania State University Press.

Peppard, Michael. 2008. "'Poetry,' 'Hymns' and 'Traditional Material' in New Testament Epistles or How to Do Things with Indentations." *JSNT* 30:319–42.

Porter, James I. 2000. *Nietzsche and the Philology of the Future*. Stanford, CA: Stanford University Press.

———. 2010a. *The Origins of Aesthetic Thought in Ancient Greece: Matter, Sensation, Experience*. Cambridge: Cambridge University Press.

———. 2010b. "Rhetoric, Aesthetics, and the Voice." Pages 92–108 in *The Cambridge Companion to Ancient Rhetoric*. Edited by Erik Gunderson. Cambridge: Cambridge University Press.

———. 2016. *The Sublime in Antiquity*. Cambridge: Cambridge University Press.

Rancière, Jacques. 2013. *Aisthesis: Scenes from the Aesthetic Regime of Art*. Translated by Zakir Paul. London: Verso.

Sanders, Todd K. 1990. "A New Approach to 1 Corinthians 13.1." *NTS* 36:614–618.

Schüssler Fiorenza, Elisabeth. 1999. *Rhetoric and Ethic: The Politics of Biblical Studies*. Philadelphia: Fortress.

———. 2000. *Jesus and the Politics of Interpretation*. New York: Continuum.

Shelley, Braxton D. 2019. "Analyzing Gospel." *Journal of the American Musicological Society* 72:181–243.

———. 2021. *Healing for the Soul: Richard Smallwood, the Vamp, and the Gospel Imagination*. Oxford: Oxford University Press.

Sorett, Josef. 2016. *Spirit in the Dark: A Religious History of Racial Aesthetics*. Oxford: Oxford University Press.

Stendahl, Krister. 1975a. "The Charismatic Movement and the New Testament." Pages 17–28 in *What the Spirit Is Saying to the Churches*. Edited by Theodore Runyon. New York: Hawthorn.

———. 1975b. "Glossolalia: The New Testament Evidence." Pages 12–28 in *The Charismatic Movement*. Edited by Michael P. Hamilton. Grand Rapids: Eerdmans.

Stroud, Ronald S. 2013. *The Sanctuary of Demeter and Kore: The Inscriptions*. Corinth 18.6. Princeton: American School of Classical Studies at Corinth.

Thiselton, Anthony C. 2000. *The First Epistle to the Corinthians: A Commentary on the Greek Text*. Grand Rapids: Eerdmans.

Thomson, S. R. Forthcoming. "Languages and Language Varieties: Early Christianity in Its Linguistic Context: Barbarian Languages." In *Language and Culture in Early Christianity: A Companion*. Edited by Tim Denecker. Orbis Supplementa. Leuven: Peeters.

Tupamaho, Ekaputra. 2020. "'I Don't Want to Hear Your Language!' White Social Imagination and the Demography of Roman Corinth." *Bible and Critical Theory* 16:64–91.

Tyrrell, George. 1909. *Christianity at the Crossroads*. London: Longmans, Green.

Versnel, H. S. 2002. "The Poetics of the Magical Charm: An Essay in the Power of Words." Pages 105–58 in *Magic and Ritual in the Ancient World*. Edited by Paul Mirecki and Marvin Meyer. RGRW 141. Leiden: Brill.

———. 2013. "Prayers for Justice, East and West: New Finds and Publications Since 1990," Pp. 275-354. *Magical Practice in the Latin West: Papers from the International Conference held at the University of Zaragoza, 30 Sept.–1 Oct. 2005*. Edited by Richard L. Gordon and Francisco Marco Simón. Leiden: Brill.

Winckelmann, Johann Joachim. 2006. *History of the Art of Antiquity*. Translated by Harry Francis. Los Angeles: Getty Research Institute.

Wire, Antoinette Clark. 2003. *The Corinthian Women Prophets*. Eugene, OR: Wipf & Stock.

Wynter, Sylvia. 1987. "On Disenchanting Discourse: "Minority" Literary Criticism and Beyond." *Cultural Critique* 7:207–44.

Responses

On Polycentrism, Simultaneity, and the Priority of Ethical Urgency: The Example of Walker's *Appeal*

Timothy A. Joseph

It would be a gross understatement to say that when our group of scholars in New Testament studies and classics gathered on November 6, 2020, forces of separation and division were encroaching upon us. The deadly crisis of the COVID-19 pandemic compelled us to hold the conference apart from one another over Zoom. The results of the US presidential election held three days earlier were in the balance, with the only certainty being that new and greater expressions of division would emerge over the ensuing months. The backlash to ongoing efforts to reckon with both the country's and our various institutions' histories of oppression of minoritized groups also loomed large.

Then there was the simple fact that scholars of classics and the New Testament—who in many cases concentrate on the same historical periods and same geographical areas and on works written in the same ancient languages addressing many of the same issues—rarely confer. As addressed in the volume's introduction and in the chapters by Denise Kimber Buell and Laura Salah Nasrallah, for a host of reasons—long-ago aesthetic assessments, the professionalization of the disciplines, and plain old siloed incuriosity, to name a few—the two fields have long been divided.

These contextual factors brought an unavoidable weight and urgency to our work together and, I think, proved to be productive. From the conference and from reading the revised papers in the ensuing months, I came away with three emphases that I intend to bring to my scholarship, teaching, and thinking about curricular design.

I am thankful to Nikolas Churik and Judith Hallett for advice as I worked on this response and to Dominic Machado for helpful suggestions on a draft.

1. Polycentrism

In her paper on the Nubian *Kandake* Amantitere, Gay L. Byron writes of the need for "a polycentric interpretive framework that expands the literary and cultural imagination of the ancient world." Given that a preponderance of extant literary sources are elite and male (with a disproportionate number originating from many of the same geographical points, such as Athens and Rome), the task of bringing other voices—and thus other centers—into view is not without challenges. But the turn in Byron's essay from a reference in Acts 8 toward an inquiry into Nubian governance and customs shows us a way toward this polycentrism. Other papers in this volume point in similarly helpful ways toward bringing more ancient stories to the center. Joseph A. Marchal puts into focus the wayward stories of sex laborers that we can discover through close reading of Paul's letters and of Pompeian graffiti. In her reading of Paul's letters in their immediate context, Candida R. Moss brings to the fore the experiences of those with physical disability, including perhaps Paul himself, and the participation of enslaved scribes in the literary process. Nasrallah shows another path toward multiple centers when, pursuing Paul's reference to speaking in tongues at 1 Cor 13:1 and building off the aesthetic critique that Emma Amos expresses in *Measuring, Measuring*, she centers nonelite *voces magicae* from curse tablets and offers an aesthetic appreciation of these ritualistic expressions. Yii-Jan Lin points to the importance of excavating how decentering occurs in her treatment of the ways in which apocalyptic frameworks have been used, in ancient times and our own time, to exclude immigrants from the center, both physically and rhetorically.

2. Simultaneity

In her talk at the conference, Nasrallah brought up the interpretive possibilities made available by the concept of simultaneity articulated by the poet Derek Walcott. In a discussion of his 1990 poem *Omeros*, the legacy of ancient Greek culture, and artistic history more broadly, Walcott (1997, 241) said, "If you think of art merely in terms of chronology, you are going to be patronizing to certain cultures. But if you think of art as simultaneity that is inevitable in terms of certain people, then Joyce is a contemporary of Homer" (see further Haubold 2007, 44–45; Pinnix 2019). There has been a flourishing of work in reception studies by scholars in classics over the past few decades (see, e.g., the volumes edited by Martindale and

Thomas 2006; Brockliss, Chauduri, Lushkov, and Wasdin 2012; and Moyer, Lecznar, and Morse 2020; Greenwood 2016; and *Classical Receptions Journal*, established in 2009). Walcott's lens of simultaneity offers a related but more radically achronological approach to those aiming to look in new ways at the cultural and ethical touchstones between ancient societies and later times and places. Such an approach can lead us to greater attentiveness to artistic "freshness" (Walcott 1997, 240) and to understand artistic exploration of the same themes and figures in different times and places as revealing of the human experience in nonlinear, nonhierarchical, and thus expansive and ever-fresh ways.

Walcott applies this term to the artistic dynamic that exists among, for example, himself, Romare Bearden, Joyce, and Homer—and, as we shall see in my consideration below of the ancient references in black abolitionist David Walker's 1829 *Appeal*, this is primarily how I find the concept of simultaneity to be helpful. But at the same time the term may be well applied to the critical approaches in many of this volume's essays. One example is Allen Dwight Callahan's trenchant discussion of the economic structures that oppressed workers at the time of the New Testament's composition in the same way they do in the twenty-first century, and of the pledges by the rich of charitable giving that, then and now, serve to buttress those structures. Callahan writes of these eras as "homologous." We might also profitably understand the lives of oppressed workers, in the ancient world and in our own time, as simultaneous; in both cases justice is, as Callahan writes, "permanently out of reach."

3. Ethical Urgency

As they de- and recenter our work on the ancient Mediterranean and address human stories and experiences that are temporally disparate yet simultaneous, the papers in this volume all put forward a strong sense of ethical urgency. I have noted the explorations of the lives and sufferings—then and now—of immigrants, sex laborers, and those with disabilities by Lin, Marchal, and Moss, respectively. Moss's centering of the experience of enslaved workers is complemented by examinations of the rhetoric of enslavement and physical conquest in the essays by Jennifer A. Glancy and Abraham Smith, to go with Callahan's treatment of enduring economic oppression and its justifications, as well as Jorunn Økland's examination of the variability of the concept of equality itself. These papers show us how to approach and interrogate issues of justice in ancient texts and culture and, crucially, how to bring our findings to bear on the divisions and injustices in our world now. The last several years have seen more scholarship in the field of classics interrogating the systems of oppression in the cultures we study and the destructive consequences, into our own time, that have come out of the celebrations of these cultures (see e.g., Haley 2009; Zuckerberg 2018; McCoskey 2019; and the online resource *Pharos*[1]). There is much more work to be done, and the pressing ethical urgency that the authors of this volume's chapters bring to their essays is instructive.

Buell's chapter makes a powerful case for each of these emphases as she advocates for scholarship and teaching that are cross-disciplinary and cross-temporal and that work to combat the racist ideologies that are built into curricula and the structures of higher education. Buell stresses that this process of "rewriting knowledge" requires the cultivation of epistemic humility. Approaches that are polycentric, open to the temporal lens of simultaneity, and forthright in conveying ethical urgency demand a decamping from the sometimes too comfortable trenches of academia and an embrace of what Buell calls partial knowing.

In this spirit I want to commit the remainder of this response to a text that is far afield from my area of disciplinary training in classical philology but points to the type of scholarly emphases that the chapters in this volume bring to the fore. The black abolitionist David Walker's (1829) *Appeal to the Coloured Citizens of the World* interweaves engagement with the New Testament and classical models in addressing the moral abomination of the practice of slavery and making the case for immediate abolition. It is a work deserving of much wider study by scholars and students of not just American history and politics but also religious studies and classics. The *Appeal*, like a work of physical art such as Amos's *Measuring, Measuring*, merits a place at the center of curricula in classics and New Testament studies, to be considered in conjunction with—that is, simultaneously with—the ancient texts that Walker engages. At the same time Walker's writing models for our scholarship and teaching, some two centuries later, the type of polycentric, achronological, and ethically driven thinking that is needed in our fields.

Walker (1796/7?–1830) was born in Wilmington, North Carolina, and spent his childhood and early adult years in the free black communities in Wilmington and Charleston, South Carolina. (Hinks 1997 is a detailed

---

1. https://pharosclassics.vassar.edu.

biography, with accompanying analysis of the *Appeal*.) By 1825 he had moved to Boston, where he worked as a used clothing salesman and was a founding member of the Massachusetts General Colored Association, which formed in 1828 and concentrated on black political organization. Walker died in August 1830; whether from sickness or as the result of an attack by white supremacist pursuers is uncertain (see Garnet 1969, vi–vii; Hinks 1997, 269–70; Crockett 2001). The latter emerges as more plausible when we consider that the *Appeal*, which was published in three editions in 1829 and 1830, was immediately identified as a serious threat to enslavers' power and was banned by government officials and legislatures in numerous states, with those aiding in its distribution threatened with punishment ranging from fines up to capital punishment.

The work is addressed to "the coloured citizens of the world, but in particular, and very expressly, to those of the United States of America," though it also includes frequent appeals directly to white readers. It contains four articles, titled (1) Our wretchedness in consequence of slavery; (2) Our wretchedness in consequence of ignorance; (3) Our wretchedness in consequence of the preachers of the religion of Jesus Christ; and (4) Our wretchedness in consequence of the colonizing plan. The critique at the heart of article 3 carries across the *Appeal*, as Walker concentrates in soaring rhetoric on the cruelty and hypocrisy of the white "pretenders to Christianity" (preface to the third edition) who enslave and dehumanize people of African descent. Elsewhere in the preface to the third edition, Walker states his purpose that "the world may see that we, the Blacks or Coloured People, are treated more cruel by the white Christians of America, than devils themselves ever treated a set of men, women, and children on this earth."

In exposing the manifestly un-Christian practices of white Christians of America, Walker builds on quotations from the Hebrew Bible (e.g., Gen 47:5–6 on 10–11; Exod 2:9–10 on 13) as well as the New Testament (e.g., Acts 10:36 [cited as 10:25–26] on 42–43; Rev 22:11 on 45; Matt 28:18–20 on 47; and Matt 18:6 on 75). He reinforces the points he draws from biblical texts with frequent references to models and analogues from elsewhere in the ancient Mediterranean world. For example, Walker opens the work's preamble by emphasizing how much greater the sufferings of the enslaved people in the United States are than the sufferings of the Israelites in Egypt, the helots in Sparta, and the enslaved under Roman rule. Walker comes back to this point in article 1 when addressing in greater detail the condition of the helots in Sparta (15–17) and then directly refuting Thomas Jefferson's well-known assertions in his *Notes on Virginia* about the superior conditions of the enslaved in the United States (17–19). At several points in this discussion Walker is sure to bring his argument about ancient and modern analogies back to Christian ethics, as on page 16:

> The sufferings of the Helots among the Spartans, were somewhat severe, it is true, but to say that theirs, were as severe as ours among the Americans, I do most strenuously deny—for instance, can any man show me an article on a page of ancient history which specifies, that, the Spartans chained, and handcuffed the Helots, and dragged them from their wives and children, children from their parents, mothers from their suckling babes, wives from their husbands, driving them from one end of the country to the other? Notice the Spartans were heathens, who lived long before our Divine Master made his appearance in the flesh. Can Christian Americans deny these barbarous cruelties? Have you not, Americans, having subjected us under you, added to these miseries, by insulting us in telling us to our face, because we are helpless, that we are not of the human family? I ask you, O! Americans, I ask you, in the name of the Lord, can you deny these charges?

This passage is representative of much of the *Appeal* as a whole: references to the classical world and to Christian principles are employed side by side, deepening and reinforcing the potency of Walker's argument. This method of complementary use of classical and New Testament models is perhaps most apparent in Walker's exploration of the theme of divine punishment. In article 3 he quotes from Rev 22:11 to underscore his point about God's punishment of the unjust:

> I tell you Americans! that unless you speedily alter your course, you and your Country are gone!!!!!! For God Almighty will tear up the very face of the earth!!! Will not that very remarkable passage of Scripture be fulfilled on Christian Americans? Hear it Americans!! "He that is unjust, let him be unjust still: and he which is filthy, let him be filthy still: and he that is righteous, let him be righteous still: and he that is holy, let him be holy still." (45)

Later, in article 4, Walker quotes the words of Jesus at Matt 18:6 when again anticipating the punishment due to enslavers and those who support them:

> Our Lord and Master said: "Whoso shall offend one of these little ones which believe in me, it were better for him that a millstone were hanged

about his neck, and that he were drowned in the depth of the sea." But the Americans with this very threatening of the Lord's, not only beat his little ones among the Africans, but many of them they put to death or murder. Now the avaricious Americans, think that the Lord Jesus Christ will let them off, because his words are no more than the words of a man!!! In fact, many of them are so avaricious and ignorant, that they do not believe in our Lord and Saviour Jesus Christ. (75)

Walker introduces this theme of divine justice in his preamble where he posits that the internal strife and suffering of the ancient Egyptians, Spartans, and Romans—the last example coming with references to harrowing historical events such as the terrors of Sulla and Catiline, the assassination of Julius Caesar, the triumvirate of Antony, Octavian, and Lepidus, and the tyranny of the emperor Tiberius—resulted from their oppression of enslaved peoples (6). After noting the more recent examples of suffering among the Spaniards and Portuguese who had propagated the practice of slavery, Walker sums up his point by stating, "they who believe that God is a God of justice, will believe that SLAVERY is the principal cause" (7, capital letters original). To Walker, the words of the New Testament and events from ancient Mediterranean history offer testimony to the same truth: divine punishment will come to those who enslave others.

In article 2, which concentrates on the importance of education, Walker keeps the theme of God's justice at the fore, this time interweaving reference to ancient Carthage and the general Hannibal, who led the Carthaginian campaign against Rome in the Second Punic War (218–201 BCE). After opening this article by underscoring that "it was sons of Africa or of Ham, among whom learning originated" (22) and that learning came to Greece and then to Rome from Africa, he pivots to highlight the story of "that mighty son of Africa, HANNIBAL, one of the greatest generals of antiquity, who defeated and cut off so many thousands of the white Romans or murderers" (22–23; capital letters are original). Walker notes that ancient Carthage, like Haitian revolutionaries in Walker's own time, had faltered because of internal divisions, and he then implores of his black readers, "Beloved brethren—here let me tell you, and believe it, that the Lord our God, as true as he sits on his throne in heaven, and as true as our Saviour died to redeem the world, will give you a Hannibal, and when the Lord shall have raised him up, and given him to you for your possession, O my suffering brethren! remember the divisions and consequent sufferings of Carthage and of Hayti" (23). In an arresting rhetorical gesture, God's justice, together with Jesus's redemptive death, are aligned with Hannibal's efforts to lead Carthage against Rome—and with the efforts of a putative future Hannibal figure in the United States.

These examples highlight how Walker dynamically welds words and imagery from the New Testament with models from the classical world of the ancient Greeks, Carthaginians, and Romans. It would be wrong to say that Walker's interweaving of the biblical and the classical was extraordinary for his time—he is writing well before the systematic separation of academic disciplines that began to take hold later in the nineteenth century and that Buell discusses in her chapter (see also the introduction to this volume). But these passages are striking in the ways they exhibit a polycentric view of the ancient world, cultivate a sense of simultaneity with the ancient past, and, to be sure, communicate an urgent ethical message. This later emphasis emerges most clearly: the *Appeal* does not dull its searing message about the evil of slavery and the barbarity that lies in an American system that does not see the humanity of African Americans.

Walker points us to a polycentric way of viewing the ancient Mediterranean by making Carthage, not Rome, the most significant actor in the Punic Wars. Our chief sources for the Punic Wars, such as the historians Polybius and Livy and the biographer Plutarch, wrote under the Roman Mediterranean hegemony that followed Rome's victory in those wars. A Romanocentric perspective is inevitable in these source texts. Walker understands the Punic Wars from the perspective not of the Romans' expansion on land and sea but from that of Africans' struggle against European oppressors. And while the characterization of Romans as white is not representative of ancient understandings of race (see McCoskey 2019, 1–34), what we see in the reference to "white Romans or murderers" here is Walker rhetorically eliding the experiences of ancient Carthaginians and African Americans of his time, conveying a sense of the simultaneity of their struggles. The "mighty son of Africa" Hannibal emerges as a representative of all people of African origins at all times, his struggle an ongoing struggle, with the arrival of another Hannibal to champion the African American cause imminent (on Walker's uses of Hannibal, see further Malamud 2019 63–65, and Machado, forthcoming). And when we recall that Walker imagines that "the Lord our God … will give you a Hannibal," we see another aspect of the *Appeal*'s simultaneity with the ancient past. The divine justice that he evokes across the work—punishing perpetuators of slavery in ancient Greece and Rome, modern Spain and Portugal, and, soon, the United States—is achronological. God's justice, Walker tells us, is bound by neither place nor temporality.

Nor is Walker's *Appeal* bound by disciplinarity or any particular hegemonic structure. The essays in this volume point to ways of extending research and teaching in New Testament studies and classics beyond divisions, in new spatial and temporal directions, toward new ethical imperatives. Thinking of this sort leads us to texts like Walker's *Appeal*, a work not only worthy of greater study but also exemplary in important ways for scholarship and teaching in our times.

Works Cited

Brockliss, William, Pramit Chauduri, Ayelet Haimson Lushkov, and Katherine Wasdin, eds. 2012. *Reception and the Classics*. Cambridge: Cambridge University Press.

Crockett, Hasan. 2001. "The Incendiary Pamphlet: David Walker's *Appeal* in Georgia." *Journal of Negro History* 86.3:305–18.

Garnet, Henry Highland. 1969. "A Brief Sketch of the Life and Character of David Walker." Pages i–vii in *Walker's Appeal, in Four Articles/An Address to the Slaves of the United States of America*. Repr. New York: Arno.

Greenwood, Emily. 2016. "Reception Studies: The Cultural Mobility of Classics." *Daedalus* 145:41–49.

Haley, Shelley. 2009. "Be Not Afraid of the Dark: Critical Race Theory and Classical Studies." Pages 27–50 in *Prejudice and Christian Beginnings: Investigating Race, Gender and Ethnicity in Early Christian Studies*. Edited by Laura Nasrallah and Elisabeth Schüssler Fiorenza. Minneapolis: Fortress.

Hinks, Peter. 1997. *To Awake My Afflicted Brethren: David Walker and the Problem of Antebellum Slave Resistance*. University Park: Penn State University Press.

Haubold, Johannes. 2007. "Homer after Parry: Tradition, Reception, and the Timeless Text." Pages 27–46 in *Homer in the Twentieth Century: Between World Literature and the Western Canon*. Edited by Barbara Graziosi and Emily Greenwood. Oxford: Oxford University Press.

Machado, Dominic. Forthcoming. "*Res Diversissimas*: A Postcolonial Reading of Hannibal's Reception." In *Handbook of Classics and Postcolonial Theory*. Edited by Ben Akrigg and Katherine Blouin. London: Routledge.

Malamud, Margaret. 2019. *African Americans and the Classics: Antiquity, Abolition, and Activism*. London: Tauris.

Martindale, Charles, and Richard Thomas, eds. 2006. *Classics and the Uses of Reception*. Malden, MA: Wiley-Blackwell.

McCoskey, Eileen. 2019. *Race: Antiquity and Its Legacy*. London: Bloomsbury.

Moyer, Ian, Heidi Lecznar, and Adam Morse, eds. 2020. *Black Classicisms in the Atlantic*. Oxford: Oxford University Press.

Pinnix, Aaron. 2019. "Sargassum in the Black Atlantic: Entanglement and the Abyss in Bearden, Walcott, and Philip." *Atlantic Studies* 16:423–51.

Walcott, Derek. 1997. "Reflections on *Omeros*." *South Atlantic Quarterly* 96.2:229–46.

Walker, David. 2015. *Walker's Appeal, in Four Articles; Together with a Preamble, to the Coloured Citizens of the World*. 3rd ed. Edited by Paul Royster. Zea E-Books in American Studies 15. https://digitalcommons.unl.edu/zeaamericanstudies/15.

Zuckerberg, Donna. 2018. *Not All Dead White Men: Classics and Misogyny in the Digital Age*. Cambridge: Harvard University Press.

Divided Worlds: How Divided Are They?

Shelley P. Haley

What are the words you do not yet have? What do you need to say? What are the tyrannies you swallow day by day and attempt to make your own, until you will sicken and die of them, still in silence?
—Audre Lorde, "Transformation of Silence into Language and Action"

My project rises from delight, not disappointment. It rises from what I know about the way writers transform aspects of their social grounding into aspects of language and the ways they tell other stories, fight secret wars, limn out all sorts of debates blanketed in their text. And rises from my certainty that writers always know, at some level, that they do this.
  For some time now I have been thinking about the validity or vulnerability of a certain set of assumptions conventionally accepted among literary historians and critics and circulated as "knowledge."
—Toni Morrison, *Playing in the Dark*

Until Lions Have Their Own Historians, the Story of the Hunt Will Always Glorify the Hunter: Africanizing History, Feminizing Knowledge
—Nwando Achebe, *Female Monarchs and Merchant Queens in Africa*

I must acknowledge that I feel a bit surreal writing this response. Indeed, as each day passes, for me the divided worlds of this volume's title is more applicable to the forces of antiracism versus the forces of antiblackness. This is deeply personal for me. Antiblackness surrounds me unrelentingly. Voter suppression laws, lack of action on the George Floyd Policing Reform Act, Haitian asylum seekers being rounded up with lassos and whips like cattle. Just the other day I read of a Black high school quarterback in Iowa who was taunted with racial slurs from the opposing players, and when he defended himself the referee ejected *him* from the game "for using profanity." As of this writing there have been no sanctions against the opposing team (*Newsweek* 2021).

As a Black woman, I encounter almost daily, indeed sometimes hourly, examples of this chasm. These range from the jaw-droppingly ridiculous, like the petition to bring back slavery that circulated at Park Hill South High School in the suburbs of Kansas City, Missouri, to the utterly ignorant and malicious, such as the censorship of children's books and young adult literature by predominantly authors of color who write about Black history and aim to empower Black, Indigenous, and other children of color. This is being carried out by the far-right group Moms for Liberty in Williamson County, Tennessee. They have condemned books about the Reverend Martin Luther King Jr., Rosa Parks, and Ruby Bridges. For the purpose of this response, however, no example is more harrowing than Donna Scott Davenport, who is a judge in Rutherford County, Tennessee. (Tennessee again!) According to a report by ProPublica (2021), Davenport "oversees a juvenile justice system in Rutherford County, Tennessee, with a staggering history of jailing children." We learn in the report that the children arrested and jailed are overwhelmingly Black. This example is central to my response for two reasons. First is Davenport's own admission that "I'm here on a mission. It's not a job. It's *God's mission*." (emphasis added). The second reason is this example parallels the case studies presented in Saidiya Hartman's (2019) *Wayward Lives, Beautiful Experiments: Intimate Histories of Social Upheaval*. In "Wayward and Willful: Twisting Figures Past *Porneia* in Paul's Letters" in this volume Joseph A. Marchal frames his analysis of *porneia* and the Pauline letters through the works of Hartman and Sara Ahmed, both critical race feminists. As a Black woman who was severely punished as a child for being willful and who now has gone on in her willful ways to apply Black feminist thought and critical race feminist theory in the most unlikely of all fields for a person like me: classics, I know how cathartic the application of critical race theory can be to destabilizing the center of classics and New Testament studies. I yearn to embrace Marchal's framing. However, I am held back by underlying assumptions of a Western epistemological framework and the erasure of the dominant infrastructure of white supremacist patriarchal discourse, a discourse that is especially crucial to understanding the brilliance of Hartman's work. She centers *Black* women as the focal point of her *narrative*. It is a *narrative* ... but it is not a *counter*narrative because that implies that it is *reactive* instead of *proactive*. Marchal claims that Hartman is "simply re-creat[ing] the lives of young Black women subject to moralizing reformist and carceral forces." There is nothing *simple* about Hartman's work, nor are the narratives re-creations. As Hartman (2008, 13) says in "Venus in Two Acts": "The promiscuity of the archive begets a wide array of reading, but none that are capable of resuscitating the girl." In this case, the solution is that white scholars need (1) to always explicitly state their social location; and (2) to racialize their discourse and not leave it to scholars of color. In the sentence above I would have preferred Marchal say *"white supremacist moralizing reformist and carceral forces."*

In his discussion of Paul's writings addressed to the gentiles, especially to the Corinthians, Marchal misses an opportunity to stress the racial differences among so-called Greeks. For example, the Corinthians belong to the Aeolian race, which had very different cultural attitudes toward gender, the body, sex, and sex work. It was *not* necessarily true in Corinth that *porneia* were enslaved or even formerly enslaved. In addition, there is the assumption of enslaved or formerly enslaved status for the people Marchal identifies as prostitutes or sex workers. What *exactly* is the evidence is that these people are enslaved? For example, in multiple places there is discussion of a person called Narcissus. What evidence is there that he was enslaved or formerly enslaved? Is it only a matter of his name or are there other markers?

That said, I found the Pauline letters fertile material for a case study for the trajectory of my own research: the application of racialized gender to ancient societies. In these epistles we find the intersection of race, gender, and class, which is at the core of the concept of racialized gender.

Marchal delves into philology, and I am not sure I fully grasp why. In this volume where most, if not all, the essays take a detached and academic tone, is Marchal being "wayward and willful" by mixing the colloquial and academic registers in his academic paper? I am not saying that Marchal has mistranslated words such as *irrumare*, but I do think some contextualization (i.e., that graffiti is necessarily quotidian and raunchy, a little like the unsanitized lyrics of the early blues) is in order here.

In her essay, "The World of *Kandake*: Foregrounding Ethiopian Queens and Empires," Gay L. Byron addresses the sins of omission, erasure, and silence that surround the women of African descent who were rulers in their nations. The truth is that within all eras of human history there have been female monarchs of African descent going back to the Fifth Dynasty of Egypt. In the New Kingdom, Hatshepsut is probably the most misunderstood female pharaoh of Egypt. The importance of the female rulers is consistently downplayed in mainstream, Eurocentric Egyptology.

There has been a persistent will to erase and erode the history of African-descended female monarchs. For example, few if any classicists or New Testament studies scholars know who Amanirenas is.[1] The title *kandake* might be slightly more recognizable to New Testament scholars because of the vignette in Acts 8:27, but they are hard-pressed to actually "say her name," as Byron implores. Unfortunately, Western historians have reduced all the holders of the title *kandake* (its problematic, Western translation is "queen mother") to their title and stripped away their names. As a result, we are slowly losing the ability to say her name and resuscitate the holder of the title from the title. The best example I have found of this comes from Adrian Goldsworthy, a white British male military historian, in his 2014 monograph, *Augustus: First Emperor of Rome*:

> In Egypt, the prefect Petronius had faced serious raids by the Ethiopians into the south of his province. He drove out the first attack but the difficulty of keeping an army in the desert caused him to pull back most of his forces. The Ethiopian *Queen Candace* [sic] again sent her warriors to attack the Romans, prompting another campaign and Roman counterattack, which this time a better-prepared Petronius extended further south.... Eventually *Candace* sought terms and Petronius referred their ambassadors to Augustus. (300, emphasis added)

Now I do not want to get too pedantic and philological, but I do want to examine Goldsworthy's syntax here. It is clear from the word order that Goldsworthy does not know or does not care that "Candace" is a title. So, in effect Goldsworthy has given us "The Ethiopian Queen Queen"! In the second sentence, he uses "Candace" alone, as if that is her given name.

He could not be bothered to do a little searching to uncover not only the meaning of *kandake* (here anglicized to Candace, which now is also a name, pronounced slightly differently), but also the *name* of this *kandake*. Scholars as far back as 1981 were able to *name* this *kandake*. Nwando Achebe (2020, 76), admittedly writing nearly a decade after Goldsworthy, says this:

> Amanirenas (ca. 40–10 BCE), who might have ruled jointly with her husband *Prince* Akinidad and reigned during a period of great prosperity (two surviving portraits from her pyramid lend clues to her rule: in

---

1. Byron herself points this out in her paper. I would add that the classicist she cites from Howard is white and has been openly antagonistic to the work of Martin Bernal.

the first she is dressed in ceremonial clothes and is spearing bound prisoners; the second portrait shows the presence of three scars under left eye, supporting the hypothesis that she might in fact be the one-eyed kandake who fought the Romans during the 20s BCE).

I assume Goldsworthy had access to the same sources as Achebe for Amanirenas, but I can only conclude that Goldsworthy did not deem this ruler worthy of any further attention.

However, look at how much more we learn about this Ethiopian ruler from a woman scholar of African descent. (By the way, Nwando Achebe is the daughter of the acclaimed Nigerian novelist, poet, and critic Chinua Achebe.) Beyond naming this *kandake*, I also appreciate that Achebe's description places the *kandake* in a politically superior position to her husband (based on titles) and establishes her as the commander-in-chief as well as a minister of state. The few details are tantalizing: What is the meaning of the scarification under her left eye? Does it necessarily mean she was "one-eyed"? If she was, did she lose that eye in a military campaign?

Did some sort of sexist historical treatment get applied to Amanirenas, or was she too obscure for Western scholars to care about? Here is a description from Jean Leclant (1981) in his chapter in *General History of Africa II: Ancient Civilizations of Africa*: "Shall we ever know whether Amanirenas or Amanishakheto was the one-eyed, 'mannish-looking' Candace who, according to Strabo, Pliny and Dion [sic] Cassius, conducted the negotiations with the Roman invaders?" Mannish-looking?! While I am not sure whether this is Leclant's translation of the ancient historians he cites, it surely falls into a sexist historical treatment and masculinization of powerful Black women.

Another female ruler who has been swept under the historical rug is Eunoë, the coruler of Mauretania with Bogudes. Whenever scholars pay any attention to Eunoë (which, frankly, is rare), they are fixated on her racial identity: scholars make much of her Greek name and struggle mightily to find some Greek ancestry for her. I have seen her described as Berber, as if that separates her from her African heritage. The ancient and medieval sources had no such misgivings: they describe her unequivocally as "Moorish." Once again, she is only of interest to ancient historians because of her connection to Julius Caesar: they apparently became lovers when Caesar arrived in Mauretania in 46 BCE prior to the Battle of Thapsus. She is often perceived as a foil to Cleopatra. Indeed, Suetonius claims she may have replaced Cleopatra in Caesar's affections. A medieval French prose work, *Faits des Romains* (*The Accomplishments of the Romans*), stresses Caesar's sexual dominance over Eunoë and describes her as "the most beautiful woman in four kingdoms, *nevertheless she was Moorish*" (emphasis and translation mine). I envision a project that resuscitates the shadowy hauntings of these neglected African queens along the lines of Saidiya Hartman's *Wayward Lives*.

This volume discusses the most urgent contemporary systems of oppression—racism, sexism, classism/economic inequity, and homophobia—and how our disciplines of classics and New Testament studies are foundational to them and complicit in their perpetuation. Each essay is powerful in its own way, but one element is sorely lacking: a condemnation of antiblackness and white supremacy, which are the originary frameworks for both our fields. In fact, three essays—Allen Dwight Callahan's "*r > g*"; Jennifer A. Glancy's "Master Jesus and the Enslaved Apostles"; and Jorann Økland's "Equality: A Modern, Ancient Greek, and Pauline History of the Concept"—simply omit any discussion of race, thus perpetuating the oppressive silencing all three of my epigraphs reference. The intersectional analysis of critical race theory is the life preserver of classics and New Testament studies. Narrow feminist or Marxist critiques, in my unsophisticated paraphrase of Duke Ellington's jazz classic, "don't mean a thing, if they ain't got race."

So, my mind turns again to antiblackness. When did antiblackness begin? Was it in ancient Hellenic societies? Was it in ancient Rome? Was it in ancient Egypt or even ancient Nubia? Was it never there but interpolated into these societies by later ones through lexicography poisoned by the bioracism and white supremacist eugenic ideology of later times? How much later? The Middle Ages? Renaissance? When and, even more importantly, why?

I have written and, indeed, I truly believe that the ancient Romans noticed skin color but did not attach negative value to it. The Romans certainly suffered from xenophobia and ethnocentrism as much as the next ancient society. But did that rise to the level of antiblackness? As an example, here is a passage from Lucretius, *Nat.* 4.1157–1160:

>atque alios alii inrident Veneremque suadent
>ut placent, quoniam foedo adflictentur amore,
>nec sua respiciunt miseri mala maxima saepe.
>*nigra melichrus est*

And lovers gird each other and urge
placating Venus, since they are afflicted
With a base passion – miserable fools
Who seldom acknowledge their own worst flaw of all.
The black-skinned girl is "tawny like the honey." (translation mine)

We are always at the mercy of the lexicon and translation, but here Lucretius, an ancient Roman author, perceives very dark brown skin as a flaw. Can we ever know how widespread such a perception was in Roman society? Can we ever trace the evolution of the preference for lighter skin tones in the ancient ideal beauty standard?

It seems to me that the disciplines of classics and New Testament studies must be partners in the project of deconstructing and decoupling our fields from the Western patriarchal epistemological framework. This is not a project of political correctness or cancel culture. But we must face head-on the fact that our respective disciplines have developed within the crucible of classist white supremacist ideology. In so doing, we restore and resuscitate those we have wittingly and unwittingly silenced and erased. I believe this book is a step in the right direction. However, we must constantly be on guard against the charge that we do this work out of the self-indulgent, self-interested quest for relevance.

Works Cited

Achebe, Nwando. 2020. *Female Monarchs and Merchant Queens in Africa*. Athens: Ohio University Press.

Goldsworthy, Adrian. 2014. *Augustus: First Emperor of Rome*. New Haven: Yale University Press.

Hartman, Saidiya. 2008. "Venus in Two Acts." *Small Axe* 12:1–14.

———. 2019. *Wayward Lives, Beautiful Experiments: Intimate Histories of Social Upheaval*. New York: Norton.

Leclant, Jean. 1981. "The Empire of Kush: Napata and Meroe." Pages 278–97 in *General History of Africa: Ancient Civilizations of Africa*. Edited by Gamal Mokhtar. Berkeley: Heinemann/UNESCO.

Lorde, Audre. 1984. "The Transformation of Silence into Language and Action." Pages 40–44 in *Sister Outsider: Essays and Speeches by Audre Lorde*. Berkeley: Crossing.

Morrison, Toni. 1992. *Playing in the Dark: Whiteness and the Literary Imagination*. Cambridge: Harvard University Press.

Newsweek. 2021. "High School Quarterback Allegedly Called Racial Slur Gets Ejected for Complaining about It." October 4, 2021. https://tinyurl.com/SBL06104f1.

ProPublica. 2021. "Black Children Were Jailed for a Crime that Doesn't Exist." October 8, 2021. https://tinyurl.com/SBL06104g1.

A Classicist's Reflections on Greco-Roman Epidemiologies of Foreignness and Categorizations of Disability

Thomas R. Martin

Professor Yii-Jan Lin dramatically demonstrates that in US history the conceptualization of disease as an invasion by immigrant others has equated them with unclean peoples—sinners to whom God denies entry to the new Jerusalem of Revelation. Conceptualizing epidemics as invasions echoes Greco-Roman thought; Livy alliteratively remarks that "A pestilence invaded the population" (*pestilentia populum invasit*; *Ab urbe cond.* 4.21.2) of the epidemic that infiltrated Rome in 436 BCE (Gardner 2019, 47, 56).[1]

As in Near Eastern tradition (e.g., Pritchard 1969), Greeks and Romans regularly associated epidemics with divine retribution for human wrongdoing (Parker 1983, 235–56; Martin 1995, 139–62; Bradley 2012; Apel 2016, 97–98). The earliest Greek literature indeed begins with Apollo inflicting a plague on the invading Greeks at Troy to punish them for treating a Trojan priest uncleanly; to survive they must purify themselves by washing and sacrificing (Homer, *Il.* 1.1–475).

Greeks and Romans frequently regarded epidemics as invading from foreign realms or having been initiated by foreigners (Pliny, *Nat.* 7.170, 26.4; Duncan-Jones 1996, 114; Flemming 2010, 21–22).[2] Athenians said

---

I am grateful to my Holy Cross colleague Tat-siong Benny Liew for the invitation to participate in this project.

This response to the stimulating papers of Yii-Jan Lin and Candida R. Moss reflects my perspective as a professional classicist and a New Testament amateur.

1. Translations of Greek and Latin are mine, unless otherwise noted.

2. Theories of other origins also existed, such as the effects of unsanitary urban areas (Courrier 2014, 104–16), or of general environmental conditions (Flemming

the Peloponnesian War epidemic came from Ethiopia (Thucydides, *P.W.* 2.48.1; Lucretius, *Nat.* 6.1141; Galen, *Ther. Pis.* 16.281)[3] or from their Peloponnesian enemies injecting drugs into Athenian wells (Thucydides, *P.W.* 2.48.2). Romans identified Babylonia as the origin of the second-century CE Antonine Plague (Hist. Aug., Ver. 8.1-4; Ammianus Marcellinus, *Res gestae* 23.6.24). The epidemic during Justinian's sixth-century CE reign reportedly migrated from Egypt (Procopius, *Bell.* 2.22.6) or Ethiopia (Evagrius Scholasticus, *Hist. eccl.* 4.29; John of Ephesus, *Chronicle* part 2[4]).

Condemning immigrants as unclean agents of disease is an attested ancient view. For example, during Commodus's reign (180–192 CE) "a pestilential disease seized Italy. The suffering peaked in Rome because the city, by its nature highly populated, was receiving people from everywhere" (Herodian, *Hist.* 1.12.1).[5] However, vitriol was more often spewed at foreigners as corrupters of indigenous mores (Xenophon, *Lac.* 14.4; Juvenal, *Sat.* 1.3; Tacoma 2016, 207–14).[6]

Finally, negative Greco-Roman reactions could reference foreigners' presumed uncleanliness: Theseus in Seneca's *Phraedra* (l. 905) calls Hippolytus, descended from Amazons, a "pestilent effluvium of an unspeakable race" (*generis infandi lues*).[7] Nevertheless, Cicero can also argue (*Off.*

2010, 22; Gardner 2019, 23–24), including extraordinary situations such as long-term effects from the massive ash fall from the eruption of Vesuvius in 79 CE (Cassius Dio, *Hist.* 66.23.3–5).

3. For text, translation, and commentary, see Pinault 1986, 60; Leigh 2016, 148–49, 245–46.

4. Translated from the Syriac version found in Pearse 2017.

5. This epidemiology seems a precedent for the modern idea of an "urban graveyard effect" (on which, see Lo Cascio 2016).

6. On the intersection of contemporary thinking and practice with modern reconstructions and representations of ancient thinking and practices, see Siapkas (2014, 66), who discusses "how modern, scholarly assumptions, ideas, and discourses concerning ethnicity have informed our conceptualizations of classical antiquity."

7. In the light of Lin's discussion of the othering of Chinese ethnicity in the United States, still a contemporary reality in my immediate family's experience, it seems appropriate to mention that this particular brand of discriminatory discourse reappears in contemporary efforts in the United States to blame others for the current pandemic; see Zimmerman 2021. Greek and Roman attitudes about the Chinese, admittedly based on very limited contact, were more complex. Pliny, for one, describes the Seres (the Roman designation of the peoples in farthest Asia) as gentle (*mites*) and disposed to avoid the company of the rest of humankind (*Nat.* 6.20); cf. Bueno 2016. Kim 2009 discusses comparative early Chinese and Greek articulations

3.11.47) that barring immigrants because they are ethnically other is unjust: "Although it is right not to allow someone who is not a citizen to exercise citizen status … to block foreigners from really having access to the city [Rome] is extremely inhuman."[8]

These texts on outsiders inform my view on Revelation's new Jerusalem. As Lin observes, entry was not a priori denied to anyone: humans from all nations, tribes, languages, and peoples can join God's "great crowd" of the saved (Rev 7:9; 19:1). The criteria for entering the new Jerusalem are moral, not ethnic: accepting God's Word and shunning the pollution of sin. People achieve this ritual cleanliness by washing their clothes in the blood of the Lamb (7:14; 22:14), turning their garments white to symbolize membership in God's army, which will ultimately conquer Satan's forces.

Revelation implies that this symbolic cleanliness is not automatically missing from those categorized as outsiders by people who see themselves as insiders.[9] Individuals' actions determine their purity, not their inherited identities. Deeds (ἔργα)—individuals' actions recorded in the book of life—are what determine their eligibility to enter the new Jerusalem (Rev 20:12; 21:27; *pace* 13:8). Those excluded remain outsiders *of their own volition* because they persist as unrepentant wrongdoers (9:20–21; 16:9, 11; 18:4). The otherness excluding them from the new Jerusalem and condemning them to eternal torment is self-determined, not something insiders impose on them for being foreigners.

---

of the "barbarian" as related to the other. Mittag and Mutschler 2010, 544–50 and Ford 2020 (esp. 56–95 and 106–29) discuss the evidence for this process in ancient Chinese and Roman thinking.

8. Cicero's words seem an eerie forerunner of William Henry Wilkins's arguments in his 1892 book *The Alien Invasion* lamenting the deleterious effects on poor citizens of "[t]he unrestricted influx of destitute aliens into the United Kingdom." Echoing (in admittedly more equivocal terms) Cicero's words, Wilkins (1892, 1, 6) agrees that "no objection can be urged against foreign immigration as a whole." The only immigrants to be rejected are those who are not "decent and cleanly [*sic*] in their habits and mode of living." Explicitly calling immigration an invasion has become a prominent feature in the discourse of contemporary political conflict in the United States; see Ulloa 2021. Noy (2000, 31–52) and Tacoma (2016, 92–104, 207–14) discuss the complicated question of whether the occasional expulsions of foreigners from the city of Rome or Roman territory were directed at specific groups and related to preconceptions about ethnic identities.

9. On Rev 21:27 and "traditional sources of defilement," see Koester 2014, 822.

This self-determination to remain sinners can bring disease. Revelation twice refers to the "infected wound" that God's avenging angel inflicts on those worshiping Satan's beast (16:2, 11). These wounds persist because the afflicted humans do not repent of their *deeds*. This emphasis on *willful* impurity is reemphasized when the angel tells John that "the critical time is near. Let the one doing wrong still do wrong and the soiled still be soiled, and let the just still do justice and the holy still be holy" (22:10–11). This passage stresses that people excluded from New Jerusalem are *not* being classified wrongdoers on the basis of discriminatory ethnic judgments. Rather, the actions they *continue to choose* settle their eternal fate (22:15). As God says, "My recompense is with me, to pay back each according to their deed (ἔργον)" (22:12).

Upping the ante from Cicero's argument about the inhumanity of discriminating against foreigners, Revelation shows that summarily excluding them from paradise contradicts God's plan. The church leaders whom Lin cites misconstrue Revelation's path for human beings of all origins to enter the new Jerusalem. Focusing on the theme of conquering others that Revelation expresses from the start (2:7),[10] these self-designated insiders ignore Revelation's teaching that people from everywhere are welcome in the new Jerusalem if they follow God's will.

If this interpretation is cogent, then we today face a troubling challenge: How can we persuade those identifying themselves as insiders that they cannot deny entry to the new Jerusalem, which they claim as their own city, to those whom they construe as Others simply on the basis of these newcomers' inherited identity as outsiders? The Greeks believed it took the divine power of *Peithō* to persuade people to change their minds. Can we find a modern goddess of persuasion to help us overcome inhumane discrimination?[11]

Professor Moss's thought-provoking arguments about disability and enslaved labor in the New Testament present me with a similar dilem-

---

10. Starting with this instance, the Perseus online database identifies seventeen appearances of the verb νικάω in Revelation: Rev 2:7, 11, 17, 26; 3:5, 12, 21 [×2]; 5:5; 6:2 [×2]; 11:7; 12:11; 13:7; 15:2; 17:14; 21:7.

11. Dow (2015) analyses Aristotle's views about the emotional component in persuasion, which is increasingly emphasized in modern studies of the challenges of persuading people, especially those outside our own circle. Perloff (2020), in a popular textbook, emphasizes the complexity of persuasive communication in contemporary settings.

ma.[12] As with discrimination against immigrants, there is much to contemplate today on these issues, from "an awareness of disability studies" being "essential in Classics and the Humanities more widely" (Adams 2021, 1), to the exception clause of the Thirteenth Amendment to the US Constitution still allowing "a new form of slavery through convict leasing" that exacerbates "the denial of equal citizenship and impeded access of unalienable human rights to African-Americans" (Tyner and Fry 2020). What evidence from Greco-Roman antiquity might be good to think with about our contemporary situation concerning (to paraphrase Moss) people living with the consequences of impairments and an imposed absence of autonomy of their labor?[13]

Greeks and Romans recognized the diversity of human disability.[14] Their reactions could be equally diverse. For example, in some communities, fathers could without penalty abandon infants judged deformed—a fatal decision for many of these unfortunates (Kelley 2007, 36–39; Dillon 2017, 167–69; Laes 2018, 23–28, 34–35).[15] By contrast, classical-era Athenian democracy supported men with disabilities who possessed only limited financial resources (Dillon 1995, 2017, pace Rose 2017).

Considerations of space limit me to two examples from Greco-Roman literature illustrating these themes. Both appear in our earliest evidence for representations of those with disabilities in Greco-Roman antiquity: Homeric poetry (Brockliss 2019).

---

12. In my discussion, I use the terms *disability* and *disabled* in the hope that this decision will not be interpreted as implying a categorization of those so designated as falling short of externally imposed social and cultural norms of appearance and patterns of activity. For a recent news article about experiential perspectives on this terminology, see Wong 2019. It seems appropriate in the context of Moss's opening remarks to say that my immediate family's experiences continue to reveal the inaccuracy and injustice of preconceptions associated with ableism.

13. For "good to think with" as a frequent English translation of Lévi-Strauss's phrase *bonnes à penser* (1962, 128), see Garber 2012, 96–97.

14. As Lisa Trentin states, "In [Greco-Roman] antiquity there was no clear distinction between a deformity and a disability, nor were there any precise Greek or Latin equivalents to these modern designations. Nevertheless, the ancients did have an extensive vocabulary to describe various phenomena of deformity and disability" (2011, 195). See also Albl 2007; Kelley 2007, 32–35; Garland 2010, 1–9; Penrose 2015; Laes 2017a; Rose 2017, 143–48, revising Rose 2003; Samana 2017.

15. Controversy over the morality of decisions to put deformed or unwanted fetuses and infants to death of course continues to this day (Singer 2011, 123–90, esp. 162–67; cf. Robinson 2017; Giubilini and Minerva 2013; Kaczor 2020, 61–91).

Hephaestus occupies a special place in studying disability in antiquity (Rinon 2006; Kelley 2007, 35–41; Garland 2010, 61–63, 79–84, 113–14; Leas 2018, 165 n. 84): he is divine, parthenogenetically born, and physically disabled (Hesiod, *Theog.* 927–929, 945; *Hymn. Apoll.* 316–317; Park 2014). Our sources report he was either born with deformed legs and feet or suffered this permanent condition after crashing to earth when either Zeus or Hera, motivated by shame and anger, threw him off Olympus (Homer, *Il.* 1.590–594; 18.393–405; *Hymn Apoll.* 318; Bazopoulou-Kyrkanidou 1997; Brennan 2016).[16] At the same time, Hephaestus possesses supreme engineering proficiency (Homer, *Il.* 1.607–608; Hesiod, *Theog.* 929). "Famously skilled," he benefits humas by teaching them "distinguished works" (*Hymn Heph.* 2–5). Nevertheless, the other gods laugh derisively at him for serving them while limping (Homer, *Il.* 1.571–600).

Homer also presents a human counterpoint to Hephaestus as an embodiment of both disability and agency: Thersites, a Greek warrior at Troy with a deformed body. He speaks up in a meeting on whether the Greeks should continue the war. His fierce criticism of the Greeks' leader Agamemnon "speaks truth to power."[17] Consequently, Thersites receives a severe beating and humiliating mockery both for his nonstandard appearance and his blunt words (*Il.* 2.211–77).[18]

Strikingly, Achilles—Thersites's explicit opposite in physiognomy and social approval—had earlier made the same argument with equal ferocity (*Il.* 1.121–187; Postlethwaite 1988). Why, then, is Thersites "the most shameful and deformed man who came to Troy" (*Il.* 2.216; 248–249), while Achilles is "the best of the Achaeans" (*Il.* 1.244; Nagy 1999)?

In short, the denigration of Thersites stems from his outspokenness as a "blame persona," but this trait also reflects how Thersites being a person with a deformity gives him a "sub-standard" physiognomy as compared to a "naturally beautiful body" (Marks 2005, 4–7, citing Nagy 1999, 215, 222–26, 253–62; Goodey and Rose 2013, 18, 26; Garland 2010, 80–81; 2017, 154–55; Thumiger 2017, 271–72). Thersites is prescient and active, as are other figures with disabilities in ancient Greek culture (Kelley 2007,

---

16. On shame associated with disabilities, see Garland 2017, 155–56; Gevaert 2017, 216–19; Laes 2018, 30–31, 182–87.

17. On the Black gay Quaker Bayard Rustin as the originator of this phrase and its adoption by the American Friends Service Committee, see M. T. Edwards 2017.

18. For the conflict among Thersites, Achilles, and Odysseus as competition among the socially elite rather than class conflict, see Marks 2005.

43–44).[19] Still, he is derided as ugly and deformed (as defined by others), an inferior being according to the social convention of the "natural body" (on which see Martin 1995, 1–37, esp. 25–37).[20]

Hephaestus and Thersites illustrate a diversity of opinion on whether deformities and disabilities came as punishment for wrongdoing (Garland 2017, 157–59; Laes 2018, 113, 183–84). Hephaestus committed no offense meriting a disability, but Thersites contravened the restrictive norms of his society. The New Testament can link a disability to wrongdoing (Matt 9:2–8, 32–34; Mark 2:3–12; Luke 5:17–26; John 5:2–15; 9:1–12), but it does not link any disability from sin to Paul's comment about his anomalous letters (Gal 6:11, Ἴδετε πηλίκοις ὑμῖν γράμμασιν ἔγραψα τῇ ἐμῇ χειρί), to which I now turn.

A variety of ancient commentators on this verse interpret it as showing Paul's keenness to guarantee his epistle's authenticity because forged letters contradicting his teaching were circulating (2 Thess 2:1–2), and the Galatians had diverged "to another gospel" (Gal 1:6; Albl 2007, 152).[21]

---

19. For others, see, for example, the lame archer Philoctetes (Gagnon 2016) and the blind prophet Teiresias (Kelley 2007, 41–44). On blindness, see Garland 2017, 156–63; Laes 2018, 80–134.

20. Reading Homer's account leaves me unable to comprehend how Goodey and Rose can assert that today Thersites would be medically diagnosed as displaying cognitive disabilities or a behavioral disorder (2018, 43, 46).

21. There was, of course, diversity in interpretation at the level of detail, then and later. For example, Gaius Marius Victorinus (*In Epistolam Pauli ad Galatas libri duo* [PL 8:1195–96]), whose Latin translation of πηλίκοις γράμμασιν is *quantis litteris*, is somewhat of an outlier in his brief remarks on the verse because, although he stresses that Paul is identifying the letter as his, Victorinus explains that Paul wrote in his own hand to show his close friendship (*familiaritas*) for the Galatians and "from kindness" (*ex charitate*) to prevent them feeling any shame about others (scribes?) knowing that they were being corrected for their sins. On Victorinus's arguments as addressed by Augustine, see Plumer 2003, 7–33. Thomas Aquinas says Paul is stressing his authorship of the epistle "to the end, namely, that you [the Galatians] might firmly hold to the foregoing, and that knowing the epistle is sent by me, you might obey better" (translation with Latin text in Larcher and Lamb 2012, 163 [= Lecture 3, 365–66]). Much more recently, the Puritan theologian William Perkins (1558–1602), in his extensive discussion of ancient and medieval commentaries on the verse, argues that Paul is not only guaranteeing the missive's genuineness but also pointing to Paul's explanation of why he wrote *such a long letter* to the Galatians (Sheppard 1989, 534–38). Reece (2017, 73–110, 198–216, 217–38) provides a comprehensive modern discussion and extensive lists of translations and commentaries.

The anonymous author Ambrosiaster says Paul "is giving authority to his epistle" (*Auctoritatem dat epistolae suae*) by saying "I wrote in/with my own hand," as Paul wants his *litterae* to be obeyed.²² Jerome interprets the verse similarly, citing other verses where Paul refers to writing in his own hand.²³ He concludes "Paul wrote his letters in large characters because their meaning was profound and because they had been transcribed by the spirit of the living God and not by pen and ink.… And although the forms with which his epistles are signed are small, the characters are nevertheless large because of the profundity contained in them" (Cain 2010, 262).

John Chrysostom interprets the verse as showing "how much distress holds fast [Paul's] blessed soul," with Paul's reference to the "letters" having been written in his own hand indicating "matters that were especially disturbing his soul." Chrysostom believes these words mean Paul himself wrote "the entire epistle" (τὴν ἐπιστολὴν ἅπασαν), a sign of "great genuineness."²⁴ Usually, Chrysostom remarks (citing Rom 16:22) that Paul dictated his letters to another. This time, however, he did the writing not only from love, but also for "the removal of evil suspicion" that he was being deceptive in his teachings about circumcision. Chrysostom concludes that πηλίκοις indicates not the size (μέγεθος) of Paul's letters but rather their "formlessness" (ἀμορφία), which amounted to his having said, "Not knowing how to write in best form, nevertheless I was compelled to do the writing by myself, so as to stop up the mouth of the informers."²⁵

---

22. *In Epistolam Beati Pauli ad Galatas* (PL 17:392); Vogels 1969, 65. Ambrosiaster's Latin translation of πηλίκοις γράμμασιν as *qualibus litteris* anticipates that of the Vulgate Bible. On Ambrosiaster and Augustine's commentary, see Plumer 2003, 53–56.

23. *Commentariorum in Epistulam ad Galatas libri tres* (PL 26:433–35); Raspanti 2006, 218–20. Cain (2010) provides an introduction and translation. M. J. Edwards (1999, 100) encapsulates Jerome's interpretation. On Jerome and Augustine's commentary, see Plumer 2003, 33–53.

24. *In Epistulam ad Galatas commentarius* (PG 61:677–78). M. J. Edwards (1999, 100) summarizes Chrysostom's comments.

25. Chrysostom in his *Commentarius in Epistulam ad Romanos* (PG 60:680) again quotes the verse but without further interpretation. A marginal comment in a medieval manuscript says that Eusebius of Emesa (on whom see Crain 2010, 24–25), held a similar opinion about πηλίκοις referring to the "formlessness" of Paul's letters rather than to their size. See Cramer 1842, 90 n. h; cf. Swete 1880, 107 n. 9. The manuscript contains a "Catena" of commentaries on Paul's epistles from Galatians to Hebrews by

Augustine tersely comments that Paul is warning against anyone deceiving the improvident (*incauti*) with a letter in his name.[26] Theodore of Mopsuestia takes a related approach, interpreting the verse as meaning "Since [Paul] was going to attack his opponents, he used 'very large letters,' pointing out that he was neither blushing nor denying what he had said."[27]

Finally, Theodoret also interprets the verse as signaling "the entire epistle, as it seems, he wrote himself." Paul, Theodoret adds, intended to teach that people's status (ἀξίωμα) is not to be under suspicion when truth is being revealed. Theodoret concludes that some think the words πηλίκοις γράμμασιν indicate "large" (μεγάλοις) letters, while others think they refer to "bad, inferior" (φαύλοις) letters. "For I," says Theodoret as if quoting Paul, "wrote the epistle, although not writing with attention to beauty" (κάλλος).[28]

In sum, these commentators' belief that Paul wrote the letter "by himself" brings me to Moss's discussion of the issue of Paul's using a scribe for his letters. Strictly speaking, a Roman scribe (*scriba*) was a private entrepreneur or public official skilled at dictation, composition of letters and documents, and financial documentation (Hartmann 2020; cf. Blumell 2006). Skilled workers serving writers could be something quite different, as the case of Tiro reveals.[29] Employed lifelong by Cicero, Tiro possessed all the scribal competencies, but Cicero's letters document Tiro serving as Cicero's executive assistant, to use modern terminology.[30]

Chrysostom, Eusebius of Emesa, Severianus of Gabala, Theodore of Mopsuestia, and, for Hebrews, Origen (Schatkin 1970).

26. *Epistolae ad Galatas expositionis liber unus* (PL 35:2146–47); Plumer argues (2003, 230 n. 277) that Augustine's translation *qualibus litteris* indicates he interpreted the Greek to mean "what kind of letter I have written to you in my own hand" because otherwise Augustine would not have failed to comment on a phrase apparently saying "what kind of letters."

27. *In Epistulam Beati Pauli ad Galatas*. Text from Swete 1880, 107; text and translation found in Greer 2010, 162–63. The translation in the anonymous Latin version is *valde maioribus litteris*.

28. *Interpretatio in XIV epistulas Sancti Pauli* (PG 82:501). Hill 2001, 1–30 offers an introduction and translation of Theodoret on Galatians. The comment about "non-beautiful" writing sounds similar to the modern conclusion that larger, less elegantly formed letters in ancient documents indicate an author's "amateurish" hand, as opposed to that of a professional scribe (Reece 2017, x, 104).

29. The Latin word *tiro* literally means "a newly levied soldier, a young soldier, recruit" and by extension "beginner." We do not know whether this was his original name.

30. Some sixty letters from Cicero and his family and friends are addressed to or

Originally a slave of undocumented origin, Tiro was emancipated by Cicero.[31] Tiro's new status as a "freedman" (*libertus*) moved him from what Orlando Patterson (2018) calls a state of "natal alienation" and "social death" into the status of a Roman citizen with many, but not all, of the "rights" of never-enslaved Roman citizens. Tiro was now known as M. Tullius Tiro, demonstrating his link to his former owner and now (in Roman terminology) formal patron M. Tullius Cicero.[32] A freedman was expected to remain loyal and useful to whoever manumitted him, and Tiro, now Cicero's *amicus* ("friend," *Fam.* 16.16), fulfilled these socially determined obligations of the client to his patron.[33]

In his letters, Cicero says he loves Tiro, worries about his health, and misses him when away (e.g., *Fam.* 16.1, 5). Cicero also writes Tiro that he judges his talent (*ingenium*) "of the greatest" (*Fam.* 16.15). He emphasizes Tiro's literary and intellectual accomplishments, including Tiro's own literary works (*Fam.* 16.18.3). Numerous letters from Cicero and his circle (e.g., *Att.* 7.2, 5; *Fam.* 16 passim) also express deep appreciation of Tiro's work for Cicero. In fact, Cicero tells Tiro his "services" (*officia*) are "innumerable—at home, in the forum, in the city, in the provinces, in private matters, in public matters, in my studies, in my writings" (*Fam.* 16.4.3).[34]

This praise of Tiro's contribution to Cicero's own works illuminates Moss's argument. Significantly, Cicero says his own "little works" might well be called "our works" rather than "my works" (*Fam.* 16.10.2: *litterulae meae, sive nostrae*; cf. *Att.* 7.2; *Fam.* 16.1).[35] Such comments cannot

---

mention Tiro (McDermott 1972, 260). The *scriba meus* named M. Tullius referred to by Cicero (*Fam.* 5.20.1; Hartmann 2020, 50–54) is not the same person as Tiro. See the references in Münzer 1939. This Tullius had been a *scriba quaestorius* for Cicero when he was proconsular governor in Cilicia (Treggiari 1969, 200).

31. Bankston 2012 provides an informative discussion of Tiro's career; see below for his conclusion about how to categorize the relationship between Tiro and Cicero.

32. Trio was only one of a network of multiple freedmen serving Cicero, but he is by far the best documented (Treggiari 1969, 200–201; Bankston 2012, 205–7).

33. What "friendship" (*amicitia*) meant in the context of the Roman client-patron relationship is controversial. See Treggiari 1969; Saller 1982; Konstan 1995; Verboven 2002.

34. On the meaning(s) of *officia* in the context of Roman freedmen, see Saller 1982, 8–22; Konstan 1995.

35. Quintilian in his work on rhetoric (*Inst.* 10.37.1) confirms that Tiro served as what we might call Cicero's editor, as I interpret the meaning of his words [*commentarios Ciceronis*] *Tiro contraxit*.

describe a worker who serves only as a human "recorder" or "printer" for his master's prose.

Do they also suggest male Roman authors regularly acknowledged essential contributions from others of lesser social status? Or do these sentiments tempt us to accept a "happy slave narrative" of the kind denounced by Frederick Douglass?[36] Could there be other motives besides genuine respect and affection motivating Cicero's comments? Was it perhaps expected that a Roman patron who had manumitted a slave would speak positively about his new friend to prove the quality of his judgment and generosity in choosing to transform this former thing into a person with a social identity? Zach Bankston (2012, 214–16) regards Cicero's professions of affection for Tiro as sincere but nevertheless concludes "that their relationship was very Roman, meaning Tiro had a specific role and served a definite purpose, like that of an object." This objectification means that "Cicero exploited Tiro for the function of gaining and retaining power."

In sum, the evidence for Tiro and Cicero buttresses Moss's conclusion: Paul in employing writing assistants could have received substantial editorial help that he valued, but he simultaneously could have objectified them—just as, she remarks, writers today often minimize or hide the contributions others make to their works.

Surely we must do better on that front, as also with approaches to persons with disabilities and the othering of foreigners. As Saul the persecutor preached after he was transformed into Paul the apostle, reconciliation (καταλλαγή) saves us (Rom 5:10–11; 2 Cor 5:11–21). We academics must hope that reconciliation efforts by colleagues to reduce conflict and build community trust, such as the project of the Bridging Divides Initiative[37] to track and mitigate political violence in the United States, can spur us to support "God's justice" (δικαιοσύνη θεοῦ, 2 Cor 5:21) for all.

Works Cited

Adams, Ellen. 2021. Introduction to *Disability Studies and the Classical Body: The Forgotten Other*. Edited by Ellen Adams. London: Routledge.

---

36. Douglass 1845; for a modern example of this corrosive danger unfortunately pertaining to language instruction in Classics, see Dugan 2019.

37. https://bridgingdivides.princeton.edu.

Albl, Martin. 2007. "'For Whenever I am Weak, Then I Am Strong': Disability in Paul's Epistles." Pages 145–58 in *This Abled Body: Rethinking Disabilities in Biblical Studies*. Edited by Hector Avalos, Sarah J. Melcher, and Jeremy Schipper. SemeiaSt 55. Atlanta: Society of Biblical Literature.

Apel, Thomas. 2016. *Feverish Bodies, Enlightened Minds: Science and the Yellow Fever Controversy in the Early American Republic*. Stanford, CA: Stanford University Press.

Avalos, Hector, Sarah J. Melcher, and Jeremy Schipper, eds. 2007. *This Abled Body: Rethinking Disabilities in Biblical Studies*. SemeiaSt 55. Atlanta: Society of Biblical Literature.

Bankston, Zach. 2012. "Administrative Slavery in the Ancient Roman Republic: The Value of Marcus Tullius Tiro in Ciceronian Rhetoric." *Rhetoric Review* 31:203–18.

Bazopoulou-Kyrkanidou, Euterpe. 1997. "What Makes Hephaestus Lame?" *American Journal of Medical Genetics* 72:144–55.

Blumell, Lincoln H. 2006. "Scribes and Ancient Letters: Implications for the Pauline Epistles." Pages 208–26 in *How the New Testament Came to Be: The Thirty-Fifth Annual Sidney B. Sperry Symposium*. Edited by Kent P. Jackson and Frank F. Judd Jr. Salt Lake City, UT: Deseret.

Bradley, Mark. 2012. "Approaches to Pollution and Propriety." Pages 11–40 in *Rome, Pollution and Propriety: Dirt, Disease and Hygiene in the Eternal City from Antiquity to Modernity*. Edited by Mark Bradley with Kenneth Stow. Cambridge: Cambridge University Press.

Brennan, Maura. 2016. "Lame Hephaistos." *ABSA* 111:163–81.

Brockliss, William. 2019. "Out of the Mix: (Dis)ability, Intimacy, and the Homeric Poems." *CW* 113:1–27.

Bueno, André. 2016. "Roman Views of the Chinese in Antiquity." *Sino-Platonic Papers* 261. http://sino-platonic.org/complete/spp261_Roman_Chinese.pdf.

Cain, Andrew. 2010. *St. Jerome. Commentary on Galatians*. The Fathers of the Church 121. Washington, DC: Catholic University of America Press.

Courrier, Cyril. 2014. *La plèbe de Rome et sa culture (fin du IIe siècle av. J.-C.–fin du Ier siècle ap. J.-C.)*. Rome: École française d'Athènes et de Rome.

Cramer, J. A. 1842. *Catenae in Sancti Pauli Epistolas ad Galatas, Ephesios, Philippenses, Colossenses, Thessalonicenses ad Fidem Codd. MSS*. Oxford: Oxford University Press.

Dillon, Matthew P. J. 1995. "Payments to the Disabled at Athens: Social Justice or Fear of Aristocratic Patronage?" *Ancient Society* 26:27–51.

———. 2017. "Legal (and Customary?) Approaches to the Disabled in Ancient Greece." Pages 167–81 in *Disability in Antiquity*. Edited by Christian Laes. London: Routledge.

Douglass, Frederick. 1845. *Narrative of the Life of Frederick Douglass, an American Slave, Written by Himself*. Boston: Anti-Slavery Office.

Dow, Jamie. 2015. *Passions and Persuasion in Aristotle's Rhetoric*. Oxford: Oxford University Press.

Dugan, Kelly P. 2019. "The "Happy Slave" Narrative and Classics Pedagogy: A Verbal and Visual Analysis of Beginning Greek and Latin Textbooks." *New England Classical Journal* 46:62–87.

Duncan-Jones, R. P. 1996. "The Impact of the Antonine Plague." *JRA* 9:108–36.

Edwards, Mark J., ed. 1999. *Galatians, Ephesians, Philippians*. Ancient Christian Commentary on Scripture: New Testament 8. Downers Grove, IL: InterVarsity Press.

Edwards, Mark T. 2017. "When Not to Speak Truth to Power: Thoughts on the Historiography of the Social Gospel." *Religion in American History Blog*. https://tinyurl.com/SBL06104h1.

Flemming, Rebecca. 2010. "Pliny and the Pathology of Empire." Pages 19–42 in *Health and Sickness in Ancient Rome: Greek and Roman Poetry and Historiography*. Edited by Francis Cairns and Miriam Griffin. Papers of the Langford Latin Seminar 14. Cambridge: Cairns.

Ford, Randolph B. 2020. *Rome, China, and the Barbarians: Ethnographic Traditions and the Transformation of Empires*. Cambridge: Cambridge University Press.

Gagnon, Jennifer M. 2016. "Lessons in Suffering: Greek Tragedy's Teachings on Disability through Sophocles' *Philoctetes*." *New Political Science* 38:335–53.

Garber, Marjorie. 2012. *Loaded Words*. New York: Fordham University Press.

Gardner, Hunter H. 2019. *Pestilence and the Body Politic in Latin Literature*. Oxford: Oxford University Press.

Garland, Robert. 2010. *The Eye of the Beholder: Deformity and Disability in the Graeco-Roman World*. London: Bristol Classical.

———. 2017. "Disabilities in Tragedy and Comedy." Pages 154–66 in *Disability in Antiquity*. Edited by Christian Laes. London: Routledge.

Gevaert, Bert. 2017. "Perfect Roman Bodies: The Stoic View." Pages 213–21 in *Disability in Antiquity*. Edited by Christian Laes. London: Routledge.

Giubilini, Alberto, and Francesca Minerva. 2013. "After-Birth Abortion: Why Should the Baby Live?" *Journal of Medical Ethics* 39:261–63.

Goodey, Chris F., and Martha Lynn Rose. 2013. "Mental States, Bodily Dispositions and Table Manners: A Guide to Reading "Intellectual" Disability from Homer to Late Antiquity." Pages 17–44 in *Disabilities in Roman Antiquity: Disparate Bodies* A Capite ad Calcem. Edited by Christian Laes, Chris F. Goodey, and Martha Lynn Rose. Leiden: Brill.

Goodey, Chris F., and Martha Lynn Rose. 2018. "Disability History and Greco-Roman Antiquity." Pages 41–53 in *The Oxford Handbook of Disability History*. Edited by Michael Rembis, Catherine Jean Kudlick, and Kim E. Nielsen. Oxford: Oxford University Press.

Greer, Rowan A., trans. 2010. *Theodore of Mopsuestia: Commentary on the Minor Pauline Epistles*. WGRW 26. Atlanta: Society of Biblical Literature.

Hartmann, Benjamin. 2020. *The Scribes of Rome: A Cultural and Social History of the Scribae*. Cambridge: Cambridge University Press.

Hill, Robert Charles, trans. 2001. *Theodoret of Cyrus: Commentary on the Letters of St. Paul*. 2 vols. Brookline, MA: Holy Cross Orthodox Press.

Kaczor, Christopher. 2020. *Disputes in Bioethics: Abortion, Euthanasia, and Other Controversies*. Notre Dame: University of Notre Dame Press.

Kelley, Nicole. 2007. "Deformity and Disability in Greece and Rome." Pages 31–45 in *This Abled Body: Rethinking Disabilities in Biblical Studies*. Edited by Hector Avalos, Sarah J. Melcher, and Jeremy Schipper. SemeiaSt 55. Atlanta: Society of Biblical Literature.

Kim, Hyun Jin. 2009. *Ethnicity and Foreigners in Ancient Greece and China*. London: Duckworth.

Koester, Craig R. 2014. *Revelation. A New Translation with Introduction and Commentary*. AB 38A. New Haven: Yale University Press.

Konstan, David. 1995. "Patrons and Friends." *CP* 90:328–42.

Laes, Christian, ed. 2017a. *Disability in Antiquity*. London: Routledge.

———. 2017b. "Introduction: Disabilities in the Ancient World—Past, Present and Future." Pages 1–21 in *Disability in Antiquity*. Edited by Christian Laes. London: Routledge.

———. 2018. *Disabilities and the Disabled in the Roman World*. Cambridge: Cambridge University Press.

Larcher, F. R., and M. L. Lamb, trans. 2012. *Saint Thomas Aquinas. Commentary on the Letters of Saint Paul to the Galatians and Ephesians*. Edited by J. Mortensen and E. Alaracón. Biblical Commentaries 39. Lander, WY: Aquinas Institute for the Study of Sacred Doctrine.

Leigh, Robert. 2016. *On Theriac to Piso, Attributed to Galen: A Critical Edition with Translation and Commentary*. Leiden: Brill.

Lévi-Strauss, Claude. 1962. *Le totémisme aujourd'hui*. Paris: Presses Universitaires de France.

Lo Cascio, Elio. 2016. "The Impact of Migration on the Demographic Profile of the City of Rome: A Reassessment." Pages 23–32 in *Migration and Mobility in the Early Roman Empire*. Edited by Luuk de Ligt and Laurens E. Tacoma. Leiden: Brill.

Marks, J. 2005. "The Ongoing *Neikos*: Thersites, Odysseus, and Achilles." *AJP* 126:1–31.

Martin, Dale B. 1995. *The Corinthian Body*. New Haven: Yale University Press.

McDermott, William C. 1972. "M. Cicero and M. Tiro." *Historia* 21:259–86.

Mittag, Achim, and Fritz-Heiner Mutschler. 2010. "Empire and Humankind: Historical Universalism in Ancient China and Rome." *Journal of Chinese Philosophy* 37:527–55.

Münzer, Friedrich. 1939. "Tullius 15." PW 7A.1:803–4.

Nagy, Gregory. 1999. *The Best of the Achaeans: Concepts of the Hero in Archaic Greek Poetry*. 2nd ed. Baltimore: Johns Hopkins University Press.

Noy, David. 2000. *Foreigners at Rome: Citizens and Strangers*. London: Duckworth.

Park, Arum. 2014. "Parthenogenesis in Hesiod's *Theogony*." *Preternature: Critical and Historical Studies in the Preternatural* 3:261–83.

Parker, Robert. 1983. *Miasma: Pollution and Purification in Early Greek Religion*. Oxford: Clarendon.

Patterson, Orlando. 2018. *Slavery and Social Death: A Comparative Study*. Cambridge: Harvard University Press.

Pearse, Roger. 2017. "John of Ephesus Describes the Justinianic Plague." https://tinyurl.com/SBL06104j1.

Penrose, Walter D., Jr. 2015. "The Discourse of Disability in Ancient Greece." *CW* 108:499–523.

Perloff, Richard M. 2020. *The Dynamics of Persuasion: Communication and Attitudes in the Twenty-First Century*. 7th ed. New York: Routledge.

Pinault, Jody Rubin. 1986. "How Hippocrates Cured the Plague." *Journal of the History of Medicine and Allied Sciences* 41:52–75.

Plumer, Eric. 2003. *Augustine's Commentary on Galatians: Introduction, Text, Translation, and Notes*. Oxford: Oxford University Press.

Postlethwaite, N. 1988. "Thersites in the *Iliad*." *GR* 35:123–36.

Pritchard, James. B., ed. 1969. "Plague Prayers of Mursilis." Pages 394–96 in *Ancient Near Eastern Texts Relating to the Old Testament*. 3rd ed. Princeton: Princeton University Press.

Raspanti, Giacomo, ed. 2006. *Sancti Hieronymi Presbyteri Opera. Pars I: Opera Exegetica 6. Commentarii in Epistulam Pauli Apostoli ad Galatas*. CCSL 77A. Turnhout: Brepols.

Reece, Steve. 2017. *Paul's Large Letters: Paul's Autographic Subscriptions in the Light of Ancient Epistolary Conventions*. LNTS 561. London: Bloomsbury.

Rinon, Yoav. 2006. "Tragic Hephaestus: The Humanized God in the *Iliad* and the *Odyssey*." *Phoenix* 60:1–20.

Robinson, Nathan J. 2017. "Now Peter Singer Argues That It Might Be Okay to Rape Disabled People." *Current Affairs*. https://tinyurl.com/SBL06104k1.

Rose, Martha Lynn. 2003. *The Staff of Oedipus: Transforming Disability in Ancient Greece*. Ann Arbor: University of Michigan Press.

———. 2017. "Ability and Disability in Classical Athenian Oratory." Pages 139–53 in *Disability in Antiquity*. Edited by Christian Laes. London: Routledge.

Saller, Richard. 1982. *Personal Patronage under the Early Empire*. Cambridge: Cambridge University Press.

Samana, Evelyne. 2017. "The Greek Vocabulary of Disabilities." Pages 121–38 in *Disability in Antiquity*. Edited by Christian Laes. London: Routledge.

Schatkin, Margaret A. 1970. "Cramer's Catena on Galatians and Origen." *Traditio* 26:303–8.

Sheppard, Gerald T., ed. 1989. *A Commentary on Galatians: William Perkins*. New York: Pilgrim.

Siapkas, Johannes. 2014. "Ancient Ethnicity and Modern Identity." Pages 66–81 *A Companion to Ethnicity in the Ancient Mediterranean*. Edited by Jeremy McInerney. West Sussex: Wiley-Blackwell.

Singer, Peter. 2011. *Practical Ethics*. 3rd ed. Cambridge: Cambridge University Press.

Swete, H. B. 1880. *Introduction: Galatians-Colossians*. Vol. 1 of *Theodori Episcopi Mopsuesteni. In Epistolas B. Pauli Commentarii. The Latin Version with the Greek Fragments*. Cambridge: Cambridge University Press.

Tacoma, Laurens. 2016. *Moving Romans: Migration to Rome in the Principate*. Oxford: Oxford University Press.

Thumiger, Chiara. 2017. "Mental Disability? Galen on Mental Health." Pages 267–82 in *Disability in Antiquity*. Edited by Christian Laes. London: Routledge.

Treggari, Susan. 1969. "Freedmen of Cicero." *GR* 16:195–204.

Trentin, Lisa. 2011. "Deformity in the Roman Imperial Court." *GR* 58:195–208.

Tyner, Artika Renee, and Darlene Fry. 2020. "Iron Shackles to Invisible Chains: Breaking the Binds of Collateral Consequences." *Baltimore Law Review* 49:357–82.

Ulloa, Jazmine. 2021. "Stoking Fears of Immigrants Has Been Part of the Republication Platform for Decades. But Something Is Different This Time." *Boston Globe.* https://tinyurl.com/SBLPress06104k1.

Verboven, Koenraad. 2002. *The Economy of Friends: Economic Aspects of* Amicitia *and Patronage in the Late Roman Republic*. Brussels: Latomus.

Vogels, H. J., ed. 1969. *Ambrosiastri qui dicitur Commentarius in Epistulas Paulinas. Pars Tertia. In Epistulas ad Galatas, ad Efesios, ad Filippenses, ad Colosenses, ad Thesalonicenses, ad Timotheum, ad Titum, ad Filemonem*. CSEL 81. Vienna: Hoelder-Pichler-Tempsky.

Wong, Brittany. 2019. "It's Perfectly OK to Call a Disabled Person 'Disabled,' and Here's Why." *Huffington Post.* https://tinyurl.com/SBL06104n1.

Zimmerman, Jonathan. 2021. "The GOP Is Reviving the Old History of Blaming Outsiders for Disease." *Washington Post.* https://tinyurl.com/SBLPress06104k2.

Freedom, Slavery, and Beyond: A Reflection

Dominic Machado

> My work is in a sense notational—reinscribing historical experience—for a political objective. Present generations must know, at the very least, what has been known in order to achieve greater clarification and effectiveness. Just as Thucydides believed that historical consciousness of a people in crisis provided the possibility of more virtuous action, more informed and rational choices, so do I.
> —Cedric Robinson

To describe the situation that we found ourselves in when we gathered for this conference in November 2020, the term *crisis* seems apt. Beset by a raging COVID-19 pandemic, unending reports of assaults against Black lives, and the possibility of a contested election result, the world around us appeared to be in disarray. In these circumstances, it was admittedly tough to think about academic issues, namely, the necessity of bridging the seemingly nonsensical disciplinary boundaries that exist in the study of the ancient Mediterranean world. Yet, over the course of the conference and in the months since, the words of the late Cedric Robinson—the underappreciated Black political theorist who coined the terms "Black Radical Tradition" and "racial capitalism" (Thomas 2005; Kelley 2017)—on the importance of the past for dealing with crisis have helped to provide a moral foregrounding for continuing to think, write, and teach about antiquity in the present moment.

This response thus seeks to elucidate how I have made sense of this conference volume in my own efforts to find a path forward in this present moment within Robinson's powerful framework. To this end, in the first part of my reflection I want to highlight how two chapters in this volume have pushed me to rethink something that I often take as a given in my scholarship and teaching: the ontological binary between freedom and slavery in antiquity. I intend to show how by "reinscribing [the] historical experience" of slavery, Jennifer A. Glancy and Abraham Smith open up new ways of reading and thinking about even the most famous pieces of evidence, texts, and objects to which we continually return in teaching and research. In the second part of this reflection, I will contemplate the volume's political objectives and attempt to articulate its implications for the future of the study of the ancient Mediterranean world, with a view toward producing more virtuous action. I will conclude, in the spirit of my fellow contributors, by acknowledging the limits of my own thinking and sharing some questions that remain for me as we attempt to bring the vision of this volume into our lived reality.

No Longer a Slave But More Than a Slave

In her brilliant essay in this volume, Glancy demonstrates through a close reading of the third-century CE Acts of Thomas how ideologies of slavery informed early Christian thought about the relationship between Christ and his followers. While other scholars have recognized that slavery lies behind the ways that Christian texts construct hierarchical relations, Glancy takes early Christian doulology a step further by excavating what she terms the "relational ontologies" of ancient slavery. Building on Denise Kimber Buell's call to recognize that antiquity relied upon a set of ontologies very different from the sovereign self of modern liberalism, Glancy draws attention to "the material entanglement of categories of slavery and the human, an entanglement confounding any sense of the self as sovereign or discrete." She characterizes the entanglement of slavery as "intense and asymmetric transcorporeality," in which the slave and master are unequal but inseparable. The slave, as she shows through her reading of the enslaved Thomas, is subsumed into and combined with the personage of their enslaver for the latter's benefit and use.

The power of the framework of intense and asymmetric transcorporeality that Glancy develops in her essay can be seen by the way it sheds light on the practice of manumission in antiquity. Take, for instance, Jesus's famous manumission of his disciples in John 15:15 when he tells them at the Last Supper that they are no longer slaves but rather friends (οὐκέτι λέγω ὑμᾶς δούλους ... ὑμᾶς δὲ εἴρηκα φίλους). Although Jesus elevates the status of his disciples from enslaved to freed, the asymmetry of slavery remains embedded in the passage. Indeed, the sentences around Jesus's freeing of his disciples are marked by constant reference to the asymmetrical power dynamics that exist between them. Jesus uses various cognates of the verb ἐντέλλω when he tells the disciplines the conditions of their relationship (15:13: "if you keep my commands [ἐντολάς], you will remain in my love"; v. 14: "you are my friends if you do the things which I command [ἐντέλλομαι] you") and when he instructs them to love one another as he loved them (15:12: αὕτη ἐστὶν ἡ ἐντολὴ ἡ ἐμή, ἵνα ἀγαπᾶτε ἀλλήλους καθὼς ἠγάπησα ὑμᾶς; v. 17: ταῦτα ἐντέλλομαι ὑμῖν, ἵνα ἀγαπᾶτε ἀλλήλους). Additionally, the passage is replete with imperative forms (μείνατε; ἀγαπᾶτε; ποιῆτε; ἐξελέξασθε; ὑπάγητε; φέρητε; αἰτήσητε) that confirm the power dynamics of the disciples' relationship with Jesus: they must continue to do his bidding in spite of the fact that they have cast off their servile status.

It is not just the power asymmetry of the enslaved-enslaver relationship that is to remain intact after the manumission of the disciples; the transcorporeality that was part and parcel of this relationship abides as well. Immediately preceding the manumission of the disciples is the famous metaphor of the vine and the branches in which Jesus clarifies the future mission of his followers. In this analogy, Jesus is the vine and the disciples the fruit-bearing branches. The naturalism inherent in the metaphor makes clear that Christ and his disciples are, to borrow Glancy's term, organismically linked. This linkage is reinforced throughout the passage in the use of the verb μένω (to stay, remain, live in); Jesus constantly reminds the disciples that they are to be lodged in him and he in them (15:4: μείνατε ἐν ἐμοί, κἀγὼ ἐν ὑμῖν; v. 5: ὁ μένων ἐν ἐμοὶ κἀγὼ ἐν αὐτῷ οὗτος). Moreover, Jesus tells them that this entanglement is the only way for them to complete their future mission: "just as the branches are not able to bear fruit in and of itself unless they remain on the vine, nor can you unless you remain in me" (15:4: καθὼς τὸ κλῆμα οὐ δύναται καρπὸν φέρειν ἀφ᾽ ἑαυτοῦ ἐὰν μὴ μένῃ ἐν τῇ ἀμπέλῳ, οὕτως οὐδὲ ὑμεῖς ἐὰν μὴ ἐν ἐμοὶ μένητε). He reiterates this position more firmly in the following line, stating that the disciples are not able to do anything apart from him (15:5: ὅτι χωρὶς ἐμοῦ οὐ δύνασθε ποιεῖν οὐδέν). As the repetition of the verb δύναμαι (to be able, capable) in these two lines makes clear, the disciples quite simply lack the ability to act on their own. Consequently, even in their elevation from slaves to friends, the disciples have no choice but to be subsumed in Jesus and to do his will.

We find a similarly complex ontology embedded in an inscription from Delphi created just a few decades before the composition of John's Gospel. This early first-century CE inscription records the manumission of Onasiphoron from her enslaver, Sophorona (Nasrallah 2019, 69–71).

We read that Onasiphoron was sold to Apollo "with the aim of becoming 'free' and not to be claimed by anybody at any future time, and to have no obligations of any kind whatever to anyone" (ἐφ' ᾧτε ἐλευθέρα εἶμεν καὶ ἀνέφαπτος ἀπὸ πάντων τὸν πάντα χρόνον, μηδενὶ μηδὲν ποθήκουσα κατὰ μηδένα τρόπον, Fouilles de Delphes 3.6.36:6–7). The enforcement of Onasiphoron's freedom is a communal responsibility: "if anyone touches Onasiphoron in order to enslave her, … anyone at all is to have the legal right to take Onasiphoron away so that she may be 'free'" (εἰ δέ τις ἐφάπτοιτο Ὀνασιφόρου ἐπὶ καταδουλισμῷ, … ὁ παρατυχὼν κύριος ἔστω συλέων Ὀνασίφορον ἐπ' ἐλευθερίᾳ, ll. 8–10). As the repetition of the word ἐλευθέρα in these clauses make clear, there is absolutely no ambiguity as to how the community is to deal with Onasiphoron.

However, the way that the next clause constructs the relationship between her and Sophorona alerts us to a different ontological reality. As the inscription states, Onasiphoron must remain (παραμεινάτω, l. 11) with Sophorona as long as she lives. Moreover, Onasiphoron must do whatever she is ordered to do without complaint (ποιοῦσα τὸ ἐπιτασσόμενον ἀνενκλήτως, ll. 11–12) or risk punishment in whatever way Sophrona sees fit (ἐξουσίαν ἐχέτω Σωφρόνα ἐπιτιμέουσα τρόπῳ ᾧ κα θέλῃ, ll. 12–13). The language we find here matches closely with what we find in the case of the disciples; their relationship to their former master is defined by cohabitation, as indicated by the μένω compounds, and obedience through the use of imperatival forms and verbs of ordering. But what makes the continuing nature of the intense and asymmetric transcorporeality of the relationship between Sophorona and Onasiphoron most obvious is the clause that follows. We hear that Onasiphoron must provide Sophorona with a child (δότω δὲ Ὀνασίφορον Σωσάνδρῳ βρέφος, l. 13). Much like the enslaved apostle Thomas, Onasiphoron serves as a body double for her master's use. In her prospective pregnancy, Onasiphoron's body becomes the vessel through which Sophorona has a child, but in spite of her corporal participation in the production of the child, it is in no way hers. Although Onasiphoron is ἐλευθέρα, she remains inseparable from and unequal to Sophorona.

Glancy's framework of ontological relationality reveals that in these two texts manumission did not fundamentally alter the relationship between the formerly enslaved and their enslaver. The intense and asymmetric transcorporeality of master-slave relations remained until one of the two parties involved died. Nor was the situation that we find in these two examples exceptional. The Onasiphoron inscription is just one of many manumission documents in the Greek world that contained a *paramonē* clause bidding the formerly enslaved to remain with their master (Zelnick-Abramovitz 2005, 222–45; 2018, 377–402; Kamen 2013, 32–42; 2014, 281–307; Sosin 2015, 325–81). Similarly, Roman legal texts featured a similar conceit, which Roman jurists refer to as *operae*, in which former slaves were to continue to perform duties for their former master so long as they both lived (Mouritsen 2011, 51–65; MacLean 2018, 37–39). If an intense and asymmetric transcorporeality remained intact for the formerly enslaved after manumission, what then did it mean to become ἐλευθέρα? Did the term ἐλευθέρα simply connote a positive concept that spoke to new rights and privileges that came to the newly manumitted but did not reflect the obligations that came with it? Or did it speak to a communal, rather than ontological, relationality that defined how the newly manumitted was to be treated by the larger community? Whatever the case, it is clear that freedom in the context of manumissions with *paramonē* provisions is not what it initially seems to be.

The use of slavery as a tool to construct power relations in the world of the New Testament also takes center stage in Smith's contribution to this volume. In his incisive essay, Smith shows that slavery as metaphor and practice, together with "Rome's visual technologies of power," enabled members of the Roman elite to control social relations and craft their own historical narratives. As Smith demonstrates, the Romans not only frequently deployed the visual language of slavery on major monuments throughout the empire to signal their position as masters of the inhabited world but also drained the human and financial capital of conquered peoples to build such monuments to their power. Playing on James Scott's famous "arts of resistance," Smith labels this particular sinister combination of tactics as the Roman "arts of domination."

Smith's way of reading the monumental logics of Rome's imperial program, however, is more than just an insightful description of Roman expressions of power. People living within the Roman Empire and long after it also made use of these powerful visual scripts to frame their place within the worlds they inhabited. As such, Smith's framework provides us with new ways of reading the power relations encoded on ancient monuments. Once again, the Onasiphoron inscription provides fertile ground for investigation. Indeed, in the second to last line of the inscription, we hear that the "sale is to be deposited as required by law: one copy engraved on the Temple of Apollo, the other taken to the public archives of the city by the Secretary Lysimakhos son of Nikanor" (τίθεται τὴν ὠνὴν κατὰ τὸν νόμον, τὴν μὲν εἰς τὸ ἱερὸν τοῦ Ἀπόλλωνος ἐνχαράξασα, τὴν δὲ ἑτέραν διὰ τοῦ γραμματέως Λυσιμάχου τοῦ Νικάνορος εἰς τὰ δημόσια τῆς πόλιος γράμματα, Fouilles de Delphes 3.6.36:14–16). What we find in this clause is a record not just of the archiving practices of Delphic manumission inscriptions but also evidence of their role in the construction of the monumental logic of the Temple of Apollo at Delphi. The Onasiphoron inscription was one of nearly 1,350 manumission inscriptions that were incorporated as part of the precinct of the Temple of Apollo at Delphi; these inscriptions have been found as part of the temple's polygonal terrace wall, on the temple itself, and on the nearby theater (Kamen 2014, 285).

Much like a triumphal monument that made manifest Roman domination by depicting the chattel acquired through conquest, the collection of physical evidence for Apollo's possession of thousands of slaves the temple precinct made clear the god's power. But while the visual idiom upon which Rome's and Apollo's claims to power rested was the same, the means by which they achieved the power was different. It was not through conquest but by religious power (and legal fiction) that Apollo gained possession of these slaves. As such, Apollo's position of power neither threatened nor was threatened by Roman imperial domination. The assertion of Apollo's might, however, though instantiated by theology, had impacts that reached beyond religion. The Temple of Apollo at Delphi was intimately connected with Greek identity and history. Indeed, from the seventh century BCE, it had served as a Panhellenic sanctuary where Greeks from all city-states were welcome and its oracle was consulted by Greeks and non-Greeks alike for its wisdom (Fontenrose 1978; Maurizio 1997, 308–34; Scott 2014). Furthermore, the temple housed countless dedications commemorating Greek military victories, among which particular pride of place was given to joint victories over barbarians such as the Persians and the Gauls. In the time of the Roman Empire, the temple was thus a reminder of what it meant to be Greek and of a great Hellenic past. Thus, the use of the visual idiom of slavery to assert Apollo's power worked to strengthen feelings of Greek collective identity in a time when Greek political and social power had begun to wane without directly challenging Roman rule. The implication here is an arresting one: the practice of slavery and its commemoration provided a comfort to people who were struggling to cope with a loss of power, a point to which we will return to later on in this essay.

Smith's framework helps us locate resistance in ancient monuments as well. Case in point is the famous tomb of the freed baker and contractor

Marcus Vergilius Eurysaces and his wife, Atistia. This massive trapezoidal travertine tomb, which was erected in the last decades of the first century BCE on the Esquiline Hill on the outskirts of the ancient Roman city, has been interpreted in a variety of ways over the last century. For some scholars, the monument represents an expression of pride that Eurysaces and Atistia felt in their *res gestae* as freedpersons (Zanker 1975; Kleiner 1977: 118–57). Others have contended the tomb was an attempt to paper over the realities of being a freedperson in the Roman world by taking recourse to a conspicuous display of wealth, much like Trimalchio does in the *Satyrica* (Whitehead 1993, 299–325). A third group has sought to step away from looking at the monument in light of the fact that those commemorated are freedpersons and rather has argued that the tomb reflected elite concerns with exemplarity and encyclopedism (Hackworth Peterson 2003, 230–57; Jones 2018, 63–107).

What all these readings miss, and what we can see thanks to Smith's analysis, is that the tomb contradicted the monumental logic that the Roman elite tried to encode in the cityscape. The monument offered viewers a different narrative of how one might achieve prominence in Roman society. It was not, as other monuments in the Roman cityscape made clear, necessary to win great military victories or hold political office to become part of Rome's collective memory: one could do it even as a baker. What this meant was that it was possible even for the enslaved, again in spite of monumental claims about their alleged inferiority to their Roman masters, to achieve cultural prominence. What's more, the fact that the tomb of Eurysaces and Atistia was one of the largest, if not the largest, monuments in late republican Rome spoke to the possibility of even surpassing their enslavers and thereby uprooting the social ordering that the Roman elites worked so hard to maintain.

The narrative of disrupting social order emerges from the form of the monument. The tomb was an ode to bread making: the monument's north face features eleven massive portholes that represent the bowls into which wooden bread kneading machines would have been placed (fig. 1), and a narrow frieze running along the top of the monument depicts in fine detail the various steps of bread production (fig. 2). Embedded in this imagery, however, was a contemporary political concern. The feeding of the masses and the provisioning of grain were a hot-button issue in the late republic and early empire, and it seems rather likely that Eurysaces and Atistia grew wealthy because of it (Kleiner 1992, 105). Even though Roman elites had conquered the world, they were still dependent on freedpersons like

Eurysaces and Atistia to keep the populace happy and ensure their privileged political position within society, forcing the viewer once again to call into question the self-proclaimed dominance of the Roman elite. If, as Smith claims, "the visual arts of domination ... added yet another layer of brutality to the presence of slavery itself," the tomb of Eurysaces and Atistia responded by showing that there were alternative narratives available.

Fig. 1. South façade of the Tomb of Eurysaces and Atistia. User:Livioandronico. Wikimedia Commons. CC BY-SA 4.0.

Fig. 2. The Bakery Frieze. User: Livioandronico. Wikimedia Commons. CC BY-SA 4.0.

Old Wine, New Wineskins?

Inasmuch as Smith's essay informs us about the visual ideologies of the world of the New Testament, he also reveals that these idioms are still prominent today. Smith shows that the deep connection between slavery and power that we find in Roman monuments can still be found in monuments that stand today, not least in the Confederate memorials in the United States that have been the subject of endless political discussion. But, as Smith demonstrates, the insidious nature of this monumental logic is that it finds its way into the most unexpected of places as well. The example that Smith cites is Thomas Ball's 1876 Emancipation Memorial in Washington, DC, which depicts a clothed Abraham Lincoln holding the Emancipation Proclamation in one hand and holding the other over a shirtless formerly enslaved man who, in the words of Frederick Douglass, was "couchant on his knees like a four-footed animal." While Ball's memorial is an attempt to celebrate the end of slavery, it nevertheless "buys into the very logic of paternalism that the Confederacy supported." By thinking diachronically, Smith unveils how "binaristic othering" to justify "subordinating some over others" and thereby "represent[ing] interests of a dominant order in maintaining its hegemony" is not something of the past. Rather, it is for Smith also an exigent present concern that is intimately linked to the past. The past not only provides the script to propagate these insidious structures of power, but its distance and obscurity to the modern observer ensures that these hierarchies can replicated without detection.

The idea that Smith brings out here—that antiquity speaks to and frequently shapes the way we think about morally exigent matters of the present day—is an important theme that emerges in this volume. Through Allen Dwight Callahan's meditation on economic inequality, Yii-Jan Lin's soundings on immigration and xenophobia, Candida R. Moss's thoughts on disability, and Jorunn Økland's search for the birth of equality as a concept, we can see clearly that writing, thinking, and teaching about antiquity demand that we speak about and meditate on inequalities, past and present. We can no longer, in light of these contributions, bury our heads in ancient texts to escape the various moral conundra facing the modern world. Rather, we must, in the words of Martin Luther King Jr. in his April 3, 1968, speech "I've Been to the Mountaintop," not stop in Greece or Rome but live in the present "to grapple with the problems that men have been trying to grapple with through history" because our "survival demands that we grapple with them."

In addition to sounding a clarion call to grapple with the manifold problems that surround us, this volume also articulates how we can go about this seemingly impossible task of using our problematic past to move toward a more morally oriented future. One key strategy that emerges, time and again, throughout these essays is the power of storytelling to counter these diachronic narratives of domination. For instance, Gay L. Byron's essay on *Kandake* Amantitere, which explicitly draws on Chimamanda Ngozi Adichie's 2009 TED talk on the "danger of a single story," demonstrates the value in trying to tell multiple stories. Advocating for what she calls a "polycentric" approach to antiquity, she contends that the telling of multiple stories, in addition to "expand[ing] the literary and cultural imagination of the ancient world," also disrupts "a Western paradigm that privileges certain theological and cultural frameworks and leads to images, historical accounts, and geographical conceptualizations that marginalize" non-European worldviews in our scholarship and teaching. By working toward a history of the Nubian queenship and, in doing so, telling the stories of Nubian queens, Byron shows us that there are alternative narratives available that work to counter the institutional racism and prejudice that has long been baked into the study of the ancient Mediterranean and have subsequently become etched into the fabric of the Western world. A similar approach is elaborated in the paper of Laura Salah Nasrallah. Through a close analysis of first- and second-century CE curse tablets, Nasrallah shows how eschewing Western aesthetics and instead adopting Black and Brown visions of the beautiful and sublime can bring new ways of understanding ancient texts. These new narratives, based in alternative aesthetics, reveal how the processes of disciplinary formation were founded on racialized, gendered, and class-based notions of importance and provide us with a way to avoid reproducing these hierarchies in our thinking, writing, and teaching.

This idea of alternative stories and aesthetics from Black and Brown perspectives brings me back to Smith's reflection on Ball's monument (fig. 3) commemorating the Emancipation Proclamation. In the very same hemisphere in which we find this narrative of continued oppression and slaving in spite of emancipation, we also find a different way of telling this story in Philip Moore's 1763 Monument in Georgetown, Guyana (fig. 4). This monument, which was erected in 1976 in celebration of the tenth anniversary of Guyanese independence, depicts Cuffy, an enslaved person of West African origin, who led a slave rebellion in 1763 that culminated in a group of formerly enslaved men temporarily taking over the Dutch colony of Berbice (Kars 2020). Unlike the freedman in a loincloth who supinely thanks Lincoln for the grant of freedom, in the 1763 monument Cuffy stands tall and strong in the garb of a traditional West African warrior. His stance and clothing make clear his role as an agent of his own freedom and the necessity of warfare for his own emancipation in a non-Western idiom. The aesthetics and narrative encoded in the monument, to my mind, serve as an analogy for what we gain by stepping away from our disciplinary safe havens so that we can tell new and different stories. Like Cuffy and the people of Guyana, we can choose to construct a more equitable and just academic future by challenging old stories and telling new ones.

In the vein of Buell's call for epistemological humility in her standout essay on interdisciplinarity, I want to end my reflection with several questions that remain for me as we search for a more moral and ethical study of the past. First, if we are to think beyond the boundaries of our own discipline, how do we do so responsibly? Will spanning across time and culture unwittingly lead to the erasure of meaningful differences? Along similar lines, how do we avoid appropriating the Black and Brown cultures and histories simply as means to advance our own discipline and our own work? If such work necessitates collaboration with experts in these fields, is it fair to put pressure on these scholars, many of whom are members of marginalized groups, to take academic risks with us? Is such work even possible in the current formulation of the university, given the nature of specialized graduate training and the subsequent impact of such special-

Fig. 3. Emancipation Memorial (Washington, DC, 2014). Wikimedia. Public domain.

Fig. 4. 1763 Monument (Georgetown, Guyana). Dan Sloan. Wikimedia. CC BY 2.0.

ization on the job market? Should we expect that others can follow the path we have laid out? Whatever the answers to these questions, what I do know is that I will look to my fellow contributors for guidance in the faith that they are working in hopes of producing "more virtuous action."

Works Cited

Fontenrose, Joseph Eddy. 1978. *The Delphic Oracles, Its Responses, and Operations, with a Catalogue of Response.* Berkeley: University of California Press.

Hackworth Petersen, Lauren. 2003. "The Baker, His Tomb, His Wife, and Her Breadbasket: The Monument of Eurysaces in Rome." *Art Bulletin* 85.2:230–57.

Jones, Nathaniel B. 2018. "Exemplarity and Encyclopedism at the Tomb of Eurysaces." *Classical Antiquity* 37.1:63–107.

Kamen, Deborah. 2013. *Status in Classical Athens.* Princeton: Princeton University Press.

———. 2014. "Sale for the Purpose of Freedom: Slave-Prostitute and Manumission in Ancient Greece." *CJ* 109.3: 281–307.

Kars, Marjoleine. 2020. *Blood on the River: A Chronicle of Mutiny and Freedom on the Wild Coast*. New York: New Press.

Kelley, Robin D. G. 2017. "What Did Cedric Robinson Mean by Racial Capitalism?" *Boston Review*. https://tinyurl.com/SBL06104o1.

Kleiner, Diane E. E. 1977. *Roman Group Portraiture: The Funerary Reliefs of the Late Republic and Early Empire*. New York: Garland.

———. 1992. *Roman Sculpture*. New Haven: Yale University Press.

MacLean, Rose. 2018. *Freed Slaves and Roman Imperial Culture: Social Integration and the Transformation of Values*. Cambridge: Cambridge University Press.

Maurizio, Lisa. 1997. "Delphic Oracles as Oral Performances: Authenticity and Historical Evidence." *ClAnt* 16.2:308–34.

Mouristen, Henrik. 2011. *The Freedman in the Roman World*. Cambridge: Cambridge University Press.

Nasrallah, Laura. 2019. *Archaeology and the Letters of Paul*. Cambridge: Cambridge University Press.

Robinson, Cedric. 1999. "Capitalism, Marxism, and the Black Radical Tradition." *Perspectives on Anarchist Theory*. https://tinyurl.com/SBL06104p1.

Scott, Michael. 2014. *Delphi: A History of the Center of the Ancient World*. Princeton: Princeton University Press.

Sosin, Joshua D. 2015. "Manumission with *Paramone*: Conditional Freedom." *TAPA* 145.2:325–81.

Thomas, Darryl C. 2005. "The Black Radical Tradition—Theory and Practice: Black Studies and the Scholarship of Cedric Robinson." *Race and Class* 47.2:1–22.

Whitehead, Jane. 1993. "The "Cena Trimalchionis" and Biographical Narration in Roman Middle-Class Art." Pages 299–325 in *Narrative and Event in Ancient Art*. Edited by Peter J. Holliday. Cambridge: Cambridge University Press.

Zanker, Paul. 1975. "Grabreliefs römischer Freigelassener." *JdI* 90:257–315.

Zelnick-Abramovitz, R. 2005. *Not Wholly Free: The Concept of Manumission and the Status of Manumitted Slaves in the Ancient Greek World*. Leiden: Brill.

———. 2018. "The Status of Slaves Manumitted Under Paramonē: A Reappraisal." Pages 377–402 in *Symposium 2017: Vorträge zur griechischen und hellenistischen Rechtsgeschichte (Tel Aviv, 20.–23. August 2017)*. Edited by Eva Cantarella, Michael Gagarin, Gerhard Thür, and Julie

Velissaropoulos. Vienna: Österreichische Akademie der Wissenschaften.

Two Approaches to Equality, Inequality, and Justice in the Ancient World

Douglas Boin

After a group of Goths successfully carried out a plot to attack and punish Rome in 410 CE for the four decades of injustices they had endured as foreigners and second-class citizens, the bishop of Hippo, Augustine, was called to write a series of pastoral reflections that became *The City of God*.

After acknowledging the displacement, loss, and trauma many residents had suffered because of the Gothic attack, Augustine used the moment not to address the root of the current political problems but to develop an aggressive treatise about the evils of Roman society and the lingering allure of its pagan gods, whose worship had once united ancient Rome's multiethnic, multilingual, religiously pluralistic society. The bishop's sermonizing—he characterizes the religious life and entertainments of Roman culture as a "moral disease" (*Civ.* 1.3.3)—brims with the confidence of a Christian writing thirty years after zealous politicians had already imposed the Christian faith on Roman cities, two decades after a bloody civil war had foreclosed any return to classical ideas of toleration.

Yet in a world beset by barbarian attacks, Augustine explains, the true and faithful Christian would have to wait patiently before biblical values completely transformed society. Christians dismayed by lingering signs of pagan values should focus, in the meantime, on aspiring to become residents of heavenly Jerusalem, where a perfect Christian society would reign after their lifetimes and where they would be enrolled as the kingdom's "future citizens" (*cives futuros*) (*Civ.* 1.3.5).

Neither in his twenty-book manifesto about this idyllic future church nor in his corpus of letters or sermons written at the time does Augustine ever address the inequities of Roman citizenship that existed in Roman law for foreigners like the Goths (see Boin 2020, 171–72).

1. Moral Lessons and the Limitations of the Classical World

A fierce desire to interrogate ancient injustices provides the impetus for Jorunn Økland's and Allen Dwight Callahan's contributions on inclusion and exclusion in the civic sphere and on economic exploitation. The picture that emerges from their classical world, with its patent gender biases, uneven enfranchisement, and its canyons of class divides, may not look like the whitewashed model of a respectable citizenry with noble values that held the awe of Enlightenment minds or America's founders. But this is history composed with clinical detail and lyricism, both raw and provocative, and it speaks loudly against the backdrop of contemporary immigration debates and amid calls for more policy changes in the United States to address widening economic disparities.

Økland's study explores the Greek concept of *isotēs*, a word usually rendered as "equality," to illuminate key differences between ancient and modern definitions of the idea, particularly as it applies to the investigation of ancient gender relations. Økland's quest to sift and sort out what the ancients thought of this notion of "equal worth," as she suggests we translate *isotēs*, leads her through Plato, Aristotle, Plutarch, and Paul and to the surprising revelation that authors could often understand the word in highly imprecise, even inconsistent ways. For the Greeks, it seems, equal worth was never without qualification. The fact that the concept itself was subject to "constant recharging"—sometimes deployed with qualitative connotations, sometimes quantitative ones—certainly goes far to explain the gender imbalances that constituted Athenian democracy. Økland's essay brings the history of this tangled intellectual legacy to the fore, even as she admits that the evidence lacks any of the moral clarity a modern champion of equality might hope to find.

Callahan's reflection spotlights the appalling gulf that divided haves and have-nots in Roman times and has the power of matching a strong ethical compass with an ardent wish to repair economic injustices of our own times. With snapshots of ancient Rome's "toney dinner" hosts and the privileges afforded its elite landowners, who were cushioned by their immense reserves of disposable income, Callahan summons a range of historical experiences which, by their negative example, evoke a general feeling of helplessness that was the norm for many ancient nameless people. In this gossamer-veiled indictment of modern capitalism, the Roman Empire's "relentless capital accumulation of wealthy elites" in the first and second centuries CE launches "a runaway freight train of kleptocracy," one that both causes its society's unravelling and, not inconveniently for the author, witnesses the "birth of the New Testament."

2. The Earnestness of the Historian's Endeavor

Is there only one way to extract lessons from bygone times? Rome's great writer Livy once said that "what chiefly makes the study of history wholesome and profitable" is "that you behold the lessons of every kind of experience set forth as on a conspicuous monument" from which readers can choose for themselves "what to imitate" and what to "mark for avoidance" (*Ab ubre cond.* preface 10 [Foster, LCL]). But the uses and abuses of history, including its willingness or susceptibility to be shoehorned into contemporary political or cultural debates, still raise perennial problems, as both these modern authors are aware. And the question of how to find honest meaning in the past without distorting it beyond truth is a struggle to which even the ancients occasionally succumbed.

The situation in the 390s CE, decades before Augustine wrote *The City of God*, provides a telling example of a world on edge looking to history for guidance. It was during these years, with Gothic men flooding the northern borders to escape the civil wars that were ravaging their villages and with Gothic women begging for handouts at the gates of Roman cities to put food on their table for their children and families, that the bishop Synesius of Cyrene in North Africa penned a xenophobic manifesto advocating for the wholesale removal of foreign soldiers from Rome's army as a means to solve the rising flood of needy foreigners in Roman life.

As the bishop explained it bluntly in a scathing text entitled *On Imperial Rule*—written in the same Greek language as the New Testament and purported to have been addressed to the imperial court at Constantinople—the ease with which men like a Gothic soldier could appear at one moment as "a rough-and-tumble man" (*sisurophoros anthropos*, 15.12) and take on the guise of a smart-looking toga wearer the next spoke to an ethnic slipperiness that made the bishop uncomfortable with their increased presence in society (15.1). Suffusing his diatribe with a superiority marshaled from his own Christian faith and mixing in colorful classical tropes warning of the dangers of uncivilized barbarians, Synesius wrote that the time had come for the Roman government to "drive out these ill-omened dogs" (my translation). Never shy of a literary flourish, he cribbed the line—no doubt to the surprise of classically educated readers—from Homer's *Iliad*, where the dubious sentiment was first expressed by the Trojan Hector, who feared the Greeks (quoting Hector's speech at *Il.* 8.523–531).

An ill-tempered churchman of embarrassing political views and with a shaky grasp of Homer—who picked an analogy that put his imperialist audience on the losing side of the Trojan War—might be a helpful reminder that neither the classical nor the New Testament world occupied a higher ground on matters of justice in antiquity. Rome's moral rot did not respect our modern disciplinary divides.

Økland's and Callahan's two essays zero in on these failings, although, quite noticeably, they take very different approaches to documenting problems of injustice. Showcasing the range of methodological choices available to scholars and highlighting both the rewards and the pitfalls of recovering ancient experiences, these are helpful efforts. For while it's become a truism for most that the archives of the classical world are never as comprehensive as we need them to be, there are agreed-upon ways of accessing knowledge from the past that make facts still verifiable, claims still documentable, and history writing still possible—at least, for those who want to remain, as Livy did, engaged in finding profit from the past. And thankfully, neither of these present writers professes the studied self-absorption of the antiquarian.

Økland's conceptual approach to equality over time reveals quite clearly how frequently and how substantially many Greek male citizens were short on embracing its full potential. Plato's sense of what constituted equality, we learn, was a concept limited to achieving harmony in artistic expression, striking the perfect balance of elements. Aristotle's idea of equality was more connected to justice, though its application was rigidly bound by existing class divides and meritocratic assumptions. As the philosopher explained it in one of his amusing anecdotes, in the event of a scenario where flutes were scarce, the principles of equality should ensure that "the superior performers ... ought to be given the superior instruments" (*Pol.* 1282b [Rackham, LCL]). Privilege, in this worldview, would always trump true need. These were not conversations resembling our notions of the concept in political representation, gender advancement, or economic redress.

Yet while Økland's exploration of equality as an ideal sets the stage for thinking differently about the New Testament, where Paul's writings evoke a thinker who might have been more receptive to issues of inclusion than were earlier classical sources, Callahan's essay puts the New Testament evidence first and brings Christianity more explicitly to the forefront of a conversation about social and economic injustice in the first and second centuries. Captivity, torture, and enslavement at the hands of ruthless ancient tax collectors emerge in his frighteningly realistic retelling of Roman imperial life. Largely reconstructed from the many economically themed parables found in the Gospel of Luke—a text whose author, Callahan observes, seems to have known the life of "the wealthy and the wretched and those in between; his view of the lower rungs, however, is from above"—emerges his passionate call to address current economic chasms and the system which sustains them still.

In Callahan's history, ancient Rome's problems both remind us of our own and that the time to correct them is long past. "Future justice," he smartly explains, "is an oxymoron."

3. Social Change and the End of the Roman Empire

Callahan writes with an infectious sense of mission that wants to see the economic inequalities of the present erased, which is more than can be said about how many Greeks and Romans, Christian or otherwise, responded to the injustices of their day.

Augustine's response to the two-tiered system of political inequality of the fifth century CE—one that denied foreigners the rights and protections of Roman citizens—asked little of churchgoers other than hope and prayer for the coming of a heavenly Jerusalem, when terrestrial borders would be eliminated. Bishop Synesius was an unapologetic xenophobe, who saw the expulsion of foreigners, even Christian ones, as a form of political expediency perfectly consonant with his own Christian faith. It would seem that Callahan's moral impatience—that any justice delayed is justice denied, expressed in his searing reflection on a New Testament gospel—stands light-years ahead of the cultural world that produced those writings.

It is one thing, of course, to depict the Roman Empire as an irredeemably fallen society or to claim that, as the empire entered its second millennium around the third century CE, its "'golden age' ... was definitely finished," the unduly pessimistic assessment offered several decades ago by biblical scholar Helmut Koester in his 1982 study, *History, Culture, and Religion of the Hellenistic Age*. It is another thing to see that empire as a collection of individuals who weighed choices, saw possibilities, and debated the outcomes of their actions. Even if outmoded characterizations of the third century CE continue to hold sway over the public and scholarly imagination, a period that has been traditionally described and continues to be caricatured as one of widespread imperial crisis, the picture emerging of that era is unmistakably more complex. In the third century CE, minority groups throughout the Roman world—religious, ethnic, and otherwise, from Christians, Jews, and Mithras worshippers to Goths, Alans, and other men born at Rome's northern colonial frontiers, like Emperor Maximinus—made some of their most significant gains in social acceptance, visibility, and political influence, notwithstanding the hostility and bigotry they would often face (Moralee 2008; Boin 2015; 2017). To say Rome was finished at any one date or time brings an arrogance to the question of who was allowed to claim the status of being Roman.

Perhaps one helpful way to bridge the divide between past and present is by extending a simple generosity to the people of the classical world, one that recognizes the many ways Greeks and Romans did try to make their world better than it was—and that some did aspire to mold it into the best version of what it could have been. For every struggle or setback that women or slaves or foreigners endured in Athens, for example, by the time Rome's government was established across the Mediterranean, paths to citizenship were regularly bringing many people who had been born outside the capital and outside Italy into the empire's political community. The first century, second century, and memorably the year 212 CE when Emperor Caracalla extended citizen status to every free-born resident of Roman territory, all saw historic moments when the definition of who counted as a Roman grew bigger. Men and women of different ethnicities, different languages, and different religious beliefs became a part of that larger whole.

There's still historical meaning in choosing not to call one's government an esoteric brotherhood and preferring instead, as the Athenians did, to name it a democracy. The latter, as Økland hints, at least left open the possibility that the ancients might one day imagine a better world and maybe, with time, even realize it. Their past was not devoid of hope.

4. Facts, Argument, and the Historian's Craft

The Romans and Greeks may not have liked acknowledging their shortcomings, their political hypocrisies, or their cultural failings, which emerge in such high relief from Økland's and Callahan's essays. But the fact is they still did so, albeit perhaps as infrequently as we might like them to have done.

Around 362 CE, stability at the Roman borders deteriorated and conditions in Roman cities for foreigners and citizens warranted increasing public action. Then Emperor Julian, raised in the Christian household of Constantine, offered a pronouncement that reveals something of the heated debate that was fracturing Rome's politics. In trying times, even Julian—an emperor whose reputation would be tarnished by charges of apostasy despite the lack of one reliable piece of evidence to confirm he ever renounced his Christian upbringing—had turned to the books of Homer for moral guidance (Boin 2020b; 2020c). Reading the old bard, he had arrived at a political plan of action different from the radical exclusion of foreigners proposed, for example, by Bishop Synesius. "From Zeus come all strangers and beggars" (Julian, *Ep.* 22.430c–31b [Wright, LCL]), Emperor Julian explained, quoting the *Odyssey* (14.56). It was imperative the Roman government find a way to do good works to respond to those in need. Rome's long-standing values demanded it.

There will always be those literalists for whom "can we really know?" remains their preferred way of silencing lines of inquiry deemed risky, foolish, or uninteresting. But if there is still a reward to be found in the contemplation of history—as Livy once proposed and I still believe there is—if the circumstances behind the events, the complicated calculus that motivated a person's decision, or the ramifications of a belief or an action are to be honored with the same respect one hopes our own lives are someday afforded, then the fervent desire to describe how it really was can still offer, as truth so often will, a moment of quiet liberation. It is to the credit of these two authors that neither of their essays seems especially willing to occupy space on the sidelines of their own time. Perhaps the most straightforward way to cross a divided world is to dare to walk across it.

Works Cited

Aristotle. 1932. *Politics*. Translated by Harris Rackham. LCL. Cambridge: Harvard University Press.

Boin, Douglas. 2015. *Coming Out Christian in the Roman World*. New York: Bloomsbury.

———. 2017. *A Social and Cultural History of Late Antiquity*. Malden, MA: Wiley.

———. 2020a. *Alaric the Goth: An Outsider's History of the Fall of Rome*. New York: Norton.

———. 2020b. "Emperor Julian, An Appropriated Word, and a Different View of Fourth-Century 'Lived Religion.'" Pages 517–30 in *Lived Religion in the Ancient World: Approaching Religious Transformations from Archaeology, History, and Classics*. Edited by V. Gasparini et al. Berlin: de Gruyter.

———. 2020c. "The Memory of the Maccabees, 'Apostasy,' and Julian's Rhetorical Appropriation of *Hellenismos* as Signs of a Fourth-Century Intra-Christian Debate." Pages 48–66 in *Rhetoric and Religious Identity in Late Antiquity*. Edited by R. Flower and M. Ludlow. Oxford: Oxford University Press.

Julian. 1923. *Julian, Volume III*. Translated by W. Wright. LCL. Cambridge: Harvard University Press.

Livy. 1919. *Livy, Books I and II*. Translated by B. Foster. LCL. Cambridge: Harvard University Press.

Moralee, J. 2008. "Maximinus Thrax and the Politics of Race in Late Antiquity." *GR* 55:55–82.

Synesius of Cyrene. 1930. *The Essays and Hymns of Synesius of Cyrene*. Translated by A. Fitzgerald. Oxford: Oxford University Press.

On Being Disciplined

Katherine Lu Hsu

This response is inspired by Denise Kimber Buell's contribution to this volume, "An Argument for Being Less Disciplined." In a reflection on some of the experiences in her professional and intellectual journey, she calls New Testament scholars and classicists to embrace a position of partial knowledge and to pursue multidisciplinary work. She links these efforts to the emergence of new stories and forms of storytelling, ones better positioned to address the contemporary crises of racial injustice and climate disaster, among others, that beset our moment. Her fellow contributors to this volume answer her call with works that bring deep scholarly expertise about the ancient world to bear on issues of the present.

Buell rallies her readers to move away from the status quo of our disciplinary siloes and inherited ways of knowing. In the suggestion to be less disciplined lies an assumption that we, the audience, start from a position of being disciplined, that we *are disciplined*. As a response to Buell's essay, I would like to engage in a playful exploration of the semantic range of this implied phrase to see if it can offer us any guidance as we forge new paths ahead.

The sentence "we are disciplined" can be read in two ways. *Disciplined* can be treated as an adjective, one that describes us—in the sense of self-disciplined—as diligent, self-motivated, focused, and productive. These qualities suggest studiousness, a trait that serves us particularly well as scholars. In the context of progressing toward a doctoral degree or producing publications at a steady rate, being disciplined can be so admired as to take on the quality of a moral virtue.

But we could also consider *are disciplined* as a passive verb, where "we" are the grammatical subject that is being acted upon by an unspecified agent. In this understanding, we become subjected to discipline, that is, to punishment, correction, and training. Discipline, punishment, and scholarly training are not entirely unrelated, as Michel Foucault (1995, 156–62) shows in *Discipline and Punish*, his study of the development of the modern French carceral system. There Foucault relates the development of the prison to that of institutions like the military, asylums—and education, our field of work. To take just one example, he describes a shift in the approach to the management and organization of time at the Gobelins in the eighteenth century. By dividing up time into smaller and smaller increments and assigning stages in a progression to be evaluated through examinations, pedagogical practice became subsumed by "disciplinary time" (159). Undergraduate and especially graduate education today is still structured around a series of stages that form a progressive evolution. This control of time is itself an expression of power, creating a hierarchy of disciplinary power that renders bodies docile.

The power structures that constrain and exercise control over bodies are subjected to critical scrutiny throughout this volume. Abraham Smith examines the iconography of Confederate statues against the background of Roman visual expressions of domination and power, while Jennifer A. Glancy investigates the rhetoric of slavery and possession in early Christian discourse and the ontological destabilization that results. Joseph A. Marchal's analysis of willful and wayward bodies sheds new light on issues of consent and coercion, the latter of which is echoed in the coercive nature of gross inequality and the unaccountability of accumulated wealth in Allen Dwight Callahan's essay. Candida R. Moss treats disabled and enslaved bodies; Laura Salah Nasrallah questions inherited frameworks of beauty that pervade our disciplines; and Yii-Jan Lin shows how foreign bodies have been used to represent the threat of disease across time. Gay L. Byron's essay demonstrates the neglected stories that come into the light by shifting the geographic center of disciplinary focus, and Jorunn Økland evaluates the variability in how the very concept of equality within a society has been defined.

Each of these studies thus marshals scholarship both to reveal new understandings of the historical use of power and to unsettle the hierarchies of power that have operated within our academic disciplines. Even as our disciplines cry out for critique, reform, and even revolution, my use of discipline, here a noun, points to the education and scholarly training that makes such work possible. Discipline descends from the Latin *disciplina* or *discipulina*, which itself derives in part from the verb *disco*, "to learn." In a culture that promotes education as a path to upward mobility, the sense of learning suggests a more positive side of discipline. And who facilitates the learning process? This person is positioned as an authority over the learner, perhaps a parent, guardian, mentor, or teacher. The idea of teaching brings us back closer to the themes at hand—our dual role as continuing students of a subject and scholars and teachers within the academy.

Even though academia permits a fair amount of freedom to pursue individual interests through research and teaching, it is in other ways strictly hierarchical. The path of scholarly training requires the student to learn from and be equipped with skills by a teacher; at some point, we were all advisees of an advisor. The German terms for doctoral advisors—*Doktorvater* and *Doktormutter*—even blur the distinction between teacher and parent. Once one has earned a PhD and ostensibly is an authority in one's own right, we nevertheless bear titles such as "assistant" or "associate"; we occupy a position called "junior" to someone else's "senior." The mark of achievement is to progress from a level of lower authority to a higher level of authority, to occupy the higher roles. But this still positions us along a spectrum within an unequal relationship.

I understand Buell's challenge to be referring to our adherence to the artificial boundaries that delineate academic disciplines, the noun. Yet in thinking about discipline as a verb, I hope that we might consider how these authoritative interpersonal relationships operate and serve to constitute an academic discipline. In becoming less disciplined, can we also disrupt the hierarchies that structure and undergird our training as scholars and advancement as professionals? Whether that is through collaboration—such as the coeditorship that guides the formation of this volume—or amplification of the work of those with less seniority in academia, a less disciplined approach also requires a reassessment of how power works within the profession.

As we move within the hierarchy of academia, we come to belong to the discipline; that is, we could potentially be considered disciples. We occupy a dual role, then, that of disciple (from the Latin *discipulus*, another noun formed from *disco*) and that of teacher. How can we apply the call to be less disciplined to both of these roles? A brief glance at two examples, one from classical Greek literature and one from the Gospel of Matthew, about teachers and disciples may offer some food for thought. The Greek term for disciple is μαθητής, which likewise derives from a verb that means "to learn," μανθάνω. The label *mathētēs* was commonly applied to students at the schools of philosophy and rhetoric in the fifth and fourth century BCE. The intellectual movements associated with these schools—including the group of thinkers, orators, and teachers known as Sophists—were the source of both intellectual activity and anxiety.

Aristophanes notoriously satirized the Sophists in the *Clouds*, first performed in 423 BCE. The play presents a portrait of Socrates so damaging that Plato's Socrates claims that it prejudiced the Athenians against him almost twenty-five years later at his trial (*Apol.* 18b–e). Socrates in *Clouds* educates young men at his Phrontisterion, attracting Strepsiades, an older man who wants to learn how to escape the debts his son Pheidippides has brought upon him. When he arrives at the school, he presents himself, declaring, "I have come as a *mathētēs* to the *Phrontisterion*!" (*Nub.* 142). But Strepsiades gets more than he bargains for: when Socrates stages a debate between Worse Argument and Better Argument, Worse Argument wins and when Pheidippides does join the Phrontisterion, he learns how to justify physically assaulting his own father. In a fit of rage and frustration, Strepsiades burns the school down. Neither teacher nor disciples have much to recommend them, and the failed journey to advantage ends in a pile of rubble.

The *Clouds* pokes fun by demonstrating the outcome of an unscrupulous student making himself the disciple of a foolish teacher. Discipleship is dangerous, it turns out. And one cannot assume that discipline, in the sense of correction and training, will lead to improved outcomes. In the turn to becoming less disciplined, then, is an opportunity to assess who is disciplining us, what such discipline consists of, and what results it yields. Education is not necessarily a unidirectional progression toward intellectual and moral improvement. As we step outside traditional disciplinary boundaries to gain new insights into the ancient past and our contemporary predicaments, we must remember that the individuals who participate in disciplining, being disciplined, and the discipline matter.

The portrait of the disciples in the Gospel of Matthew offers a different angle for thinking about the position of being a disciple. As Michael Wilkins (1995, 137–41) has shown, the presentation of the disciples in Matt 13, as opposed to Mark 4, creates and emphasizes a distinction between disciples (*mathētai*) and the undifferentiated crowd (*ochlos*). Matthew 13 opens with Jesus teaching "great crowds" (*ochloi polloi*) through parables. Later, the disciples privately approach to question Jesus:

> Καὶ προσελθόντες οἱ μαθηταὶ εἶπαν αὐτῷ· Διὰ τί ἐν παραβολαῖς λαλεῖς αὐτοῖς; ὁ δὲ ἀποκριθεὶς εἶπεν αὐτοῖς· Ὅτι ὑμῖν δέδοται γνῶναι τὰ μυστήρια τῆς βασιλείας τῶν οὐρανῶν, ἐκείνοις δὲ οὐ δέδοται. ὅστις γὰρ

ἔχει, δοθήσεται αὐτῷ καὶ περισσευθήσεται· ὅστις δὲ οὐκ ἔχει, καὶ ὃ ἔχει ἀρθήσεται ἀπ' αὐτοῦ.

Then the disciples came and asked him, "Why do you speak to them in parables?" He answered, "To you it has been given to know the secrets of the kingdom of heaven, but to them it has not been given. For to those who have, more will be given, and they will have an abundance; but from those who have nothing, even what they have will be taken away." (Matt 13:10–12; NRSV)

In the parallel passage, Mark 4:10 describes the private questioners as "the ones around him together with the twelve" (οἱ περὶ αὐτὸν σὺν τοῖς δώδεκα), implying a larger group of people who associate with the Twelve. In Matthew's account, a narrower group of only "the disciples" are defined as the ones possessing the ability to understand divine mysteries and recipients of abundant gifts. In fact, we see that "everywhere in this chapter Matthew keeps the disciples and crowds separate, the latter enhancing the former's understanding through their ignorance" (Wilkins 1995, 140). While Matthew's portrait of the disciples contains both positive and unflattering aspects, the disciples are nevertheless intended to stand apart as the select. Their special status may be discerned through internal qualities (ability to understand and access to special knowledge) or external actions (demonstrated through their commitment and the cost it incurs).

To be a disciple, then, may mean more than just to be a student, a learner, or an adherent to a person or cause. While the Sophists in Aristophanes's satire took on any disciple willing to pay, in Matthew the disciples are specially chosen, gifted, and distinct from the crowd (despite often being portrayed as foolish or weak). To what extent does that appeal to us as academics: to be drawn in to something that excludes others, to be found and pronounced special and select by virtue of our knowledge and understanding? For all of us, part of the task of becoming scholars is to master an area of expertise. As we explore how to become less disciplined and work to free ourselves of disciplinary constraints, we may also lose some of the frameworks in which we can prove ourselves as belonging. Perhaps there is little lost there, but it needs to be acknowledged nonetheless.

This meander through the ideas associated with discipline has brought to light a network of relationships that surrounds the tasks of learning, teaching, accumulating expertise, and constituting academic disciplines.

These ponderings lead me to further questions we might consider together: What ethics and attitudes do we bring as disciples? What kind of disciples do we want to be, and to what end? What does our choice of teacher reflect about us, and do we reflect our teachers? As educators ourselves, who train and guide new students and introduce them to our fields of expertise, what ethics are we demonstrating for our students? Even as we seek to disrupt disciplinary boundaries with our work, we remain embedded to some extent in hierarchical arrangements. In the context of the embattled humanities, it can feel even more risky to disrupt existing structures, yet all of the contributions in this volume point toward the need for change—especially at this moment when the COVID-19 pandemic has altered the status quo. I look forward to continuing this conversation about and engaging in the work of transforming the practice of discipline and our disciplines together.

Works Cited

Foucault, Michel. 1995. *Discipline and Punish: The Birth of the Prison*. Translated by Alan Sheridan. 2nd ed. New York: Vintage.

Wilkins, Michael J. 1995. *Discipleship in the Ancient World and Matthew's Gospel*. 2nd ed. Grand Rapids: Baker.

Afterword: The Ancient World and the Ancient World

Joy Connolly

1. Habits of Unseeing

The City and the City, a novel by the speculative fiction writer China Miéville (2009), rests on the premise that the two cities of Beszél and Ul Qoma occupy most of the same topographical space while their citizens pursue separate existences. Members of each group live in a permanent silent agreement not to see members of the other: they unsee any traces of the residents, buildings, streets, and monuments that occupy their own space. At times, as the narrator describes at the beginning of the novel, ingrained discipline breaks down:

> An elderly woman was walking slowly away from me in a shambling sway. She turned her head and looked at me. I was struck by her motion, and I met her eyes.... In my glance I took in her clothes, her way of walking, of holding herself, and looking.
> With a hard start, I realised that she was not on GunterStrász at all, and that I should not have seen her.
> Immediately and flustered I looked away, and she did the same, with the same speed. I raised my head, towards an aircraft on its final descent. When after some seconds I looked back up, unnoticing the old woman stepping heavily away, I looked carefully instead of at her in her foreign street at the faces of the nearby and local GunterStrász, that depressed zone. (Miéville 2009, 12)

When a citizen of Beszél fails to unsee people or parts of Ul Qoma (or vice versa), an intimidating secret police force called "Breach" takes action to preserve the integrity of the collectively imagined irreality.

China Miéville is a scholar of Marxism whose most recent book is a study of the *Communist Manifesto*, but his novel transcends its obvious political point: that each of us chooses to unsee poverty, racism, injustice, and environmental decay on a daily basis. It examines the sources and consequences of our desire to maintain separate worlds even when the evidence of our senses tells us that our reality is an artifact of willed belief.

The present volume aims to heal the breach between the Greco-Roman world and the early Christian world that scholars have chosen to sustain since the eighteenth century, giving rise to the title of my essay. No intimidating Breach, but disciplinary structure and culture continue to police those who seek to break down the constructed barriers separating the two overlaying territories. In their thoughtful introduction, the editors of this volume examine what prevents a more regular and robust engagement between scholars of the two worlds. They rightly point to the weight of culture and history, with all its anxieties and prejudices: secular scholars' worries about the potential slant of faith-based scholarship; the eighteenth-century hierarchization of world languages, fueled by anti-Semitism and antiquarian classicism, that awarded classical Greek and Latin greater value and beauty than Hebrew and Koine Greek; and the nineteenth century rise of disciplinary specialization, with its many documentable fragmenting and isolating effects. They also acknowledge the professionalized research university's inward turn away from people and ways of reading outside the academy. They call us to integrate the worlds of the Roman Empire and early Christianity, to reconnect with the vital spark of what Edward Said (1983, 1–53, 175) called the "worldliness" of intellectual activity.

Ubiquitous, influential, the driver of complex social and political change and for many believers, the seed of personal transformation, the Christian scriptures have, can, and do, as the editors of this volume suggest, "generate different worlds in an open future." These texts deserve close study from many angles, including the historical context in which they were composed. The contributors to this volume are proof of this. Their essays populate our minds with a more accurate ancient Mediterranean, a region filled with people of various sexual identities and orientations (Marchal) and classes (Callahan), people with disabilities (Moss), and women of color (Byron, Haley), a world that troubles contemporary categories of foreign and native (Lin) and equal and unequal (Økland). These are just a few of the ways this volume enriches our understanding of a set of texts that continue to activate thought and action and to undergird the beliefs of millions of people up to the present day.

So long as we assent to the Miévillean habits of unseeing that keep scholars of early Christian texts isolated from colleagues who could help them advance their historical studies, we will continue to produce less than our best scholarship. Here, to my mind, is the most important contribution of this volume beyond the individual essays. Its insights push us to come to grips with what must be done if we wish, as the theorist Sylvia Wynter (2003) has compellingly enjoined us, to undertake a collective rewriting of knowledge as we know it: to identify the assumptions that have bent and colored scholarship of prior decades and centuries, and in a spirit of combined humility and aspiration for accuracy and clearer insight, to devise the new scholarly habits, styles, collaborative assemblages, values, and notions of merit that will allow us to remake a richer and more accurate ancient world.

Should we succeed in doing so, the fields of early Christianity and Greek and Roman studies will have done a service for all the arts and sciences.[1] We will have taken an important step toward healing not one but two Miévillean landscapes, by integrating the two worlds of classical and biblical scholarship and the two worlds of the academy and the human society whose space the academy occupies. It is the small blue marble we inhabit—the material frame for Said's worldliness—that is my concern in this essay. Scholars have the power to make worlds. To unleash that power, let us first remember that the modern research university that structures our scholarly lives was invented by, and bears the scars of, the nineteenth-century globe, dominated by the divided, competitive nations of Europe.

2. Humanistic Scholarship as an Integrative Force

What is the role of humanistic scholarship in the university today? According to Bill Readings (1996), in the nineteenth and early twentieth centuries, the university (by which he meant the north American and European research university) had a clear mission: to uphold the cultural fabric of the modern nation. The university was the "producer, protector, and inculcator" (Readings 1996, 3) of national culture in the Arnoldian sense of the word, "the best that has been thought and said." But the late twentieth century undermined this vision by bringing globalization—not only to the nation and the corporation, but to academia, as American universities and

---

1. For a helpful overview of the challenges to the twentieth century institutionalization of the disciplines, see Menand 1997; Menand concludes that that even and perhaps especially English departments cannot "continue to offer plausible raisons-d'etre without a reconception of their functions" (214).

colleges began to recruit students and faculty from around the world. Globalization meant that the historical national mission of the university was no longer tenable. In the globalized American university, Readings argues, the place of the humanities became especially precarious. Our nation-based departments of literature and culture had made us central to the old mission; but after globalization, our roles and responsibilities in the new University system, which Readings scathingly calls the system of "producing excellence," are not at all clear.

Tragically, Readings was killed in an airplane crash before he could finish his book. Its final chapters, though they are not fully polished, issue a powerful call to readers in the academy to confront the consequences of globalization. Readings was under no illusion that this would be easy. He wrote caustically:

> An order of knowledge and an institutional structure are breaking down, and in their place comes the discourse of excellence that tells teachers and students simply not to worry about how things fit together, since that is not their problem. All they have to do is get on with doing what they always have done, and the general question of integration will be resolved by the administration with the help of grids that chart the achievement of goals in achieving excellence, whatever that might be. To take responsibility for devising a new mission, instead of leaving it to corporate powers, meant constructing a new, shifting disciplinary structure that moves beyond custom and nostalgia to think the social bond without recourse to a unifying idea, whether of culture or the state. (1996, 191).

Readings's fear that administrative powers and priorities would shape the university has come true at many schools, where changes in departmental structure and curriculum have been driven by budget rather than on intellectual grounds. I share his and others' worry about the loss of a guiding mission for the humanities that is meaningful to increasingly diverse faculty and students, administrators, and the public.[2] I share his belief that faculty and students should take on this responsibility even if—perhaps especially if—they work in well-resourced institutions that are not (yet) feeling the direct pinch of budget reductions and cuts. But I disagree with

---

2. Sheldon Pollock (2016) makes a powerful argument for the redisciplinization of the humanities via a return to philology, which I see as a potentially valuable complement to my global framing.

Readings's hope to do this work without recourse to a single unifying idea. There is one unifying idea we can rescue: the world itself, the whole planet, taken as a unit.

The political theorist John Dunn (2018, 285), even as he argues for a global approach to the history of political thought, checks his readers with a warning. "Who can presume to think for a first-person plural as broad as the world's human population?" His answer: the dangers of over-reach and error are clear, but the epistemic and cultural need is so urgent that we must try; we must forge new groups to think together across borders of discipline, area study, nation, language, and continent, to test what we can do.

Dunn's emphasis on new gatherings brings me, as often in my work, to the thinker Hannah Arendt. In her essay "Introduction *into* Politics," Arendt (2005, 128) wasn't talking about the humanities, but her words are relevant and useful nonetheless: "If someone wants to see and experience the world as it 'really' is, he [sic] can do so only by understanding it as something that is shared by many people, lies between them, separates and links them, showing itself differently to each and comprehensible only to the extent that many people talk about it and exchange their opinions and perspectives with one another, over against one another."

Arendt is talking about world-making—the creation of a shared world of thought, creativity, experiment, and common purpose, the place where the exchanges key to democratic politics can happen and where the individuality of human beings is made visible and their value thus preserved. She saw the purpose of the university as enabling world-making, thanks to its ability to convene people across generations around the activity of talking together about texts, ideas, and works of art.

For Arendt, to stop thinking, to be thought-less, as she believed Nazis such as Adolf Eichmann became thought-less, is to lose the world, and this means losing the public space we humans hold in common. To think, to be thoughtful, is to keep building and preserving the plural world of human affairs. She took from Kant the conviction that thinking allows us to handle human unpredictability and plurality because it leads to the enlargement of the mind, increasing the thinker's ability to understand the world from different perspectives, and to form judgments on the basis of that understanding. So she enjoined educators to teach not "how to live the good life," not morals or belief systems, but rather "what the world is like" and how to talk about it. This education would make students "world-builders" "in love with the world," in her phrase, committed to repairing and renewing it (Duarte 2000).

Consider the promise of this high purpose against Readings's story about mission loss in the contemporary university. Now consider our disciplinary structure—in particular our division into departments that reflect nineteenth century Euro-American priorities, interests, and values, and the humanistic scholarly habit of privileging solitary study and writing. Now ask: do these structures and practices meet the needs of the world today?

So far, well-funded institutions have for the most part decided to preserve the national and linguistic divisions of languages and literatures and histories. Many under-funded institutions have gone global, creating departments of World Literature and World Culture and Humanities, but these changes are often driven by dollars rather than intellectual mission, and faculty are understandably slow to find virtue in this administrative top-down remapping of their collegial communities. Virtually all selective research institutions demand regular publications of articles and a single-author monograph as the evidence of scholarly merit at the key moments of tenure and promotion—preventing scholars from pursuing the time-consuming acquisition of foundational skills after they have left graduate school and undermining the collaborative work necessary for comparative, transregional, and transcultural scholarship (see Guillory 2007; Hall 2007).

Meanwhile, our planet is getting smaller, thanks to technology, access to travel, and economic and academic globalization. Especially as groups historically separated by space come into closer and closer contact with one another, the work that urgently needs to be done is the work of bridging national, linguistic, cultural, and religious divides. Making this priority the grounding principle of the way we group ourselves and design curricula would mean giving equal time and energy to preserving the specificity of human experience in the groups humans have formed over time *and* to connecting, communicating, comparing, contrasting, and mutually understanding the results of our studies in their global context.

This priority would also empower scholars from groups historically underrepresented in our disciplines—whose ancestors have been, or who themselves continue to be, marginalized or ignored when they introduce new approaches to producing or circulating knowledge. Hold in your minds a smaller scale picture than the planet: consider humanistic scholarship as a house. The foundations are laid and the first walls constructed by scholars of past generations; as time passes, scholars build additions. The house gets larger over time. It stops being a place primarily for people

Afterword: The Ancient World and the Ancient World

to live and becomes a thing of beauty that we preserve for its own sake. We paint it, we adorn it; we build porches and parapets; we see how high we can build our towers and how detailed and lovely we can make the ornamentation. We devise gates that test mastery and close off access to parts of the structure. We do all this because we can. There may be nothing wrong with each step in the construction. But at the end of the day, the house of humanistic scholarship must be a place where people can live.

One of the most exciting developments in the humanities over the past thirty years or so is how scholars have come to treat the activity of inviting more people into the house. When I was a graduate student in the 1990s, well intentioned behavior mostly amounted to this dictum for admissions and faculty search committees: "open the doors and let different people in." Nearly thirty years later, the paradigm has changed for the better. A critical mass of faculty, students, and administrators understand that when you open the doors wide enough, you need to redesign the whole house. From a house whose doors and windows we push open, we are moving to something closer to a stoa or a *hutong* or even, perhaps, simply a cleared field marked only by moveable boundary stones.

Each contribution to this volume is an example of one of three new directions in humanistic scholarship that have emerged over the past few decades that help build a new house of scholarship—by people of color, queer people, people who grew up in poverty, people for whom access to education was difficult in their early years and is never taken for granted as they grow older. Taken together, they amount to a quiet revolution—and they make it easier to imagine and undertake humanistic scholarship in a global frame.

First, scholars are pursuing a wider range of ways to circulate knowledge, including multimedia publications, graphic novels, podcasts, writing that incorporates personal stances, creative writing, and memoir, and writing that expresses the fruits of collaborative research. This volume includes several essays that frame the argument in personal terms, making the stakes clear. It sets up dialogues of statement and response between and among scholars that extend the give-and-take of the conference to the written artifact—a mode of organization that invites readers into the conversation and preserves a dynamic, generous sense of openness to the proceedings. Several authors acknowledge the challenge of working across languages and regional histories, a challenge best met by collaborative work, to which the academic humanities, committed to a single-author model, usually fails to grant due recognition.

Second, reflecting a trend I see adopted in particular by the emerging generation of scholars, in a mode that has gained greater traction since the Great Recession of 2008–2009, these essays root themselves in the world and its concerns. Understanding equality, rights, and identity by exploring alternatives in ancient texts are hallmarks of this volume.

Third, comparative, transnational, transregional, and transtemporal scholarship, which frames questions at the margins or on the borders of states. Such projects compare the "I" in a lyric poem written in Uzbekistan with one in Sao Paulo, or concepts of criminal justice in ancient Assyria and China, or economic developments in agrarian cultures across the global south—or conceptions of rights in Roman texts and Christian ones.

These three directions are difficult or impossible to pursue in isolation. They involve acts of cocreation. Anyone who has done this work can tell you about its enormously generative effects—often unpredictable and difficult to contain within the seminar timetable or the traditional disciplinary graduate seminar or the semester calendar. Each of these directions, and their emphasis on collaboration, relationality, and context, have the potential (and often do) respond constructively to the critique of the European thought-world made by scholars like Sylvia Wynter (1987), who points out that "our present arrangements of knowledge were put in place in the nineteenth century" to serve the interests of imperialist Europe (cited in Chuh 2019, 1).

Scholars have been doing this work for decades. But for many reasons, much of it—work that is collaborative or written in the vernacular or expresses itself in activity beyond peer reviewed publications—tends to run into problems when it encounters the rules and habits of the university as it is currently institutionalized. Given the challenges ahead of us, this is a serious problem that deserves our close collective attention. Faculty pursuing the directions above are not rewarded as they deserve. The path is much smoother for traditional monographs and articles on more and more highly specialized topics that fit within recognized disciplinary borders.

Many scholars, particularly scholars of color, women, scholars who were first in their families to go to college, queer scholars, scholars from poor families, and immigrant scholars, will put this point more bluntly. These scholars feel pressured not only to produce ever more specialized knowledge, but to do so in isolation and in an artificial language that limits their audience and impact. Worse, the system demands that they assimilate themselves into structures designed to perpetuate worldviews in which they are marginal, excluded, or devalued. As Wynter would say, the distinctive contributions of minoritized perspectives and discourses risk being lost.[3] The limited forms of acceptable scholarly expression build walls between scholars and the communities they hope to reach—putting beyond their reach (as Arendt would say) the world they are trying to build in common.

The great virtue of this volume is that it accelerates acceptance of plurality in scholarship. It adopts a plural approach to defining what counts in the production and circulation of knowledge—one that takes seriously the goals of inclusive world-making and transformation on a global scale, rather than one that imitates the national and linguistic divisions of the world. The achievement of the contributors should prompt us all to think differently about doctoral education, the requirements for tenure and promotion, the forms scholarship is permitted to take, and the shape of the scholarly groupings in the university.

One of the major obstacles to change in the humanities is ourselves: our passions and comfort zones. The arts and science professoriate in American research universities is overwhelmingly white and comes from better-off, well-educated families. A 2021 study of over 7,000 faculty across eight disciplines in the arts and sciences showed that today's PhDs grew up in households with incomes roughly 25 percent above the United States median (Morgan et al. 2022). It also showed that faculty are twenty-five times more likely to have a parent with a PhD.

My point here is not simply that we need to continue diversifying the professoriate in terms of race, ethnicity, and class, though we must do so—but that our universities are filled with scholars who are thoroughly acculturated to its design, reward structure, habits of thought, and styles of speech and writing. We feel at home in the research university as it is currently designed. Although we are often overworked, we love what we study and are (with some good reasons) resistant to change, since for decades now, change has seemed driven by dollars instead of academic priorities. Committed to our doctoral students' success in landing academic posts, we tend to recommend risk-averse approaches to scholarship—familiar topics and forms of circulating knowledge like those I mentioned above: the conference paper, the peer-reviewed article, the university press monograph.

---

3. Other guiding stars for this argument include Gayatri Spivak, Kandice Chuh, Roderick Ferguson, and Grace Hong.

But staying the course is not an option. Consider the steeply falling numbers of faculty lines and humanities majors.[4] In the mid 1970s, between 2,500 and 3,000 jobs were advertised in the Modern Language Association (MLA) Job List. By the end of the 1980s, that number had increased to nearly 4,000 posts per year. The financial crisis of the late 1980s led to a sharp drop, but with the economic recovery, the numbers increased again, beating out the 1970s highs … until the crash of 2008–2009. The total number of posts fell abruptly from about 3,500 in 2008 to 2,000 posts just two years later. Numbers have fallen further since. Just under 1,600 jobs were posted in 2019; in 2020, just over 1,400. For the first time since the 1970s, when these numbers were first tracked, faculty lines have not grown as the economy recovered.

The 2008 crash also brought down the majors count. And once again, for the first time in history, while the economy has improved—especially for the wealthiest Americans, virtually all of whose kids go to college—the humanities numbers have not. Louis Menand summarized the picture in the *New Yorker*: "between 2012 and 2019, the number of BAs awarded annually in English fell by 26 percent, in philosophy and religious studies by 25 percent, and in foreign languages and literature by 24 percent. In English, according to the Association of Departments of English … research universities like Brown and Columbia took the biggest hits" (Menand 2021). Just 8 percent of students entering Harvard in 2021 reported that they intend to major in the arts and humanities; not long ago that number was close to 20 percent. We all know exceptions like creative-writing and philosophy. But we should not be content with a few exceptions or small gains. Undergraduates should be flocking to the humanities—and in particular, to the study of a set of ancient texts that continue to exert visible influence on the planet today!

The good news is that like the contributors to this volume, many scholars are trying to "think different," to quote the Apple advertisement, in the hope of reaching more students and with the grand purpose of revitalizing the creation of knowledge by reframing its scope. They are rooting their scholarship in issues of public concern and interest. They are improving their explanations of how policy-irrelevant scholarship is crucially valuable as an expression of care for our world. They are tackling bigger questions by working in collaborative groups organized explicitly to advance our knowledge by pushing back on outdated disciplinary rules.

---

4. The material in this and the following paragraph appears in Connolly 2022.

The challenges to scholarly transformation in the university are considerable. Our structures carry a heavy load of history; our ecosystem is huge, fragmented, and brutally competitive. Let us keep our eyes on the great purpose and promise of humanistic scholarship: to study an integrated ancient world that resists the pressure of struggling states to remake themselves by unseeing the interconnected worlds of the past.

Works Cited

Arendt, Hannah. 2005. "Introduction *into* Politics." Pages 93–200 in *The Promise of Politics*. Edited and with an introduction by Jerome Kohn. New York: Schocken.

Chuh, Kandice. 2019. *The Difference Aesthetics Makes: On the Humanities "After Man."* Durham, NC: Duke University Press.

Connolly, Joy. 2022. "Let's Open Our Eyes and Leap." *TAPA* 152.1:15–23.

Duarte, Eduardo. 2020. "Thinking in Dark Times: Learning to Repair and Renew Our Common World." Pages 136–50 in *Hannah Arendt on Educational Thinking and Practice in Dark Times*. Edited by Wayne Veck and Helen M. Gunter. New York: Bloomsbury Academic.

Dunn, John. 2018. "Why We Need a Global History of Political Thought." Pages 285–310 in *Markets, Morals, Politics: Jealousy of Trade and the History of Political Thought*. Edited by Béla Kapossy, Isaac Nakhimovsky, Sophus Reinert, and Richard Whatmore. Cambridge: Harvard University Press.

Guillory, John. 2007. "Second Thoughts on the Notion of Raising Standards." *Profession*: 77–82.

Hall, Donald E. 2007. "A More Capacious View of Scholarship." *Profession*: 83–88.

Menand, Louis. 1997. "The Demise of Disciplinary Authority." Pages 201–19 in *What's Happened to the Humanities?* Edited by Alvin B. Kernan, William Bowen, and Harold G. Shapiro. Princeton: Princeton University Press.

———. 2021. "What's So Great about Great-Books Courses?" *The New Yorker*. December 13. https://tinyurl.com/SBL06104q1.

Morgan, Allison C., Nicholas La Berge, Daniel B. Larremore, Mirta Galesic, Jennie E. Brand, and Aaron Clauset. "Socioeconomic Roots of Academic Faculty." *Nature Human Behaviour* 6 (2022): 1625–33. https://www.nature.com/articles/s41562-022-01425-4.

Miéville, China. 2009. *The City and the City*. London: Macmillan.

Pollock, Sheldon. 2016. "Areas, Disciplines, and the Goals of Inquiry." *Journal of Asian Studies* 75.4:913–28.

Readings, Bill. 1996. *The University in Ruins.* Cambridge: Harvard University Press.

Said, Edward W. 1983. *The World, the Text, and the Critic.* Cambridge: Harvard University Press.

Wynter, Sylvia. 1987. "On Disenchanting Discourse: 'Minority' Literary Criticism and Beyond." *Cultural Critique* 7:207–44.

Wynter, Sylvia. 2003. "Unsettling the Coloniality of Being/Power/Truth/Freedom: Towards the Human, after Man, Its Overrepresentation—An Argument." *The New Centennial Review* 3:257–337.

Contributors

Douglas Boin, trained in classics, is Professor of History at Saint Louis University (USA) and the author, most recently, of *Alaric the Goth: An Outsider's History of the Fall of Rome* (Norton, 2020). An expert on the religious world of ancient Rome and on society and culture in the later Roman Empire, with research appearing in the leading national and international journals of his field, he is currently codirecting an archaeological project with the British School at Rome in Umbria, Italy.

Denise Kimber Buell is Cluett Professor of Religion at Williams College (USA). Her research asks how contemporary and ancient concerns affect the interpretation and reconstruction of early Christian history and texts, with particular attention to race, ethnicity, gender, and relations between humans and nonhumans. Her work appears in multiple articles as well in *Making Christians: Clement of Alexandria and the Rhetoric of Legitimacy* (Princeton University Press, 1999) and *Why This New Race: Ethnic Reasoning in Early Christianity* (Columbia University Press, 2005).

Gay L. Byron is Professor of New Testament and Early Christianity at Howard University School of Divinity (USA). Her scholarship focuses on the origins of Christianity in ancient Ethiopia. She is the author of *Symbolic Blackness and Ethnic Difference in Early Christian Literature* (Routledge, 2002), coeditor of *Womanist Interpretations of the Bible: Expanding the Discourse* (SBL Press, 2016), and coeditor of *Black Scholars Matter: Visions, Struggles, and Hopes in Africana Biblical Studies* (SBL Press, 2022). For 2021–2022, she was a Visiting Faculty Fellow in the Franklin Humanities Institute at Duke University (USA). Her current book project focuses on Ethiopian manuscripts and early Christianity.

Allen Dwight Callahan is an independent scholar, media commentator, and creative consultant in the United States. He has taught biblical languages and literatures at the Harvard Divinity School and has served as Associate Chaplain at Brown University and as Theologian in Residence at Metropolitan Baptist Church in Washington, DC. He is the author of three books and over two dozen scholarly articles and has been a featured contributor in documentaries aired on PBS, the History Channel, and the Discovery Channel.

Joy Connolly began her service as President of the American Council of Learned Societies (USA) in July 2019. Previously, she served as Provost and Interim President of The Graduate Center at the City University of New York, where she was also Distinguished Professor of Classics. She has held faculty appointments at New York University (where she served as Dean for the Humanities from 2012–2016), Stanford University, and the University of Washington. Joy is a member of the American Academy of Arts and Sciences. She has published two books with Princeton University Press on Roman political thought and rhetoric and over seventy articles, reviews, and short essays, including for media such as *Bookforum* and the *Times Literary Supplement*.

Jennifer A. Glancy is Professor of Religious Studies at Le Moyne College (USA). She is the author of *Slavery in Early Christianity* (Oxford University Press, 2002), *Corporal Knowledge: Early Christian Bodies* (Oxford University Press, 2010), and *Slavery as Moral Problem: In the Early Church and Today* (Fortress, 2011). Her current book project couples analysis of slavery in early Christian writings with assessment of twenty-first-century discourses about what it means to be human.

Shelley P. Haley is the Edward North Chair of Classics Emerita at Hamilton College (USA). Her BA is from Syracuse University, and she received her PhD in Classical Studies from the University of Michigan. In 2021, she served as President of the Society for Classical Studies, the first African-American woman to do so in the Society's 153-year history. Widely acclaimed as an expert on Cleopatra, Haley's current research centers on recovering the constructions of race and gender in ancient Rome by applying the theoretical framework of critical race feminist theory.

Contributors

Caroline Johnson Hodge is a Professor in the Department of Religious Studies at the College of the Holy Cross (USA). She is the author of a book entitled *"If Sons, Then Heirs": A Study of Kinship and Ethnicity in Paul's Letters* (Oxford University Press, 2007). Her current research documents evidence for a Christian household cult before Constantine and highlights the roles of Christian women and slaves in household rituals.

Katherine Lu Hsu is Assistant Professor of Classics at College of the Holy Cross (USA). She is the author of *The Violent Hero: Heracles in the Greek Imagination* (Bloomsbury, 2021) and coeditor (with David Schur and Brian P. Sowers) of *The Body Unbound: Literary Approaches to the Classical Canon* (Palgrave Macmillan, 2021) and has written about Greek literature, papyrology, and graphic novels. She has taught previously at Brooklyn College (City University of New York), where she was director of the intensive Latin/Greek Institute.

Timothy A. Joseph is Professor of Classics at the College of the Holy Cross (USA), where his research and teaching concentrate on ancient Greek and Latin literature, as well as the reception of ancient ideas and models in the United States. His publications include *Tacitus the Epic Successor* (Brill, 2012) and *Thunder and Lament: Lucan on the Beginnings and Ends of Epic* (Oxford University Press, 2022).

Tat-siong Benny Liew is the Class of 1956 Professor in New Testament Studies at the College of the Holy Cross (USA). He is the author of *Politics of Parousia* (Brill, 1999) and *What Is Asian American Biblical Hermeneutics?* (University of Hawaii Press, 2008). He also edited *Postcolonial Interventions* (Sheffield Phoenix, 2009), *Reading Ideologies* (Sheffield Phoenix, 2011), and *Present and Future of Biblical Studies* (Brill, 2018). Liew is also the series editor of T&T Clark's Study Guides to the New Testament (Bloomsbury).

Yii-Jan Lin is Associate Professor of New Testament at Yale Divinity School (USA). She is the author of *The Erotic Life of Manuscripts: New Testament Textual Criticism and the Biological Sciences* (Oxford University Press). Her forthcoming book, *Immigration and Apocalypse: The Revelation of John in the History of American Immigration* (Yale University Press), focuses on apocalypticism and the use of Revelation in the political discourse surrounding American immigration—both in utopian conceptions of America and violent exclusion of foreigners.

Dominic Machado is an Assistant Professor of Classics at the College of Holy Cross (USA). He is an ancient historian who studies the perceptions and realities of nonelite group behavior (collective action, dissent, and resistance) in the Roman world. He is also interested in the role that classics plays in the modern world and has published papers on topics on questions of diversity and inclusion in publication practices and the racialized reception of antiquity in the twentieth and the twenty-first century.

Joseph A. Marchal is Professor of Religious Studies and affiliate faculty in Women's and Gender Studies at Ball State University (USA). He has published ten books and edited collections, most recently *Appalling Bodies: Queer Figures before and after Paul's Letters* (Oxford University Press, 2020), *After the Corinthian Women Prophets: Reimagining Rhetoric and Power* (SBL Press, 2021), and *Bodies on the Verge: Queering Pauline Epistles* (SBL Press, 2019). They are currently serving as chair of Society of Biblical Literature's first-ever Committee for LGBTIQ+ Scholars and Scholarship and founding coeditor of *QTR: A Journal of Queer and Transgender Studies in Religion*.

Thomas R. Martin is the Jeremiah W. O'Connor Jr. Professor in the Department of Classics at The College of the Holy Cross (USA). His teaching and scholarship concern Greek and Roman history, biography, numismatics, and the manuscript tradition of Josephus in Latin. He is the author of, among other books, *Ancient Greece. From Prehistoric to Hellenistic Times* (Yale University Press, 2nd ed. 2013) and *Ancient Rome: From Romulus to Justinian* (Yale University Press, 2012). He is one of the founders of the online Perseus Digital Library. For general audiences, he has appeared in filmed documentaries on ancient Greece and Rome and written numerous book reviews for the History Book Club.

Candida R. Moss is the Edward Cadbury Professor of Theology at the University of Birmingham (UK) and a Research Associate at the Institute for the Study of the Ancient World in New York. Moss's research focusses on martyrdom, resurrected bodies, disability studies, and enslaved literate workers and early Christianity. The award-winning author of seven books and dozens of articles, Moss's publications include *Divine Bodies: Resurrecting Perfection in the New Testament and Early Christianity* (Yale University Press, 2019) and the forthcoming coedited volume *Enslavement, Writing and Power in the Ancient Mediterranean* (Oxford University Press).

Laura Salah Nasrallah is Buckingham Professor of New Testament Criticism and Interpretation at Yale University (USA), with a joint appointment in the Department of Religious Studies and the Divinity School. She is author of *Ancient Christians and the Power of Curses: "Magic," Aesthetics, and Justice* (Cambridge University Press, forthcoming), *Archaeology and the Letters of Paul* (Oxford University Press, 2019), *Christian Responses to Roman Art and Architecture: The Second-Century Church amid the Spaces of Empire* (Cambridge University Press, 2010), and *An Ecstasy of Folly: Prophecy and Authority in Early Christianity* (Harvard University Press, 2003).

Jorunn Økland, trained in classics and theology, is Professor of Gender Studies in the Humanities and Professor of New Testament at the Centre for Gender Research and at the Faculty of Theology, University of Oslo (Norway). Serving on the Translation Committee of the Norwegian Bible Society, she has been Chair of the Revision of the Norwegian Bible (appearing in 2024). From 2016 to 2021, she also served as the Director of Norwegian Institute at Athens, Greece. In English language, she has authored *Women in Their Place: Paul and the Corinthian Discourse of Gender and Sanctuary Space* (2004), and coedited volumes such as *Marxist Feminist Criticism of the Bible* (2008). Recent English-language publications include: "The Celebrity Paratexts: The 1 Corinthians 14 Gloss Theory before and after *The Corinthian Women Prophets*" in *After the Corinthian Women Prophets* (see above under Marchal), and "Women's Bravery: Jane Dieulafoy, Queen Parysatis, and the Reception of the Persian Empire in Nineteenth Century France" in *The Hunt for Ancient Israel* (Equinox, 2022).

Abraham Smith is Professor of New Testament at Perkins School of Theology/Southern Methodist University (USA). His research interests include ancient and modern slavery, violence studies, and African American biblical hermeneutics. His most recent publications include *Mark: An Introduction and Study Guide—Shaping the Life and Legacy of Jesus* (Bloomsbury, 2017). *Black/Africana Studies and Black/Africana Biblical Studies* (Brill, 2020); and "Incarceration on Trial: The Imprisonment of Paul and Silas in Acts 16" in *Journal of Biblical Literature* 140 (2021).

Ancient Sources Index

Old Testament/Hebrew Bible

Genesis
- 1:26 — 227
- 47:5–6 — 283

Exodus
- 2:9–10 — 283

Song of Songs
- 1:51 — 251

Isaiah
- 53:7–8 — 65

Deuterocanonical Texts

2 Maccabees
- 6 — 110

New Testament

Matthew — 14, 339–40
- 5–7 — 13
- 5:46 — 209
- 9:2–8 — 303
- 9:9–13 — 209
- 9:32–34 — 303
- 11:19 — 209
- 13 — 340
- 13:10–12 — 340–41
- 17:24 — 209
- 18:6 — 283–84
- 18:15–17 — 209
- 18:21–35 — 163
- 21:31–32 — 209
- 22:15–22 — 209
- 22:36–40 — 19
- 25:14–30 — 163
- 25:31–46 — 161
- 28:16–20 — 16, 283

Mark — 14
- 2:3–12 — 303
- 2:14–15 — 209
- 4 — 340
- 4:10 — 341

Luke — 132, 207–9, 212–13
- 1:1 — 213
- 1:3 — 213
- 3:12–13 — 210
- 5:17–26 — 303
- 5:29 — 209
- 9:51—19:28 — 207
- 10:25–37 — 19, 208
- 12:13–21 — 208
- 12:16 — 207
- 12:26 — 207
- 13:6–8 — 208
- 14:1–33 — 208
- 14:12–13 — 207
- 14:47–48 — 208
- 15:1–10 — 208
- 15:32 — 207
- 16:1 — 207
- 16:1–11 — 208
- 16:13 — 207
- 16:14 — 208
- 16:19–31 — 208, 210

Ancient Sources Index

Luke (cont.)		16	140, 145
16:20–21	207	16:1–16	114, 141–42
17:7	207	16:22	113, 304
18:2	207		
18:9–14	207, 210	1 Corinthians	14, 125, 131, 133, 145,
18:18–30	208	247, 256, 261	
18:23	207	1–4	256, 266
18:35	207	1:17–25	223
19:1–10	207–10	4:20	236
19:11–27	163, 207–8	5–6	140
		5:1	134
John	14, 209	5:4–5	141
5:2–15	303	5:9–11	134, 141
9:1–12	303	6:9–10	124, 141, 236
15:4–5	317	6:9–16	134, 141
15:12–17	316–17	6:18	134, 136
		6:19–20	136
Acts of the Apostles	268	7	128, 134, 143
1:8	65	8	223
8	77, 280	9:22	233
8:26–40	65, 77	11	128, 256
8:27	71, 292	11–14	131, 267
8:31	65	11:7–9	227
8:35	65	11:17–25	233
8:37	67–68	11:21–22	223
8:39	65	12:7–10	108
9:1–19	108	12:28	256, 259
10:36	283	13:1	247, 256, 258–61, 268–69, 280
12:12	66	14	256
12:25	66	14:18–19	259, 269
13:13	66	14:23	256
15:36–40	66	14:33a–36	267
16:22–23	107	15:25	236
20:4	146	15:50	236
21	78	16:17	145
		16:21	106
Romans	14, 125, 131–33		
1:11–13	133	2 Corinthians	141
1:18–28	124	5:11–21	307
5:10–11	307	8	233
6:6—7:25	136, 157	8:13–15	231, 233
7:4	158	9:22	233
7:5	133	12:1–6	108
7:7–25	132, 156		
14:17	236		

Ancient Sources Index

Galatians	106, 131, 144, 158	2:7	300
1:6	303	2:9–10	190
1:10	158	2:11	300
2:19–20	107	2:13	190
3:20	235	2:17	300
3:27–28	235	2:20	193
4:1–7	157	2:26	300
4:29	157	3:4	91
5:21	236	3:5	300
6:11	106, 303	3:10	190, 192
6:14	107	3:12	300
6:17	107	3:17	91
6:19	157	3:19a	91
		3:21	192, 300
Ephesians	114	4–5	192
		4:1	190
Philippians	14, 131, 240	5:5–6	192, 300
2	140	5:6	191
2:6–8	132, 166, 232	5:9	191
2:12–16	131, 134, 136	6–16	192
2:25–30	143–44	6:1–16:21	192
4:2–3	144	6:2	300
4:18	143–44	6:5–8	98
		6:9	190–91
Colossians	114, 232	6:15	193
4	233	7:1	193
4:1	232–33	7:9	94, 299
4:15	146	7:14	91, 190, 299
4:18	106	9:7	98
		9:20–21	299
2 Thessalonians	106	10:2	193
2:1–2	303	10:7	193
3:17	106	11:1–2	191
		11:7	192, 300
Philemon	159	11:18	193
		12:11	192–93, 300
Revelation	14, 85, 94, 97, 99, 189, 191, 297, 299–300	13:7	192, 300
		13:8	191, 299
1:1	190, 193	13:10	192
1:5	191	13:16–18	19
1:9	190, 192	14:2	192
1:9–20	192	14:4	91
2–3	192	15:2	192, 300
2:2	192	15:3	193
2:3	192	16:2–6	91, 300

Revelation (cont.)	
16:9	299
16:11	299
17–21	192
17:1	190
17:2	91
17:6	91
17:14	300
18:4	299
18:8	98
18:12–13	191
18:24	191
19:2	193
20:12	299
21:2	19
21:7	300
21:9–10	190
21:27	83, 87, 299
22:1–3	92, 190, 193
22:6	190, 193
22:8	190
22:10–12	91, 283–84, 300
22:14–15	91, 299–300

Papyri

P.Mich.	
3.188	111
10.583	111
10.584	111
11.605	111

P.Oxy.	
42.3070	144
56.3860	112

Other Ancient Sources

Acts of Thomas	155, 159–70, 316
Ambrosius, *In Epistolam Beati Pauli ad Galatas*	304
Ammianus Marcellinus, *Res gestae*	
23.6.24	298

Aristophanes, *Nubes*	
142	340

Aristotle, *De anima*	252

Aristotle, *Eudemian Ethics*	
1241b	158

Aristotle, *Politica*	227
1254a.8	16
1255a	181
1260a	158
1260a–1260b8	176
1277b33–1278a40	176
1282b	332
1282b	227–28
1283a	229

Augustine, *Aethiopia credet Deo*	77

Augustine, *De civitate Dei*	
1.3.3–5	329

Augustine, *Epistolae ad Galatas expositionis liber unus*	305

Augustine, *On Imperial Rule*	
15.1	331
15.12	331

Augustus, *Res Gestae*	188–89

Aulus Gellius, *Noctes atticae*	
19.8.15	23

Cassius Dio, *Historia Romana*	
66.23.3–5	298

Celxus, *De medicina*	
6	109–10

Chariton, *De Chaerea et Callirhoe*	
8.8.4	108

Cicero, *De finibus bonorum et malorum*
5.2   177

Cicero, *De officiis*
1.128–129   176
3.11.47   298–99

Cicero, *De oratore*
1.126   112

Cicero, *Epistulae ad Atticum*
7   306

Cicero, *Epistulae ad familiares*
5   306
16   306

Cicero, *Epistulae ad Quintum fratrem*
2.2.1   109

Cicero, *In Catilinam*
2.22   176

Cicero, *De republica*
2.46   186

Cicero, *Tusculanae disputations*
5.112   110
5.113   110

CIL
4.1389   146
4.1825a. Add. 212   142
4.2259   145
4.2275   145
4.2266   145
4.8897   146
4.9027   146

Columella, *De re rustica*
1.9.8   114

Digesta
41.2.3.12   168

Dio Chrysostom, *Commentariorum in Epistulam ad Galatas libri tres*   304

Dio Chrysostom, *Commentariorum in Epistulam ad Romanos*   304

Diodorus Siculus, *Bibliotheca historica*
1.33   74

Dionysius of Halicarnassus, *On Composition*   264–67

Erasmus, *Desiderius*   9, 12

Eusebius, *Historia ecclesiastica*
2.15.1–2   66

Eusebius, *Praeparatio evangelica*
5.1.9   84

Evagrius Scholasticus, *Historia ecclesiastica*
4.29   298

Fouilles de Delphes   318, 320

Gaius Marius Victorinus, *In Epistolam Pauli ad Galatas libri duo*   303

Galen, *De captionibus*
2.90   281

Galen, *De theriaca ad Pisonem*
16.281   298

Gregory of Nyssa, *Commentarius in Canticum Canticorum*   77

Herodian, *Historia de imperio post Marcum Aurelium*
1.12.1   298

Herodotus, *Historia*
7.194.1–3   108

Hesiod, *Theogonia*
  927–929 ... 302

Historia Augusta, Heliogabalus
  29.3 ... 115

Historia Augusta, Verus
  8.1–4 ... 298

Homer, *Iliad* ... 19
  1.121–187 ... 302
  1.475 ... 297
  1.571–600 ... 302
  1.590–594 ... 302
  1.607–608 ... 302
  2.211–277 ... 302
  2.216 ... 302
  2.248–249 ... 302
  8.523–531 ... 331–32
  18.393–405 ... 302

Homer, *Odyssey* ... 17
  14.56 ... 335

Homeric Hymns, *Hymn to Apollo*
  316–317 ... 302

Homeric Hymns, *Hymn to Hephaestus*
  2–5 ... 302

Irenaeus, *Adversus haereses*
  3.1.1–3 ... 191
  4.20.11 ... 191

Jerome, *Epistulae*
  108.24.1 ... 262

John of Ephesus, *Chronicle* ... 298

Josephus, *Antiquitates judaicae*
  19.332 ... 236

Josephus, *Bellum judaicum*
  2.379 ... 186
  5.446 ... 189

  7.218 ... 189

Julian, *Epistulae*
  22.430c–31b ... 335

Juvenal, *Sat*
  1.3 ... 198

Livy, *Ab ubre condita*
  preface ... 331
  1.43.5 ... 23
  3.28 ... 186
  4.21.2 ... 297
  45.18.1 ... 18

Lucius Annaeus Florus, *Epitome rerum Romanorum*
  2.33 ... 186

Lucretius, *On the Nature of Things* ... 19
  4.1157–1160 ... 294–95
  6.1141 ... 298

Marcus Aurelius, *Meditations* ... 17

Martyrdom of Polycarp ... 110

Ovid, *Ars*
  1.509–522 ... 176

Ovid, *Tristia*
  4.2.43–46 ... 186

Philo of Alexandria, *De specialibus legibus*
  3.159–162 ... 204

Plato, *Apologia*
  18b–e ... 340

Plato, *Leges*
  2.667d ... 228
  ... 226

Plato, *Phaedo* ... 13

Plato, *Phaedrus*		Sophocles, *Antigone*	14, 18
240c	227		
		Sophocles, *Oedipus Rex*	19
Plato, *Republic*	234		
		Stobaeus, *Floreligium*	
Plato, *Symposium*	14	4.209	115
Pliny the Elder, *Naturalis historia*		Strabo, *Geographica*	
6.20	298	17.1.54	69
7.170	297	17.2.2	75
11.149	110		
26.4	297	Suetonius, *Divus Augustus*	
		79.2	109
Pliny the Younger, *Epistulae*			
7.21	109	Suetonius, *Vespasianus*	
52.12	176	7.2–3	110
Plutarch, *Praecepta gerendae reipublicae*		Tacitus, *Agricola*	186
18.6	229		
		Theodore of Mopsuestia, *In Epistulam*	
Procopius, *De bellis*		*Beati Pauli ad Galatas*	305
2.22.6	298		
		Theodoret, *Interpretatio in XIV*	
Pseudo-Clementine, *Recognitiones*		*epistulas Sancti Pauli*	305
8.29.3–4	262		
		Thucydides, *Historia belli peloponnesiaci*	
Pseudo-Plutarch, "On Monarchy, Democracy, and Oligarchy"	229–30, 234	1.1.22	204, 213
		2.48	89
3.1	230	2.48.1–2	298
Quintilian, *Institutio oratoria*		Trimalchio, *Saturica*	321
5.9.14	176		
5.11.10	193	Virgil, *Aeneid*	17
10.37.1	306		
		Virgil, *Georgics*	19–20
Rhetorica ad Herennium	112	4	106
3.12.22	176		
		Xenophon, *Respublica Lacedaemoniorum*	
Seneca, *Phaedra*	298		
		14.4	198
Seneca the Elder, *Controversiae*			
1 praef. 9	176		
Sicilian Breton, *De divitiis*			
12.2	204		

Modern Authors Index

Achebe, Nwando 70–71, 289, 292–93
Ackerknecht, Erwin H. 87
Adams, Ellen 301
Adichie, Chimamanda Ngozi 67, 324
Adler, Eric 4–5, 9, 19
Agamben, Giorgio 155, 158–59, 161
Agnew, J. H. 3
Ahmed, Sara 10, 40, 125, 128–32, 290
Albl, Martin 301, 303
Ameriks, Karl 2
Amos, Emma 248–49, 255–56, 268, 280, 282
Anders, Charlie Jane 39, 59
Annas, Julia 234
Apel, Thomas A. 88, 90, 297
Appadurai, Arjun 257
Arendt, Hannah 347, 351
Armstrong, Richard H. 14
Armstrong, Amaryah 144
Arthurs, Joshua 250
Asante, Molefi Kete 72
Ascough, Richard S. 144–45, 239
Ashby, Solange 68, 71
Ashenburg, Katherine 88
Atherstone, Andrew 12
Attridge, Harold A. 160, 162, 166
Aune, David 191
Bailey, Randall C. 133
Bakhtin, Mikhail H. 16
Baldwin, James 210
Ball, Thomas 194, 323
Bankston, Zach 306–7
Barclay, William 114
Barker, Stephen 14
Barr, David L. 191

Bartchy, S. Scott 181–82
Barthes, Roland 111
Bassi, Karne 20, 22
Baumgarten, Alexander Gottlieb 252–53
Baumgartner, Kabria 47
Bazan, B. Carlos 2
Bazopoulou-Kyrkanidou, Euterpe 302
Bazzanna, Giovanni 156, 158, 170, 266
Bearden, Romare 251, 281
Bell, Andrew J. E. 185
Bell, Dorian 6
Bell, Sinclair 184
Bellis, Alice Ogden 251
Belvedere, Apollo 254
Bentley, Jerry H. 9
Berlinerblau, Jacques 19
Bernal, Martin 76, 292
Berry, Diana Ramey 165
Best, Paul 212
Bhambra, Gurminder K. 54
Blair, Elena Duvergès 229
Blanton, Ward 8
Bledstein, Burton J. 10
Bloom, Harold 14
Blount, Brian K. 91
Blum, Edward 254
Blumell, Lincoln H. 305
Bock, Darrell L. 4
Bodel, John 113, 179
Boer, Roland 222
Bohlinger, Travis 99
Boin, Douglas 6, 11–13, 20, 24, 329–36
Bond, Sarah 7, 250
Bonnet, Charles 72
Bonnett, Max 160

Modern Authors Index

Bookidis, Nancy 263
Borgen, Peder 7
Borges, Jorge Luis 9
Børresen, Kari E. 223–24
Boruchoff, David A. 19
Botha, Pieter, J. J. 13
Botting, Eileen Hunt 20
Bowden, John 99
Boyarin, Daniel 8
Brace, C. Loring 85
Bradley, Keith 180–84
Bradley, Mark 297
Brand, Dionne 58
Bray, Gerald R. 131
Brennan, Maura 302
Brettler, Mark Zvi 8
Briggs, Sheila 132, 183
Brockliss, William 281, 301
Brooten, Bernadette 19, 41, 53–54, 57, 107, 124, 183, 234
Brophy, Alfred L. 45
Brunner, O. 219
Bryce, James 18
Buckland, W. W. 162
Buckner, Candace 106
Buell, Denise Kimber 21, 24, 39–64, 124, 138, 155–58, 166, 247, 253, 255, 279, 282, 286, 316, 325, 337, 339
Bultmann, Rudolf 131
Bregman, Rutger 204
Brown, J. T. 108
Brown, Thomas J. 194
Bueno, André 298
Burke, Sean D. 66, 176
Burstein, Stanley 73
Burton, Paul 20
Butler, Judith 127, 222–23, 231, 239–40, 253
Butler, Octavia 39, 56
Butler, Shane 261–62
Byron, Gay L. 22, 24, 40, 54, 65–82, 89, 130, 183, 251, 280, 291–92, 324, 338, 344
Byron, Lord 253
Cain, Andrew 304
Callahan, Allen Dwight 40, 182, 190, 203–16, 281, 294, 324, 330, 332–34, 338, 344
Cameron, Averil 255
Camp, John McK. 231
Campbell, Beatrix 220–21, 240
Campbell, James T. 45
Cancik, Hubert 219
Carey, Greg 190–91
Carson, D. A. 5
Carter, Warren 13, 17
Castelli, Elizabeth 260
Chandler, John W. 47
Chapman, Honora 6
Charles, Ronald 183
Chauduri, Pramit 281
Chazan, Robert 8
Cheah, Pheng 22
Chow, Rey 15
Chuh, Kandice 255–56, 350–51
Clark, Elizabeth A. 48
Clavel, F. 84
Cobb, L. Stephanie 110
Cody, Jane M. 187
Coetzee, J. M. 18
Cohn, Samuel 84
Coles, Robert 210
Collins, Chuck 211
Collins, Derek 263
Collins, John J. 7, 108, 190
Cone, James H. 132
Connolly, Joy 343–54
Connolly, William E. 22, 24
Conybeare, Catherine 12
Conze, Werner 235
Cook, A. B. 5
Coolidge, Mary 95
Courier, Cyril 297
Cox, Karen L. 194
Craig, John 213
Cramer, J. A. 304
Crane, Susan A. 2
Crawley, Ashton 252, 255–58, 261, 269
Crenshaw, Kimberlé 66
Crosby, Molly Caldwell 88

Crossan, John Dominic	188	Elm, Susanna	13
Crossley, James G.	20	Emberling, Geoff	72–73, 76
Currie, William	89	Engberg-Pedersen, Troels	8, 266
D'Angelo, Mary Rose	142, 144	Engel, A. J.	2
Dann, Otto	219–20, 236, 239	Euben, J. Peter	15, 20, 22
Darnton, Robert	112	Eurell, John-Christian	259–60
Darwin, Charles	52	Evans, Hubert	16–17
De Jonge, Casper	265, 267	Eyl, Jennifer	266
De Souza, Philip	188	Fairweather, William	7
De Vos, Craig Steven	144	Faraji, Salim	77–78
Deissmann, Adolf	113–14	Farrar, Frederic W.	108
Denecker, Tim	262	Farrington, Lisa	248
Denison, Jim	99	Felder, Cain Hope	66, 77
Denton, Daniel	86	Ferguson, Roderick	250, 351
Derrida, Jacques	13–14, 21	Finley, Moses I.	177–80, 182
Descartes, René	224, 252	Finnis, John	19
deSilva, Daniel	192	Fisher, Marjorie M.	68–72
Dillon, Matthew P. J.	301	Fitzmyer, Joseph A.	8
Donaldson, Terrance	8	Flannery, Helen	211
Douglas, Mary	88	Flemming, Rebecca	137, 297
Douglas, Kelly Brown	255	Fontenrose, Joseph Eddy	320
Douglass, Frederick	175, 194–95, 307, 323	Formisano, Marco	255
Dow, Jamie	300	Fotopoulos, John	268
Du Bois, W. E. B.	75, 194	Foucault, Michel	4, 9, 14–15, 123, 338
Duarte, Eduardo	347	Fox, Arminta	141, 259
Duff, Arnold Mackay	178	Frankfurter, David	263
Dugan, Kelly P.	307	Fraser, Nancy	221–22, 239–40
Duncan-Jones, R. P.	297	Fredriksen, Paula	8
Dunkelgrün, Theodor	6	Freud, Sigmund	14
Dunn, John	347	Friedrich, Nestor Paulo	192
Durkheim, Émile	10	Friesen, Steven J.	191
Dwoskin, Elizabeth	99	Fry, Darlene	301
Eagleton, Terry	14–16	Frye, Northrop	14, 111
Eastman, Susan	132	Fukuda-Parr, Sakiko	219
Ebbeke, O. G.	3	Gadza, Elaine	253
Edwards, James	23	Gafney, Wilda C.	66
Edwards, M. T.	302, 304	Gager, John G.	6
Ehrhart, Samuel D.	94	Gagnon, Jennifer M.	303
Ehrman, Bart	112, 114	Gaisford, Dean	17
Widinow, Esther	263	Gallia, Andrew B.	177
Eisenbaum, Pamela	133	Garber, Marjorie	301
Eliot, T. S.	5	Gardner, Catherine	234, 297–98
Elliott, J. K.	160	Garland, Robert	301–3
Ellis, Heather	2, 4	Garrett, Susan	193
		Garrison, Irene Peirano	12

Modern Authors Index

Gamwell, Lynn	14	Hall, Donald E.	248
Garlake, Peter	74	Hall, Edith	23
Garnsey, Peter	158	Halperin, David M.	123
Gaventa, Beverly	66, 78, 132	Hammermeister, Kaim	252–53
Georgi, Dieter	254	Hardt, Michael	19
Gerber, Albrecht	114	Hardwick, Lorna	20
Gerdmar, Anders	8	Harlow, Barbara	17
Gevaert, Bert	302	Harper, Kyle	135
Gibbon, Edward	17, 88, 204	Harper, Kyle	184
Gilbert, Gary A.	187	Harris, Leslie M.	45
Giubilini, Alberto	301	Harris, William V.	112, 260

Glancy, Jennifer A.   24, 40, 107, 135–36, 140, 144, 155–73, 183–84, 193, 281, 293, 316–17, 338

		Harrison, Stephen	20
		Hartin, Patrick J.	163

Hartman, Saidiya   40, 58, 125–30, 136–37, 140–41, 144, 162, 290–91, 294

Glazebrook, Allison	135	Hartmann, Benjamin	113, 305–6

Harrill, J. Albert   107, 156, 162, 179–80, 183

Godsey, William D.	6		
Gold, Martin B.	96	Harvey, Paul	254
Goldhill, Simon	4, 6–7, 12, 50	Hattersley, Michael E.	7
Goldsmith, Kenneth	112	Haubold, Johannes	280
Goldsworthy, Adrian	292–93	Haynes, Joyce	69–70
Goodey, Chris F.	302–3	Heerink, M. A. J.	20
Gordon, Richard	264	Hegel, Georg Wilhelm Friedrich	7–8, 75
Gorodeisky, Karen	253		
Gosepath, Stefan	218, 224–26, 239	Hellevik, Ottar	219
Graetz, F.	93	Hengel, Martin	7
Grafton, Anthony	2, 6	Hidalgo, Jacqueline	105, 127
Gratiosi, Barbara	250	Higgins, Lesley	12
Graybill, Rhiannon	145	Hill, Robert Charles	305
Green, Ashbel	88	Hilton, John	17
Green, Mira	137	Hinchliff, Peter	12
Greenwood, Emily	54, 250, 281	Hinks, Peter	282
Greer, Rowan A.	305	Hintze, F.	68, 72
Grieser, Alexandra	251–52	Hisey, Alan J.	108
Gross, Ariela	162, 165	Hitchcock, F. R. M.	260
Gruen, Erich	6	Hodge, Caroline Johnson	1–38, 134
Guillory, John	348	Hoke, Jimmy	132
Gupta, Nijay K.	13		
Gurd, Sean	253, 261	Hölderin, Johann Christian Friedrich	252
Gwynne, G. J.	108		
Gwyther, Anthony	190	Honig, Bonnie, H.	14
Habinek, Thomas	112	Hong, Grace	351
Haines-Eitzen, Kim	113	Hope, Valerie	185, 188
Hajdin, Mane	224	Hopkins, Keith	181

Haley, Shelley P.   24, 39, 41, 53–55, 57, 67, 124, 250, 255, 282, 289–96, 344

		Hopkins, Pauline	56
		Horsfall, Nicholas	112, 116

Horsley, Richard   13, 107, 179, 182, 191
Houston, Drusilla Dunjee   71–72
Howard, Thomas Albert   2
Howard-Brook   190
Howley, Joe   112–13
Hsu, Katherine Lu   24, 337–42
Hughes, Jessica   109
Huntington, Samuel P.   20
Hurtado, Larry   9
Inglehart, R.   219
Ipsen, Avaren   135, 137
Irigaray, Luce   14
Ivarsson, Frederik   133–34
Isaac, Benjamin   53
Jackson, Zakkiyah Iman   155, 157, 170
Jacques, Jeremiah   99
James, Marlon   39
James, Patrick   4
Jemisin, N. K.   39
Jennings, Willie James   250, 256
Jensen, Liz   39
Jensen, Uffa   6
Johnson, Luke Timothy   5, 13
Johnson, Walter   165
Johnson, William A.   112
Johnston, Jay   251–52
Jones, Christopher P.   12, 193
Jones, James H.   93
Jones, Nathaniel B.   321
Joseph, Timothy   1–38, 279–88
Joshel, Sandra R.   176, 181, 183
Jowett, Benjamin   12
Junior, Nyasha   108
Kaczor, Christopher   301
Kallis, Aristotle   250
Kamen, Deborah   124, 138–40, 142–45, 183–84, 319–20
Kampen, Natalie Boymel   188
Kant, Immanuel   347
Kars, Marjoleine   325
Kartzow, Marianne   159, 163
Käsemann, Ernst   131
Kearney, Richard   14
Keddie, G. Anthony   187, 189
Keel, Terence   52
Keller, George Frederick   97
Khawaja, Noreen   247
Kim, Yung Suk   67
Kittredge, Cynthia Briggs   131
Keats, John   253
Keita, Maghan   72
Keith, Chris   107
Kelley, Shawn   254–55, 301–3, 315
Kim, Hyun Jin   298
King, Martin Luther, Jr.   213, 324
Kiple, Kenneth   93
Kiple, Virginia   93
Kippenberg, Hans G.   219–20
Klawans, Jonathan   92
Klein, Herbert S.   2
Klein, William   260
Kleiner, Diane E.   321
Klijn, A. F. J.   160
Kloppenborg, John S.   8, 236, 238–39
Knust, Jennifer   132, 135, 276
Koester, Craig   190, 193, 299
Koester, Helmut   204, 333
Kolstø, Pål   6
Konstan, David   251, 254, 306
Koselleck, Reinhart   218–19
Kotrosits, Maia   250, 254
Kousser, Rachel   185
Kraus, Thomas J.   3
Kraut, Alan M.   86–88, 92, 96, 99
Kraybill, J. Nelson   188
Kuehnast, Kathleen   177
Kwok Pui-lan   133
Lachmann, Karl   12
Laes, Christian   301–3
Lalitha, Jayachitra   16
Lamb, M. L.   303
Lambert, Michael   17–18
Lampe, Peter   142
Lang, Mabel   231
Langton, Daniel R.   8, 14
Larcher, F. R.   303
Lasswell, Harold   212
Lavan, Myles   185–86
Leclant, Jean   293
Lecznar, Heidi   281

Lee, Erika	98	Marks, J.	302
Leonard, Miriam	5, 7, 14	Markel, Howard	94
Lepore, Jill	16	Markovits, Daniel	228
LeVen, Pauline	262	Marrou, Henri	255
Levene, Mark	39	Marshall, Jill	237–38
Lévi-Strauss, Claude	301	Marshall, John W.	8
Levin-Richardson, Sarah	124, 138–42, 144–45	Martin, Clarice J.	66, 135–36, 145, 191
		Martin, Dale B.	135, 182, 297, 303
Levine, Amy-Jill	8	Martin, Thomas R.	24, 297–314
Levine, Molly	76	Martindale, Charles	280
Libero, Lorentana de	110	Marx, Karl	179, 344
Liew, Tat-siong Benny	1–38, 133, 297	Mather, Cotton	86
Lin, Yii-Jan	8, 24, 41, 83–104, 280–81, 297–98, 300, 338, 344	Mather, Increase	86
		Mattern, Susan P.	187
Lintott, Andrew	191	Matthews, Dylan	204
Lipsius, Richard A.	160	Matthews, Shelly	128, 132
Littman, Robert J.	89	Maurice, F. D.	3–4
Lo Cascio, Elio	298	Maurizio, Lisa	320
Locke, John	224	Mazama, Ama	72
Long, Thomas L.	84	Mbembe, Achille	257
Longstaff, Thomas R. W.	3	McCammon, Sarah	19
Lopes, Rodolfo	225–26	McCoskey, Denise	41–43, 53, 282, 286
Lopez, Davina	176–77, 187–90	McDermott, William C.	306
Lorde, Audre	110–11, 289	McKeown, Niall	178, 180–81
Lovelace, Vanessa	66, 130	McKnight, Scot	5
Loveless, Natalie	255	McMaster, Geoff	99
Lugones, Maria	57	Meier, G. F.	252
Lushkov, Ayelet Haimson	281	Melcher, Sarah	107
MacAskill, Ewen	19	Melosi, Martin V.	87
Macgregor, G. H. C.	7	Menand, Louis	345, 353
Machado, Dominic	24, 286, 315–28	Mendelssohn, Moses	252
MacLean, Rose	319	Mendonca, Megan	11
Madison, James	203	Metzger, Bruce	112
Maillot, Aristide	248	Meyer, Birgit	251, 258
Malamud, Margaret	19–20, 43, 54, 75, 286	Michelakis, Pantelis	20
		Miéville, China	343–45
Mandela, Nelson	18	Mill, John Stuart	111
Manhardt, Laurie Watson	108	Millar, Fergus	237
Marchal, Joseph A.	19, 24, 40, 123–54, 183, 280, 290–91, 338, 344	Miller, Anna	235–38
		Miller, Patricia Cox	267
Marchand, Suzanne	43, 51	Miller, William I.	88
Marcus, Bernard	211	Minerva, Francesca	301
Marganne, Marie-Hélène	109	Mitchill, Samuel Latham	90
Mariev, Sergei	255	Mittag, Achim	299
Mark, Joshua J.	68, 70	Modica, Joseph B.	5

Montserrat, Dominic	144	Ober, Josiah	15
Moore, Philip	325	Økland, Jorann	24, 41, 217–46, 281, 294, 324, 330, 332, 334, 338, 344
Moore, Stephen	5, 8, 11, 43, 57, 193		
Moralee, J.	334	Okorafor, Nnedi	39
Morgan, Allison, C.	351	Oldson, William O.	6
Morgan, Robert	4	Olyan, Saul	107
Morris, Jeremy	3, 46	Ong, Hughson T.	8
Morrison, Toni	289	Orrells, Daniel	54
Morse, Adam	281	Ortega, Mariana	57
Morse, Samuel, F. B.	92	Osiek, Carolyn	236
Moss, Candida R.	24, 41, 91, 105–22, 280–81, 297, 301, 305–7, 324, 338, 344	Owesen, Ingeborg	224
		Padilla Peralta, Dan-el	77, 250
Most, Glenn W.	2, 6, 12	Page, Hugh, Jr.	78
Moten, Fred	257	Parchami, Ali	17–19
Mothoagae, Ithumeleng D.	17	Parham, Marisa	66–67, 78
Moule, C. F. D.	114	Park, Arum	302
Mouritsen, Henrik	319	Parker, Angela N.	107, 132
Moxnes, Halvor	15	Parker, Grant	18, 53–54
Moyer, Ian	281	Parker, Johnson	165
Müller-Sievers, Helmut	12	Parker, Robert	297
Müller-Wille, Staffan	219–20	Parsons, Mikeal C.	107
Münzer, Friedrich	306	Patterson, Orlando	168, 179–80, 182, 306
Murnaghan, Sheila	176		
Mutschler, Fritz-Heiner	299	Peers, Glenn	255
Myerowitz Levine, Molly	54	Penrose, Walter D., Jr.	301
Myles, Robert J.	4	Pentcheva, Bissera V.	262
Naas, Michael	21	Peppard, Michael	260
Nagy, Gregory	302	Perkins, Judith	110, 159
Nakamura, David	99	Perkins, William	303
Nanos, Mark D.	8	Perloff, Richard M.	300
Nasrallah, Laura Salah	24, 40, 113, 136, 144, 247–77, 279–80, 317, 324, 338	Perry, Jonathan S.	177–78
		Pesthy, Monica	162
Negri, Antonio	19	Petersen, Lauren Hackworth	183, 321
Nelson, R.	255	Phillips, Jacke	68, 70–71
Newson, Ryan Andrew	194	Piketty, Thomas	203, 206
Neutel, Karin	234	Pinault, Jody Robin	298
Ngai, Sianne	256	Pinnix, Aaron	280
Nicholas, Barry	168	Pippin, Tina	193
Nicolet, Claude	187	Plumer, Eric	303–5
Nietzsche, Friedrich	214, 251, 254	Pollock, Sheldon	346
Nooter, Sarah	261	Ponessa, Joseph	108
Noy, David	299	Pormann, Peter E.	22
Nussbaum, Martha	19	Porter, James I.	5, 251, 265–67
O'Connor, Murphy	114	Poser, Rachel	76
Oakes, Peter	142, 144	Postlethwaite, N.	302

Modern Authors Index

Powell, John H. 88
Pritchard, James B. 297
Proper, Emberson Edward 88
Punt, Jeremy 5
Quigley, Muireann 164
Ramsby, Teresa R. 187
Rancière, Jacques 251–53
Rathbone, Dominic 109
Readings, Bill 345–48
Reay, Brendon 113
Record, Robert 224
Redondo, Jordi 6, 8
Reece, Steve 107–8, 111, 113–14, 303, 305
Reimarus, Hermann 2
Reinhartz, Adele 8, 78
Reisner, George 72
Renan, Ernst 207
Reynolds, Benjamin E. 190
Richards, E. Randolph 113–14
Richlin Amy 123, 136
Richmann, Christopher 19
Rinon, Yoav 302
Robinson, Nathan J. 301
Rodgers, Zuleika 6
Rojas-Flores, Gonzalo 191
Roller, Otto 114
Rose, Martha Lynn 109–10, 301–3
Rosenberg, Charles E. 93
Rosenthal, Franz 22
Rousseau, Jean-Jacques 225
Roynon, Tessa 54
Rummel, Erika 12
Rustin, Bayard 302
Sadler, Rodney S., Jr. 22
Said, Edward W. 16, 21, 344–45
Salés, Luis J. 71
Saller, Richard P. 184, 306
Samana, Evelyne 301
Samuelsson, Gunnar 108
Sandage, Scott 195
Sanders, Todd 260–61
Santini-Ritt, Mimi 69–70
Satlow, Michael L. 193
Savage, Kirk 195

Schäfer, Peter 6, 8
Schatkin, Margaret A. 305
Schein, Seth L. 23
Schelling, Friedrich Wilhelm Joseph 252
Schipper, Jeremy 107–8
Schlegel, Friedrich 254
Schüssler Fiorenza, Elisabeth 20, 53–54, 125, 136, 142, 237, 254, 259
Schweitzer, Tyrrell 254
Scott, James C. 175, 319–20
Scott, Joan, W. 225
Scroggs, Robin 19
Segal, Alan F. 8
Segovia, Fernando F. 20
Seitz, Christopher R. 23
Sen, Amartya 218
Sevenster, Jan Nicholaas 8
Severy-Hoven, Beth 187
Shaner, Katherine A. 107, 132, 144, 183
Sharpe, Christina 55, 57–59, 128
Shelley, Braxton 258, 261, 269
Sheppard, Gerald T. 303
Sherwood, Yvonne 8, 11, 43, 57
Shinnie, P. L. 72
Sick, David H. 12
Sider, Robert D. 21
Singer, Peter 301
Sinopoli, Carla M. 54
Smil, Vaclav 19
Smith, Abraham 24, 40, 66, 77, 175–202, 281, 316, 319–25, 338
Smith, E. H. 89–90
Smith, Mitzi J. 16, 67, 130, 132, 158–59
Smith, Shanell T. 128, 140, 193
Snowden, Frank 69, 73
Sobrino, Jon 4
Sontag, Susan 83–84
Sorett, Josef 255
Sosin, Joshua D. 319
Spickard, Paul 86
Spittler, Janet 169
Spivak, Gayatri Chakravorty 22, 351
Spring, Gardiner 83, 92
Starr, Raymond J. 112

Ste. Croix, G. E. M. de	203, 205	Vogels, H. J.	304
Stendahl, Krister	133, 261	Vogt, Johannes	177
Sterling, Gregory	8	Vogt, Joseph	178–79, 181–82
Stillinger, Jack	111	Voinot, Jacques	109
Stock, Wiebke-Marie	255	von Tischendorf, Constantin	3
Stott, John R. W.	108	von Wilamowitz	251
Stout, Arthur B.	96	Wadman, Meredith	83
Stover, Timothy J.	20	Wake, Peter	7
Stowers, Stanley K.	5, 133, 235	Walcott, Derek	280–81
Strauss, David Friedrich	3, 8	Walker, Alice	130
Stray, Christopher	9	Walker, David	281–87
Strobel, A.	114	Wallach, John R.	15
Stroud, Ronald S.	263	Walsh, Robyn Faith	115
Stuckenbruck, Loren T.	190	Walters, Tracey	54, 124
Stuurman, Siep	225	Ward, Julie K.	234, 238
Swete, H. B.	304–5	Wardle, David	17
Tacoma, Laurens	298–99	Wasdin, Katherine	281
Taylor, Charles	14	Watson, Patricia	109
Thatcher, Tom	3	Weinstock, Stefan	186
Thiselton, Anthony C.	260–61	Wells, Richard	14
Thomas, Darryl C.	315	Welsby, Derek A.	68, 72
Thomas, Eric A.	127	Westermann, William Linn	178, 181
Thomas, Page A.	3	Wet, Chris L. de	159, 166
Thomas, Richard	281	Wheeler-Reed, David	135
Thompkins, Daniel P.	178	White, Jonathan, W.	195
Thornton, Russell	86	Whitehead, Alfred North	11, 321
Thumiger, Chiara	302	Wiedemann, T. E. J.	179
Timpanaro, Sebastiano	12	Wilder, Craig Steven	46–47
Tolnay, Stewart E.	93	Wilkins, Michael	340–41
Török, L.	68, 72	Wilkins, William Henry	299
Treggiari, Susan	306	Williams, Catrin	3
Trentin, Lisa	109–10, 301	Wilson, Brittany	66
Tupamahu, Ekaputra	256	Winckelmann, Johannes	248, 251, 253–54
Turner, Nigel	107–8		
Twomey, Jay	14	Winsburg, Rex	112
Tyner, Artika Renee	301	Wimbush, Vincent	20, 41, 52, 54–55, 57
Tytler, James	90	Winterer, Caroline	4, 9
Ulloa, Jazmine	299	Wire, Antionette	131, 136, 141, 237, 259
Underwood, Doug	19	Witherington, Ben, III	109
van Straten, Folkert T.	109	Witzke, Serena S.	135
Varone, Antonio	147	Wolf, Friedrich August	6
Vasunia, Phiroze	17	Wong, Brittany	301
Verboven, Koenraad	306	Woodruff, Archibald	190
Verrips, Jojada	251, 258	Wynter, Sylvia	39–40, 51–52, 55, 58, 255–56, 345, 350–51
Versnel, Henk	263, 268		

Yamauchi, Edwin M.	71–72
Yarboro Collins, Adela	191, 268
Youtie, Herbert C.	106
Yellow Horse, Aggie J.	99
Yong, Amos	107
Yovel, Yirmiyahu	7–8
Yung, Judy	98
Yusoff, Katherine	58
Zahn, Theodor	107–98
Zanker, Paul	321
Zelnick-Abramovitz, R.	319
Zetzel, James E.	2, 6
Zimmerman, Jonathan	298
Zuckerberg, Donna	20, 282

Subject Index

#SayHerName, 65–66
ability, ableism. *See* disability
abolition, 46–47, 74, 281–82
adoption, 157
aesthetic, -s, 68, 184, 227, 247–48, 250–69, 279, 295, 324–25, 338
    critique, 256, 280
    racial, -ized, 255, 258
affect, -ive, 127, 129, 132, 138, 143, 145
    queer affect, 132
Africa, 17, 22, 46, 52, 65–68, 71–78, 84, 194, 255, 257, 283, 285–86, 289, 291–92, 325, 331
    African diaspora, 55, 157
    African women, 77–78, 248, 291, 293
    Africana studies, 44, 53, 72
    Afrocentrism, 56
African American, 43, 47, 67, 74, 93, 258, 286, 301
agency, 132, 137–38, 183
alienation, 182, 184, 190, 306
American Colonization Society, 46–47
American Council of Learned Societies, 24, 156
American Philological Association, 48
Amherst College, 47
androcentrism, 221
animality, 84, 157, 181, 183, 186, 323
anthropogenesis, 155
anthropology, 5, 156
anti-Judaism, 2, 6, 8, 133, 344
anti-Semitism. *See* anti-Judaism
antiracism, 42, 124, 128, 130, 289
apocalypse, 83–84, 86, 90–91, 97, 99, 127, 131, 143, 190–91, 204, 206, 280

apologetics, 4–5
appropriation, 325
archaeology, 11, 50, 72–73, 78, 183
art, 50, 252, 254–55, 280, 332, 345
    history, 248
Asian, -ness, 99
    Asian American Pacific Islander, 59, 99
    Stop AAPI Hate, 99
assemblage, 158, 164–65, 169–70
assimilation, 94, 162, 350
authority, 10, 16, 18, 125, 141, 146, 187, 194, 230, 237, 304, 338–39
    biblical, 5
    scientific, 52
    women's, 241
Axum, 53
Azusa Street, 268
baptism, 65–66, 77, 157–58, 160, 170, 210, 235
barbarian, 133, 187, 251, 284, 286, 299, 320, 329, 331
Beyond Canon project, 247
Black, -ness, 43, 46, 58–59, 73–74, 77, 84, 89, 93, 126, 157, 178, 251, 255, 257, 268, 281–83, 290, 295, 315, 324–25
    antiblackness, 289, 294
    Black feminism, 53
    Black women, 54, 126, 290, 293
Black Lives Matter, 78
blindness, 69, 109–10, 303
body, -ies, 110–12, 128, 131–32, 134, 157–59, 161, 165, 167–70, 184, 191, 204, 221–22, 248, 256–58, 262, 265–66, 291, 303, 338

Boston Museum of Fine Arts, 72, 76
Brazil, 181, 266
Bridging Divides Initiative, 307
British Museum, 69–70
Buffet, Warren, 206, 212–13
Caesar, 13, 69, 109, 186, 285, 293–94
canon, -ical, -ization, 15, 21, 52, 114, 141, 144, 207, 247–48
capitalism, 12, 40, 221, 239, 330
   racial, 315
censorship, 290
census, 212
China, -ese, 94–96, 98, 299
Christian, -ity, -ization, -s, 2, 4–5, 7, 15, 42–43, 45, 47–51, 65, 71, 79, 84, 92, 110, 159, 190, 204, 258–59, 283–84, 329, 331–35
   anti-Christianity, 83
   early Christianity, 49, 67–68, 77–78, 107, 155, 157–58, 182–83, 189, 217, 226, 230, 234, 238, 260, 262–63, 316, 344–45
   European, 51
   identity, 167
church, 2–4, 96,
   Black, 258
citizenship, 41, 48, 96, 99, 139, 176, 189, 191, 205, 217, 225, 228–31, 234–36, 299, 301, 329–30, 334–35, 343
   naturalization, 96
civilization, civilized, 20, 52, 74–75, 227, 331
class, -ism, 114, 179, 181, 203, 213, 232, 236–38, 291, 294, 325, 330, 332, 351
   aristocracy, 205, 230, 254
   working, 205, 281
classification, 21, 84, 165, 195, 248, 297
Cleopatra, 293
climate crisis, 40, 58, 206, 344
coercion, 129, 131, 135, 137, 140, 143–45, 159, 163, 338
College of the Holy Cross, 23
colonialism, 16–20, 22, 45–47, 85–88, 94, 114, 116, 133, 146, 248, 253, 256–57, 283, 334

colorism, 73, 295
Columbia University, 178
Columbus, Christopher, 16
comparative studies, 175, 177, 179–81
conquest, 192–93, 299, 321
consent, 129, 131, 137, 143–45, 338
conversion, 66, 78, 260
COVID-19, 19, 22, 59, 84, 99, 105, 211, 222, 279, 315, 342
criminalization, 126
critical race theory, 290
   critical race feminism, 290
criticism, 3–5, 12, 50, 52
   form, 3
   historical, 3–4, 52, 54, 67, 259
   literary, 5, 14
   narrative, 5
   source, 2–4, 12
   textual, 2–3, 8, 12
crucifixion, 107, 158, 189, 193
cultural memory, 177, 184, 193–94, 321
curriculum, 4, 48, 282, 346
curse tablet, -s, 262–64, 270, 280, 324
democracy, 217, 222, 229, 231, 233, 237–38, 330, 334
demons, 89
desire, 128–29, 132, 135–36, 138–39, 141, 143, 184, 262
disease, 19–20, 41, 83–88, 90–94, 96–99, 108, 298, 300, 329, 338. *See also* plague
disability, 13, 24, 57, 59, 83, 88, 105–11, 115, 224, 251, 255, 280–1, 297, 300–3, 307, 324
   critical disability theory, 108
   religious model of disability, 108
   studies, 105
disciple, -ship, 208, 318, 341–42
discourse, 10, 85, 106, 112, 155, 157–9, 176–7, 184–5, 187, 207, 227, 237, 254, 266, 290–1, 298, 338, 346
displacement, 49
diversity, -ification, 56, 346, 351
domination, dominance, 84, 123, 156–59, 161, 170, 175, 179–80, 183–85, 187, 189, 191–93, 203, 319–20, 322–23, 338

Subject Index

economy, -ics, 12–13, 40, 77, 84, 110, 114, 205–7, 219, 222, 228, 252, 324, 330, 333, 348, 350
    inequality, 23–24, 207, 214, 281, 324, 330, 333, 351
ecumenism, 3
education, 4–5, 41, 43, 46, 52–53, 56, 233–34, 264, 283, 285, 315, 324–25, 331, 337–42, 345–49
    doctoral, 42, 45, 56, 337, 339, 351
    graduate, 44, 325, 338, 348–49, 350
    seminary, 45, 50
    undergraduate, 41, 44, 338, 352
Egypt, -ian, 42, 66, 69, 72–73, 75–76, 89, 112, 283, 285, 291–92, 294, 298
ekklēsia, 41, 217, 232, 235–38, 240–51, 267
elitism, 56, 112, 137, 139, 175–78, 180–81, 184, 187, 189, 191, 205, 214, 261, 264, 266, 269, 280, 321–22, 330
embodiment, 115, 123–24, 127, 145, 157, 164, 262, 265
empire criticism, 5
Enlightenment, 2, 7–8, 52, 225, 330
environmental studies, 44, 59
epidemic, -iology, 83–84, 86, 297
epistemology, 40, 57, 258, 290, 325
equality, 40, 74, 159, 217–41, 301, 318, 324, 329–30, 332, 338, 344, 350
    gender, 219, 224, 226, 228–29, 234, 240–41
equity, 223
eschatology, 88, 90, 239
ethic, -al, -s, 1, 4, 15, 39, 41, 44, 125, 156, 210, 223, 227–28, 234–35, 279, 281–84, 287, 325
Ethiopia, 53, 56, 65–72, 75, 77–78, 89, 251, 291–92, 298
ethnicity, 13, 40–42, 56, 66–67, 72, 74, 77, 167, 178, 224, 236, 251, 253, 299–300, 331, 334, 351
eugenics, 294
eunuch, 65–67, 77–78
Europe, -ean, 52, 55, 76, 85–86, 93–95, 218–19, 221, 224, 250, 345, 348, 350

Europe, -ean (*cont.*)
    Eurocentrism, 53, 67, 291, 350
exclusivity, 23, 39, 96, 320, 335
execution, 161, 165, 204, 283
exorcism, 160–61
exploitation, 105, 116, 307
faith, 2–3, 5
fantasy, 162–63
feminism, 14, 42, 59, 124, 126, 128, 130, 136, 220–22, 224, 234, 290, 294
Feminist Sexual Ethics Project, 54, 57
feminization, 124, 289
fiction, 39–40, 59, 343
    speculative, 39, 59, 343
Floyd, George, 289
Forbes, 211
foreign, -er, -ness, 85–87, 93, 95, 97–99, 231, 297, 299–300, 307, 329, 331, 333, 335, 338, 343–44
formalism, 5
freedom, 126–27, 129, 139, 219, 232, 315, 318–19
French Revolution, 225
friendship, 229, 303, 307, 317
Gates, Bill and Melinda, 206, 212
geography, 74
gender, 13, 40, 44, 57, 66, 79, 123–24, 127, 133, 135–36, 176, 181, 187–88, 190, 193, 217, 219–20, 224–28, 233–37, 240, 247, 253, 257, 265, 289, 330, 332
    slippage, 176
genocide, 194
gentile, 133–34, 145, 291
Germany, 4, 186, 194, 253
global, -ization, 345–48
glossai, 256, 259–63, 267–70
Goths, 329, 331, 334
Greece, 6, 22, 75, 89–90, 176, 181, 217, 225, 286, 319–20
    Athens, 179, 217, 230–31, 233, 238–39, 301, 330, 334
    Carthage, 285–86
    history, 320
    literature, 18, 43, 73, 110, 210, 297, 339

Subject Index

Greece (cont.)
  mythology, 14, 302
  Sparta, 225, 230, 283, 285
Hagar, 144, 157
Haiti, 88, 285, 289
Hamilton College, 53
haunting, 66, 78, 254
Hawai'i, 46
Hebrew Bible, 23
hegemony, -ic, 55
Hellenism, -ization, 7–8, 68, 72, 74, 79, 294
hierarchy, -ization, 17, 23, 66, 74, 124, 145, 156–58, 168, 170, 217–48, 223, 225, 233–37, 251, 254, 261, 281, 316, 321, 323, 235, 332, 338–39, 342, 344
  gender, 241
historical Jesus, 3, 107, 254
history, 3, 6, 11, 41, 50, 53, 55–56, 67, 72–75, 79, 125–26, 156, 175, 177, 179, 186, 194, 204, 218–20, 226, 237, 239, 250, 279, 285, 289, 297, 315, 319, 324–25, 331, 333, 335, 344, 347–49, 353
  counterhistory, 125, 128, 130, 181
historical consciousness, 2
HIV/AIDS, 84
housing, 222
Holocaust, 8
homophobia, 294
humanism, 5, 9, 14, 51, 56, 58, 179, 345, 348–49, 353
humanities, 9, 41, 44, 47, 50, 52, 56–58, 224, 250, 301, 346–49, 352
human, -ity, -ization, 40, 52, 55–56, 75, 132, 145, 155–59, 166, 168, 170, 179, 204, 207, 232, 256, 268, 281, 286, 300, 316
  dehumanizing, 183, 283
  nonhumanity, 40, 157, 159, 170, 268
hybridity, 40
ideology, 13, 52, 72, 113, 115, 187, 189, 193, 213, 239, 261, 282, 294
identity, 14, 66–67, 95, 112, 165–7, 183, 227–28, 231, 299–300, 320, 344, 350
  racial, 45

immigration, -nts, 83, 85–87, 94–96, 98, 280–81, 297, 299, 301, 324, 330, 350
imperialism, 18–19, 22, 124–25, 177, 188–89, 237, 250, 332, 350
  visual imperialism, 176–77, 322
incarceration, 18, 98, 126, 160–61, 165, 168, 188, 290–91, 338
inclusivity, 3, 68, 217
India, 17–18, 22, 54, 160, 164, 167
indigeneity, 45–46, 49, 58, 85, 290, 298
  indigenous studies, 44
individualism, 40
Institute for Signifying Scriptures, 55, 57
interdisciplinarity, 24, 57, 325, 337
intersectionality, 146
institution, -alization, 9, 16, 45, 79
invasion, 83, 96
Iraq, 19,
Islam, 20, 22, 83, 92
  Islamophobia, 20
Italy, 298
Iudaios, -oi, 189
Jefferson, Thomas, 284
Jerusalem, 65, 160, 189, 191, 209
  new/New, 19, 85–86, 91, 94, 99, 297, 299, 329, 333
Jim Crow, 48
Journal of Biblical Literature, 105
Journal of Feminist Studies in Religion, 54
Judea, 187
Judaism/Jewish, -ness, 6–8, 20, 71, 92–94, 98, 110, 113, 124, 160, 235, 334
  and Hellenism, 13
  studies, 6
justice, 1, 56, 66, 190, 211, 213, 226–28, 231–34, 240, 268, 281, 290, 300–301, 330, 332–33
  divine punishment, 90–91, 134, 284–86, 297, 303, 307
  gender, 228
  racial, 41–42, 56, 337
  social, 68, 219
kandake, 65–72, 74–78, 280, 291–92, 324
kinship, 143
kleptocracy, 205, 213, 330

knowledge, 10, 17, 39, 41, 289, 337, 346, 351
  blackened, 58
  production of, 9–10
  rewriting of, 41, 345
  scientific, 93, 98
Kush, 53, 68–69, 72–73, 77–79
kyriarchy, 125
land ownership, 203, 330
language, 3, 7–8, 50, 111, 219–20, 224, 250, 261–64, 266–67, 289, 344, 347–50
  African, 17, 53
  Aramaic, 111
  French, 13, 225
  Greek, 3–7, 17, 48–50, 111, 224, 331, 344
  Hebrew, 111, 344
  Latin, 5, 11, 17–18, 48–50
  Norwegian, 223–24, 231, 240
  translation, 12–13
  Urdu, 17
law, 50, 133, 135, 162, 168, 179, 181, 228, 237, 329
liberal arts, 47, 252
liberalism, 105, 156, 218, 222, 224, 241, 316
liberation, 5, 19, 157, 222, 323, 325
liminality, 66
Lincoln, Abraham, 194, 323
linguistics, 3, 6, 9, 11–12, 250, 351
literacy, 107, 112, 114
Louisville Institute, 123
lynching, 132
Mainz Academy of Science and Literature, 178, 181
maleness, 40, 47, 53, 66, 176, 188, 193, 248, 251, 253–56, 265, 280
Manifest Destiny, 94
marginalization, 24, 49, 76, 78, 136–37, 139–41, 145–46, 324, 338, 348, 350
masculinity. *See* maleness
martyrdom, 110, 160, 163
Marxism, 205, 218, 222, 294, 343
McFarland Center for Religion, Ethics, and Culture, 23

meritocracy, 228, 332
Meröe, 68, 70, 73–74, 77–78
Miami University, 42–43
migration, 93, 125, 141, 164
minority, -ization, 43, 78, 141, 203, 279, 334
mission, -ary, 18–19, 49, 86, 108, 110, 114, 160, 290, 317, 333, 345–46
military, 13, 19, 67–69, 71, 74, 77–78, 83, 185, 187, 191, 230–31, 320–21, 338
  divine army, 299
misogyny, 156, 176, 221, 234, 294
modernity, 43
monarchy, 208, 230, 236
  queens, 66–71, 77–78, 289, 291–94, 324
moral, -ity, -izing, 4, 83–85, 91, 97, 126, 176, 183, 190, 192, 218, 290–91, 299, 301, 323, 325, 329–30, 333, 337, 340, 347
  sexual, 135
Moses, 14, 211
mujerista, 59
multiculturalism, 15
music, 257–58, 262, 264, 269
mythology, 3,
narrative, 59, 83, 319, 337
  counternarrative, 125–26, 290, 322, 324
National Republican, 195
nationalism, 7
  white, 193–94
nation, -ality, 44, 57, 228
Native Americans, 45–46, 86
  Mohican nation, 45, 49
nativism, 88
neoliberalism, 12, 221–22, 257
New York Daily Tribune, 96
New York Times, 212
Nigeria, 293
Nubia, 40, 66–68, 70–73, 76, 78–79, 280, 294, 324
numismatics, 187, 192
obedience, 130–31, 136, 143, 317
Oberlin College, 46

Subject Index

objectification, 144, 162–65, 168, 184, 307
oligarchy, 230
Onesimus, 159
ontology, 155–57, 159, 170, 316
oppression, 22, 24, 40, 129, 131, 175, 279, 281–82, 294
  economic, 281, 330, 333
other, -ing, 85–86, 129, 133, 195, 298–300, 307, 323
Oxford University, 194
pagan, -ism, 83, 329
Palestine, 20
parable, 207–8, 210, 333, 340
passion, 133–34, 139, 252, 295
paterfamilias, 208, 250
paternalism, 195, 323
patriarchy, 176, 220–21, 290, 295
patronage, 306–7
penetration, 123–24, 138
persecution, 95, 108, 190
Persia, 230
perversity, 128–29, 133, 135, 140, 146, 206
Pharisee, -aism, 208, 210
philanthropy, 206, 211–14
philology, *see* linguistics.
philosophy, 10, 14, 20, 47, 49–50, 157–58, 193, 220, 224–26, 228, 233–34, 238, 252, 269, 339, 352
people of color, 58, 75, 255, 282–83, 290, 324–25, 349–50
plague, 84–85, 91, 94, 96–98, 298. *See also* disease
pleasure, 135, 163, 226–27, 264
poetry, 4, 253, 260, 262, 264–65, 301
police, 343–44
politic, -al, -s, 1, 13, 16, 19–20, 22, 44, 50, 52, 68, 71, 74, 77–78, 90, 125–26, 131, 136, 176, 185, 188, 218, 223–24, 226, 227–31, 237, 250, 252, 255, 283, 299, 316, 320, 332, 334–35, 347
  of memory, 194
  political violence, 307
polycentrism, 280, 282, 286, 324

Pompeii, 137–39, 141–44, 280
porneia, 124, 130, 134–36, 140–41, 146, 290–91
Portugal, 285–86
positivism, 9, 16
possession, 156, 159–61, 170, 266
posthumanism, 156
power, 21–22, 40, 59, 66, 76, 131, 135, 137, 139, 159, 161, 170, 175, 179–80, 182, 194, 203, 237, 240, 250, 252, 255, 262, 264, 268, 307, 316–17, 319–20, 323, 330, 338–39, 345
poverty, 87–88, 91, 97, 110, 126, 161, 182, 203–5, 210, 230, 299, 335, 344, 350
prejudice, 8, 251, 261, 267, 324, 344
Priapic protocol, 123
primitivism, 94
privilege, 72, 181, 233, 319
professionalization, 2, 4, 8–10, 15–16, 48, 279
  of knowledge, 11
propaganda, 175–77, 184, 188–89, 192, 195, 213, 319, 322. *See also* technology of power
psychology, 14, 49
Puck, 92–94
purity, 91–92, 94, 125, 297, 300
  sexual, 93
Queen of Sheba, 70–71, 75
queerness, 124, 128–30, 349–50. *See also* sexuality
queer studies, 59, 124, 127
rabbinics, 204
race, racism, racialization, 7–8, 16, 18–19, 40–44, 52–53, 55–56, 58, 72, 74, 76, 84–85, 95, 125, 133, 167, 220, 247, 250–51, 253, 257, 282, 289, 291, 294, 298, 315, 324–25, 337, 351
  institutionalized racism, 76
Reconstruction, 48
religion, 17, 49–50, 52, 57, 213, 219, 258, 261, 283, 320, 348
  Greco-Roman, 5, 191–92
  religious studies, 352
Renaissance, 9, 12, 50–51, 294

reparations, 213
research, 58–59, 339
resistance, 130, 138, 181–83, 189–90, 205
respectability, 124, 127, 141, 146
rhetoric, 8, 19, 99, 124, 126, 131–32, 136, 143, 237, 240, 250, 263, 266, 269, 283, 338
rights, 19, 180, 185, 220, 222, 227–28, 231, 301, 318–19
   free speech, 238
   LGBTQIA+, 221
   press, 222
   voting, 289
   women's, 234, 238
ritual, 263, 269–70
Romantic, -ism, 111, 115, 252–54
Rome, Roman Empire, 18–20, 22, 69, 71, 75, 77–79, 140, 158, 175–76, 181, 183, 187, 190, 193, 204–5, 283, 285–86, 292, 294, 297, 319, 321–22, 330–35
   literature, 73
   Pax Romana, 18
   Republic, 185, 321
   Roma, goddess, 187–88
   Romanocentrism, 286
   Romosexuality, 124
   whiteness, 286
sacrifice, 297
science, 3, 9, 16, 50, 59, 84, 93, 157, 206, 224, 345
   and racism, 294
   biology, 8
   mathematical, 224
   natural, 50
   social, 10, 50–51, 59
scribes, 41, 105–8, 111–15, 280, 305–6
secular, -ism, -ization, 50–52, 228
self-control, 134, 139
sensation, sensory experience, sensual perception, 146, 251–52, 257–58, 269
Septuagint, 227, 235, 238
sex, -uality, 13, 15, 19–20, 24, 44, 84, 91, 123–24, 126–28, 133–35, 138–39, 143, 176, 224, 227, 229, 233–34, 291, 344, 349–50

sex, -uality (*cont.*)
   promiscuity, 94
   sex work/labor, 96, 125–26, 135–38, 140–46, 184, 205, 280–81, 291
   sexism. *See* misogyny
   sexual exceptionalism, 124, 133
   sexual vulnerability, 176, 183
   trafficking, 221
silence, 289, 294–95, 335
sin, 91, 96, 109, 133, 136, 157, 299
skepticism, 2, 4
slavery, 13, 18, 24, 46–47, 54, 56, 58, 74, 88, 106–7, 112–16, 124–29, 132, 135–37, 141–45, 155–70, 175–83, 185–86, 189, 191, 193–94, 208, 217, 226, 228, 230, 232–33, 235, 237–38, 280–86, 291, 300–301, 306, 315–19, 321, 323, 334, 338
   freedperson, 113, 306, 321, 325
   literacy among enslaved, 114
   manumission, 306, 316, 318–20
   slave revolution/rebellion, 88
   enslaved Christians, 183
   enslaved persons as prostheses, 113, 166, 318
social location, 291
social mobility, 66, 182
socialism, 233
Society of Biblical Literature, 48
Society of Classical Literature, 42
solidarity, 233
Sophism, 339–41
South Africa, 18
Spain, 16, 285–86
specialization, 8–9, 15, 48, 56, 344
spirit, 157, 159, 170, 256, 265, 267
status, 13, 58, 107, 110, 112, 134, 142, 176, 179, 227, 229, 267, 269, 305, 307, 334, 341
   servile, 317
stereotyping, 125, 136, 176, 183, 193
stigma, -tization, 83, 133, 145–46
stoicism, 214, 225, 238, 266
struggle, 126, 131, 136, 203, 205, 213, 286, 331

subjugation, 16, 58, 131, 137, 139, 146, 162, 169, 187, 203, 229, 317, 323
sublime, 266, 324
submission, 129, 131–32, 143, 162–63, 230
suffering, 110, 190, 252, 283
  as redemptive, 110
supersessionism, 8
surveillance, 176
survival, 66, 83, 105, 324
taxation, 205, 208–10, 214, 333
teaching, -ers, 58–59
technology, 2, 107, 115, 194, 348
  of accessibility, 107
  of power, 175–77, 184, 189, 195, 319
  visual, 175–77, 184, 319
tenure, 44
theology, 5, 12, 51, 67, 85–87, 204, 255, 261, 263, 320, 324
  as oppressive, 110
tongues, speaking in. See *glossai*
trauma, 128, 329
Tuskegee experiment, 93
transcorporeality, 158–59, 318–19
Trump, Donald, 99
United Kingdom, 17–18, 50, 67, 74, 186, 220, 299
  Britannia, 187
Unite the Right rally, 194
United States, 16, 18–19, 41, 45, 49, 56, 68, 75–76, 83, 85, 88, 90–99, 125, 132, 162, 165, 194, 207, 219, 250, 279, 283–84, 286, 297–99, 323, 330, 345–46, 348
  American exceptionalism, 90–91, 94
  Civil War, 177–78, 194–95, 323–35
  Confederacy, 177, 194–95, 323, 338
  Constitution, 301
  patriotism, 98
  South, 162, 178, 181
university, -ies, 4, 9–11, 15–16, 18, 44, 50, 257, 325, 345–47, 351
  press, 48, 351
  private, 49
University of Cape Town, 194
University of Regensburg, 247

urban spaces, 125–26, 136, 140, 145, 297–98
utopian, 40
value, -s, 221, 232, 234–35, 239, 260, 329, 335, 347, 350
violence, 21, 48, 99, 107, 127, 129, 135, 138, 140, 159, 161, 180–81, 183, 186, 193, 203, 213, 230, 266, 307
  sexual, 184, 194, 230
virtue, 193, 212, 316, 326, 337, 348
voces magicae, 262–64, 267, 280
war, 20, 83, 85, 188–89, 237, 266, 331
  as metaphor, 83
Wasp, The, 96
wayward, -ness, 123–46
wealth, 71, 76, 106, 182, 194, 203, 206–10, 212–14, 229–30, 233, 281, 330, 351
  inherited, 205, 208
  redistribution of, 222, 233
West, -ern, 9, 22, 40, 52, 67, 255, 290, 295, 324
West Indies, 88–89
will, -fulness, 123–46, 159, 162–63, 166, 168–69, 262, 290–91, 300, 317, 331, 344
  divine, 136
  free will, 164
Williams College, 41, 43–49, 51, 56
womanism, 59, 66, 130
women, 54, 66, 124, 126, 137, 176, 193, 217, 225–27, 230, 234, 236–38, 241, 267, 334, 350
  of color, 344
  queens. See monarchy.
World War I, 51
white, -ness, 40, 45, 47, 52–53, 55–56, 73, 75, 77, 85, 92–93, 95–96, 98, 248, 250, 254–56, 268, 283, 291
  supremacy, 16, 47–49, 124, 250, 283, 286, 294
  women, 59, 106
xenophobia, 92, 294, 324, 331
Zacchaeus, 212

CPSIA information can be obtained
at www.ICGtesting.com
Printed in the USA
LVHW071252250623
750655LV00006B/10